A SURVEY OF CHRISTIAN ETHICS

A Survey of
Christian Ethics

EDWARD LeROY LONG, Jr.

New York   Oxford
OXFORD UNIVERSITY PRESS

First published by Oxford University Press, New York, 1967
First issued as an Oxford University Press paperback, 1982

Library of Congress Cataloging in Publication Data

Long, Edward Le Roy.
  A survey of Christian ethics.

  Includes bibliographical references and index.
  1. Christian ethics.   I. Title.
[BJ1201.L6   1982]   241   82-8266
ISBN 0-19-503242-X (pbk.)

Printing (last digit): 9 8

Printed in the United States of America

Preface

The relationship between Christian faith and moral decision has been the subject of perennial discussion and inquiry. When men of faith examine ethical issues they are driven to serious and prolonged reflection. Such reflection often finds its way into written form, where it stands for others to share, evaluate, and criticize. Many of the great theological works of Christian history deserve study for both doctrinal and moral insights. Many available studies of Christian ethics treat this material in an historical manner, often by presenting selected portions from great classics.

In addition, the field of Christian ethics as a contemporary discipline is comprised of a vast and varied literature in which ways of understanding the classics as well as different approaches to the present are set forth in many perspectives and many degrees of detail. A number of present books add to the discussion by developing their own definitions of the proper relationship of faith to ethics.

While no single book can hope to do everything required in Christian ethical study, there is a need for a book which surveys the field of Christian ethics in order to develop a comprehensive appreciation of the wide variety of approaches found in both the historical and the contemporary materials. Rather than constructing its own internally systematic point of view, such a book should look for the patterns that have perennially appeared in the analysis of these issues. It should introduce the reader to such patterns without being primarily concerned to argue that he should embrace a particular one of them.

Any study of methodology must do more than paraphrase what others have said. It must devise a typology for purposes of clarifying and organizing a vast body of material. The categories presented in a typology are not inert, but serve to point out relationships and to create understandings. They are, in themselves, something of a systematic construct, but a systematic construct to be measured by its capacity to illumine issues and point to the essential features of given systems and the relationships between them.

Typologies are best understood as prisms, which spread out the components into separable entities within a band, rather than as sorting boxes.

into which completely distinct units are arbitrarily placed. Perhaps the word *motifs* is better than the word *types* for describing the categories employed in this analysis. Whereas *types* often implies mutually exclusive systems which claim independence from other ways of dealing with the same issues, *motifs* can be used to denote trends which can exist together, as simultaneous elements within a whole. Individual thinkers can more easily exhibit two motifs in a single view than they can combine two different types into a whole.

In the beginning of his famous study *The Methods of Ethics*, Henry Sidgwick presented this understanding of his task:

> There are several recognized ways of treating this subject [of ethics] none of which I have thought it desirable to adopt. We may start with existing systems, and either study them historically, tracing the changes in thought through the centuries, or compare and classify them according to relations of resemblance, or criticize their internal coherence. Or we may seek to add to the number of these systems: and claim after so many unsuccessful efforts to have at last attained the one true theory of the subject, by which all others may be tested. The present book contains neither the exposition of a system nor a natural or critical history of systems. I have attempted to define and unfold not one Method of Ethics, but several: at the same time these are not here studied historically, as methods that have actually been used or proposed for the regulation of practice: but rather as alternatives between which the human mind seems to me necessarily forced to choose, when it attempts to frame a complete synthesis of practical maxims and to act in a perfectly rational manner. Thus though I have called them natural methods, they might more properly be called natural methods rationalized, because it is perhaps most natural to men to guide themselves by a mixture of different methods more or less disguised under the ambiguities of language. The impulses from which the different methods take their rise exist to some extent in all men; and the different claims of different ends to be rational each man finds urged and admitted by his own mind in different states and attitudes.[1]

Much that Sidgwick has said about his approach applies, with appropriate modifications, to this book. The motif patterns discerned here are "theological methods rationalized" in the sense that we believe the motifs that have been discerned are perennial options which have been present and will remain present in Christian thinking about moral issues. Some of the motifs appeal more strongly to certain thinkers than others. Some thinkers declare themselves for single motifs while they are criticized from the standpoint of considerations arising from other motifs. Unless this writer is mistaken, any Christian ethical thought can be described by using the motifs here delineated, singularly or in concert with one another.

What, then, is to be said about other interpretative schemes? They may be useful and even helpful for certain purposes. A scheme for drawing the contrast between individualistic and communal types of ethics could illumine the way in which different moral schemes handle the relationship of the individual to the group. Or, distinctions between different kinds of Christian ethics might be described in terms of ethics of the first, second, and third persons of the Trinity. Other distinctions have been drawn in terms of a contrast between indicative and imperative ethics. Except as these alternative classifications illumine special issues, they can, we believe, be subsumed under the deliberative, prescriptive, and relational ways of formulating the ethical norm and the institutional, operational, and intentional ways of implementing ethical decisions.

Because this study covers such a broad field it may look shallow in comparison with depth studies of specific issues and most certainly is shallow in its treatments of specific figures. Its attempt to be comprehensive has forced it to compromise with thoroughness in the discussion of individual systems of thought. It is hoped that such impressions as it gives of the historical and contemporary figures with which it deals are fair and legitimate as far as they go, but the use of a motif to characterize certain aspects of a particular perspective should not obscure the integrity of a man's thinking as set forth in his own writings. This study should both inspire and aid the reader to seek his own knowledge of the different men by reading their primary works.

The preparation of a volume like this is quite beyond the capacity of any one person to undertake and complete without the help of others. The original suggestion for a book of this kind came from my colleague, Clyde A. Holbrook. While we canvassed the possibilities several times, he should be credited with what is good in the idea but not held responsible for the final form in which it appears. Time—a necessity in today's academic world—was made available by a research status leave from Oberlin College and a fellowship from the John Simon Guggenheim Memorial Foundation. Office facilities and access to library materials were furnished by Drew University, which extended gracious hospitality during a year spent pleasantly on its campus. A number of friends, including Drs. James Luther Adams, John C. Bennett, David M. Graybeal, William A. Johnson, Paul L. Lehmann, Michael Novak, H. Shelton Smith, and Kenneth Underwood, read the manuscript in early drafts and suggested significant revisions. Their interest in an undertaking of this nature has sustained my spirits while bringing it to completion. Others who helped prepare the copy and insure its accuracy include Dr. Robert Beach and his associates at the Library of Union Theological Seminary, Rev. Paul Rahmeier, Miss June Wright, and my wife. I am deeply grateful for the many kinds of assistance given by these institutions and individuals.

Thinking about moral issues from the perspective of Christian faith should never cease. What has already been done is but prologue to what must yet be undertaken. The world is moving, faith is pilgrimage, and the intellectual enterprise must both report and challenge what transpires. Perhaps this analysis can contribute to ongoing discussions about the Christian understanding of moral responsibility.

Oberlin, Ohio   E. L. L., Jʀ.
December 1966

Contents

I
The Varieties and Functions
of Ethical Discourse

I

Ethics and Values in Philosophy and the Social Sciences

Theological ethics pursues its work in relation to many other disciplines and cannot be understood apart from them. In some cases theology borrows concepts from other disciplines; in other instances it arrives at its own insights by translating for its use concepts and categories which have originated elsewhere; in still other situations it rejects the approaches of other disciplines. The rejection of other insights by theology does not mean that there is no relationship involved, since the arguments of those who vigorously deny the value of other disciplines for thinking about moral issues from a Christian perspective are often as dependent upon the disciplines they reject for the formulation of the issues as are the arguments of those who look to such disciplines for positive contributions.

Christian ethical reflection has long been carried out in relation to moral philosophy. The relationship between these two branches of inquiry has sometimes been very close and at other times been quite distant; sometimes friendly, at other times hostile. It is impossible to understand Christian ethics without some appreciation of philosophical ways of dealing with moral issues. In more recent years, moreover, there has been an increasing relationship between Christian ethical thought and the social sciences. The growing importance of this relationship makes it necessary to consider the ways in which value considerations can be involved in the scientific analysis of social function. In order to understand Christian ethics as a field of discourse, it is important to have at least a bird's-eye view of ethical discourse as found in moral philosophy and the social sciences.

Philosophical Discourse Concerning Ethics

In the opening chapter of a popular textbook on philosophical ethics the following description is given of the nature of moral philosophy:

3

> . . . ethics seeks to point out to men the true value of life. Ethics asks
> and attempts to answer such questions as: What values are most
> worthwhile? Why is one act better than another? No person can live
> a satisfactory life who has not set up for himself some scale of values.
> Ethics is a study of human values. It attempts to stimulate the moral
> sense, to discover the true values of life, and to inspire men to join in
> the quest for these values.[1]

Traditional approaches to moral philosophy have been interested in
providing men with guidance for the conduct of life. They have regarded
the reason as a sufficient guide to moral conduct even though they differ in
their understandings of how the reason functions. These approaches to
moral philosophy have a long and honorable history. Plato believed that
the soul perceives the highest good under certain circumstances—
circumstances in which the soul is no longer chained to the particularity
of sense experience. Not every soul, to be sure, attains full and complete
knowledge of the good, but Plato held that the human reason is capable
of the necessary and sufficient insight to know the true content of human
obligation.

Aristotle, though he was early dependent upon the Platonic influence,
came to define the highest good, not in some detached way perceived by
the soul when isolated from sense experience, but in terms of happiness.
He put it this way in his *Nicomachean Ethics:*

> Happiness, then, is something final and self-sufficient, and is the end of
> action. . . . However, to say that happiness is the chief good seems a
> platitude, and a clearer account of what it is is still desired. This might
> perhaps be given, if we could first ascertain the function of man.[2]

The last phrase in this quotation, which invites rational inquiry into the
function of man, indicates that Aristotle understood moral decision in
terms of a wider knowledge of what man is and how he acts. Aristotle
seemed confident that such an inquiry is possible and that its results are
important for ethical choices. When men come to understand what is truly
excellent then they can achieve well-being.

Confidence in human reason as a source of moral standards reached a
high point in the eighteenth and nineteenth centuries, though these centuries also brought forth several sharp criticisms of this confidence. In
John Stuart Mill we find a deep conviction that the rational individual
can confidently know the difference between right and wrong by the
application of his intelligence to the question: "What is good for the
greatest number of people?" Mill believed, as did many men after him,
that liberty is an essential and crucial condition for the exercise of this
judgment.

The clearest, and perhaps most successful, attempt to found an ethical standard upon rational deliberation apart from other bases of judgment is found in the ethics of duty set forth by Immanuel Kant. Kant attempted to make *a priori* ethical judgments, that is, judgments based upon the reason acting apart from any traditional authority or experimental investigations. "Act on the maxim," said Kant, "that you could will to become a universal law." He went on to amplify his statement with the following explanatory maxim: "So act as to treat humanity whether in thine own person or in that of any other, in every case as an end withal, never as a means only." These two formulations, taken together, constitute the categorical imperative and were proposed as rational principles having a self-evident moral authority. Kant's purpose was to provide an unassailable rational basis for making moral decisions. He sought to make ethics autonomous, to begin with a rational ethic as the foundation upon which to build religion. His work has influenced, either positively or negatively, much subsequent thinking about the relationship of ethics and religion, especially in Protestant circles.

Traditional approaches have never resulted in agreement concerning the values which ought to guide human conduct. The efforts to find such values have been many, the proposals legion, and the arguments about their adequacy often bitter as men have struggled to see how reason provides men with knowledge of the good. Many men have sought to classify the kinds of answers that the traditional philosophical approach has given to the ethical question. These classifications constitute a shorthand for dealing with the various ways that men have rationally inquired into the nature of the good life. While these classifications are not exhaustive, they are instructive. They can be suggestive even when they oversimplify the carefully wrought arguments of the men and systems which they abstract. One of the classic efforts to examine the methods used by philosophical ethics was made by Henry Sidgwick of Cambridge University.[3] Sidgwick suggested three primary methods to be characteristic of philosophical ethics. *Intuitionism* refers to those schemes which, like Plato's, hold that moral imperatives are self-evident presuppositions of rational thinking. The other two views reject the contention that the rational man is aware of self-evident maxims and argue that only when happiness in a broad and profound sense is taken as a goal can the norms of ethics be derived. *Egoistic hedonism*, which is the second basic type of approach, understands such happiness in terms of the well-being of the individual, somewhat as Aristotle seems to have done. Universal hedonism, or *utilitarianism*, thinks about the greatest good for the greatest number of people, following in the path exemplified by Mill.

Sidgwick's classification has had wide use but not universal acceptance. Many other attempts have been made to speak about the different sorts of moral philosophy, even those types which have expressed the traditional search for the good life. In a textbook published at the turn of this century we find the following types described: theistic, intuitional, utilitarian, evolutionary, and eclectic.[4] Some of these categories correspond to those proposed by Sidgwick, but others seek to point to quite different approaches to the ethical enterprise. Questions can surely be raised about the overlapping of these five types. Cannot a theistic ethic appear in one of the other forms as well? Might not an evolutionary ethic seek a utilitarian goal? Is not an eclectic ethic really a combination of other types? It does not seem that this fivefold classification adds anything to the basic types proposed by Sidgwick. For thinking about the traditional types of philosophical ethics, intuitionist, hedonistic, and utilitarian types seem basic.

If, however, philosophical ethics are classified in terms of the mode in which they set forth the norm, another type of distinction can be drawn. This distinction draws attention to a contrast between teleological and deontological types of philosophical ethics. Teleological types of moral philosophy ask questions about human conduct in terms of a conception of the good toward which right conduct supposedly contributes. They ask, "What is the proper end of man?" Deontological types of moral philosophy deal with human conduct in terms of a conception of duty which is considered to be imperative because it is right. They ask, "What is the content of obligation?" This difference has sometimes been described as the difference between asking "What is the good in an ultimate sense?" and "What is the right in an obligatory sense?" C. D. Broad gave the classical description of these two types—a description proposed as a modification of Henry Sidgwick's classic study of *The Methods of Ethics:*

> Deontological theories hold that there are ethical propositions of the form: "Such and such a kind of action would always be right (or wrong) in such and such circumstances, no matter what its consequences might be." This division corresponds with Sidgwick's Intuitionism in the narrower sense. Teleological theories hold that the rightness or wrongness of an action is always determined by its tendency to produce certain consequences which are intrinsically good or bad. Hedonism is a form of teleological theory. It is plain that teleological theories can be subdivided into *monistic* and *pluralistic* varieties. A monistic theory would hold that there is one and only one characteristic which makes a state of affairs good or bad intrinsically. A pluralistic theory would hold that there are several independent characteristics of this kind. Hedonism is a monistic teleological theory. I think that a similar subdivision could be made among deontological theories. It might be held that all the various moral rules recognised by a deontological theory are determinate forms of a single rule, or at any rate that they all answer to a single necessary and sufficient criterion. This seems to have been Kant's view. Such a theory is mo-

nistic. A deontological theory which held that there is a number of independent moral rules would be pluralistic.[5]

Aristotle and Kant have been mentioned in connection with the traditional interest of philosophical ethics in the power of reason to guide men to the good life. The same individuals who in one sense stand on common ground stand on opposing grounds when measured by another set of categories. Aristotle, for example, thought of ethics as the determination of behavior in relation to an end, or *telos*. He defined the good of man in terms of happiness, a happiness understood in relation to the whole function and purpose of man. Kant, on the other hand, looked at duty in a deontological manner. He was concerned to know the right thing to do in every circumstance and as a matter of duty. Even when he urged men so to act that they might will their action to become universal, he was not dealing with universality in a teleological manner.

The contrast between teleological and deontological ethics colors even the use of these ideas in theological morality. Religious moral systems, like that of Roman Catholicism, that are based upon the philosophical work of Aristotle develop very different features than do the theological ethics, like those of Protestant liberalism, that are inspired by Kant. While both make use of philosophical forms in their work, and both stand in contrast with theological ethics that reject the place of philosophical judgments, they cannot be equated. In one, moral reasoning thrusts toward a determination of conduct in relation to an end, or purpose, such as the well-being of man. In the other, the content of duty is derived from a categorical norm, such as love. If pressed either might assent to the idea that the good of man is served by love, or that love is required for the good of man—but the crucial implications of the order in which these two factors are mentioned cannot be overlooked. The Thomistic theologian who finds excitement in the long discussion of the end or purpose of man in the third book of the *Summa Contra Gentiles* and who accepts it as the necessary precondition of valid ethical analysis, is in a different thought-climate from the post-Kantian Protestant who takes his clue for moral duty from exhortations based upon the Sermon on the Mount.

The religious man is apt to reshape the issue between the teleologist and the deontologist. He is prone to inquire whether the action to which he feels constrained is in keeping with the moral purposes of the universe (or of God, its Creator and Sustainer). Popular judgments often take this to be a question as to whether or not there is a God, but they oversimplify and obscure deeper issues. The issue is whether or not moral action is backed by the very nature of reality itself. In Confucianism the issue is just as alive in nontheistic terms as it is alive in theistic terms in other religions. One can ask whether the universe is friendly to moral action without necessarily postulating a God to embody the friendliness. One can also conceive of God in a teleological manner, as a structural and unchangeable embodiment of certain values, or one can conceive of God as one who makes his will known in relationship to occasions and duties of particular circumstance.

Confining himself to the theological form of these two positions, W. G. MacLagen has proposed the term *contextual* for the view that the universe must be friendly to the doing of our duty if there is to be any sense in doing it. He has used the term *aetiological* for the contention that a teleological meaning need not be present with which to justify a particular moral decision.

> The supposition of a friendly universe is naturally, even if not inevitably, given a theistic form: our concern, anyhow, is with it only in that form. It is because this is God's world and only because it is God's world that it is reasonable to follow the path of duty, without condition or reservation, wherever it may lead. This is the pattern of what I call the contextual explanation of the claim of duty. The aetiological explanation, on the other hand, treats our sense of duty as a kind of "hearing God addressing and commanding us." The claim on us is authoritative and absolute because and only because God is its source. However independent of our recognition of this fact our sense of the claim may be it remains a sort of absurdity until it is understood in these terms.[6]

It would seem most likely that the idea of divine sanction for moral behavior can be held in philosophical terms only if there is a predictable pattern to the nature of God's sanction for moral action. If one comes to think of God's will as without any structural dependability in supporting either the good or the right, then the problem of using philosophical terminology to describe that will would become increasingly difficult. Both the teleological and the deontological forms of traditional moral philosophy tend to think of morality in terms of fixed and dependable principles rather than in terms of a capricious exercise of an unstructured will.

Another issue within moral philosophy which requires mention and preliminary exploration is the issue between the idealistic tradition in philosophy itself and the pragmatic-empirical tradition. When the term *moral philosophy* is used, the idea of a deductive reason, which starts from ideals and essences and moves to the examination of conduct in their light, is often supposed. However, as every student of philosophy knows, the philosophers have in their midst articulate exponents of a pragmatic approach which begins with the examination of human activity and moves inductively to a crystallization of general norms. The empirical tradition often appeals to a universal moral sense, a *consensus gentium moralis*, as a source for moral judgment. It looks for the common features of morality in all traditions, hoping thereby to distill from them a conception of right and wrong. Or, it looks for a more limited range of meaning which can be embraced, not because it meets the canons of good sense when measured by rational idealism, but because it is helpful to men in concrete daily decisions. Perhaps we might suggest that the category of experience becomes uppermost in the empirical-pragmatic tradition whereas the category of reason is uppermost in the idealistic schools. The idealist is interested in reason as the source of generalization; the pragmatist is interested in experience as a source of generalization. Both, however, accept reflective and analytical generalization as a crucial source of moral guidance.

All forms of traditional moral philosophy, despite their differences, have tended to believe that the reason can and should provide men with the insights by which they can lead a good life. They have adopted different explanations concerning how these insights should be derived and formulated but they have not challenged the basic intent of moral reasoning to guide human conduct. But the belief that moral reason is a valid source of insight about right behavior has not been shared by all philosophers in the past nor is it universally accepted in our day. In the same cultural period in which Plato was writing his dialogues, the Sophists, like Thrasymachus and Callicles, were raising doubts about the capacity of man to arrive at a rationally adequate determination of the good. They suggested that factors like group mores and subservience to authority work to determine how men behave irrespective of the judgments of reason. Since then many philosophers have been uncertain whether they should make normative judgments about the good. A contemporary text on philosophical ethics, reflecting this uncertainty, defines ethics as *the critical study of standards for judging the rightness or wrongness of conduct.*[7] While this seems traditional enough, its author goes on to point out that the phrase "standards for judging" can refer either to standards which "might be used" for judging or standards which "ought to be used" for judging and throws to the student himself the decision as to which interpretation he prefers to adopt.

The traditional view of ethical discourse as the road to the good life has been sharply challenged in the twentieth century. Stephen Toulmin has suggested that moral thinking can be classified by three categories. The first of these is the *objective* approach, which seeks to ascribe a property to those things or acts which are considered to be morally right or good. The second of these is the *subjective* approach, which finds the clue to ethical meaning in the attitudes of those who adhere to particular standards. Toulmin criticizes both views. The objective approach, he argues, cannot finally sustain its view that ethical actions have objective qualities.

The subjective approach, by emphasizing the purely arbitrary character of individual or group preferences, furnishes no good grounds for ethical choices, since the preferences may well contradict each other. A third approach, which he calls the *imperative* approach, is a reaction against the first two but not a break from them. It is the youngest of the three approaches and has often been viewed as an entirely new way of understanding the ethical enterprise. According to this view

> Ethical concepts . . . correspond neither to processes "in" the object nor to processes "in" or "in the mind of" the speaker: there is no quality and no response which can plausibly be taken as that to which our value-sentences refer. . . . In contrast to those sentences of the form "So-and-so is X" which give information of some kind, the whole force of ethical statements (according to him [i.e. the imperative type of thinker]) is *rhetorical*. They are, he asserts, disguised imperatives or ejaculations; our least misleading ethical utterances being those like "Good!," the cry of joy, and "Naughty!," the command to desist.[8]

Close scrutiny of Sidgwick's categories in comparison with those of Toulmin will show that the focus of attention has shifted. In Sidgwick we are concerned with the kind of answers men give to the query, "What is the good which enables men to achieve their fulfillment?" In Toulmin we find the questions so constructed as to reveal an underlying interest in the problem of scrutinizing ethical statements as assertions of fact or feeling. Philosophical discourse as carried on by Sidgwick is quite different from philosophical discourse as seen by Toulmin. There has been a shift of emphasis tantamount to a change of purpose. Toulmin goes on to examine the function played by ethical reasoning in human life, and his conclusions suggest that moral reasoning is valuable for the comparison and analysis of ethical statements rather than for the assertion of particular standards.

The challenge to the traditional view began in 1903 with the publication of G. E. Moore's *Principia Ethica*[9] and has gathered momentum and complexity ever since. Moore's chief effort was devoted to showing that the term *good*, like the term *yellow*, represents a simple concept which is known rather than defined. Consequently, efforts to define the good by reference to some natural reality, such as evolution or happiness, are fallacious. Moore conceded that men should obey rules that are generally practiced since such obedience leads to happiness. This may sound like a concession to the necessity of adjusting men to the demands of their culture, but Moore saw it as a proper conclusion of moral reasoning. Despite this adherence to aspects of the traditional view, Moore was instrumental in focusing the attention of the philosophical world upon the function of ethical language and the meaning of ethical terms.

Following Moore, other thinkers have argued that while the nature of the right act can be known intuitively it is impossible to give reasons why this or that act is good. W. D. Ross[10] and H. A. Prichard[11] have argued the futility of trying to ground the right upon arguments which justify particular acts by reference to their eventual consequences. A right act is right on its own terms, since the idea of right is an ultimate and irreducible notion which cannot be defined. The common man can perform the right act without reflective investigation of its probable consequences if universalized.

Another challenge to the traditional view, perhaps even more radical than the challenge proposed by Moore and Ross, has been called "the emotive theory of ethics." According to this view, set forth by Toulmin as his third category, ethical statements are made for the purposes of expressing approval or disapproval and thus influencing behavior. Early expressions of this view can be found in C. K. Ogden and I. A. Richards[12] and in articles by R. B. Braithwaite and W. H. F. Barnes. Later expressions can be found in A. J. Ayer[13] and Charles Stevenson.[14] Ayer's work is an outgrowth of his involvement with the Vienna Circle of logical positivists and tends to reject all ethical statements as nonsense—not in the everyday meaning of that term which implies foolishness, but in a sophisticated meaning which implies nonverifiability. Stevenson, however, is concerned to make as much use of ethical language as possible while at the same time acknowledging its fundamentally emotive character.

The intricacies which arise in the arguments between the various modern approaches to ethics deserve attention in another context and there is insufficient room here to examine them with any degree of adequacy.[15] It is clear, however, that there has been a shift within moral philosophy from the practical interest in conduct—in the good life—to the theoretical interest in ethical statements as assertions of verifiable truth. Moritz Schlick, one of the Vienna Circle, once set this contrast forth in the sharpest possible terms—terms which heighten a distinction between the traditional and analytical approaches to these issues.

> . . . ethics is a system of *knowledge,* and nothing else; its only goal is the truth. Every science is, as such, purely theoretical; it seeks to understand; hence the questions of ethics, too, are purely theoretical problems. As philosophers we try to find their correct solutions, but their practical application, if such is possible, does not fall within the sphere of ethics. If anyone studies these questions in order to apply the results to life and action, his dealing with ethics has, it is true, a practical end; but ethics itself never has any other goal than the truth.
>
> So long as the philosopher is concerned with his purely theoretical questions, he must forget that he has a human interest as well as a cognitive interest in the object of his investigation. For him there is no greater danger than to change from a philosopher into a moralist, from an investigator into a preacher.[16]

In an effort to avoid the complexities of traditional moral philosophy, to transcend the seeming impasse between intuitionalists, utilitarians, and other schools, analytical philosophy has focused attention upon a more limited and manageable issue: "What is the nature and function of ethical discourse?" But even here we get a variety of answers, including R. M. Hare's modification of most of those views which have already been mentioned.[17] Much that has been done is highly significant for understanding the issue examined, but it has not attained that degree of publicly verifiable agreement which ethics as "a science" or even the study of ethical language as "a science" might be hoped to reach.

The outlooks so hastily surveyed above represent developments within but one branch of contemporary philosophy. Traditional metaphysical approaches to reality commonly associated with the search for the good life in moral philosophy have been challenged by existentialism as well as by the work of the logical positivists and the linguistic analysts. In speaking about philosophical discourse as related to ethics we must therefore take account of the work of men like Kierkegaard, Heidegger, Sartre, Buber, and Berdyaev as well as the work of men like Moore, Ewing, Ayer, Schlick, and Hare.

And so we find ourselves, not with two great camps, but with three. Allegiance to the traditional method remains. Enthusiasm for the problems of analysis attracts its own band of adherents. Existentialists render a verdict which includes the same judgment as that of the analysts in rejecting metaphysical foundations but places something very different in their stead. Moreover, between the two contrasting rejections of traditional approaches a wide and inexplicable gulf seems to exist. The analysts, and those concerned about the issues which they raise, live in a world of discourse and interchange which takes little or no account of what is being thought by the existentialists; the existentialists, in turn, often ignore the world of the analysts—or at least write as if the analysts did not exist. Even an observer like Thomas E. Hill, who seeks for comprehensive fullness in the making of typologies, omits the existentialists from his exhaustive study *Contemporary Ethical Theories*.[18]

Existentialism, like analysis, is a methodology rather than a set of conclusions. Moreover, to define it precisely would be to violate its own distrust of thinking about reality in terms of static essences. Kierkegaard would judge it "comic" to begin a discourse with the phrase: "The essence of existentialism is. . . ." Nevertheless, one has to abstract in order to review, to condense in order to describe. It is impossible to think of existentialism without describing certain tendencies to which it gives expression.

Existentialism as a way of moral reasoning seriously qualifies the traditional search for universality as the hallmark of the satisfactory ethical norm. Its objection to the category of the universal rests upon the bondage of the universal to the spectator attitude, which seems to existentialists to contradict the very nature of the ethical situation itself. The existentialist is concerned with the involvement of each man in the situation to which he himself must respond. To require of him a detachment, born of the drive for reason to stand in aloof judgment in order to preserve its autonomy, is to destroy the integrity of the participant in ethical decisions. The price paid for detachment is very high—it may even be the destruction of concern about the consequences of moral reasoning for human life and conduct. Indeed, the existentialists might well point to the position of a man like Schlick as the inevitable outcome of the search for impeccable objectivity. The price for making universally verifiable statements about ethics is removal from the ethical situation itself.[19]

Existentialism owes much to the thought of Søren Kierkegaard. Summarizing his importance, William Barrett observes the crucial role involvement played in the thought of this pioneering Dane:

> . . . it may take philosophy a long time to absorb the full import of what [Kierkegaard] has to say about the ethical as a level of our human existence. In the traditional kind of ethics philosophers are concerned with analyzing the concepts of good, bad, right, and wrong, and with deciding to which things or kinds of things these predicates may be attached. This is a purely formal kind of analysis; indeed, in modern times philosophers have shifted their inquiry to an analysis of the language of ethics. Such linguistic analysis does not in the least require that the man who makes it himself exist ethically. It is thus perfectly possible—and in fact often happens—that a philosopher who has worked out a complete theory of values in the abstract may yet remain in a childish or donnish existence that has never felt the bite of the ethical upon it. One's values may thus be all down on paper, but one's actual life goes on as if the ethical did not exist. A formal theory of ethics would be perfectly empty if it were not for the fundamental act of ethical existence by which we let values come into our life. The fundamental choice, says Kierkegaard, is not the choice between rival values of good and bad, but the choice by which we summon good and bad into existence for ourselves. Without such a choice, an abstract system of ethics is just so much paper currency with nothing to back it up.[20]

It is easy to parody existentialism as a radical individualism, but this is at best a very partial understanding of its purpose and is more often a gross distortion of the case. The existentialist does ask about the standing ground of the individual. He looks upon the individual as the participant within a situation, not as a spectator who enunciates norms. The existentialist does emphasize the need for seeing ethical judgments in relation to particulars rather than as derivations from overarching universals. He does underscore the role of presuppositions and the element of "faith" as ingredients in the decisions which men make about matters of conduct. But he also talks about community. He looks at the relationships in which the individual arrives at decisions. He studies the consequences of decision in relation to the actual involvements in which a man stands enmeshed. Buber, whose thought about ethics surely includes relationship, belongs to the existentialist movement. To characterize him as an individualist is to confound the meaning of terms!

In the exploration of its understandings, existentialism has employed a number of terms to describe dimensions of the human situation. These terms often describe that which prevents the attainment of the ethical fulfillment rather than describe the positive content of an ethical goal. Some of the terms, like the word *freedom*, are taken from traditional thought and given radical implications. Other terms describe a human situation seen through different eyes. *Anxiety, depth experience, crisis, emptiness*, and *nothingness*, have appeared frequently in the literature of the movement. Or, positively stated, the term *authentic selfhood* has become one key with which the existentialist pursues his quest for the good life.

These phrases bring to ethical discourse a new dimension, not merely a dimension of individual involvement but a dimension of urgency, of encounter, of agony, and of release. There is a psychological overtone to discussions carried on with these phrases, but it is not a scientific inquiry concerning the nature of adjustment or mental health. The contrast between the existentialists and the analysts is symbolized by the contrast between the terms *nothingness* and *nonsense*. The latter, employed by the analysts, implies a judgment as to the knowledge status of a statement. The judgment is rendered in a detached manner and can be publicly demonstrated. The analyst is concerned about the public character of his assertions; he hopes for common consent to the conclusion that certain sorts of statements are nonsense. Nothingness, however, describes a state that is entered or escaped. It has experiential implications; those who know what nothingness means do so from an encounter with its reality. There can be neither detached consideration nor universal agreement as to the meaning of nothingness, apart from the experience it entails. Nor is this an empirical means to the validation of a proposition. It is an invitation to a standing point.

The relationship between existentialist types of moral philosophy and religious approaches to the moral question has been no less complex than the relationship between traditional and analytical moral philosophies and religious thought. If there has been a tendency in the past to relate theological ethics to traditional moral philosophy, a tendency that still persists in conservative Roman Catholic thought, there has been a tendency in our time to relate theological reflection about ethical issues to existentialism. This has been particularly true in schools of Protestant thought identified with the neo-Reformation tradition and is often coupled with a labored rejection of traditional moral philosophy. The same theologians who find existentialism a satisfactory vehicle for religious ethics usually regard the analytical modifications of traditional philosophy with some suspicion. It is only recently that explorations into the import of analytical philosophy for theological understanding have been initiated, but there are grounds for thinking some insights may come from this endeavor for clarifying the nature of moral statements.

We shall return many times to the discussion of the relationship between philosophical discourse about ethical norms and religious discourse about these same questions. The issue is perennial. Meanwhile, we must examine how the thinking of social scientists bears on ethical issues, for it is not only in relation to philosophers that theological thinkers have formulated their views of ethical problems, even though philosophical thought has admittedly played the prominent role in the examination of the issues and in its influence upon the discourse of theological ethics.

Discourse about Values in the Social Sciences

Moral philosophy has been a function of human thought for almost as long as has articulate and reflective thinking about religious matters. It has been used and rejected for centuries, both in the Western and non-Western traditions. The social sciences, however, are younger. Fewer men have devoted lifetimes to building syntheses between the social sciences and theology than have conceived great edifices of speculative thought combining theology with philosophy. Moreover, the social sciences have arisen in a period of Western history when the relationship between the theological enterprise and the intellectual enterprise has been one of rift and suspicion rather than cooperation and synthesis. Indeed, the social sciences have arisen from progenitors, like Comte, whose judgments concerning the validity of religion have been especially negative. It therefore should be no surprise to find that materials dealing with the relationships between sociological theory and theological thought are far less prevalent or developed than materials dealing with the relationships of moral philosophy to theological ethics. Separation rather than unity, and indifference rather than contempt have generally marked the relationships between social theory and theological reflection. This may well account for the fact that the two disciplines, despite a few individuals who have been concerned about their theoretical relationship, have never enjoyed a marriage nor been racked by the agonies of a divorce.

To be sure, there have been many practical working relationships developed between sociology and religion. The use of sociological tools, such as the statistical survey, has often been a part of the working equipment of men engaged in, or teaching about, the life of the church in society. But many times men who have engaged in this kind of study have been oblivious to, or disdainful of, the theological enterprise as a reflective discipline. The result has been that in many theological institutions there has been a division, often sharply drawn, between two fields: one called by such names as Christian ethics or moral theology; the other, social ethics, church and community, or Christian sociology. In recent times, however, there has been increasing evidence of interest in the theoretical relationships between the social sciences and theological ethics among teachers of Christian social ethics.[21]

There is also at present a tremendous interest within the field of the social sciences themselves in the theoretical complexities that attend the creation of frameworks for understanding the nature of social function. This interest comes to a focus but not to a consensus in Robert K. Merton's book *Social Theory and Social Structure*,[22] but a number of significant works in contemporary sociology are concerned with the same problem. The writings of Howard Becker, Kingsley Davis, Talcott Parsons, and Pitrim A. Sorokin are probably the best known.[23] Among the issues that figure in the discussions are questions concerning the adequacy of conceptual models for the description of social realities, whether or not standardization of theory is necessary and desirable between the various practitioners of the art, and—for our study a most crucial question—the role of values and ultimate commitments in the ordering and functioning of society. In social psychology we have questions as to the nature of the self and its relationship to the social context.

The discussion of these theoretical questions is going on within the social sciences themselves, but with no consensus concerning how they should be answered. Indeed, there is even argument about whether they should be posed. Some observers draw a distinction between the social sciences, which adhere strongly to a descriptive analysis of societal function, and the political sciences, which enter more directly into considerations of questions with valuational overtones. In a strong statement of the view that valuational discussion has no place in the social and political sciences, Maurice Cowling has this to say:

> Those who want this sort of political science want something they cannot have. The assurance that prejudices are principles, preferences reasons, and the arbitrary opinions they adopt a rational expression of the universal law, is something political science cannot supply. But, if an ethically commanding science is an impossibility, an ethically indifferent philosophy is not. If political science in this sense is an

illusion, political explanation, whose function is not to guide, exhort or preach, whose conclusions command to no particular line of action and whose object is simply to understand, is neither illegitimate nor undesirable.[24]

Cowling says the same thing about the role of sociology and flatly declares "if any . . . sociologist accepts the claim that sociology has a normative function in relation to social policy, then the claim he is accepting is illegitimate."[25]

Or consider Peter Berger's thrusts, aimed at all the participating elements in a false society. Berger is less concerned to argue that social scientists should concern themselves with values than that inevitably they do so, often with unfortunate effects. Speaking of the professional social workers, he points out that they often reinforce the value structure of the police despite their theoretical aversions to doing so. Moreover, the theories of the social sciences appear to Berger as helps to the erection of "a fairly viable observation tower on society" but are always in danger of becoming objects to which the social scientists give allegiance rather than the tools they use for understanding reality. In biting words Berger contends,

> If one would go on now and discuss in detail the factional disputes between different schools of the same academic discipline, and the surrealistic distortions of reality to which such vested interests drive their adherents, the comedy would take on the character of a savage farce. Suffice it to say that the scholarly cloak of the social scientist is anything but a safe protection against the hazards of ideological befuddlement.[26]

A third quotation will round out the evidence upon which to make certain systematic observations. It comes from William E. Kolb, a sociologist who has been especially concerned about the role of valuational questions in the social sciences.

> This, then, is the nature of modern sociological orthodoxy. It provides a tool for the understanding of societies other than one's own and perhaps a weapon if some of these societies are to be fought. It is a basis for the acceptance of one's own society and for the development of specialized disciplines which can help that society function more effectively in limited areas. It is not an instrument of social criticism either with respect to the relationship of the content of ultimate value systems to universal human needs or with respect to the degree to which any society is an instrument of the powerful for the achievement of their own purposes. Nor, finally, is it a basis for hope for those who believe that men are ultimately responsible for choosing their own destiny and shaping their own lives. Men are creatures shaped by value systems and their mechanisms of instrumentation, incapable of

criticism except when society fails its task of socialization or delivering the goods.[27]

There is obviously a difference between the attitudes of the authors we have cited. The difference is a witness to the presence of a controversy. It is the nature of the controversy in which we are interested. To what extent are valuational commitments wise and needful in the development of social theory? To what extent does social theory shape and influence the determination of valuational commitments in society?

In the quotations above we find different answers to these questions. Cowling wants the separation clear in order that the integrity of the social sciences be preserved. According to this view, an adequate understanding of the function of social institutions can be derived without facing the question as to how such functioning should occur. It is for politicians and not political scientists to give direction to a culture. The law is shaped by legislatures and courts, not by legal theorists. Students of culture and law observe the nature of such decisions and their consequences in society, describing what they see rather than prescribing what they wish would take place. To breach the line between the descriptive and the evaluative is a major distortion of the function of the academic social scientist.

The author of the last quotation seems to be saying that the difficulty lies in the failure of the social scientists to give sufficient attention to the valuational element. It will not do, he seems to argue, to keep the detached aloofness demanded by Cowling. Not only is it impossible, as the limited ways in which valuational considerations creep into sociology show, but it is undesirable to pursue social analysis without social criticism and thorough consideration of the values upon which society is to be founded. Kolb argues, not only in the essay cited but in other papers, that choices of nonempirical values by freely responsible human beings must be studied as necessary factors in the development of social theory. He extends Parsons' use of value commitments as given factors in social functioning, but criticizes Parsons for treating such value commitments as neutral givens rather than as elements over which man has freedom of choice. Moreover, he hopes that sociological analysis can provide some guidance in enabling men to make choices about value systems.

Berger is an iconoclast. He denies by implication Cowling's thesis, suggesting that sociology has never really functioned as a purely detached science. He raises questions about Kolb's program by contending that the valuational ingredients of sociology are often fictional and perverse rather than helpful and constructive. Instead of dialogue he engages in polemics, with both the sociologists and the religious leaders the object of his bitterly incisive complaints. His stance as a prophet may leave him homeless, though he may have a claim to insight which transcends the categories of both sociology and religion. Of this we can be sure, his efforts will be valuable in helping us to see the inadequacies of a value ignorance as well as the perversions of premature conclusions about value loyalties and value commitments.

There may be something of a contrast between what is happening in philosophical reflection about ethics and what may be happening in the social sciences. Philosophy, with a long history of metaphysical attempts to define the substance of the good life, has tended to turn in recent decades to systems of thought which delimit its role, to tighten its conceptual task. Sociology, with a shorter history and a more extensive identification with a strictly limited, even positivistic, conception of its task, is being prodded to discuss the possible broadening of its function. There is flux in both disciplines; they are pregnant with exciting possibilities, but they are likely to be equally suspicious of theologians who arrive to function either as midwives or as executioners for ideas in controversy.

While theologians may need to stay out of the domestic controversies of the social sciences, they must not ignore what is happening within them. To the extent that social analysis is a valid, even a fruitful, window through which to view the functioning of society, the religious man can gain from it wisdom concerning the role he can play in living out his ethical obligations. Moreover, the religious man is interested, at least within the Christian tradition, not only in the functioning of the specifically religious ingredients of society, but in the functioning of the culture itself. Dietrich Bonhoeffer, John A. T. Robinson, and others who have underscored the need for Christian worldliness help us to see that the responsibility of the religious man is not to work merely through the sacred dimensions of life, but through all its structures and processes for the accomplishment of those things to which he is ultimately committed. He must know, not only about rites and ritual, but about civil rights and righteousness. He must realize, not only what ought to be done, but how it can be made real.

It can also be hoped that modest, yet meaningful, contributions to the social sciences can continue to appear from the pens of theological scholars. A perusal of texts in the sociology of religion will show that a work like H. Richard Niebuhr's *Social Sources of Denominationalism*[28] has received wide reading in several academic disciplines. Robert Lee's "reply" to the Niebuhr work may find similar usefulness in calling attention to opposite factors at work in church life.[29] Such works not only interpret the church as felt from inside to those who view it entirely from outside but they focus attention upon specific issues and problems and help those within the church to better understand its functioning. Because of this specific focus they do not represent a general sociology of the church, but the contribution they do make need not be depreciated on this account.

The contribution of anthropology must surely be considered in a discussion of ethical discourse in the social sciences. The most narrowly defined sort of anthropological study concerns itself with primitive cultures. Ruth Benedict's *Patterns of Culture* deals with three cultures: the Zuñi cultures among the Mexican pueblos, the Dobu culture near the Trobriand Islands, and the Kwakiutl culture of Vancouver Island. Near the very beginning of her work, Miss Benedict declares that "the distinguishing mark of anthropology among the social sciences is that it includes for serious study other societies than our own."[30] To study other cultures requires the anthropologist to refrain from evaluation of another cultural system by the standards accepted in his own. This is not to say that knowledge of other systems is valid merely as an abstract exercise in gathering a compendium of information, for Miss Benedict takes elaborate pains to point out that knowledge gained from studies of other cultures can, for example, be crucially useful in combatting racial bigotry and prejudice at home.

It is sometimes supposed that a study of primitive cultures is a clue to the origin of civilized ethical and religious patterns. This supposition is often nurtured by the tendency of the uninformed to equate primitive and ancient, to assume that an inquiry into patterns of behavior found among the former is a clue to the patterns that have been passed through by high civilizations. But a primitive culture is unindustrialized, nonliterate, and not necessarily ancient or new. Primitive refers to living extant patterns, not historically discarded ones. To find polygamy among a living culture today does not demonstrate that all cultures have moved from polygamy to monogamy as they have matured. As Miss Benedict puts it, "the use of primitive customs to establish origins is speculative."[31]

Bronislaw Malinowski has declared that "anthropology, as the science of man at large, as the most comprehensive discipline in humanism without portfolio, was the last to come."[32] He goes on to point out that many disciplines contribute to the methodology of the anthropologist, since the nature of "culture" is unveiled by the insights of many disciplines. He places anthropology closest to the humanistic studies, as an inquiry into the meaning of man. But, like Benedict, he emphasizes the implicit valuational purpose in the work of the anthropologist.

> As a scientific moralist fully in sympathy with races hereto oppressed or at least underprivileged, the anthropologist would demand equal treatment for all, full cultural independence for every differential group or nation, no political sovereignty for any tribe, state, kingdom, republic, or empire.[33]

Anthropology has experienced some of the same methodological upheavals as philosophy and sociology. It has become increasingly technical. This shift can be seen by comparing the classical work of L. T. Hobhouse, *Morals in Evolution*,[34] with a work like that written by Florence R. Kluckhohn and Fred L. Strodtbeck entitled *Variations in Value Orientations*.[35] Hobhouse seeks simply to tell the story of the evolution of ethical ideals. His categories are like those of the general historian and require no particular knowledge of technical terms in order to be meaningful. His book, like the work of Edvard Alexander Westermarck entitled *The Origin and Development of Moral Ideals*[36] has been a continuing help to those interested in the growth and development of moral practices. But Hobhouse may be accused of impinging evolution as a pseudo-metaphysical category of Western thought upon the evidence, and must be read with allowance for that perspective.

In the Kluckhohn and Strodtbeck volume, however, the emphasis is upon relativity—in accordance with which the investigator seeks to understand the moral behavior and ethical reflection of the cultures he is studying in terms of the assumptions of the observed cultures rather than his own. This approach results in a more self-consciously developed sort of methodology. We might wonder whether a concept of relativity is any less culturally induced than a concept of evolutionary development, but that would take us afield. In reviewing the various words used by modern anthropologists for the source of valuation, Kluckhohn and Strodtbeck write:

> The concepts of relativity which are critically important to the development of the theory presented in this volume are those of the anthropologists who regard a knowledge of the basic assumptions of a people as indispensable to the interpretation of concrete behavior. Of the variety of terms invented to designate the central core of meanings in societies the most familiar are "unconscious system of meanings" (Sapir), "unconscious canons of choice" (Benedict), "configurations" (C. Kluckhohn), "cultural themes" (Opler), and "core culture" (Thompson). "Basic personality type" (Kardiner and Linton) is an equally familiar concept which has similarities to those just mentioned but differs from them in having a more definitely psychological focus. Still another and more recently formulated concept is that of "world view" (Redfield).[37]

Understandings in all academic disciplines are in flux. Specialization has made it difficult to keep up with the fast moving changes in the different academic fields, though it has not made it impossible to try to keep a running acquaintance with the general scope of what has been going on outside one's special field. This discussion has tried to indicate the broad sweep and major motifs in philosophical ethics and in the social sciences which are significant for an understanding of ethical discourse. This subject must be considered even though the scope of the remarks has been preliminary and limited.

2

Religion, Morality, and Christian Ethics

If we are to understand the form and character of a religious ethic, we must develop some guides for the possible ways of understanding religion as well as for the possible meaning of ethical discourse and behavior. Only thus can we adequately think about the relationship of ethics and religion.

The Relationship of Ethics and Religion

No discussion of the relationship of religion to morality can ignore Henri Bergson's *Two Sources of Morality and Religion*.[1] In this book Bergson talked about two kinds of morality and two kinds of religion. He explored the interrelationship between them in both philosophical and sociological terms. He saw customary morality as that social obligation which functions as a cohesive bond within an existing social order. It dominates a "closed society" in which things are accepted as they are given, in which there is no critical assessment of prevailing practices. Customary morality is related to static religion, which serves to sanctify and entrench the *status quo*. Static religion provides the final sanction for customary morality and employs palliatives and magic to exercise this function.

Whereas Bergson held that customary morality tends to sanctify the existing order and to perpetuate the *status quo* he also felt that there is a creative morality in relation to which religion plays another role. This kind of morality involves aspiration toward an ideal. It challenges existing customs in a prophetic manner because it draws its inspiration from beyond the present situation. It is most effectively practiced in an "open society." Bergson found the mystic to exemplify both creative morality and dynamic religion, since the mystic transforms the situations of which he is a part by transcending the limitations of matter and time. Static religion and customary morality are never entirely replaced by dynamic religion and creative morality. The tension between them persists in all situations in which the more dynamic forms arise. However, without the dynamic and creative elements the social function of religion is negative and disheartening. With them there is a greater promise of social health.

In another classic study Rudolph Otto interpreted religion as the sense of awe before a special reality.[2] He contended that religion involves a unique, nonrational experience of the Holy in which man is confronted by the *Mysterium Tremendum*. The confrontation is mysterious because it involves "the wholly other"; it is tremendous because "the other" portrays a sense of overpowering impact, the feeling of urgency, the dimension of awe. Much that Otto said about this "wholly other" applies to the concept of the sacred, the concept of a unique dimension of experience that is peculiarly "religious."

Otto tended to pull religion and morality apart, placing morality in a sphere of rational experience and religion in the nonrational realm. Indeed, moral earnestness and rigor can be a definite threat to the mystical dimension of religious experience. Sin, for example, is not merely disobedience to a norm or violation of the divine will, but becomes an experience of finitude and inadequacy before the Holy.

The differences between Bergson and Otto illustrate contrasts which appear in a discussion that has grown increasingly complex and sophisticated since they did their pioneering work. The kinds of distinctions made by Bergson have been elaborated and expanded by Robert L. Calhoun.[3] According to Calhoun, religion can appear in different expressions, ranging from assent to cognitive propositions that may have few implications for behavior to a commitment that involves personal surrender. Likewise, moral obligation can appear on different levels: habitual conformity to mores; sanctioned conformity to laws; the preference of duty for its own sake; and conduct which is an authentic response to the acknowledgment of an intrinsic and sovereign good. The relationship between religion and morality is most fruitful when the highest kind of religion is coupled to the highest kind of moral obligation. When this happens, religion contributes a sense of humility in the moral person and a sense of community among seekers after justice and truth. Calhoun's delineation of these issues certainly carries the discussion beyond the oversimplified view that "ethics provides the reasons for choosing the 'right' course; religion helps us to put our *hearts* into it."[4] For Calhoun, not only does religion provide the motive and sustaining force for executing moral decisions, it carries men through the vicissitudes and temptations of life and introduces the experiences of judgment and forgiveness.

Otto's approach has also been given subsequent expressions, particularly in the discussion about the nature of religion as carried on in the phenomenological, or scientific, study of religion (*Religionswissenschaft*). This discipline, less widely known than moral philosophy or the social sciences, describes religious phenomena in terms of the meaning which such phenomena have to those who participate in them as believers. It studies ideas and experiences of the sacred, constantly resisting the reduction of the sacred to other categories. As Mircea Eliade, one of the contemporary exponents of this approach has said, "To try and grasp the essence of a [religious] phenomenon by means of physiology, psychology, sociology, economics, linguistics, art or any other study is false; it misses the one unique and irreducible element in it—the element of the sacred."[5]

While there is no universal agreement among phenomenologists concerning the relationship of religion and morality, their very understanding of religion results in a general consensus that ethical requirements are religious when they are held to be divinely commanded as sacred obligations. In his study *The Meaning of Religion*, W. Brede Kristensen contends that the ethical and ritual prescriptions in the book of Exodus, the Code of Hammurabi, and the Avesta are religious in nature because they are taken as sacred obligations. In these religious codes no distinction is drawn between laws that refer only to man's conceptions of the social good and laws which refer to the worship and treatment of the divine. For example, contractual obligations are considered binding, not because of the intrinsic importance of a man's word to a stable society, but because they are inviolable in the eyes of God. Adherents of a given faith may even accept injunctions which they take to come as divine commands although they seemingly contradict what men normally regard as good. Pointing to the book of Job Kristensen studies the conflict between the content of an ethical norm as understood by man and the divine will as set forth by God. Job claims to be righteous according to the ethical norms he honors as a man but discovers that God's sacred will prevails in a different manner. According to Kristensen, the book of Job declares

> . . . that true human wisdom consists of godly fear and righteousness. That is [man's] law of life. The law which God follows is an inscrutable mystery for man, and he does not need to concern himself with it . . . if God accepts human righteousness as pleasing to Him, this is not because ethical conduct or moral law have autonomous value. Moral law has absolute authority because God has ordained it and ascribes value to it. That is the cardinal point: the belief of the pious man in the value of righteousness is subordinate to his belief in the sovereign, almighty, and omniscient god.[6]

God's will, and not the ethical claim, is the decisive element. God's will is subject to no judgment, even the judgment of "the good" as defined by normal ethical standards. Kristensen is not suggesting that religious demands always contradict the normally ethical—but the possibility that they will do so must be acknowledged. God often requires the same righteousness that ethical men would themselves cherish, but He is not bound to do so. Hence, a religious morality is always one in which the priority for valuation is placed upon the divine will, not upon an independent ethical criterion.[7]

The phenomenological approach can never fully avoid the tendency to think of religion as something added to ethics rather than something which is an inherent feature of the ethical itself. Geradus Van der Leeuw, in his classic phenomenology of religion, *Religion in Essence and Manifestation*, seems to acknowledge the possibility of an ethic arising on its own terms, but such an ethic is basically different from religion. Religious morality is more like custom, resting upon the sanction of some external power.

> Observance of the potency of life, tabus, and purifications, the obligations of worship and the other demands of Power upon life, together constitute usage, tradition and custom, whose sphere of operation is more extensive than that of law. Custom then is essentially religious, because it is the endowing with form of fear and awe before superior power . . . morality may derive its own claim either from some quite independent principle, as it has been sought to do again and again in the modern world, or else it rests, exactly like custom, on the demand of Power.[8]

In an attempt to combine insights from the phenomenology of religion with insights from an analytical philosophy, Ninian Smart has created an elaborate discussion of the role of religion in relation to ethics. Smart prefers the term *spiritual* to the term *religious* but uses both terms in his discussion. He acknowledges the common meaning of the term *religious* with its reference to the notion of God and the institutional paraphernalia of worship and ritual. But he sees "spiritual" dimensions in nontheistic doctrinal schemes and in metaphysical beliefs that have overwhelming power upon their adherents without benefit of institutional backing.

Smart admits that moral propositions are considered by most religious men to be intimately related to religious commitments. An ethic is religious when it is held to be by its adherents. Religious men must make this identification consciously—an ethic is not religious if it is unacknowledged as such. The religious man appeals to doctrinal affirmations in defense of ethical judgments, whereas the nonreligious man appeals to what he takes as self-authenticating human values. The resultant action may be the same: "I think it can be claimed that . . . appeal to God's Will or to the doctrine that man is made in the divine image will not yield any different result from simple appeal to the principles that suffering is an evil and that men are to be treated compassionately and benevolently."[9] (Smart concludes that moral judgments can be arrived at apart from religious authority, at least as he understands such authority.)

Those who relate their ethical decisions to religious factors do so, Smart contends, in three main "strands," or patterns. In the *numinous* strand religion provides a spiritual sanction for duty which can be and has been formulated by ordinary reflection. In this strand religion makes into a spiritual concern values and attitudes which are also found in the mundane realm, though it may alter their quality in the process. Work becomes prayer, obedience to elementary rules of fair play becomes obedience to God's will, and humility becomes abasement before the Holy One. In this numinous strand men move from ethical insights attained from their common experience to a situation in which these insights are given sacred meaning. The spiritual is superimposed upon the moral, and by this very imposition runs the risk of seeming to offer "eccentric" or unusual reasons for justifying actions.

In the *mystical* strand one goal becomes of overriding importance. It functions as the *summum bonum* which actually upsets all contending values in order to achieve its dominance. This goal often is an ascetic one, in which celibacy and renunciation of worldly goods are practiced in order to attain a future end. This kind of religious ethic leads to a radical recasting of the value structure of the believer in contrast to the value structures of nonreligious men. It also tends to engender a claim on the part of the mystic that he has the highest sort of morality, a morality which transcends the normal distinctions between good and evil.

In the third pattern, which Smart calls the *incarnation* strand, an earthly appearance of a deity provides the moral example by which the religious man measures his daily conduct. The attempt of the religious man to respond in fidelity to the paradigm-example is incalculably effective in creating and sustaining moral earnestness. Those who approach the behavior patterns that have been made real in the incarnation of the divine being thereby become saints, who in turn inspire more response to the paradigm. Christianity, in which the Incarnation occurs in a single, unique man, presents the paradigm as sinless. Jesus Christ reflects the divine without blemish. While this single incarnation gives clear focus and direction to the believer, its very purity places him under the highest possible demand.

Smart's categories introduce breadth and diversity into the phenomenological approach and describe variations that are obscured by the definition of the sacred as an imposed external reality which functions only to sanction ethical actions. But, even for Smart, religion is something external to ethics. This external function of religion in relation to ethical choice looks to many men like authoritarianism, like an irrational devotion behind fanatical causes, like resistance to valid human efforts to create community between men. There are many thinkers who regard religious morality as unacceptable by virtue of the very qualities that the phenomenologists make definitive.

Paul Tillich has proposed a very different way of thinking about religion and morality, a way that rejects all dichotomies between reason-determined and faith-determined ethics. He wrote that "religious principles dwell within the principles of moral action" and that "morality is intrinsically religious, as religion is intrinsically ethical. . . ."[10] For Tillich, there is a religious dimension in the moral imperative itself. This religious dimension in the moral imperative is the element of the unconditional, which is present within the intrinsic claim of the moral impulse itself and not merely as the obligation to obey an external command. Moral impulses arise from matters of great concern when normative issues are present. If no striking or important consequences are involved, there is no moral issue. Tillich charged that analytical inquiry into semantics of ethical language, such as carried on today by some philosophers, cannot understand the element of concern that is crucial to morality. He also complained that a pure existentialism, which makes decisions mere matters of preferences, undercuts the normative aspect of ethics.

According to Tillich, religion often errs, gravely and demonically, when it functions as the sanction for action that does not of itself have the ultimate nature of a genuine concern. Tillich called this "graceless moralism" and criticized much popular preaching and even serious theologizing for perverting the ethical impulse. There is a danger in the subordination of the ethical to the sacred, as Tillich noted when he observed "that the unconditional character of the moral imperative is its religious quality. No religious heteronomy, subjection to external commands, is implied if we maintain the immanence of religion in the moral command."[11]

Tillich's analysis stands in distinct contrast with that of Kristensen and the other phenomenologists. Perhaps the distinction between them should be described as follows: For Kristensen, the religious element (the sacred) is something which is "added to" the ethical dimension as a sanction for it. For Tillich, the religious element (the unconditional) is something which inheres alike within the ethical and the religious realms. Tillich made this distinction clear in suggesting that the phrase "the Will of God" must be interpreted in a new way.

> It is not an external will imposed upon us, an arbitrary law laid down by a heavenly tyrant, who is strange to our essential nature and therefore whom we resist justifiably from the point of view of our nature. The "Will of God" for us is precisely our essential being with all its potentialities, our created nature declared as "very good" by God, as in terms of the Creation myth. He "saw everything that he made." For us the "Will of God" is manifest in our essential being; and only because of this can we accept the moral imperative as valid. It is not a strange law that demands our obedience, but the "silent voice" of our own nature as man, and as man with an individual character.[12]

Tillich and Kristensen disagree, not only about what makes an ethic religious, but about the very nature of religion itself. Kristensen thinks of religion by grouping different phenomena (such as prayer, sacrifice, ritual) into patterns which make up religion in terms of its observable features. In looking at the various factors belonging to the *genus religiosus,* the values that such beliefs and practices have for their adherents are given significant attention, but these are not judged as right or wrong with the tools of phenomenology, since the fact that they are considered valid by their adherents is an ingredient of the phenomenon. Tillich's definition of religion involves the concept of "ultimate concern." Within this definition "god" is understood as that which exercises dominant influence over men by virtue of their submission to its formative power. This influence need not be in the form of a supernatural being (with flowing beard and shining halo) or even a supernatural authority, but may be that which is functionally prior to, or formative of, all the thinking-acting of the believer. It is, therefore, not an object of belief which can appear or disappear without fundamentally affecting the situation of the believer, but is his very "ground of being." This "ground of being" cannot be changed without totally restructuring existence. Religion involves that aspect of life best described as "man's ultimate concern." "Man is unconditionally concerned about that which conditions his being beyond all the conditions in him and around him. Man is ultimately concerned about that which determines his ultimate destiny beyond all preliminary necessities and accidents."[13]

Neither of these views by itself is adequate to describe all that appears as Christian ethics. In some forms of the Christian ethic the norm is sanctioned by religious authority functioning "externally." For example, some Christians accept the Decalogue of Moses or the Sermon on the Mount as taught by Jesus because they come from the Bible or were taught by religious leaders of great authority. But in other forms of the Christian ethic the intrinsic moral claim of a norm coincides with the religious impulse. Under such conditions the Decalogue and the Sermon on the Mount capture the allegiance of men because they commend themselves by their own ethical content as well as by virtue of their source. To insist that religious morality must be confined to one of these rubrics is to judge what is proper or creative religion rather than merely what is religion in general. It is to raise issues which properly belong to the theological enterprise.

Theological Discourse about Ethics

Theology is the reflective, articulate elaboration of the meaning of faith based upon the explicit acknowledgment of a commitment. There may be religious behavior without such reflection but not theological ethics. For a given thinker or given tradition the explication and elaboration of a faith structure in theological terms may do more than merely identify a standing ground, but it must at least do that. It will also justify the standing ground and provide criteria for choosing between otherwise diverse and confusing patterns of thought and action. The point of view from which diverse evidence is scrutinized determines the way in which that evidence is sifted, analyzed, and finally understood. In theological inquiry about ethics, we are concerned about the effect of supreme loyalties upon men's views of right and wrong.

Unreflective action, however much it may be governed by a single object of devotion, is not theological analysis. Most ethical discourse is undertaken within a framework of presuppositions which function much as does a faith-commitment, but we cannot rightly consider such discourse to be theological if it does not examine its commitments. Moreover, it may well belong to theological analysis to ferret out the unexpressed and unacknowledged grounds upon which men in other disciplines make their judgments and interpret their assertions. This process can be friendly when it seeks merely to bring to light matters otherwise ignored; it becomes polemical when men claim exemption from the standing ground of a faith-commitment and must have their commitments and assumptions pointed out.

In approaching its task theology must relate itself in some fashion to the range of ethical discourse represented by the various philosophical and descriptive disciplines. It may do this by rejecting them as unable to provide either form or guidance for its work. It seldom does this merely by ignoring them. Karl Barth stands as a contemporary exponent of the view that theological ethics must take its authority solely from a revealed command of God. For Barth, theological ethics proceeds without depending upon or acknowledging normative elements in other ethics. No reason above the command of God can be given for obedience to the command. Ethics is a branch of dogmatics. "True man and his good action can be viewed only from the standpoint of the true and active God and His goodness."[14]

Barth's problem arises when he seeks to talk about ethics within the limits imposed by his theological methodology. How is he to talk about the true and active God? He might use biblical materials, as he sometimes does. But Barth's discourse about ethics is not simply an exegesis of biblical materials. He quotes biblical texts and refers to biblical themes, but he does not structure his presentation around a biblical pattern. Indeed, his primary category for the structuring of ethical discussion is freedom; his subcategories are freedom before God, freedom in fellowship, freedom for life, and freedom in limitation. His general thesis consists in the statement that "the goodness of human action consists in the goodness with which God acts toward man,"[15] but his means for describing this goodness clearly exhibits great familiarity with much general human discourse about ethics.

In fact, "general" ethics may become a clue to the inherent features of the divine demand, though no particular sort of ethical reflection—such as existentialist philosophy—encompasses this demand adequately. What has been denied entrance at the front door (especially in Chapter VIII of Volume II,2 of the *Dogmatics*) is admitted through the side door (Chapter I of Volume III,4). The contributions represented by "general ethics" must be kept subordinate to the considerations from dogmatics, but they can be employed for expository purposes. "In books and lectures ethics can be treated independently, that is, in external separation from dogmatics, so long as it is presupposed that this separation is understood and treated as purely technical, and therefore that dogmatics is not detached from its ethical content and direction and that the question of dogmatics remains paramount and decisive in ethics."[16]

Another way of considering the relationship of theological discourse to other forms of discourse about ethics is to consider theological discourse as a source of supplementary guidance. This supplementary guidance may be of two qualities. In St. Thomas Aquinas it is different in nature, so that what is seen theologically in revelation is taken to complement what is known philosophically through reason. Theological discourse about ethics supplements general human discourse about ethics by providing a body of insight and knowledge with very special qualities. In this sort of relationship the innately different quality of theological discourse is preserved as fully as it is preserved in Barth, but it extends and supplements other sources of judgment instead of remaining aloof from them.

A. C. Knudson acknowledges the special subject matter of theology without postulating any methodological difference between it and philosophical discourse.

> In its method of validation [Christian or theological ethics] does not differ from philosophical ethics. But it emphasizes, as the latter does not, the ethical teaching of Scripture and of the Christian church. It approaches the whole moral problem from the religious point of view, and hence deals with such questions as those above noted in a way and to an extent that would hardly seem fitting in general ethics. Its standpoint is that of the church. It concentrates attention on those moral problems in which the church has been and is primarily interested, and hence is as much entitled to be regarded as an independent discipline as is theology.[17]

The peculiar focus of attention described by Knudson may actually create special problems for his view that there is no basic difference between philosophical and theological methodologies. To stand within the church, to be interested in the problems peculiar to its life, and to adopt the religious point of view in confronting moral questions may well entail something a bit distinct from philosophical reasoning. Knudson's problem seems to be the reverse of Barth's. Barth postulates a sharp dichotomy between theological discourse and general discourse about ethics and then seems to make a tentative place for general discourse for which there is really no theoretical slot in his scheme of things; Knudson postulates similarity between philosophical discourse and theological discourse and then mentions a number of factors for which philosophical discourse has no seeming place. Perhaps the complexities of theological discourse as actually used defy their simple classification as completely distinct from or fully equivalent to other forms of ethics discourse.

The theological consideration of ethical matters also contributes a vocabulary which is apparently distinctive. Words like *grace, sin, judgment*, and *eschatology* are seldom heard except in theological works. These words have relevance for moral issues and for the analysis of the moral situation even though they may not be rightly considered as merely ethical in their meanings and connotations. Take, for instance, the word *sin*. It involves some idea of wrongdoing, of violating rules or sacred trusts. These common views of sin are essentially moralistic, overly concerned with the ethical implications of the term. The ideas of sin as misplaced allegiance, as ruptured fidelity, as pretension and pride, are not at first evoked in non-theological discourse. With its category of sin theological inquiry takes the normal categories of ethical experience—standards and their violations—and unfolds a new set of meanings. These meanings are not necessarily discontinuous with ordinary experience, nor are they confined to the specific experiences that are to be had within ecclesiastical structures. They are meanings which are explored with the aid of theological discourse as it seeks to explore the commitment it professes to a particular world-view. They are meanings relevant to the analysis of loyalty configurations and the description of the quality of human relationships in regard to what is held to be of surpassing worth.

There is a communal experience involved in the use of most theological language. Hence, there can be very little theological language apart from some relationship to a community of faith to which that language is relevant. For those who stand in the Christian tradition this community is the church. But to stand within the church means many different things, even to Christians, and the debates are long and bitter as to how this standing point is to be understood. The communal experience becomes subject to analysis and scrutiny even by those for whom it is an object of allegiance and a means of identification. H. Richard Niebuhr has caught the interplay between the communal and the critical in this relationship.

To be in history is to be in society, though in a particular society. Every view of the universal from the finite standpoint of the individual in such a society is subject to the test of experience on the part of companions who look from the same standpoint in the same direction as well as to the test of consistency with the principles and concepts that have grown out of past experience in the same community. A theology which undertakes the limited work of understanding and criticizing within Christian history the thought and action of the church is also a theology which is dependent on the church for the constant test of its critical work. Being in social history it cannot be a personal and private theology nor can it live in some non-churchly sphere of political or cultural history; its home is the church; its language is the language of the church; and with the church it is directed toward the universal from which the church knows itself to derive its being and to which it points in all its faith and works.[18]

There is yet another way to characterize theological reflection about ethics. It may be regarded as the transvaluation of ethical discourse. The meaning of transvaluation can be seen in a case study. For field work as part of his training, a seminary student was assigned to a settlement house in a slum neighborhood and given the task of acting as "big brother" to a gang of street ruffians. The very first night on the job he found himself with a group that was planning a switch-blade raid on a rival gang, and he was asked to go with the group. All the training of the student, his inclination to fair play, his respect for the law, his abhorrence of violence, were at odds with the assigned task of getting to know the members of the gang as persons bound together by trust and mutual respect.

There were at least four possible courses of action open to the student. Not only was it necessary for him to choose whether or not to go on the raid, but he had also to consider what sort of a relationship to maintain with the gang under either condition. There were different ways of going and different ways of refusing to go. The student could, of course, have walked out in a self-righteous huff, condemning the boys in forceful language as naughty street urchins. The stronger the moral convictions of the student about law and order the more tempting this course of action. "Mother taught me," he might say, "to keep out of trouble; my minister, to do what Jesus would do; my scoutmaster, to obey the law and be morally upright; my school teacher, to live up to my ideals." If he pursued this course of action, the seminary student would presumably return to the field work office for another assignment, breaking all relationship with the gang.

A second possible course of action would have involved saying to the boys in the gang, "I can't participate in this, but I'll wait here for you and if any of you get in trouble I'll come to the police station and help bail you out. I'll have hot chocolate ready when you get back."

Or, the student might have carefully explained to the boys why he considered the raid socially dangerous and morally questionable, yet have said in effect, "I'm part of your outfit; if as a gang you decide to go, I'm going also. I'll accept any blame that comes our way. I hope we don't get into any trouble. Play it cool and avoid difficulty. However, if the cops come, be reasonable and polite. Let me do the talking and see what happens if we treat the cops squarely."

A fourth way of meeting the situation might find the student saying to the boys, "Let's get the other gang and give 'em what's coming to them! Run if the cops come. Give me a razor to protect myself."

If this situation is analyzed from the moral perspective that gang raids are wrong, the distinctive alternatives are to go or not to go. The first and second courses of action are "morally" right; the third and fourth, "morally" wrong. In judging what he should do, the student might well decide he can have no part of the raid. The question as to whether he quits the job, or stays at the settlement house to prepare hot chocolate is secondary to the primary decision not to be personally involved in a moral wrong.

If this situation is analyzed from another perspective, a perspective which regards the fostering and maintaining of a relationship to the boys in the gang as the leader's main responsibility, then other courses of action may be judged valuable. The student may feel he must go along on the raid in order to create the possibility of fruitful relationships with the group, perhaps even according to the fourth mode of action. He may decide the risks involved in accepting the group's plans are worth taking for the sake of creating the future rapport needed in a leader/confidant.

To analyze this situation in terms of the relationships involved rather than in terms of the moral standing of the deed planned is to transvaluate the ethical situation. Presumably something of this sort is portrayed by the Gospel accounts in which Jesus eats with publicans and sinners and in which Jesus treats lightly the Sabbath law in order to render needed human service. What happens in each case is that a new constellation of values and considerations gets introduced into a situation, forcing quite different judgments as to what ought to be served by any response to it.

The meaning of transvaluation has been more abstractly described by H. Richard Niebuhr, who wrote about the moral implications of faith in the God made known in Jesus Christ. To acknowledge faith in this God is to submit every known human value to his judgment; to be willing to abandon every humanly cherished value to the value that is acknowledged in Him. This does not require, however, that human values be rejected or ignored. The theological enterprise does not produce a self-sustaining and internally consistent alternative to human values which can be embraced without continued relationships to them. Instead, it takes human values and the moral law and gives them a new seriousness and a new dimension of application. The theological enterprise does not come forth with additional considerations supplementing that already known on other grounds. Instead, it reconstitutes the human stuff already known into a new reality. Human knowledge is not rejected; it is not superseded; but "universalized and intensified until it is reborn."[19]

From this flow many new perspectives on the ethical enterprise. Obedience to God overrides every earthly value claim; no creaturely thing is to be served as absolute, yet every creaturely thing is to be embraced as a concern. Moral obedience is no longer to be restricted to the circle of those who reciprocate in kind, but extends to enemies and all in need. This involves, not the acceptance of a new and more stringent law embraced in the manner of the old and less demanding law, but a new embrace of the old law which by its very totality reforms and recreates that law in new dimensions. Even the man who adheres to the law is judged and cleansed as he comes to see his continual perversion of the very thing to which he gives allegiance.

> So the revelation of the person may be said to involve the republication of the moral law. But what is republished is an original edition that had been hopelessly corrupted by a multitude of wretched translators and conceited scholars of whom we Christians doubtless are the worst. . . . The original edition of the moral law is not handed to us in definitive form through any act of revelation. Let us rather say that when the lawgiver is revealed with his intentions the reasoning heart is granted the rudiments of a scholarly equipment by means of which, with much pain and labor, it may through all its history work at the restoration of the fundamental text. That this reason will often be led astray by evil imaginations and that it will introduce new corruptions is also certain in the light of a revelation which shows up man's sinful self even as it discloses the personal goodness of God.[20]

The transvaluation of which Niebuhr spoke sets ethical discourse into relational terms. Niebuhr used the terms *relative* and *relativity* but, as Paul Ramsey observes, *relational* and *relatedness* more nearly describe his position. Value is determined by the persons or beings for whom something is good; it is not a rigid category of right. The seminary student, to return to the illustration, would judge his actions in terms of their consequences-in-relation to the group with whom he is thrown in contact. He would not measure his actions by abstract preconceptions of innately right and innately wrong behavior.

We have discussed three understandings of the theological enterprise with illustrations drawn from modern Christian thinkers. We might also have chosen thinkers from the past history of Christian thought. The pattern of rejection by theology of the contributions of other insights was early seen in Tertullian. Denying the value of philosophy for Christian faith he exclaimed in famous lines, "What has Jerusalem to do with Athens?" The pattern of transvaluation was early seen in Augustine, who took the thought of the Greek philosophers and transformed it to Christian purposes. Origen could be classified as a supplementalist, who added Christian vocabulary to systems borrowed from the thought world of his day.

To approach ethical issues with an acknowledged fidelity to a faith-commitment does not give uniform answers to previously unsolved problems. It even raises new questions as to how the faith commitment is to be related to other branches of human thought. The very multiplicity of understandings which arise in relationship to this issue constitutes much of the data with which the theologian must deal. Even when he seeks to present his own point of view as the most satisfactory solution to certain issues, he does so in relation to the thought of other theologians. He who cannot engage in dialogue dare not enter the theological enterprise. He who does not dare to enter is likely to ignore a most fundamental ethical issue—the issue as to the grounds from which life is viewed and in terms of which response to it is made.

Christian Ethics as Norm and Act

In dealing with ethical questions men who are loyal to a particular tradition seldom concern themselves with acquiring general notions about theological ethics and then proceed to apply these canons to the peculiar issues of their own traditions. Men who consider ethical questions in acknowledged relationship to faith commitments often do so in fidelity to a specific tradition. In speaking about Christian ethics, therefore, we are not speaking of a branch of theological ethics which has its methodological problems solved for it by a parent discipline. All the issues that plague theological ethics plague Christian ethics as well, with the addition of special issues that arise out of the special features of Christian experience. Like any form of theological ethics, Christian ethics deals with a wide range of concerns that are related to an acknowledged faith commitment. Like any form of theological ethics it deals with these concerns in a variety of ways, at times sharply debating the relative merits of the different ways. There is no hierarchical pattern, moving from general to philosophical to theological to Christian ethics—with issues appropriate to each category settled prior to the adoption of the next category. All the considerations which arise in relation to ethics-in-general arise also in relation to Christian ethics-in-particular.

To insist that Christian ethics is marked by great diversity is not to deny the right of any thinker to advance an argument in support of some particular perspective as the most satisfactory Christian solution to an issue. Such arguments form the very stuff of which the discipline is made. As a field of scholarly endeavor, theology must acknowledge the existence of divergent views and explore the implications of arguments between them. It must permit and encourage individual thinkers to arrive at independent understandings and to justify them in dialogical relationship to each other and to the tradition within which the theologian works. Theologians do this, not by ignoring their own positions or refusing to define their standing ground, but by finding how their conclusions relate to the range of views advanced by others in claimed fidelity to different traditions.

To emphasize the diversity and to survey the possibilities in Christian ethics is the necessary point of beginning. It is a necessary point of beginning because there are those who expect Christian ethics to be a monolithic reality. This expectation is sometimes harbored by those who are unacquainted with theology and who jump to the conclusion that authority, tradition, and dogma conspire to prevent any sort of diversity. This expectation is also harbored by those who insist that a particular formulation of the ethical question is the only legitimate expression of the Christian ethic. To emphasize the existence of diversity is to guard against misinterpretation by those who fail to recognize its existence. It is also to guard against the attacks of those who would overcome it by arbitrary authority.

But the issue cannot be left with diversity alone. " 'Christian' then would be only a family name, and have no reference to an integrity which unites Christians in all ages."[21] In discussing the problem of "the one and the many" in Christian ethics, Waldo Beach and H. Richard Niebuhr wisely insist that something more than a mere compendium of arguments must be discovered. Without ignoring the many contrasts within the field—contrasts between ethics of obligation and ethics of aspiration, between law and freedom, between Christ and the world—these authors focus the unity of Christian ethics upon the two commandments of love for God and love for neighbor.

> Within the variables of Christian ethical theories, there is a constant *triadic* relation—the "vertical" relation of the believing and acting self to God, and the "horizontal" relation of the self to other selves—a relation in which God is, so to speak, the "middle term." How and why the neighbor is loved depends on how and why God is loved. Thus, in Jesus' summary of the law, the Second Commandment, to love the neighbor, is described as like or part of the First.[22]

It is clear from this quotation that Christian ethics has something to do with the Bible. It is in the Bible that the two commandments are set forth. They are first given in the book of Deuteronomy; they are repeated by Jesus as a summary of the law. But here, so to speak, the agreement stops. To say that Christian ethics has something to do with the Bible is not to define just how this relationship is to be understood. Christians have argued for centuries concerning how to understand both the content and the authority of the Bible, and Christian ethics both reflects and helps perpetuate the arguments. Does the Bible set forth its ethical implications as demands voiced directly by God, as ideals that are compatible with the conclusions of metaphysical philosophy, as the portrayal of events to which men are to respond from the depth of their own selfhood, or by picturing the life and heroic death of a leader to be emulated? While Christians may be one, or nearly one, in their acknowledged fidelity to the Bible, they are surely many in their understandings of the role played by the Bible in the determination of ethical decisions.

It is also clear from the quotation from the work by Beach and Niebuhr that Christian ethics has something to do with allegiance to God, especially to God as known and revealed in Jesus Christ. It is God's will that is made known in the Commandments. It is love for God that furnishes the essential relationship of the faithful man. But to say that Christian ethics has something to do with God as made known in Jesus Christ is to leave unexplored the ways in which the nature and self-disclosure of God are to be understood. Is God a structure of essential goodness by which all ethical values are to be measured? Is He the source of authority for certain laws, or One who acts in history with a freedom that makes possible the freedom of the faithful man to meet contingent situations in fidelity to Him without bondage to law? Does Jesus Christ reveal God's will by acting out a life of moral rectitude and sacrificial heroism which binds his followers to perform similar acts, or does he portray the love of God in redeeming men so that they can respond to the world about them in the freedom of their authentic calling to love their neighbors in a pattern appropriate to their own situation? Does the revelation require adherence to a supernaturalistic idea of God or will the categories of "ultimate concern" or "the ground of being" adequately support the ethical imperatives involved? Does belief in God require explicit acknowledgment of his existence to accompany every action or does the "secular" realm of worldly chores provide as full and as true a means of service to God as life in a monastery?

A final element evident in the quotation is the concept of love. Christian ethics has something to do with love. This term is most commonly employed to describe the character of the Christian life. Those who wish to be more explicit prefer the transliteration of the Greek word from the New Testament, *agape*, for which a near equivalent in English is "self-giving" or "outpouring love." This love is for God and for neighbor; the extent to which it may permit a concern about the self is cause for great debate. Does it stand alone, in distinct contrast to other forms of love, such as *eros*, the Greek word for self-regarding love which takes satisfaction from the object of its regard and affection? Is love a possibility for men to follow in all, or only in some, relationships of life? Is it fulfilled or contradicted by justice? Can the exercise of love include resort to violence as the effort to protect the neighbor, or does love include as legitimate only nonviolent sorts of persuasion? These are the questions which arise, along with many others, to perplex and agitate those who begin the pilgrimage into Christian ethics by starting with the realization that love is its central concept.

There is another term which forms a prominent ingredient in the Christian ethic. It does not appear, except perhaps by implication, in the summary made by Beach and Niebuhr. There are men who would deny it as a necessary consideration in the crystallization of a Christian ethic, even though by so doing they must take issue with a prevailing motif in the tradition. The concept of the community or fellowship of believers, in which the heritage is known and through which the tradition is kept real, figures in a Christian ethic. Christian ethics is related to the church. For some it is inseparable from the church. But to mention the church is to require another definition. Do we mean the visible social institution on the corner, complete with bazaars, steeple, and perhaps even air-conditioning? Do we mean the body of loyal followers of Jesus Christ, those who really do his will? Do we mean a priesthood which has the power of absolution and through this power exercises subtle restraints and influence upon the behavior of the membership? Do we mean the preaching of the word and the administration of the sacraments by which fidelity to the tradition is maintained and the grace of Jesus Christ made real in the world of the present? Do we mean a special group of elected or appointed elders who are charged with authority and power to administer discipline in a functioning social organism? Do we mean the culturally conditioned institution which seems adept at compromising and perverting every moral and spiritual reality to which it tries to point? The church is no exception to the rule that each time one adds a defining concept to Christian ethics he opens up a host of issues for debate and argument.

Those who are appropriately modest in dealing with Christian ethics acknowledge this diversity in developing their own points of view. Some years ago, Reinhold Niebuhr wrote a book called *An Interpretation of Christian Ethics*.[23] This title has frequently been cited with appreciation as a sign of Niebuhr's realization of the relationship of his own outlook to the diversity we have portrayed. Likewise, E. Clinton Gardner writes in the opening chapter of another book: "The present interpretation of Christian ethics is offered, therefore, not as a definitive treatment of the subject but rather as one approach to Christian ethics."[24] Gardner argues that the flavor of a particular ethic will be determined by the nature of the theological perspective from which it is written. Jesus gave his followers neither a systematic theology nor an ethical system, and consequently great variety has occurred in men's efforts to explore the meaning of his life, death, and resurrection.

Other writers are less modest. Carl F. H. Henry declares:

> The ethics of Hebrew-Christian theistic revelation commends itself to logical thought because its coherence avoids the conflicts which lurk in the speculative accounts of the moral claim. It rises above the interior contradictions of secular ethics and provides a new integration of the legitimate elements of the moral situation.[25]

We should be amiss, however, if we take Henry's declaration that the thrust toward uniformity and agreement is a mark of the orthodox theological camp of which he is a member. Andrew R. Osborn, an admirer and student of Schleiermacher, and a strong advocate of the scientific method in Christian ethical reflection, held tenaciously to the view that all interpretative disagreements in Christian ethics ought finally to be overcome. Osborn insisted that there is no fundamental difference between the truths of observation as known by natural reason and the truths of revelation as known from the Bible. "When there is apparent disagreement, the difficulty becomes an occasion for the more exact investigation of the meaning of both. The solution will come with clear knowledge. It is an axiom that, rightly understood, scientific knowledge and revealed truth are in complete accord."[26]

We cannot transfer to ethical reflection the divisions of thought usually associated with theological points of view. To be sure, Roman Catholic, liberal Protestant, fundamentalist, and neo-orthodox approaches to Christian faith each manifest certain characteristics in their handling of the ethical question. But these divisions of the theological spectrum are more accurately reflective of attitudes toward the question of revelation and authority than of the attitudes involved in ethical analysis. In the chapters that follow we shall explore at greater length the peculiar motifs for the ethical question as these find expression in the thought of different theologians. It is only by such a procedure that we can deal with a field in which, for example, a conservative view of Scripture and a reliance upon a so-called scientific method would both call for the end of diversity within the field of ethical analysis.

Despite the many differences between Christians concerning how ethical matters are to be understood, they seem to be agreed about the responsibility of the believer to act upon his ethics as well as to think about them. P. H. Nowell-Smith, writing from a philosophical perspective that claims to be concerned only with theoretical knowledge about moral information, rightly observes that the traditional metaphysical interest in the good life is shared by religious ethics. No religious ethic will finally be content merely to arrive at verified statements that such and such a moral principle is true. The inner thrust must be present to act upon the principle in fidelity and responsiveness to its claim as a guide to action.

There are many ways of saying this within the Christian tradition. Jesus observed that men shall be known by their fruits. He had harsh words for those who admitted knowledge of the law but had not observed it. Paul Ramsey once remarked that "Christian ethics as a *theory* is always an interruption of Christian action,"[27] and went on to insist that interest in theory must never truncate action. James Gustafson declares, "the study of ethics can never replace the personal responsibility to act—in relation to the action of God and the actions of other men."[28]

Two elements constitute the roots of the ethical enterprise. Ethics involves theory and practice, ends and means, standards and applications. It is not clear that a separation between these two aspects of the problem is as real in life as it can be made in theoretical discourse. Men often reflect upon what they have done following their actions, or at least during their actions. They move by impulse and conditioning as well as by analysis and deliberation. They may even employ means to implement their ideals that are difficult to reconcile with the ends they profess to serve. Nevertheless, whether in sequence, in combination, or in seeming detachment from one another, the elements of standard-setting and decision-implementing constitute twin foci of the ethical enterprise. Only a few philosophers, who take special pains to limit their analysis artificially, deny this twin character of the moral task.

In the structure of this work we have chosen to deal separately with these two aspects of the ethical problem. Any discursive analysis must employ categories and classifications to explore the variety and complexity of human ideals and actions. It must abstract from vast complexities some manageable framework with which to set forth its understandings. There is a logic to a pattern which starts with questions as to how ethical standards are determined and moves to questions as to how ethical decisions are implemented. This logic does not imply that all men make decisions in this order. It simply justifies this procedure for the discussion of issues.

To suggest that Christian ethics is concerned with both norms and actions, with standards and structures, with discourse and with acts is not to suggest that all the questions and complexities occur on the first of these levels. The achievement of constructive actions does not result from simply exhorting men to actualize what they have thought about reflectively. There are just as many questions regarding the best ways to implement ethical decisions as there are about what norms should guide and govern ethical action. There is a good deal of theoretical analysis involved with regard to applications, as well as norms. Critical inquiry is required in both areas. To be sure, consideration of norms will find itself in conversation with philosophical questions; consideration of strategy is likely to be in conversation with issues confronted in the social sciences. In some cases this distinction is reflected in a difference between Christian ethics and social ethics, between moral theology and Christian sociology. Any distinctions of this sort, valuable as they may be for organization of curricula or specialization of interest, must ultimately be subordinate to the more inclusive task of portraying Christian ethics as both a search for wisdom about the nature of the divine imperative and a shrewdness in the capacity to implement what it requires.

II
The Formulation of the Ethical Norm

3

Reason as a Source of Moral Judgments

This chapter discusses the use of reason as a source of moral judgments in Christian ethics. The next chapter discusses the use of philosophical categories for the statement and elaboration of Christian norms. In the first approach, Christian ethics is subsumed under the rubrics of philosophy; in the second, valid elements in philosophical ethics are appropriated and bent to the service of theological commitments. In the first, a rationally autonomous philosophy is the master of Christian judgment; in the second, moral philosophy is the tool of Christian ethics. In both cases, however, deliberative and rational judgments are used to formulate the ethical norm, and general principles or ideals are used for judging actions to be right or wrong.

Enough has already been said in Chapter 1 to suggest that moral philosophy is not a monolith to which Christians may turn for a single unified set of judgments about moral matters. Some philosophers prefer an empirical-pragmatic rather than an idealistic basis for judgments. Still others doubt that reason can furnish valid judgments of normative character without at least some degree of guidance from religious revelation. The deliberative motif in Christian ethics is not a single approach that always comes to the same answers and overcomes all disagreements by the use of reason, but it is a varied set of procedures for deriving ethical ideals from or with the aid of the reason and for judging acts in light of general principles and concepts of the good.

Clear but Partial Use of Reason: Aquinas and Scholastic Catholicism

Saint Thomas Aquinas based his ethics on a carefully reasoned discussion of the end of man in relation to the providence of God. He acknowledged the validity of the God-given reason as a source of ethical guidance:

> . . . it is clear that the rational creature alone is directed to its actions
> by God, not only in what befits the species, but also in what befits the

individual. For everything is for the sake of its operation, since operation is the ultimate perfection of a thing. Therefore each thing is
directed to its action by God, according as it is subject to the divine
providence. Now the rational creature is subject to the divine providence as being for its own sake governed and cared for, and not, as
other corruptible creatures, for the sake of the species only. For the
individual that is governed only for the sake of the species is not
governed for its own sake, whereas the rational creature is governed
for its own sake, as we have made clear. Accordingly, rational creatures alone are directed by God to their actions for the sake, not only
of the species, but also of the individual. . . .
Besides. The rational creature is subject to the divine providence in
such a way, that not only is it governed thereby, but is able to know
something of the nature of providence; so that it is capable of exercising providence and government in relation to others.[1]

Thomas did not understand the reason to be autonomous, a law unto itself.
Man can be guided by reason because there is reason in God which governs
the usefulness of reason for man. To be sure, unreasonable men pervert
their own nature and obscure the divine wisdom. But these men can be
judged faulty in their use of reason because they do not follow the measure
of true rationality known in divine providence.

Reason in Thomas is not simply the servant of revelation, assigned only
to the task of explicating truth given by some other means. Reason does
have a contribution to make to ethical knowledge, apart from revelation.
Natural man can derive a partial, yet valid, knowledge of God by the use
of his reason. He can also make valid judgments between good and evil
as he uses his reason in governing his relationship to others. Other factors,
such as revelation, have an important place, but they never contradict or
overturn what is validly understood on rational grounds.

The discussion of human action which dominates the second part of the
first book of the *Summa Theologiae* is a highly rational analysis of moral
choice and its consequences. In this analysis Thomas considers the sense
in which human acts are voluntary. Without freedom the rational will
cannot be held responsible for its judgments. Intention, choice, and
consent are important ingredients in the moral decision.

External acts may be said to be good or evil in two ways. First,
in regard to their genus, and the circumstances connected with them.
Thus, the giving of alms, if the required conditions be observed, is
said to be good. Secondly, a thing is said to be good or evil from its
relation to the end; and thus the giving of alms for vainglory is said
to be evil. Now, since the end is the will's proper object, it is evident
that the nature of good or evil, which the external act derives from its
relation to the end, is to be found first of all in the act of the will,
whence it passes to the external act.[2]

Not only is the free decision of the will important, but the motive which is cherished by the will affects the necessary judgment of an external act. Deeds are judged by motives and intentions as well as by nature and content. Not only must the rational man act freely, in knowledge of the quality and consequences of his actions, but he must act with the right intentions as well. "It is therefore evident," wrote Aquinas, "that a good or evil act deserves praise or blame in so far as it is in the power of the will; that it is right or sinful according as it is ordered to the end; and that its merit or demerit depends upon the recompense for justice or injustice towards another."[3] Thomas held that a false will can spoil a good deed, but he did not suggest that a right intention can necessarily make a wrong act into a righteous deed.

Thomas considered the capacity to exercise wise moral choice to be an intellectual virtue. In the exhaustive consideration of habits, virtues, and vices found in Question 58 of the *Summa Theologiae* Thomas defined prudence as "the right reason about things to be done."[4] Prudence is an intellectual virtue, involving the use of the reason in the application as well as the determination of standards, in the area of specific choice as well as in the enunciation of general principles. Prudence is an acquired intellectual habit which appears in those who have trained themselves in the wise analysis of practical decisions. It involves plain common sense as well as attention to ideals and norms. It involves many of the elements of sound deliberation. As one contemporary writer phrases it, "Moral deliberation, as the name implies, is an intellectual process of weighing the various possible actions which may be done, under the actual circumstances which can be foreseen, in the light of the end to be obtained."[5]

Prudence is one of four cardinal virtues known to man through the reason and involving the reason as a ground of virtue itself. It is joined by three others:

> For the formal principle of the virtue of which we speak now is the good as defined by reason. This good can be considered in two ways. First, as existing in the consideration itself of reason, and thus we have one principal called *prudence.*—Secondly, according as the reason puts its order into something else, and this either into operations, and then we have *justice,* or into passions, and then we need two virtues. For the need of putting the order of reason into the passions is due to their thwarting reason; and this occurs in two ways. First, when the passions incite to something against reason, and then they need a curb, which we thus call *temperance;* secondly, when the passions withdraw us from following the dictate of reason, *e.g.,* through fear of danger or toil, and then man needs to be strengthened for that which reason dictates, lest he turn back, and to this end there is *fortitude.*[6]

In Aristotle and in other Greek thinkers we meet these same virtues as *wisdom, justice, temperance,* and *courage.* These four virtues can be shared by all men in consequence of their status as rational beings. Aquinas took them from the classical tradition, left them grounded in reason, but gave them an interpretation of his own.

Having set forth the four natural virtues known to man by reason and representing the application of reason to moral questions, Thomas went ahead to describe three virtues that are known by revelation and sustained by supernatural grace.

> . . . the theological virtues direct man to supernatural happiness in the same way as by the natural inclination man is directed to his connatural end. . . .

> . . . in relation to both intellect and will, man needed to receive in addition something supernatural to direct him to a supernatural end. First, as regards the intellect, man receives certain supernatural principles, which are held by means of a divine light; and these are the things which are to be believed, about which is *faith.*—Secondly, the will is directed to this end, both as to the movement of intention, which tends to that end as something attainable,—this pertains to *hope*—and as to a certain spiritual union, whereby the will is, in a way, transformed into that end—and this belongs to *charity.*[7]

These three virtues of faith represent a new element which is added to the natural virtues without changing or contradicting them. By setting forth these theological virtues Thomas went beyond (or above) the realm of rational morality to the sphere of revelation. Moral reason functions to show men one sort of virtue; in prudence it becomes itself a virtue. Faith functions to show men another sort of virtue; it is itself a virtue.

In dealing with the concepts of law and obligation, Thomas used a similar scheme for dividing the natural and the supernatural levels. There are four levels of law. The highest position in a graded hierarchy is occupied by eternal (or divine) law, which is found in the wisdom of God and is the prototype or exemplar from which all other law is drawn. Then there is natural law, or that portion of the divine law that can be known by all rational men. Below this come the human or enacted law of particular jurisdistions, and church law.

Human or enacted law must accord with the principles of natural law or it cannot bind the conscience of the rational man. A city council can no more bind the conscience of the rational man to believe that stealing and treachery are right than it can make water run uphill by passing an ordinance declaring gravity reversed. Since natural law is based upon man's use of reason, all men are under obligation to it whether or not as individuals they understand its rootage in the divine law. Just because certain men do not understand stealing to be wrong does not mean that the proper use of their reason would not lead them to see that it is wrong if they were so instructed. ". . .[A]s regards the common principles whether of speculative or of practical reason, truth or rectitude is the same for all, and is equally known by all. But as to the proper conclusions of the speculative reason, the truth is the same for all, but is not equally known to all."[8]

Church law is divided into two parts. The old law, coming from the Old Testament, includes the Decalogue and the codes that arose as part of its interpretation. The new law, coming from the New Testament, includes the admonitions of the Gospels. The Decalogue contains both ceremonial and moral precepts, and it covers the judicial reason evidenced in the casuistical sections of the Exodus codes. The moral part of the Decalogue, of course, follows the natural law and is therefore binding upon all men. The ceremonial aspects of the Decalogue, however, are primarily for those who stand within the community of faith. Likewise, the new law contains both the obligatory precepts, which are the theological virtues of faith, hope, and charity and are binding upon all Christian believers, and the counsels of perfection, which are to be followed by those who are called to more rigorous obedience in devotion to the Gospel. The counsels include poverty, chastity, and obedience.

The appreciative understanding of reason and its role found in Thomas may seem to be a surprising contrast to authoritarian and legalistic aspects of the Roman Catholic tradition. The Roman Church has not always been fully confident that the natural reason of man can be trusted to know the content of the natural law without guidance from divine and ecclesiastical teaching. Pope Pius IX, in treating these issues in the *Syllabus of Errors* of 1864, specifically condemned the view that philosophical and moral insights can be obtained by reason alone, in ignorance of the authoritative teaching of the Church. His declarations have caused considerable apprehension about the Church's position on natural law among those who do not own allegiance to the Church as an authoritative teacher. They seem to preclude the possibility that men can wrestle with ethical questions in a free market place of ideas assured that their conclusions will be judged only by the canons of rational cogency.

Moreover, since the Church holds that natural law is based upon reason it believes that such law binds all men, not merely those who assent to the faith. Consequently, many Catholic scholars contend that the Church has both a right and a duty to advocate such human legislative law as conforms to the natural law, and that a state can enforce such laws upon all men precisely because they reflect the universally binding requirements of reason. This argument has often been employed in defense of Catholic efforts to have birth control by "artificial" means prohibited by civil statute. It raises problems because other members of the same political jurisdiction regard the practice of birth control to be a positive responsibility of the rational man.

Legalism can enter Catholic morality through the rational evaluations of degrees of guilt that are made in the penance system of the confessional. Two degrees of sin are distinguished: mortal sin involves a serious transgression and has been committed with the consent of the will; venial sin is less serious or has been committed without the free and deliberate consent of the will. The calculation of guilt and the analysis of conduct which determine the status, severity, and consequences of sin, together with appropriate means of making restitution for its commission, are forms of deliberation, but the process may result in an increasingly prescriptive legalism.

The use of reason as a source of moral guidance within a clearly defined range of ethical judgments is a continuing mark of most Roman Catholic teaching. Hence, a contemporary Catholic theologian states the case for rational deliberation and defines its province as follows:

> . . . the Catholic approach to morality is influenced by these profoundly moving convictions: that man, by his reason can know what is right and can guide his moral behavior accordingly; . . .
> Man, alone among the creatures of the earth, has intellectual knowledge; man, alone of all the creatures of the earth, conceives his acts in terms of obligation. He does not only say, "I do," or "I do not": he says, "I ought," and "I ought not." The basic principles of morality, therefore, are not the characteristics of a particular religious faith. There are the norms, universally recognized, by reasoning men: do good and avoid evil; thou shalt not wantonly kill another man; care for the children you have begotten; respect the aged; reverence the dead, etc.[9]

Much contemporary Roman Catholic thinking builds upon Thomistic insights in order to emphasize the unchanging character of objective moral judgments. According to this interpretation, the morally right action can be determined with rational certainty about what is objectively valid. "All moral education is aimed at instructing the individual to recognize the objective norm that should govern his behavior. This is the difficult task of moral teaching and moral learning."[10]

To be sure, deliberation and analysis is required, but such deliberation is a rational process for determining the good act and its consequences. In a contemporary textbook of Catholic morality, Vernon J. Bourke explicates this process as follows: Man moves through a series of deductive efforts to arrive at a moral judgment. The first level of judgment is synderesis: "The good is to be done"; the second, the judgment of moral science: "It is good to help others in distress"; the third, the impersonal particular judgment: "This drowning man should be helped"; the fourth, a personal particular judgment: "I should save this drowning man"; the fifth and final rational choice of action: "I will save this man now."[11] At no point in this process does the chain of rationality break. The movement is from first principles through moral rules and objective reasons to particular choices demanded by the conscience. Even in the choices demanded by conscience reason weighs the circumstances of the situation to judge that a particular course of action is feasible. An unwise or foolish act of heroism, leading to two drownings instead of one, would not be required.

The papacy has frequently lent its authority to the side of Catholic thinking which emphasizes the importance of objective moral teaching. Instruction from the holy office dated February 2, 1956, carried this point of view into administrative edict. Earlier encyclicals, especially *Humani generis* in 1950, criticized existentialism and strongly reaffirmed a traditional metaphysical philosophy set forth in objective rational principles and unchangeable norms. Pope Pius XII emphatically endorsed the role of principles and moral norms based upon reason. In his first encyclical letter he wrote:

> Before all else, it is certain that the radical and ultimate cause of the evils which We deplore in modern society is the denial and rejection of a universal norm of morality as well for individual and social life as for international relations; We mean the disregard, so common nowadays, for the forgetfulness of the natural law itself, which has its foundation in God, Almighty Creator and Father of all, supreme and absolute Lawgiver, all-wise and just Judge of human action.[12]

There are many problems which defy the neat picture of moral certainty implied by the foregoing approach. While the general features of traditional Roman Catholic morality are well established, arguments persist about the implications of such teaching for specific decisions. The doctrine of the just war, for example, is being re-examined by many theologians in light of the destructive consequences of atomic weapons. Similar questions arise about the legitimacy of right to work laws and about birth control. Even when papal pronouncements are made about contemporary social problems, the moral theologians find themselves faced with the need to interpret the pronouncements.

It is unfortunate that the deliberative motif in Roman Catholicism has too often been seen through the conservative interpreters. They read Thomas in a rigidly scholastic way. Meanwhile, other theologians are reading Thomas in a different way and developing a more flexible moral theology. Bernard Haring admits that "modern situation ethics represents in effect a reaction against an all too rigidly rationalistic ethic of essences, an ethic which was not able, in its knowledge of the essence identical in all and in the fixed and permanent bond of obligation, to recognize that which lies beyond, namely, that which is irreplaceable and non-transferable in the individual and in the situation."[13] Karl Rahner has labored to develop an existential ethics which, while it maintains the belief in objectively valid moral norms, also notes the difficulty inherent in the human perception of such norms on given occasions. What ought to be done on a specific occasion cannot lie entirely outside the universal norms, yet it cannot be merely the deductive consequence of a general principle. Thus Rahner declares:

> It would be absurd for a God-regulated, theological morality to think that God's binding will could only be directed to the human action in so far as the latter is simply a realization of the universal norm and of a universal nature. If the creative will of God is directly and unambiguously directed to the concrete and the individual, then surely this is not true merely in so far as this individual reality is the realization of a case of the universal—rather it is directed to the concrete as such, as it really is—to the concrete in its positive, and particularly its substantial, material uniqueness. God is interested in history not only in so far as it is the carrying out of norms, but in so far as it is a history which consists in the harmony of unique events and which precisely in this way has meaning for eternity.[14]

By combining formal assent to the validity of essentialistic ethics with acknowledgment that some truth may lie in the corrective emphasis that a situational ethics sets forth, Rahner and Haring manage to remain orthodox without being rigid. Unlike Ford and Kelley,[15] Fitzpatrick, or John A. Ryan[16] who feel called to fight the battle as a defense of objective norms, Rahner and Haring obviously feel the pull in the opposite direction. But despite the extensive, imaginative, and sensitive manner in which they set forth their views and the frequent deference shown to the corrective element acknowledged in relational ethics, both men stand within deliberative Thomism. Their modifications of Thomism are a welcome contrast to the rigid interpretations too long used in Catholic circles, but they never break with the dependence upon reason and law as these belong to the morality of obligation found in Thomas himself.

Varieties of Sovereign Reason in Protestant Ethics since Kant

Protestants divide very sharply concerning the role played by reason in the theological enterprise. The role of reason in the determination of ethical norms is consequently a matter of considerable debate. There are Protestants who affirm an even broader role for moral philosophy than Aquinas did; there are other Protestants who regard practically all moral philosophizing as the invasion of a false and misleading element in the moral life of the believer.

The clearest and least ambiguous way to adopt moral philosophy is to accept the reason as a sole and sufficient source of moral guidance. This approach has been especially strong in the liberal Protestantism built upon the philosophy of Kant. In the first quarter of this century Edgar Sheffield Brightman was one of the best known American exponents of this view and Hastings Rashdall one of the better known British spokesmen. Both of these men worked in acknowledged allegiance to the Christian tradition, but they demanded that the moral judgments of Christians be subjected to the thorough scrutiny of reason. Thus, Brightman declared:

> In one sense it is clear that the moral law is more fundamental than religion. Religion and morality were so intertwined in their origins that it is impossible for us to determine which was which in primitive times. But for civilized and reflective man religion has the distinctive meaning of the worship of a divine power that is believed to be good. Now, it is impossible to regard any being as good, unless one has some conception of what "good" is; and that conception is one's ethics.[17]

Similarly, Hastings Rashdall, following a long discussion of attempts in his day to question the adequacy of reason in the area of moral deliberation, wrote as follows:

> We have, then, discovered no reason in the arguments of the super-moral Religionists for abandoning the position that the end prescribed to man by his own moral consciousness must be part of the true end of the Universe. That there is one absolute standard of values, which is the same for all rational beings, is just what Morality means. Nothing less than that is implied by the idea of absolute value which underlies the simplest moral judgment, when its implications are analyzed and reflected on.[18]

Rashdall shared with many philosophical moralists a conviction that moral law possesses an objective validity. He granted that some men do not acknowledge the moral law and that mankind has been slow to grasp its content, but he insisted that failure of mankind fully to know the content of the moral law does not refute the existence of such a law. "Morality is no more affected by its gradual development, or by the fact that infants and very low savages may not possess the notion at all, than the validity of mathematical axioms is affected by the fact, if it be a fact, that some savages cannot count more than ten, or that mathematically deficient minds—sometimes very brilliant minds in other ways—cannot follow the simplest geometrical reasoning."[19]

This insight echoes a series of ideas that appeared in Christian theology with special vigor even before the work of Immanuel Kant. Rashdall acknowledged his indebtedness to Bishop Joseph Butler (1692-1752), who

found Christian truth established in nature as well as revelation and who saw moral obligation as an essential feature of the rational order of things. Butler's thinking, however, was mainly directed to stemming the tide of an even more radical insistence upon the place of reason. This appeared in the deists, whose doubts concerning special revelation were never accompanied by doubts concerning the existence of a moral order and the obligation of each man to live in accord with it. Indeed, English deism of the eighteenth century took as a tenet of rational religion belief in a reward and punishment scheme in a next life, operating in relation to the moral actions of the individual in this one.

A classic American treatment of Christian ethics as the work of sovereign reason is found in a volume first published in 1892 in the International Theological Library. Its author, Newman Smyth, was for many years the pastor of the Center Congregational Church on the New Haven green and influenced both Yale and the larger American theological world. In his book Smyth presented a very clear case for basing Christian ethics upon an autonomous moral deliberation. It is proper to speak of Christian ethics as a science. It may begin by examining the biblical record and the life and power of Christ, but it must take into account data from all spheres of human life. Christian ethics "is the science of the moral contents, progress, and ends of human life under the formative Christian Ideal."[20] In subsequent editions Smyth rephrased his views, but remained convinced to the end that the truths of Christian ethics will harmonize with all possible knowledge.

Smyth was sceptical of any effort to base Christian ethics upon revealed or dogmatic theological considerations alone. Thus, Christian ethics as a science takes precedence over revealed theology as a source of understanding of religious and ethical truths.

> Reason is called sooner or later to think out ethical-religious truths under metaphysical conceptions, and the dogmatic theology of the Church is the reasonable endeavor to harmonize the truths of Christianity in a system of thought. But whatever may be the function of theology, the primary ethical elements of religion should be distinguished, and not allowed to become lost or confounded, in any system of divinity which may be built up philosophically, or taught with authority in the creeds of the Church. Christian ethics must be allowed to follow closely, and should remain true to the ethical-religious consciousness, without prevention or prejudice from Christian dogmatics. Moreover, whatever postulates Christian ethics may borrow from Christian theology, it must bring these to its own moral tests and judgment.[21]
>
> Still less can we allow in Christian ethics any dogmatic belief which would put in bonds the Christian ethical principle itself;—as, for instance, the tenet that morality is dependent upon the divine will,

that the distinction between right and wrong is a created distinction, which God might have willed otherwise. Christian ethics cannot consent to commit suicide in any supposed interest of theology.[22]

Smyth struggled against the introduction of arbitrary elements into the analysis of ethical issues. He considered theology to be such an arbitrary element whenever it tries to contradict the insights of the ethical-religious consciousness. But the ethical-religious consciousness also judges philosophical method, so that any philosophical ethic which ignores the Christian element stands open to criticism as a truncated and inadequate understanding of the human situation. Any account of man must be judged inadequate if it does not seek to enter into the spirit of Christ and bring "all its analysis and theories of man's moral life to the light of the luminous ethical personality of Jesus Christ."[23] To do this fulfills reason rather than suspends it; completes rather than contradicts the philosophical enterprise. The distinction between philosophical and Christian ethics "tends to disappear as the philosophy of an age becomes Christianized, and the Christianity of an age becomes rational and real."[24]

Confidence in reason as the main, if not the sole source of religious insights has made other appearances in American religious thought. In orthodox Unitarianism, as represented by William Ellery Channing, reason was used to judge which aspects of biblical teaching might be accepted. The use of reason within orthodox Unitarianism was probably more suited to refuting classical theological ideas, such as the doctrine of the Trinity, than to setting forth a constructive system of its own. In transcendentalism, however, as represented eloquently by Ralph Waldo Emerson, the reason acquired an even more dominant role with respect to morals. The transcendentalists affirmed the existence of a rational order that men can know directly. They shifted from a combination of biblical and rational insights to belief in a rational order that men can know intuitively. This order involves not only intellect but emotions, not only knowledge of a benevolent cosmic spirit but knowledge of a moral order with direct authority and appeal to man's reason.

It is helpful to think of reason as conceived by the transcendentalists as an intuitive ability to perceive the divine order directly, without revelation and even without elaborate investigation and analysis. Intuitive reason should not be considered as different or as antithetical to autonomous reason, but as a special form of sovereign reason. Emerson set forth the concept in these words:

> The law which Ethics treats is that we mean by the nature of things; the law of all action which cannot yet be stated, it is so simple; of which every man has glimpses in a lifetime and values that he knows of it more than all knowledge; which whether it be called Necessity or Spirit or Power is the law whereof all history is but illustration;

is the law that sits as pilot at the helm and guides the paths of revolutions, of wars, of emigrations, of trades, of legislation, and yet is fully exemplified in all its height and depth in the private life of every man.[25]

Emerson affirmed the rational structure in both the natural world and the moral order. In his famous "Divinity School Address" he suggested that men naturally desire to attune themselves to the divine laws of morality. He found Jesus to be a religious genius who exhibited in his own life a peculiar capacity to know and understand the divine moral structure but who cannot be understood in terms of having a special status. All men, therefore, discover in and by themselves the same values Jesus understood. In this discovery the look is forward to new insights, not backwards in subservience to some authority whose insights are at best but partial. In a later essay on worship he stated the same theme this way:

There will be a new church founded on moral science; at first cold and naked, a babe in a manger again, the algebra and mathematics of ethical law, the church of men to come, without shawms, or psaltery, or sackbut; but it will have heaven and earth for its beams and rafters; science for symbol and illustration; it will fast enough gather beauty, music, picture and poetry. Was never stoicism so stern and exigent as this shall be. It shall send man home to his central solitude, shame these social, supplicating manners, and make him know that much of the time he must have himself to his friend. He shall expect no cooperation, he shall walk with no companion. The nameless Thought, the nameless Power, the super-personal Heart—he shall repose alone on that. He needs only his own verdict. No good fame can help, no bad fame can hurt him. The Laws are his consolers, the good Laws Themselves are alive, they know if he have kept them, they animate him with the leading of great duty, and an endless horizon. Honor and fortune exist to him who always recognizes the neighborhood of the great—always feels himself in the presence of high causes.[26]

Emerson's reliance upon an intuitive rather than an analytical reason, which gave preference to the reasons of the heart over the reasons of the mind, to feeling over understanding, was hardly more acceptable to the Unitarianism of a traditional stripe than to the Christianity of the orthodox traditions. Today his writings are more apt to be studied in a literature class than in a theology course. As a product of his time, Emerson gave expression to the optimism of the era and found it bolstered by confidence in a benevolent God of cosmic support. His use of philosophical virtues— beauty, prudence, love, heroism, intellect—as means for setting forth his thinking about religious ethics gives us yet another illustration of the many ways in which a deliberative ethic can be developed.

The thinking of men like Newman Smyth and Ralph Waldo Emerson has ceased to be influential in the current scene. The books of Newman Smyth are sometimes seen on the library shelves of older preachers, but his ideas are seldom mentioned in contemporary sermons. The works of Emerson are read in high-school English courses, but these are usually opaque to theological subtleties. But if Newman Smyth's book is gathering dust on library shelves, a little volume by Paul Tillich, entitled *Love, Power, and Justice,* is in print and gathering converts. Much has happened between Smyth and Tillich, and to set the two men into a similar mold requires that the reader be warned about the passage of time and the movements of ideas by which they are separated. In general, however, it can be said that moral philosophy was being rigorously challenged in Tillich's day in a way it was not being challenged as Smyth wrote. To be sure, Smyth wrote during the incubation of fundamentalism, but fundamentalism did not engage in discussions about this particular issue. It had other enemies, higher criticism, evolution, and the social gospel, against which to vent its feelings. In Tillich's day, however, moral philosophy had come in for specific attack, either in a radical way that regarded Christian morality as having nothing to gain from philosophical ethics, or in a modified way that regarded the ideals of Christian ethics as seriously qualified by human sin. Questions were raised, for example, concerning the relationship of love and justice. They were said to exist in radical tension with each other, at dialectical cross purposes that are hardly in harmony with a view that each is a rational virtue, a reasonable ideal.

In *Love, Power, and Justice,* Tillich was trying to base each element directly upon a rational foundation. He called this an "ontological foundation," but its affinities with philosophical procedure are obvious.

> Therefore the search for the basic meaning of love, power, and justice individually must be our first task, and it must be carried out as a part of the search for the basic meaning of all those concepts which are universally present in man's cognitive encounter with his world. Traditionally they are called principles, structural elements, and categories of being.[27]

Tillich was criticizing the contrasts drawn between love and justice, between love and power. He believed that when these are ontologically conceived, and that when the fundamental character of each is traced back to its grounding in the nature of being, that the tension between these different ethical concepts is removed.

> Love and power are often contrasted in such a way that love is identified with a resignation of power and power with a denial of love. Powerless love and loveless power are contrasted. This, of course, is unavoidable if love is understood from its emotional side and power from its compulsory side. But such an understanding is error and

confusion. It was this misinterpretation which induced the philosopher of the "will-to-power" (i.e., Nietzsche) to reject radically the Christian idea of love. And it is the same misinterpretation which induces Christian theologians to reject Nietzsche's philosophy of the "will-to-power" in the name of the Christian idea of love.[28]

Tillich's ontological definition of love involves the idea that love is the power of unity which seeks to overcome separation and estrangement. Love, therefore, is itself a power seeking to reunite that which has been estranged by separation. Love can only reunite those things which are essentially united in their ontological being. Similarly, both power and justice are rooted in the nature of being. Power is defined as the capacity of a thing to exist, and justice, as the form that being takes. Since these elements are all rooted in the same ontological foundation, there is no serious tension between them. Love does not do more than justice demands, but love is the ultimate principle of justice. "Love reunites; justice preserves what is to be united. It is the form in which and through which love performs its work. Justice in its ultimate meaning is creative justice, and creative justice is the form of reuniting love."[29]

Tillich rooted his ethical thinking about love, power, and justice in an ontology of being. While this assured each concept a status of its own, Tillich did not intend this to split rational ethics apart from faith any more than he intended to subject ethics to a religious authority imposed from without. Rightly used, faith can deepen and enrich the rational consciousness of law and community known to all men. In the resultant theonomous situation, reason naturally considers the depth dimensions which are the concern of faith. This is preferable to an autonomy in which ethical reasoning is a law to itself (often fighting against faith) and a heteronomy in which the ethical is subjected to an external authority (often submitting to faith against its inherent impulses). In pursuing his task Tillich willingly embraced existentialist as well as traditional modes of philosophical thinking, accepting from each insights useful for grounding ethics in ontology. Consequently, he was not chained to any traditional metaphysic binding his ethical thinking to fixed categories of right and wrong. It may be among Tillich's greatest triumphs to have understood the contributions that properly come from the integrity of a sovereign reason without having to fight for a complete autonomy in the rational process. If reason can function in correlation with faith, avoiding both hostility and submission, then a very profound deliberation is possible in Christian ethics.

4
Christian Norms in Philosophical Categories

One of the formative influences upon religious thought in the twentieth century was a series of lectures delivered at the turn of the century by Adolph Harnack to a group of students at the University of Berlin. In their English translation they are entitled *What is Christianity?* Even though these lectures are concerned with the nature of the Gospel, they give us a clue to the way in which Harnack viewed ethical questions. Harnack felt that religion and morality are very closely related. He wrote:

> . . . Jesus combined religion and morality, and in this sense religion may be called the soul of morality, and morality the body of religion. We can thus understand how it was that Jesus could place the love of God and the love of one's neighbour side by side; the love of one's neighbour is the only practical proof on earth of that love of God which is strong in humility.[1]

From the very first page of his book Harnack drew attention to the similarity between Socrates and Jesus—to the disparagement of neither. His whole treatise was informed by the assumption that the Gospel itself makes sense to any rational man, Christian or not. Harnack paid much attention to the life and teachings of Jesus and the subsequent development of the church, but in understanding these he employed the categories of philosophical idealism rather than the kerygmatic imagery of the New Testament.

Harnack saw no conflict between philosophical reason and religious understanding. They accomplish much the same result in different ways. Jesus and Socrates both contribute to our understanding:

> Plato, it is true, had already sung the great hymn of the mind; he had distinguished it from the whole world of appearance and maintained its eternal origin. But the mind which he meant was the knowing mind; he contrasted it with blind, insensible matter; his message made its appeal to the wise. But Jesus Christ was the first to bring the value of every human soul to light, and what he did no one can any more undo. We may take up what relation to him we will· in the history

of the past no one can refuse to recognize that it was he who raised humanity to this level.[2]

Harnack's way of expressing the Christian norm draws heavily upon the categories of philosophical reason. According to Harnack, Jesus recognized "the infinite value of the human soul."[3] But Harnack did not use this phrase alone for the description of the Christian norm. He also used the biblical word *love*. Indeed, Harnack thought of love as a single, necessary, unified, and universal whole. "[What Jesus recognized as the moral principle] reduces to *one* root and to *one* motive—love. He knows of no other, and love itself, whether it takes the form of love of one's neighbour or of one's enemy, or the love of the Samaritan, is of one kind only."[4]

Harnack spoke of the principle of love as a legitimate moral standard for all men to follow. He laid great stress upon the right motives for ethical action. Love and mercy should be done for their own sake and not as means to an end. In "the higher righteousness," set forth in the Sermon on the Mount, Harnack found a primary emphasis upon the intention of the moral act, the inner motive. He freely interpreted Gospel admonitions, such as the counsel to poverty, in accordance with canons of good judgment and moderation. For example, Harnack noted that Jesus taught the danger of riches and even counseled poverty for his followers. But he pointed out that poverty as such is not a sensible norm, and in a digression urged ministers and missionaries "to concern themselves with property and worldly goods only so far as will prevent them being a burden to others, and beyond that to renounce them."[5] This describes a prudent poverty—a poverty within the limits of good sense.

Harnack's use of philosophical categories for the discussion of Christian norms leaves the exact relationship between moral philosophy and the Gospel unexplored. In leaving this question unresolved, Harnack stood in the footsteps of Friedrich Schleiermacher, who likewise argued that both moral philosophy and religious ethics come to similar conclusions by somewhat different paths.[6] At no point, however, did Harnack actually subordinate the Gospel to the considerations of reason.

Many subsequent thinkers have followed the lead of Harnack in using moral ideals as a vehicle for presenting Christian norms without letting the philosophical method become the master of Christian thinking. On the popular level, works by Georgia Harkness[7] and Sidney Cave[8] illustrate this tendency. A somewhat more rigorous work by Albert Knudson interpreted the teachings of Jesus by means of the philosophical category of principles. According to Knudson,

> What and how many principles should be included in the fundamental ethical teaching of Jesus is a point on which there may be

differences of opinion. But there are two concerning which there could hardly be any question. One is the principle of love, and the other the principle of moral inwardness or moral perfection.[9]

Knudson's discussion of the principle of perfection is especially illuminating. He contended that Christian perfection is really more basic than Christian love, since it is by the thrust toward perfection that love itself comes to fruition. It is for this reason that the church has often used the term *perfect love*. Knudson also took pains to extricate the idea of perfection from monastic and ascetic overtones. Because self-realization has a place within the principle of love, it also has a place within the concept of perfection. "We may, then," he wrote, "define the Christian ideal as self-realization through self-renunciation and through the aid of the Divine Spirit."[10]

Different thinkers have proposed different philosophical categories for the Christian norm, and they have differed with respect to the number of philosophical categories deemed necessary to describe that norm. Harnack used one category—the principle of love, interpreted as respect for the infinite value of the human soul. Harkness seems to follow his lead, though she has spoken of many New Testament themes as well as of the central idea of love, and she has emphasized the theistic context. Knudson made two principles basic, setting love and perfection side by side as twin aspects of Christian morality. Yet another modern theologian, George Thomas, has turned to moral philosophy for several categories with which to describe Christian imperatives. Calling for the critical acceptance and transformation of moral philosophy by Christian thinkers, he has declared, "Christians can derive help from moral philosophy in formulating principles for the determination of their *duties* to their neighbors and in defining the virtues which constitute character."[11]

Thomas explores the relationship of hedonism and utilitarianism to Christian ethics. The Christian parallel to happiness is blessedness. This cannot share the aims of selfish hedonism, but it is compatible with the view that man's well-being can include the enjoyment of honorable pleasures.

> Although [the idea of blessedness] is inconsistent with the humanistic view that happiness through exercise of one's natural capacities is the primary aim of life, it is not opposed to the humanistic ideal of developing one's natural capacities, using them creatively, and enjoying the happiness which normally accompanies this activity. However, it points to a deeper and purer joy which is independent of all natural pleasure and happiness and which can be maintained despite the loss of these because its source is in God. Since it is not bestowed by nature or achieved by man, it cannot be taken away by the indifference of the one or the frailty of the other.[12]

In considering duty as a philosophical concept which may be used for Christian purposes, Thomas first examines the categorical imperative of Immanuel Kant and acknowledges the important contribution of Kant in filling men with awe before the moral law. However, duty for its own sake leads to legalism, and men must proceed to a higher conception of righteousness in which duty is understood in relationship to the service of persons in love rather than merely as an obligatory impulse.

Thomas includes in his discussion both teleological ethics and deontological ethics. In considering value he compares the objective theory of Nicolai Hartmann with the subjective theory of Ralph Barton Perry. He rejects both theories of value in their extreme forms but tries to preserve the significance of each when taken in moderation.

The Christian character that Thomas describes is a composite of many admirable virtues borrowed and transformed from philosophical ethics, almost always taken in moderation and made new in the grace of God in Jesus Christ. He found meaning for Christians in a great number of values, including truth and friendship. The idea of love is not given exclusive attention; however, it has the unique task of transforming all philosophical ideals into viable expressions of neighborly concern and service to God. In love the antagonism between law and liberty is overcome. The Christian ethic is absolute in its demand that we love our neighbors at all times and in all circumstances, but relative in its requirements as to how we determine our duty. We can take the contingent and changing factors of each circumstance into account as we determine how love is to be exercised, and in doing so we rely upon the deliberation which is characteristic of moral philosophy at its best.

Many of those thinkers who speak about the relationship of moral philosophy and Christian ethics draw a contrast between two roots of our Western heritage. One, represented by the biblical tradition, stands for covenantal obedience and moral rigor. The other, represented by the classical tradition, stands for the search after virtue that is based upon wisdom and understanding. The use of Greek categories for Christian norms has been evident in most of the individuals discussed in this section. In Aquinas the Greek virtues stand for the norms of natural morality, the biblical virtues for the norms of supernatural morality. Respect for beauty, heroism, and intellect are among the categories met in Emerson. For Tillich power and justice were as important as love, and all three were based on ontological considerations. George Thomas transvaluates concepts such as virtue, duty, and happiness (well-being) in his consideration of the relationship between moral philosophy and Christian ethics.

An interesting and somewhat unusual variation to this set of categories was proposed some years ago by H. W. Garrod, a tutor of Merton College, Oxford. He considered the interplay between Greek and biblical elements in most discussions of moral philosophy and then made this comment:

No one sitting down to write a history of architecture would dream of confining his treatment of the subject to, let us say, the Greek and Byzantine styles. A professedly comprehensive treatise upon architecture which omitted all mention of Gothic would be thought to be the work of a lunatic—of a lunatic in aesthetics. In just the same way it seems to me to be a kind of ethical lunacy to write a treatise upon morals in which nothing is said of the influence upon the conduct of life of the ideas of the peoples of Northern Europe. Yet this is what our professors of ethical theory one and all consistently do. They discourse to the full extent of their knowledge upon Greek morality; they discourse, beyond the extent of their own or any man's knowledge, and abandoning experience completely, upon Christian morality. But they leave out of account altogether what I may venture, for want of a better name, to call Gothic morality.[13]

According to Garrod, the ideal Christian type of man is the saint, who searches for holiness; the ideal Greek sort of man is the φρονιμos,[14] who exemplifies understanding and intelligence. To this Garrod added the knight, who exemplifies rigor and manhood, whose virtues include chivalry and a sense of honor. "These two ideals, chivalry and honor, are neither Greek nor Christian. I take them to be the peculiar property and creation of the northern races. I may call them the cardinal virtues of Gothic morality."[15]

There may be a faint semblance here to the complaint lodged by Nietzsche against Christian morality. Garrod preferred to identify himself with the Reformers and quoted Œcolampadius in expressing disgust for the meek virtues. Garrod argued that the virtues of chivalry and honor are very much a part of Western morality, and we should openly acknowledge their importance. His essay is astringent and provocative; it impels a second look at traditional formulations; but it has gathered around it no group of kindred spirits to take up the cause.

When men talk of principles in moral philosophy, they naturally think of Greek ideals. Garrod has challenged this tendency from one perspective. Another challenge to this tendency was proposed by Andrew R. Osborn, one-time professor in the Biblical Seminary of New York. Like Garrod, he was impatient with the Greek contribution, but for different reasons. Osborn felt that the Greek heritage obscures the distinctive character of the Christian ethic. The Christian ethic must be rooted in the same demand for absolute obedience to God that is found in the Hebrew ethic. "Its source and standard are not human excellence, but moral order derived from God, the eternal reality."[16]

Osborn's belief in the reality of a moral order led him to assert the possibility of a "scientific" method in ethics, in which the actual moral law rooted in the very structure of existence is discovered in the same way that the laws of the physical universe are discovered by the physical scientist. These objective principles are related to God's righteousness as portrayed in the Bible. It is because God is righteous that creation is harmonious and because creation is harmonious that there is an objectively real moral order in which truth and justice operate and wickedness is punished. In a strange admixture of doctrinal adherence to biblical authority and professed allegiance to the scientific method, Osborn described his conception of Christian ethics:

> Christian Ethics, believes, therefore, that in the lives and the teaching of the prophets of Israel, in the life and teaching of Jesus, and in the lives and teaching of his disciples there is to be found a unique and authoritative statement and exemplification of the principles underlying conduct. Its method is to use the principles discovered from these sources as standards whereby to judge and interpret the facts which it has discovered from its observation of life and its analysis of the process of history. In its inquiry into the moral phenomena of life it uses the method of strict scientific investigation, and welcomes all facts which the moral and social sciences have discovered. Only it does not limit itself to these; it brings also to its task the results of its own investigation into the eternal principles underlying human conduct as these are set forth in the Bible. Thus it provides the knowledge and the guidance which our modern world with its lapsed standards of morality needs for its spiritual recovery.[17]

The use of the category of principles provided Osborn with a method for understanding biblical teaching in changing occasions. Biblical teaching contains examples of legislative codes which change with time and circumstance. But the principles behind the legislation remain fixed. Hence the specific biblical codes do not bind, but the principles behind them do. Speaking of students just beginning their study of Christian ethics, Osborn suggested that one of their sources of difficulty and confusion lay in the fact that they

> were looking for rules and regulations, which would give specific direction on particular problems, instead of seeking universal principles, under which these problems could be brought. Once it is clear [to them] that the Ten Commandments and the Sermon on the Mount were summaries of religious and moral principles, and not codes of rules, and that it was possible to find in the Old and New Testaments principles of conduct applicable to life in every age they began to see how the guidance and authority they desired could be found.[18]

There is change and evolution in ethics as codes are reinterpreted, but there is no change in the intention of ethics as reflected in its principles. Osborn examined each of the Ten Commandments separately as the statement of a permanent, unchanging principle—a principle derived from the biblical tradition rather than from Greek speculation. Thus, while Osborn spoke of principles, permitted deliberation concerning their meaning in changing circumstances, and warned against the danger of hardening biblical ethics into codified form, he professed strict allegiance to the biblical roots of the Christian ethic. The unchangeable moral principles come from God; ". . . to cast Christian ethics into a Greek mold obscures its distinctive character."[19]

In analyzing the deliberative motif in Christian ethics, one must take care lest the function of reason be too narrowly conceived. In some forms of a rational ethic the deductive reason, logically doing its work upon the implications of first principles, is pictured too exclusively in terms of a theoretical and abstract rational process which issues in propositional statements concerning the nature of the good. Paul Ramsey invites us to see natural law in broader terms, claiming that some of its able modern exponents have revised natural law so as to base it upon a full human response to the innate claims of the right rather than merely upon a deductive exercise of the mind. In discussing Jacques Maritain and Edmond Cahn, the first a lay Roman Catholic philosopher, the second a professor of law, he finds a remarkable agreement in their understanding of the significance to be attached to that innate sense of right and of wrong which seems to reside within the sensitivities of humanity itself.[20]

Ramsey's interpretations of Maritain and Cahn provide us with a window upon his own developing thought, which exhibits in a special way a post-critical affirmation of in-principled love as the most fruitful statement of the Christian ethic. The promise of this outlook has been present from his first writings; its flower has become increasingly full with each new major work. Ramsey stands as one of the clearest evidences that the deliberative motif is by no means dormant in contemporary Protestant ethics, despite the sustained and rigorous attacks upon it. He also tends to show us that a deliberative approach to the formulation of ethical norms can slide over into a prescriptive approach in its efforts to provide specific content to its principles.

In his first major book, *Basic Christian Ethics*, Ramsey sets forth a conception of Christian love essentially compatible with philosophical idealism, yet distinctively clear in its own rigor. Ramsey notes the rootage of Christian love in the righteous will of God and in the redeeming work of Christ and clearly contrasts Christian morality with any kind of code morality. He ends by giving Christian love this essentially abstract philosophical definition: "disinterested love for the neighbor."

The adjective *disinterested* means the elimination of prudent regard for self. Ramsey's interpretation breaks with self-realization theories as espoused by men like Knudson. It breaks with any theories of distributive justice which include the self as one claimant for existing goods. The neighbor is to be loved radically for his sake, since only through such a radical denial of the self can the neighbor be truly served in his need and the broken situation of humanity healed. Utilitarian ethics can cement and preserve existing societies on the basis of mutuality or on the basis of a legitimate balancing of self-love with neighbor love, but broken community can only be healed by the reconciling work of a radically disinterested love.

> The importance of keeping community intact can hardly be over-estimated. Nevertheless, creating community among men where none now is, the task of reconciling man with man, is a still more important problem. As regards it, "if you love those who love you . . . And if you salute only your brethren, what more are you doing than others? Do not even the Gentiles the same?" (Matt. 5:46,47.) If you love only within societies held together by mutual self-interest, what more are you doing than others? Does not even Bentham the same? If you love only for the sake of some increment in value, loving yourself and others alike, what more are you doing than others? Does not even Mill the same? If you follow natural rational intuition, uninstructed by Christ, in considering yourself and others each as similar "cases" to whom distribution of goods should be given, what more are you doing than others? Does not even Sidgwick the same? These all alike assist perhaps in conserving life in community, but they can hardly bring an isolated or hostile man into community with you or you with him.[21]

Basic Christian Ethics argues a case from which Ramsey could have moved two ways. He might have continued to emphasize the radical character of Christian love, especially its refusal to countenance the reasonable place for self-interest which most philosophical ethics provide. Instead, he has moved in his subsequent thinking to greater utilization of philosophical insights for his understanding of Christian love and its strategies. In doing so, he has built upon the professed acceptance of philosophical idealism found in this early book.

Ramsey's case for disinterested love of the neighbor involves the transvaluation of philosophical concepts by shifting the focus from the self to the neighbor.

> Christian ethics raises no fundamental objection to definitions of *value* given by any school of philosophical ethics. Hedonism, for example, or the theory that pleasure alone is the good, may be incorrect on philosophical grounds, but if true there would be nothing unchristian about it. Christianity makes no essential attempt to transform a person who believes there is no good in life but pleasure into one who believes there are other goods besides pleasure. Its concern is to turn a hedonist who thinks only of *his own* pleasure into one who gives pleasure (the greatest good he knows) to his neighbors.[22]

The question "Whose good?" demands that a Christian determine to which neighbor he is obliged to show disinterested love. The answer to this question involves the search for social policy, since social policy determines how and to whom love is transmitted. In determining social policy, philosophy is a useful ally but a bad master. At one place Ramsey says that "contemporary Christian ethics must make common cause with the ethics of philosophical idealism. We must become debtors to the best insight available at the present stage of thought."[23] At another he observes,

> . . . while Christian love makes alliance or coalition with any available sources of insight or information about what should be done, it makes *concordat* with none of these. Christian love must, indeed, enter into such alliances; it must go in search of some social policy. Yet in the relationship between Christian love and the principles of an acceptable social ethic, Christian love remains what it is, dominant and free. It does not transform itself into the coin of any realm, though it enters every realm and becomes debtor to the Greek and to the barbarians.[24]

Ramsey acknowledges a basic truth in the conception of natural justice found in philosophical ethics. He prefers this idea to the concept of natural law, which has sometimes been overly rigid in its formulations. While natural law cannot fully encompass all the demands of Christian love, the Christian would in any case acknowledge a sense of justice and charity akin to that portrayed by natural law theories. We are not to be disconcerted if the Christian sense of justice coincides with insights into justice provided by philosophical understanding.

Ramsey has set forth his conception of "in-principled love" in many places. While much of Ramsey's later writing has been concerned with problems of implementing ethical decisions, in the course of each discussion he has explored the theoretical grounds of just action. This is true of his discussion of the just war, the sit-in movement, and problems of natural law. Ramsey has become critical of situational ethics expounded in recent years. His understanding of principles has included increasing emphasis upon the definition of right acts demanded by such principles. In his discussion of modern warfare Ramsey declares: "Love posits or takes form in principles of right conduct which express the difference it discerns between permitted and prohibited action, and these are not wholly derived from reflection upon the consequences."[25] In a discussion of Christian responsibility in sexual relationship, he notes "he is a poor constructive ethicist who, without much argumentation, rules out the possibility that rules of action may still be fashioned by hearts instructed by Christ to know what love itself implies."[26] In a comment upon modern ethical theory, he says, "Christian love would [not] be halted, lamed, or blinded, or Jesus Christ any less the lord of life, if there are more ethical principles to be found in the land of the living than is allowed by certain contextual or situational ethics."[27]

It is difficult to know what should be said about the vast body of preaching and writing produced as a result of Harnack's influence. Perhaps the homiletical discussions of these issues should be ignored in any serious effort to understand Christian ethics in an academic context. But is the scholar charged only with analysis of what other scholars say, or does he find his quarry in the common parlance of the world as well as in the more precise discourse of the academy? The popular homiletical discussions may have been more critical in influencing men's thinking about these matters than the technical discourses. Even when they are vague in their intentions and uncritical in their use of terms, they mold the thinking of the Christian movement. Two examples will suffice. In his preaching of an ethic of love, Harry Emerson Fosdick often used the terms *principle* and *sensible* to characterize the ethical teachings of Jesus as centered in the Sermon on the Mount. Fosdick sought to arouse enthusiasm for, and devotion to, the love ethic of Jesus. He described love as a possible, though difficult, way to live in the world.[28] In somewhat the same vein, Toyohiko Kagawa wrote about the virtues of love and decried its absence from common life. Kagawa admitted that Jesus had no philosophy of love and interpreted love in somewhat mystical terms even though he referred to it as a "law." In speaking of love Kagawa employed terms like *self-sustaining, universal, transcendent, eternal,* and *the Holy of Holies.* While he described love as breaking out of the philosophical categories, he was nevertheless dependent upon such categories for describing it.[29]

The thought of Reinhold Niebuhr contains an attack upon liberal theological ethics as found in the legacy of Harnack, but the attack is made with categories very similar to those used in liberal thinking. He takes the form in which the ethic of love had been set forth in the liberal tradition and declares it to be an historical impossibility. In lifting the norm above the reach of man's likely capacity to fulfill it in a world in which all human actions are corrupted by sin, Niebuhr employs language and a conceptual framework that belongs to the very tradition he is undercutting.

In chapter four of his book *An Interpretation of Christian Ethics,* Niebuhr speaks of "the relevance of an impossible ethical ideal." He characterizes Christian love as an "impossible possibility," coining one of the most frequently quoted phrases in theological ethics. With this phrase Niebuhr is trying to say that Christian love is always relevant to human life, but that it is also always beyond full human attainment. Niebuhr's discussion of Christian love is set forth in terms of philosophical idealism but is at the same time critical of such idealism.

The dimension of depth in the consciousness of religion creates the tension between what is and what ought to be. It bends the bow from which every arrow of moral action flies. Every truly moral act seeks to establish what ought to be, because the agent feels obligated to the ideal, though historically unrealized, as being the order of life in its more essential reality. Thus the Christian believes that the ideal of love is real in the will and nature of God, even though he knows of no place in history where the ideal has been realized in its pure form. And it is because it has this reality that he feels the pull of obligation. The sense of obligation in morals from which Kant tried to derive the whole structure of religion is really derived from the religion itself.[30]

Niebuhr has expressed serious reservations about much of what he wrote in this early work. In one place he has gone so far as to disavow almost the whole work,[31] but in writing a new preface for the paperback edition of the work published in 1956, he indicates that his greatest reservations have occurred with respect to his understanding of the relationship between love and justice. Whatever changes Niebuhr has experienced in his understanding of love, of justice, and of the relationship between the two, the basic framework of abstract thought in which he has cast his discussions of the radical nature of love has remained fairly typical of his approach.

Niebuhr has not, for example, abandoned his view that love is "disinterested" and "sacrificial" though he has come to admit a relationship between sacrificial love and mutual love in terms of the distinction between the eschatological (which places it at the end of history) and the historical (which may take place now).[32] This means that Niebuhr is no more willing to declare the historical impossibility of sacrificial love than he is willing to admit the possibility of remaking social life by sacrificial love alone. This theme has become a source of great difficulty for his interpreters because of its very dialectical character, and an especially inviting target for his critics.

Niebuhr has always pointed to Jesus Christ as the source of our understanding of love, both to His teachings and to His redemptive work on the Cross. Niebuhr's emphasis has shifted from Christ's teaching to Christ's redemptive work with the passage of time and with the shift in the theological climate in which he worked from that of the social gospel to that of various neo-Reformation movements. In the early book, *An Interpretation of Christian Ethics*, his view is stated this way: "The ethic of Jesus is the perfect fruit of prophetic religion. Its ideal of love has the same relation to the facts and necessities of human experience as the God of prophetic faith has to the world."[33] In *The Self and the Dramas of History* we read: "The fact is that the revelation of the 'Cross of Christ' does not superimpose, but merely clarifies, the truth about man's situation when ultimately considered. The situation which is clarified by the Christian faith can be validated by common experience."[34]

The role which Niebuhr assigns to "man's essential nature" or to "common experience" in the understanding of Christian love (*agape*) has been variously interpreted by students of Niebuhr's thought. Ramsey, who wants to include Niebuhr in a tradition of modified natural law, finds much in this concept to parallel the thinking of Jacques Maritain, in which the human inclination toward appreciation of the moral good is considered as an important source of moral knowledge. Niebuhr, of course, has serious strictures to deliver against traditional rational versions of natural law and the false use of natural law to bolster partial insights with the cloak of immutable universality. He has gone so far as to dismiss Thomistic versions of natural law as the religious sanctification of a medieval social structure. If we are to speak of an equivalent to natural law in the thought of Niebuhr about those given structures of personality and meaning known by common experience, it is important to couple the concept with the qualifications of traditional natural law which Niebuhr himself has made so frequently.

Gordon Harland, who interprets Niebuhr's ethics in terms of the christological dimension, suggests that man's essential nature is perceived by the natural man as a lack. Since we first experience the moral requirement as obligation and claim, to which we know in our hearts we have not measured up, it is only when our essential nature is revealed to us through the *agape* made known on the Cross, that we see ourselves as we were meant to be. Essential manhood is revealed to us through Christ. Niebuhr "is seeking to show that the *agape* of the Cross is verily the law of man's true nature. In this sense the Cross 'clarifies, but does not create, a norm which is given by the very constitution of selfhood.' "[35]

Niebuhr cannot be understood as either a rationalist or as an irrationalist. He refuses to demand the neat logical consistency of a metaphysical idealism; he equally refuses to dismiss the large realm of coherence and intelligibility which man can know and use for his own good. In the dialectical encounter between rationality and irrationality, between coherence and incoherence, men are to work out their understandings of life with neither pretensions to omnipotence nor despair of meaningful knowledge. In an essay published three different times, Niebuhr explores this dialectical pattern. He looks at the idealist tradition in Christian theology, running from Origen, through Aquinas, the Christian Platonists, Renaissance humanists, and liberal Christianity, and rejects this tradition by saying:

> It is obviously perilous to the content of the Christian faith and to the interpretation of life to place such a reliance on the coherences

and rationalities, the sequences and harmonies, of nature and reason. But the perils in the other direction are vividly displayed in contemporary as well as older Christian existentialism. The primary peril is that the wisdom of the Gospel is emptied of meaning by setting it into contradiction to the wisdom of the world and denying that the coherences and realms of meaning which the cultural disciplines rightfully analyze and establish have any relation to the Gospel.[36]

The tension between love and justice in Niebuhr's thinking has been a perennial theme. It is easily misunderstood, especially if the difference between Niebuhr and Brunner, who intensifies the contrast, are not carefully noted. Justice is not a substitute norm for use in situations in which love does not work. Niebuhr's thinking cannot be confused with the outlooks of those who postulate situations, such as a law court, in which justice and its own demands must be uppermost and exercised without regard for love. Justice is the functional expression of love in its effort to adjudicate competing claims, and hence is a necessary aspect of every social policy. It is demanded by love, yet also seems to negate love at any point where it is taken as satisfactory—immune from the judgment which love renders over every existing achievement. Moreover, apart from love, justice is crude and degenerates into calculation and even the mere balance of power. Balances of power, however, cannot be ignored by the Christian who must devise a social policy which brings tolerable harmonies between conflicting groups. Love both demands these balances of power and judges their inadequacy. Social actions cannot be judged by an independent norm of justice which functions for the difficult or impersonal situations in which love will not work.

Man's reason has a role to play in his search for justice. Reason helps him to weigh claims; it enables the conscience to awake to social evil which ought to be corrected; it keeps the door open for new and fresh evaluations. But reason is also subject to limitations and even to corruption. It may become the instrument by which self-interest is rationalized rather than judged. It cannot be used as an alternative to power. Niebuhr's strictures against the optimistic hope of the Renaissance tradition, in which reason was extolled as a means to eliminate the conflicts between conflicting systems of power, are among the most severe strictures in his writings. He is fully consistent in his refusal to countenance any view of love as a simple possibility and any view of reasonable justice as a road to utopia.

There are many expressions of philosophical procedure and in-principled deliberation in the Christian tradition which have not been covered in this section. Moreover, deliberative procedures are often found in relationship to other motifs. Anders Nygren, for example, exhibits deliberative as well as relational understandings in his treatment of Christian love. The Reformers, especially Calvin, show many features of a deliberative approach even though their thought is better understood by other categories. Deliberative elements can appear in connection with prescriptive and even with relational approaches. In this section we have set forth clear and obvious examples of the deliberative motif in order to portray the use of reason and moral philosophy in Christian thinking about ethics.

Section B: The Prescriptive Motif in Christian Ethics

5

The Prescriptive Motif and Its Biblical Forms

To say "Love thy neighbor as thyself" is to set forth a different form of ethical maxim than to say "Give a cup of coffee to everyone who knocks on your door." The first sets forth a principle; the second specifies a type of expected behavior; the first invites deliberation about the means necessary to express love for the neighbor; the second states how the neighbor is to be treated. The first has the advantage of flexibility, the danger of vagueness; the second has the advantage of offering specific guidance, the danger of hardening into a set of rigid requirements that cannot be changed to fit the unusual situation. The first elicits a seemingly unlimited range of demands which arise in the course of its intended fulfillment; the second leaves little question as to what is required in order to live up to one's moral obligation in a specific situation but does not say much about duties to the neighbor in a wider context.

Almost every religious tradition has, in some way or another, developed a series of ethical injunctions as guidance for its adherents and set them forth as practical, specific, and detailed prescriptions for conduct. Such prescriptions have the advantage of answering the question so often asked by men, "*What do I do* to be good (or, to obtain salvation)?" Hence the ancient Hebrew was instructed to offer release of male slaves at the end of six years; the Shaker maid was told that she might not begin her ironing until she could see without burning a candle in the room; the Hindu Brahmin was forbidden to eat with untouchables; and the orthodox Muslim was admonished to avoid boasting, blasphemy, and slander. In some traditions the theological heritage furnishes a possible judgment upon code morality—a judgment not found within the theological outlook of other traditions—but the presence of code morality is practically a universal phenomenon in man's religions, and its presence cannot be ignored even in places and traditions in which it has been decried.

In his study *Christ and the Modern Conscience* Jacques LeClercq speaks of two elements in Christian ethics. Both elements are present, he argues,

73

in Christian considerations of the moral life. The one, called "wisdom morality," has many marks of a deliberative ethics, such as we have already explored; the other, called "code morality," is equally important even though it may not quite measure up to the quality of the first.

> The [ideas] of code morality and wisdom morality are fundamental; they are keys. We shall be coming across them constantly in the course of our inquiry. For the moment, it will be enough to remember that code morality is a popular ethics applying to a people and depending on the voice of a master who lays down the rule, and that it is thus obligatory on those believers who do not aspire to an ideal which is itself ethical. It corresponds, in short, to a parting of the ways between the moral rule which a man must respect in order to satisfy the master, and thus obtain the recompense he desires, and immediate personal satisfaction, which lies on another path. Wisdom morality, on the contrary, is an ethics corresponding to the aspirations of the man who aspires to a perfect life.[1]

The feature of code morality to which LeClercq points is its obedience "to the voice of a master who lays down the rule." The element of authority is nearly always present in code morality, whether in the form of a religious precept given as the revealed will of a deity, or in the form of statutory and enforcement regulations which accompany the legislation of a community. The legislation of a commonwealth or state, frequently called the code, is a compendium of legislation together with specified provisions for its enforcement. Even though all religions hope that their adherents will willingly and cheerfully do the divine will, and most governments hope for cooperation from their citizens, the code in which certain acts are either prescribed or prohibited is backed by an implied authority with power to punish violations.

A number of terms have been proposed to describe the kind of norms LeClercq calls "code morality." For instance, John Murray proposed the term *principles*, which he applied to "objectively revealed precepts, institutions, commandments, which are the norms and channels of human behavior."[2] We obviously cannot adopt this phrase, for we have used the term *principles* to refer to a quite different approach to the formulation of the ethical norm. It is hardly a philosopher, thinking deliberatively about the principles which govern man's search for the good life, who declares:

> The criterion of our standing in the kingdom of God and of reward in the age to come is nothing else than meticulous observance of the commandments of God in the minutial details of their prescription and the earnest inculcation of such observance on the part of others.[3]

Another word used to describe prescriptive codes is *legalism*. But the word *legalism* bears a very close relationship to the term *law*, many forms of which belong to rational and deliberative ethics. Certainly the idea of natural law is closely related to deliberative reason. While a natural law ethic may, on occasion, specify desired behavior in specific terms, it generally enunciates principles. The intent and hope of most natural law is to point to reason as a source of universally acceptable norms. Because of this, the term *law* has one kind of implication while the word *legalism* has another. It is not wise, therefore, to use either phrase as the name for a basic motif.

Still another term in this connection is *formalistic*, employed by Kenneth E. Kirk in his Bampton Lectures for 1928.[4] Kirk applied *formalistic* to the process of codification which began in the apostolic period, a process he regarded as a cleavage from the original Gospel ethic. As Kirk used the term *formalism* it is obviously polemical and derogatory; it leaves no possible room for prescriptive ways of specifying expected behavior which permit modifications for circumstance. Moreover, the word *formalism* has been used by Friedrich Paulsen to contrast with teleological. According to Paulsen a formalistic ethics "claims that the concepts good and bad, taken in their moral sense, designate an absolute quality of the will, without any regard to the effects of acts or modes of conduct," whereas in a teleological ethic "acts are called good when they tend to preserve and promote human welfare; bad, when they tend to disturb and destroy it."[5] Since this distinction has already been discussed in terms of the contrast between "teleological" and "deontological" kinds of philosophical ethics, it is well to shy from Paulsen's term in describing prescriptive norms.

One more way of dealing with these patterns was employed by the late H. Richard Niebuhr, whose book *The Responsible Self* sets forth three great patterns, or synecdoches, for the formulation of the ethical question. Niebuhr's book is so carefully wrought and his categories so nearly like those proposed here, that it is with great gratitude and extreme reluctance that we explore points at which the categories under development here differ from those set forth by his work.

Niebuhr's main purpose was to argue for the suitability of his third category, the category of responsibility. He found two other categories at work in the theoretical formulation of ethical understandings. In one, moral reasoning is portrayed by the image of man-the-maker. Such an image understands man as shaping his moral decisions in light of a goal or purpose. It represents much that is associated with teleological approaches in moral philosophy. Different men have entertained different goals— pleasure, happiness, self-realization—but they have been alike in conceiving of the moral life as the pursuit of some goal and the fabrication of the necessary procedures for its attainment. All that Niebuhr said about this type of moral reasoning we should affirm as true of deliberative ethics.

Niebuhr's second type is portrayed by the image of man-the-citizen.

Such an approach recognizes the role "of *mores*, of commandments and rules, *Thou shalt*s and *Thou shalt not*s, of directions and permissions."[6] The "citizen" of any given situation is confronted with the issue as to whether he will consent to or rebel against the requirements imposed upon him. In this image of ethics, man is *homo politicus* and the self is understood as a "legislative, obedient, and administrative" entity.[7] All these features of Niebuhr's second type would be true of what we propose to call prescriptive ethics.

The following argument may take issue with Niebuhr's second type; perhaps it only takes issue with certain individuals whom he chose to assign to it. But, from the standpoint of clarifying our own discussion, it seems important to suggest that Niebuhr's second image is more philosophical in assigning Kant to his second category; whereas, we have assigned Kant to deliberative ethics. Niebuhr may have found it easier to place Kant in the second category than we do because he saw all three of his categories as but different forms of a philosophical method. Or, he may have done it because he relied heavily upon the distinction between teleological and deontological reasoning to distinguish his first from his second pattern; whereas, we have tended to see the difference between the deliberative and prescriptive ethic more in terms of a difference between an autonomous and a heteronomous authority, between the enunciation of a general ideal and the specification of a desired behavior.

It hardly seems likely that one could hold a political unit together with the Kantian formulation of ethical duty. To be sure, Kant elaborated many implications from his formal sense of duty and found himself convinced that rational duty and the Gospel ethic had much in common. But to urge the citizen to "Act on the maxim that you could will to become a universal law," or "So act as to treat humanity whether in thine own person or in that of any other, in every case as an end withal, never as a means only," is hardly the procedure of the average traffic bureau. The citizen is more likely to be told, "Drive on the right," "Do not litter," or "Stop here on red."

While some forms of prescription are petty and brittle, others are imaginative and helpful. Moreover, both tendencies persist in the Christian formulation of prescriptive norms, and we cannot understand the scope of Christian moral teaching without taking into account the variety which has obtained and continues to obtain the allegiance of Christians. We dare not rely entirely upon the critics of code morality to guide us, for they frequently present prescriptive norms in a narrow and biased manner. Therefore we must consider the possible use of the Bible as a source of prescriptive guidance, fairly assess the extent and nature of prescription in Catholic and Protestant life, and explore how casuistries take new circumstances into account under the rubrics of codes.

Prescriptive Obligation in Biblical Terms

The Christian life has frequently been defined in terms of obedience to the prescribed requirement of biblical injunctions as found in the Ten Commandments, the Exodus Codes, the Sermon on the Mount, and other parts of the Bible. It is surprising to discover the widely divergent theological positions that have given rise to a reading of biblical ethics in prescriptive terms. While many of those who regard the Bible as a law book belong to the conservative tradition, a Protestant liberal, such as Harold Bosley, reports with keen memory the impact which the book by Charles M. Sheldon, *In His Steps*,[8] made upon him during his youth. Sheldon's book, which was phenomenally popular because it captured the imaginations of millions (and perhaps because it filled an innate longing for specific guidance), posed the ethical standard in a prescriptive form as an answer to the question "What would Jesus do?" About this, Bosley writes,

> "What would Jesus do?" impresses me as a permanently valid question for anyone who calls himself a Christian. It cuts to the heart of the meaning of being a Christian in this or any other age. Even as of old, being a Christian either means accepting Jesus' invitation to "Follow me" or it comes close to having no coherent meaning at all.[9]

C. H. Dodd is convinced that both Jesus and Paul adopted a prescriptive framework for their ethical teaching, a framework found in the Judaism of their day. Dodd's argument is no unreflective tract ignorant of the Gospel of grace-without-law proclaimed with new vigor in our day—nor does it ignore the proclamation of Good News within which the early church embodied its ethical teachings. It is a careful assertion that prescriptive elements play a role in the New Testament writings about ethical matters. Ethical action is a response to the mighty acts of God in redeeming mankind through the death and resurrection of Christ, but the kinds of moral action that are appropriate to the mighty acts are specified in prescriptive terms. Dodd maintains that the early church saw to it that the kind of behavior expected of Christians was spelled out for their guidance and not left to the whim of the spirit or to the sense of appropriateness cherished by the new converts. Dodd argues that Paul, far from trusting the personal judgments of his followers to guide them to morally acceptable behavior, thundered orders to his converts:

> . . . the orders are severely practical and commonsense. The Christians of Thessalonica are to observe decent self-control in sexual relations, to respect the rights of others, to do their best to love their neighbors, and to be honest and industrious, so as to maintain a reasonable standard of living without having to keep appealing for charity (like some

Christian communities Paul knew too well). Paul's teaching, then, had its feet well on the ground.[10]

Using the methods of form criticism, Dodd shows that there is a body of ethical teaching which appears in much the same form and tone in I Thessalonians, Hebrews, and I Peter and which was taught in the New Testament church as part of the tradition. This teaching rendered its moral instruction in specific terms and provided "a scheme of practical precepts for everyday living."[11] Not only did the early church proclaim what Christ had done for the redemption of man; it also kept alive the moral instruction of its risen Lord and Master as a guide to the conduct expected in his followers.

The Gospel sayings which reflect the teachings of Jesus are basically prescriptive indications of proper Christian behavior. Matthew clearly intended that the Sermon on the Mount should be understood as law, since he placed the collected sayings of Jesus in analogous relationship to the Mosaic law of the Pentateuch. Even though the Gospel writers reformulated the teachings of Jesus for their own purposes, the prescriptive features of the teaching were not obscured. Dodd willingly speaks of the "Law of Christ." He declares that "Jesus Himself set forth a substantial number of ethical precepts, and these precepts are couched in markedly authoritative tone, and are accompanied by solemn warnings that they are intended to be obeyed."[12]

Dodd likewise characterizes the moral instruction of Paul in prescriptive terms. He shows that Paul's moral exhortations are "perfectly straightforward general maxims which you could transfer directly to the field of conduct."[13] They are capable of literal application. He argues that Paul understood the Gospel in terms of new law, even though he sounded warnings against the shortcomings of law. These warnings from Paul have been used by some theologians in the Reformation tradition to argue that Paul threw over the law, a position Dodd rejects. Dodd is opposed to any interpretation of Paul in terms of Augustine's dictum "Love God and do as you please." This he feels can be "seriously misleading" and may result in "barren sentimentality."[14]

Dodd knows that he upholds a currently unpopular interpretation of New Testament ethics, but insists that a prescriptive understanding of moral obligation is essential to the experience of "repentance" upon which the Gospel depends for its promise of grace. Dodd builds his case for using the teachings of Jesus as a guide for the conduct that should be expected from his followers with full recognition of the arguments against his point of view. He also finds that he must wrestle with the problems which have always occupied the followers of Jesus who seek to apply his teachings in daily decisions. Dodd draws a distinction between precepts and codes.

Codes provide precise and foolproof instructions for every detailed situation that may arise. Precepts—particularly of the type found in the teachings of Jesus—"differ markedly from much of the contemporary rabbinic teaching, which aimed precisely at producing a foolproof scheme of rules and regulations in obedience to which man might conform to the law of God in all likely contingencies."[15] Yet the precepts are concrete and instructive; they are more than broad generalities. They clearly specify the *quality* and *direction* which any act must take in order to be an expression of Christian love. Unless an act, however lowly or partial, has the same direction specified by the precepts, it does not constitute Christian behavior. ". . . the goal may be still far off. But the demand that our action in concrete situations shall have *this* direction and *this* quality is categorical."[16]

This sophisticated modern statement shows that the use of the Bible as a source of prescriptive ethical guidance need not be marked by rigidity and narrowness. At times Dodd speaks as an ethicist, concerned about the theological dimensions of ethical judgments; at other times he writes more as a New Testament exegete, concerned to report findings from the literature itself. Perhaps the spokesman for an ethical point of view is driven to see a more unified picture in New Testament ethics than the exegete. The former must argue a position and cherish some consistency; the latter can accept the ambiguities and complexities that may be present in the biblical materials themselves. There is no reason, however, for the two functions to be entirely split apart, or for the representatives of one group to ignore the work of the other.

The technical problems that relate to the interpretation of biblical thought are numerous. Does the portrayal of Jesus in Luke abrogate the picture of Jesus based upon Matthew? Did Paul christianize the Stoic tradition, as Morton Scott Enslin has argued?[17] Did Jesus intend his teaching to be understood as a guide to behavior, as Hans Windisch suggested?[18] Are the ethics of Jesus to be understood as legislation for a future kingdom or for the interim prior to a cataclysmic end of this world?[19] Was Wilhelm Herrmann right in his view, echoed many times since, that the literal observance of Jesus' commands is impossible?[20] If so, are we to conclude that the purpose of Jesus' teachings is to shock, exhort, and vivify the truth so as to impel his believers to action? Can the use of law as a means to obtain salvation be rejected without also rejecting the place of law as a guide to the moral behavior of the Christian who is justified by faith? Any adequate exploration of these issues must come in other works, for discussion of these is bound to persist at length and with vigor. Our purpose here is limited. It is to show that some men see the teaching of the New Testament in prescriptive terms, even in face of many onslaughts against this view from contemporary Protestant writers.

Another way of exploring the legitimacy of prescription in Christian ethics is to deal with the obligations of Christians to keep the law of Moses. To what extent is Christian morality to include concern for the moral (and to a lesser extent) the ceremonial law of Moses? George A. F. Knight has argued that Christ did not abrogate the requirements of the Old Testament law, and that although Christ is the end or fulfillment of the law he is not its destroyer. Speaking of how Christ builds upon the Mosaic law, using precepts from the *Torah*, Knight observes:

> He who is the *end* of the Law himself now empowers it to unfold its true meaning and produce its predestined effect in a new fulness of vitality in the life of the man who is joined with him. But when he does this with the precept in question, Christ does not thereupon offer the believer a new law or a new precept that he himself is inventing on the spot. He is offering him an ancient precept from the law of Moses. And this is true even of the so-called "Eleventh Commandment" which we are inclined to attribute to Christ alone, but which our Lord is merely quoting out of Deuteronomy and Leviticus. This means that it is in fact the law of Moses which is the original Word of God, but that it is Christ, the living Word, who is the agency that releases the potentiality within it.[21]

Christian groups in several periods of the life of the church have regarded the Bible as a source of moral law in prescriptive terms—treating the Bible as a law book. Such groups have found in the law of Moses and the ethic of the New Testament a guide for Christian behavior, even a clue to the nature of the church's own life. Many of these groups have been Protestant, since the Bible occupies an especially authoritative place in Protestant thinking. But even before the Reformation there were individuals looking to the Bible as the source of ethical norms in the prescriptive sense. The pre-Reformer, John Wyclif, sought to reform the life of the church in accordance with the law he found in the Gospel. Unlike Luther, Wyclif never came to believe in justification *sola fide*, and hence never came to challenge the law in the same way that Luther did. However, he did take the ethical teachings of the Bible very seriously and proposed them as the criteria by which the reform of the church by the power of the state should be instigated and judged.

Wyclif thought of law in three forms: scriptural, natural, and the law of conscience. While all three forms of law are related to each other, it is scriptural law which is of interest to us here. Scriptural law is the "divine law of the Gospels." Each person has access to a knowledge of this law to the extent that he can read the Bible. Hence it was important for Wyclif to see that translations were prepared which opened the scriptures to the reading public, allowing each man to perceive for himself the content of scriptural law.

Several specific conclusions which Wyclif drew as he read the divine law of the Gospels are important for understanding his view of the church and the program he pursued as a pre-Reformer. In the first place Wyclif became convinced that the church should be poor. Much of his writing criticized the immense wealth of the medieval church and the privileges assumed by its clergy. Second, Wyclif held that the devotional or contemplative life must express itself in service, not in ascetic withdrawal. Poverty is not an end but a means, a means to the more adequate service of one's fellow man. Pilgrimages for special religious rites and celibacy are ruled out because they withdraw a man from service to his fellows rather than spur him to it. Third, Wyclif became convinced that power must be exercised only as a trust. If the church misuses its spiritual power by seeking unworthy ends or acquiring worldly prestige, the state is to use its power to correct the church. Last, Wyclif developed modified scruples about Christian participation in war. He ruled out the participation of the church in the crusades, in the self-righteous war for holy objectives. Wyclif argued that war must be fought in love and righteousness for corrective ends, never in anger for vindictive purposes. This affirmation of the just war in contrast to the crusade is especially interesting in light of efforts among contemporary thinkers to draw a similar distinction.

Wyclif made a list of seven bodily works of mercy which all men should perform, and also a list of seven spiritual works of mercy. The bodily works included feeding the hungry, giving drink to the thirsty, showing hospitality, clothing the naked, visiting prisoners, visiting the sick, and burying the dead. The spiritual list included teaching, counseling, reproving, comforting, forgiving, suffering, praying.

Wyclif's thought was anything but a dry and brittle legalism; it even contained a sense of identity with Christ which hinted of the evangelical spirit. There was a Christ mysticism in Wyclif, not unlike that in Saint Paul, though in the final analysis the moral law rather than the saving relationship of justification by faith remained normative. The following passage, despite its sense of abandoned obedience to Christ, clearly defines the kind of behavior that marks the Christian life and presupposes that only by following this kind of behavior, which Wyclif believed to be demanded by the New Testament, does one stand in a saving relationship with Jesus Christ.

> *Christ, not compelling, but freely counselling each man to perfect life, saith thus,* . . . "If any man will come after me, let him deny himself, and take his cross, and follow me."
> If a proud man be converted to Christ, and made meek, he hath forsaken himself. If a covetous man ceaseth to covet, and giveth his own things, he hath denied himself. If a lecherous man changeth his life to chastity, he hath denied himself; as St. Gregory saith, He denieth him-

self who forsaketh and withstandeth the unreasonable will of his flesh.
The cross of Christ is taken when despisings for the love of truth be
not forsaken, when the flesh is punished for abstinence, and when compassion and pity toward our neighbour is truly kept; when a man is
crucified to the world, and the world is crucified to him, setting at
nought the joy thereof. It is not enough to bear the cross of painful life,
except men follow Christ in virtues, not by steps of bodily feet, but by
meekness, love, and heavenly desire.[22]

Let us look, then, and see what is enjoined and commanded by the
Lord, in the law of perfect liberty, and observe it, and abstain from
what is forbidden, and from giving attention to laws newly ordained,
and this will be enough.[23]

Wyclif's suggestion that men should turn to the Bible as a source of
ethical guidance (as well as for the definition of the true nature of the
church) was accepted by many forms and branches of the Protestant
movement, and especially by the so-called left-wing of the Reformation.
The use of the Bible as a source of moral law is not confined, however, to
those branches of Protestantism in which works righteousness is stressed
more than justification by faith, for John Calvin furnishes us with one of
the most visible cases in which moral requirements are understood prescriptively from the biblical teachings.

Calvin's adherence to the doctrine of justification by grace is beyond
dispute and undergirded all that he said about the place of the law, but it
did not lead him to doubt the value of the law as a source of normative
ethical judgment. Like Irenaeus, Calvin saw no opposition between the Old
Testament law and the Gospel; Christians are subject to both. Citing Paul
as his authority, Calvin suggested that Christ is the fulfillment of the law,
not its negation. Christians are not called to oppose law-as-such, but only
the idea that salvation can or should be earned through works of righteousness performed under the law. Calvin himself stated the proposition in
these terms:

In another place, [Paul] states that "the law was added because of
transgressions"; that is, to humble men, by convicting them of being
the causes of their own condemnation. Now, this being the true and
only preparation for seeking Christ, the various declarations which
he makes are in perfect unison with each other. But as he was then
engaged in a controversy with erroneous teachers, who pretended that
we merit righteousness by the works of the law—in order to refute
their error, he was sometimes obliged to use the term *law* in a more
restricted sense, as merely preceptive, although it was otherwise connected with the covenant of gratuitous adoption.[24]

Calvin fought the same battle that Paul fought against those who used
the law as a program for righteousness. The first use of the law is to con-

vict men of their failure to live up to the righteousness of God which it sets forth. Law in this sense is "like a mirror, in which we behold, first: our impotence; secondly, our iniquity, which proceeds from it; and lastly, the consequence of both. . . ."[25] But not all men find the law a pedagogue to repentance. The law functions for them in a second sense. It holds them in restraint, because they fear the penalties which flow from disobedience to the law. These men may actually resent the requirements of the law and rebel against the divine authority that it represents, but even so, evil is restrained in the social order by this functioning of the law. A third use of the law, of special interest for this inquiry, is a creative one. It offers positive, prescriptive, and helpful guidance to the saints, as well as the guidance for good living by which they show forth their gratitude toward the saving grace of God which they have known.

> The third use of the law, which is the principal one, and which is more nearly connected with the proper end of it, relates to the faithful, in whose hearts the Spirit of God already lives and reigns. For although the law is inscribed and engraven on their hearts by the finger of God,—that is, although they are so excited and animated by the direction of the Spirit, that they desire to obey God—yet they derive a twofold advantage from the law. For they find it an excellent instrument to give them, from day to day, a better and more certain understanding of the Divine will to which they aspire, and to confirm them in the knowledge of it. As, though a servant be already influenced by the strongest desire of gaining the approbation of his master, yet it is necessary for him carefully to inquire and observe the orders of his master, in order to conform to them. Nor let anyone of us exempt himself from this necessity; for no man has already acquired so much wisdom, that he could not by the daily instruction of the law make new advances into a purer knowledge of the Divine will. In the next place, as we need not only instruction, but also exhortation, the servant of God will derive this further advantage from the law; by frequent meditation on it he will be excited to obedience, he will be confirmed in it, and restrained from the slippery path of transgression.[26]

Calvin took pains to set forth the content of biblical law for the guidance of the faithful. Chapter eight of the second book of the *Institutes* expounds the moral law and its content, following the ten precepts of the Decalogue. The catechism of the church at Geneva, used for the instruction of children, contained a section on the law, which also expounds the meaning of the Ten Commandments. In the catechism the minister declares:

> . . . although we never satisfy the law in this earthly pilgrimage of ours, yet we shall not consider it to be superfluous, because it demands such strict perfection from us. For it shows us the mark at which we

ought to aim and the goal to which we must strive; that each of us, according to the measure of grace bestowed upon him, may try to conform his life to the highest rectitude, and by assiduous care make more and more progress.

To this, the catechumen replies, "That is my opinion."[27]

In his commentaries upon the Bible, Calvin explores the meaning of God's word, including the function of that word in making known to the faithful the ways in which God intends men to act. The faithful man delights in the law—it is no slavish subservience to a code which impels him to show his gratitude to God, but a right behavior which excites and impels the believer into obedience and trust. "Only those who come happily to the study of the law, who enjoy its teaching, who think nothing more worth while or pleasanter than to make progress in it, are qualified students of the law." A bit later Calvin declares, "For it is silly for us to wag our ears like asses, and confess God with mouth and lips only. Men truly progress in God's school when they form their lives by his teaching, when they have their feet ready to walk, to follow wherever he calls."[28]

In making the Ten Commandments basic to his ethical understanding, Calvin set himself against those groups in his day which contrasted the law of Moses with the law of Christ. Calvin would have no part of an evangelical law which contradicted or entirely superseded the Decalogue and sharply condemned those who "rashly explode Moses altogether, and discard the two tables of the law."[29] Calvin held that Christ restored the law of Moses to the genuine purity it had before the Pharisees had obscured it with falsehoods and blemishes.

Calvin was seeking to make a place for the law without succumbing to legalism. To illustrate: the third commandment specifies "Thou shalt not take the name of the Lord, thy God, in vain." Calvin held that this law requires us to hold the name of God sacred, which means to use the divine name in valid oaths and proper contexts—not to forswear its use completely. The Anabaptists, however, substituting a new evangelical law, "Swear not at all," actually set the teaching of Christ in the Sermon on the Mount against the teaching of the Father in the Decalogue. Calvin argued that Christ was condemning the way in which the scribes and Pharisees used oaths, not condemning the use of oaths in valid and legitimate contexts. Calvin's method takes the Decalogue seriously while at the same time it refuses to take the Sermon on the Mount legalistically. It calls for sober and balanced judgment about the proper use of oaths, a judgment informed by profound understandings of what it means to use oaths in a legitimate way.

Luther used two senses of the law, only hinting at a third, whereas Calvin spoke of law in three functions. In a twofold use of the law a distinction is made between the law as a teacher in Christ, which brings men to repentance, and law as a source of civil regulation, which governs men's conduct. In a triple use of the law, found in Melanchthon initially, and more fully in Calvin, a distinction is made between the law as leading to repentance, the law as a source of restraint for sinners (negative civil function), and the law as guidance for believers (positive civil function). Luther took the civil function of law in its basically negative sense and subordinated it to the theological use of the law as a teacher in Christ. Luther taught that the use of the law as guidance is not to be compared in significance to the value of the law as a goad to repentance. Calvin, in making a distinction between the way sinful men respond to the prescriptive features of law (as requirements they resent) and the way in which redeemed men see the prescriptive features of law (as guidance they welcome), was able to make a positive place for law in the life of the believer which simply could not be placed into the twofold scheme that Luther made for separating the civil or prescriptive use of the law from the theological, i.e. pedagogical, use. Luther hinted at a triple use of the law when he noted that the pious man and the impious man read the civil prescriptions of law very differently, but he never developed the fullblown conception which in Calvin provided the way of making the law a source of welcome and positive moral guidance for the believer.[30]

Men have debated whether Calvin was respecting the content of Christ's teaching or misunderstanding its intention by setting up the third use of the law. George Thomas is representative of Calvin's critics, who feel that the Swiss Reformer overstressed the place of law. He holds that

> It can hardly be denied that Calvin's ethic is primarily an *ethic of law* rather than an ethic of love. This is due to his failure to grasp the radical and unique character of Christ's teaching. He is right in insisting that Jesus did not mean to lay down a "new law"; but he is wrong in holding that Jesus merely "purified" the "old law." As we have seen, Jesus sought to express the absolute will of God which had been only partially revealed in the law of Moses. The fact that he quotes the two-fold law of love from the law of Moses does not imply that love occupies the same place in his ethic as in that of the Pentateuch, or that it is merely a "summary" of the Ten Commandments. The meaning of the law of love for Jesus must be derived from a study of all he said and did, including his death on the Cross. Such a study discloses that his ethic is not an ethic of law, even when love is included as the primary law; it is an ethic of love, which accepts and makes use of laws only insofar as they embody the demands of love.[31]

In contrast, a number of contemporary thinkers like John Murray and C. F. H. Henry, have kept alive the Calvinistic idea of biblical law as a source of prescriptive guidance and have done so with a rigor that may itself have transformed Calvin's own intentions. Murray believes that the ethics of the Bible are to be respected in all their prescriptive particulars. Henry feels that the Bible is to be taken seriously as a source of specific ethical guidance. In an extended discussion of the difficulties arising when either philosophical idealism or relational relativism is used to state the Christian norm rather than the prescriptive detail of biblical teaching, Henry reasserts the view that Scripture is the only infallible rule of faith and practice.

> Love, as the Bible exposits it, is not something as nebulous as moderns would have us think. The New Testament knows nothing of lawless believers in Christ. No believer is left to work out his moral solutions by the principle of love alone. He has some external guidance from Divine revelation. The early believers were not delivered from an obligation to obey the precepts of the law. The life of love which Christianity proclaims is centered in love for the Living God who has revealed his will, and only to the extent that love impels the believer to fulfill God's revealed will is it genuinely of the Holy Spirit. Love is in accord with the biblical ethic when it devotedly seeks to obey fully the Divine commands.
>
> The content of love must be defined by Divine revelation. The biblical revelation places the only reliable rule of practice before the community of faith. What the Bible teaches gives trustworthy direction to love of self, of neighbor, of God. The pages of the Bible are filled with an interest in good fathers and children, good husbands and wives, good neighbors and friends, good rulers and subjects, good states and the good life, and the feeling of love even in the regenerate believer is inadequate to chart the whole implication of the moral life.[32]

Henry finds the particularization of the moral life—his term for prescriptive guidance—in the revelation of both testaments. The Mosaic law dominates the Old Testament; the Sermon on the Mount, the New. Henry admits that there is a difference between perpetual obligations and temporary obligations under the disclosure of the Old Testament and that there is a growing, or progressive, disclosure of God's will for man with the change in eras. But the foundational norms are found in the Ten Commandments, which are binding upon Christians in both the religious and ethical dimensions. The "two-tables" of the law, the first specifying duties to God, the second, duties to neighbor, cannot be separated. The prophets explore with deeper understanding the ethical instructions set down in the Ten Commandments. In dealing with the New Testament and the central summary of the teachings of Jesus in the Sermon on the Mount, Henry not only portrays Jesus as friendly to Old Testament law, but he finds the Sermon on the Mount to be important for the factual guidance that it offers. "The Sermon remains valid not only in the disposition it intends, but in its precepts and commandments."[33] Henry declares that the requirements of the Sermon on the Mount are to be understood by the redeemed man as providing that view of moral imperatives rooted in the creation itself.

> The historic Reformed view is that the Sermon is an exposition of the deeper implications of the moral law, and hence a statement of the practical way in which *agape* is to work itself out in daily conduct here and now. The Sermon expresses therefore the only righteousness acceptable to God in this age or in any. As such, the Sermon condemns the man in sin, is fulfilled by Christ's active and passive obedience, and serves as the believer's rule of Christian gratitude in personal relations.[34]

Henry explores the rest of the New Testament for the same sort of particular guidance that he finds in the Sermon on the Mount. Because the Bible sets forth in particular terms what it means to fulfill the love of God there is no reason why any man "need be in doubt about what inner attitudes and pursuits are approved by God, and what are condemned."[35] Henry admits that the connection between biblical precepts and everyday decisions are not always easy to see, and that Christians may not always agree concerning what the biblical ethic requires in each specific decision of life. Therefore, "even consecrated Christians, devoted to the will of God, and seeking the guidance of the Holy Spirit in applying the ethics of inspiration in their immediate situation, have had to confess at times that some other biblical principle should have been applied, or that a mistake was sincerely made."[36]

Henry affirms the mutuality rather than the opposition of Gospel and law. He speaks of the threefold function of the law under political, pedagogic, and didactic categories—though in doing so he changes the order Calvin assigned to these three functions. Henry acknowledges the Holy Spirit to be a necessary source of Christian impulse toward the good life. But the degree of rigor and demand for consistency, the polemical tone and assertion of authority, are more evident in Henry than in Calvin. Perhaps Calvin would have developed such a tone had he addressed himself to the issues and antagonists which Henry confronts in the present age. It may be one thing to affirm the place of law in contrast to Luther and the evangelical radicals of the sixteenth century; it is another, perhaps, to write against the nontheistic naturalists and existentialists of the twentieth.

The position represented by John Murray, Carl Henry, and Gordon H. Clark[37] may be an unsatisfactory continuation of the Calvinist heritage and an unattractive statement of Christian morality, but it should not be dismissed on the wrong grounds. It is not petty nor is it foolish. It intends to bring life under a clear sense of the divine will. It believes that prescription is necessary because it alone can guide men in the actual conditions of

life. It feels that moral righteousness must be clear and basically unchangeable by circumstance. While it must be remembered that conservative
evangelicalism does not represent the only possible understanding of biblical ethics, its moral view flows naturally from a plenary doctrine of
inspiration and it argues seriously for a rigorous sense of the divine law.

6

Prescriptive Codes in the Christian Tradition

Whether or not a prescriptive process is at work in the New Testament writings, there can be no doubt of its prominent position in the writing of the Apostolic Fathers in the second and third centuries of the Christian era. While there are differences in the degree of codification among individuals, the general features of the apostolic period are clear. About them Kenneth Kirk remarked:

> St. Paul's indignant wonder was evoked by the reversion of a small province of the Christian Church to the legalist spirit of Jewish religion. Had he lived a half-a-century or a century later, his cause for amazement would have been increased a hundredfold. The example of the Galatians might be thought to have infected the entire Christian Church; writer after writer seems to have little other interest than to express the genius of Christianity wholly in terms of law and obedience, reward and punishment.[1]

Several teaching manuals in the early church set forth the Christian life as a choice between good and evil and provided a detailed list of behavior related to each. *The Doctrina* indicates how the Christian should behave by providing a long list of expected and a long list of prohibited actions, setting into contrast the way of life and the way of death. These lists explicitly rule out wrong attitudes, such as pride, greed, sourness, and the holding of a grudge as well as wrong actions, such as theft, lying, and causing divisions. They rule out certain practices that are related to magic and sorcery, the use of enchanting potions and the practice of astrology. These practices lead to idolatry, the attempt to get something through manipulative means rather than by conforming to the will of God. There are also passages in *The Doctrina* that reflect a folk wisdom, a practical level of advice. In 4:5 we find "Do not keep stretching out your hands to receive, and drawing them back when it comes to returning." The impression left by reading *The Doctrina* is of a well-intended description of the sober, God-fearing, humble life as the Christian should live it. It is a

89

life that involves devotion and earnest moral effort and to which there are no magical short cuts.

The teaching found in *The Doctrina* is amplified by that found in *The Didache*, in which there is more evidence of familiarity with the Old Testament law. *The Didache* sometimes states a rigorous demand, then settles for a partial fulfillment. "If you can bear the Lord's full yoke, you will be perfect. But if you cannot, then do what you can" (6:2). "If you do not have running water, baptize in some other. If you cannot in cold, then in warm" (7:3). "Welcome every apostle on arriving, as if he were the Lord. But he must not stay beyond one day. In the case of necessity, however, the next day too. If he stays three days, he is a false prophet" (11:5). This sort of advice, representing as it does common-sense responses to contingent circumstances, shows the beginning of a casuistry at work in the codified teaching of the early church.

These manuals call for a kind of life that can be recommended to all men and can be lived in the world; their teaching is not ascetic. They commend the humility of the Christian life as one of obedience to the Old and New Testament ethics, but they do not set forth this obedience in christocentric terms. The ethic here is tough and sober, but not impossible; it urges men to guard their associations with evil men lest they be led astray by those who follow the way of darkness. However, these teachings also seem shallow and dry, lacking specifically Christian inspiration.

Other apostolic writers widened the separation of the morally righteous from the morally impure and used the law, even Mosaic law, as a central aspect of the Christian ethic. In the letter bearing his name, Barnabas broke with the content of the Mosaic law, but not with its methodology. In doing so he made use of a common principle of scriptural interpretation, the allegorical method.

> Now, because Moses said, "You shall not eat swine or eagle or hawk or crow or any fish that does not have scales on it," he had three teachings in mind. Further, he says to them in Deuteronomy, "And I will set forth my ordinances to this people." So, then, God's command is not that they should not eat, but Moses spoke in the spirit. This, then, is why he mentioned the swine: "You shall not associate," he means, "with men who are like swine," that is, when they are in luxury, they forget the Lord, but when they are in want they acknowledge the Lord, just as the swine when it is feeding does not know its master, but when it is hungry it squeals, and when it has been fed, it is quiet again. "Neither shall you eat the eagle or the hawk or the kite or the crow"; you shall not, he means, associate with or come to resemble such men as do not know how to provide their food by toil and sweat, but lawlessly seize what belongs to others, and while pretending to live in innocence, watch and look about to find whom they can plunder in their greed, just as these birds are the only ones that provide no food

for themselves, but sit idle and seek ways to eat the meat of others, since they are pests in wickedness. "And you shall not eat," he goes on, "sea eel or polyp or cuttlefish." You shall not, he means, associate with such men and come to resemble them, who are utterly ungodly and already condemned to death, just as these fish alone are accursed and swim in the depths, not swimming on the surface like the rest, but living in the mud at the bottom.[2]

Exhortative moral teaching is found in many early Christian writings, including a second-century sermon entitled "Second Clement" and the work of Irenaeus, *Against the Heresies*. These writings make clear that law has a place in the Christian life, and while they are less specific than *The Doctrina* and *The Didache*, the righteousness they require of Christians is defined in a prescriptive manner. Moreover, in Second Clement obedience to the law of faith as well as the law of morals is necessary to salvation. In Irenaeus, doctrinal correctness, as well as moral rectitude, is called for as the law of both Testaments is made central for the Christian life.

> As in the law, therefore, and in the Gospel [likewise] the first and greatest commandment is, to love the Lord God with the whole heart, and then there follows a commandment like to it, to love one's neighbour as one's self; the author of the law and the Gospel is shown to be one and the same. For the precepts of an absolutely perfect life, since they are the same in each Testament, have pointed out [to us] the same God, who certainly has promulgated particular laws adapted for each; but the more prominent and the greatest [commandments], without which salvation cannot [be attained], He has exhorted [us to observe] the same in both.[3]

In the medieval life of the church, prescriptions appeared for the correction of offenses against standards of behavior as well as for the specification of proper Christian conduct. A body of legislation was developed, often by tradition and the decisions of respected individuals rather than in actual deliberative assemblies. This legislation has been preserved for us in the documents which deal with penance in the medieval period.[4] These documents contain not only careful definitions of specific sins that should be avoided by Christians, but provision for the expiation of such sins through an elaborate set of prescribed punishments. The nature of these documents can be illustrated by the decisions of an Irish abbot named Cummean which date from the middle of the seventh century. These are collected into eleven sections, each concerning a particular type of sin. The first deals with gluttony and is mainly concerned with prohibitions against drunkenness. Drunkenness involves a penance of forty days on bread and water for priests, seven days for laymen. The same penance is prescribed for the person who tempts the culprit to drink, even "for the sake of good fellowship." If the stupor benumbs the individual's organs of speech, a special fast is added to the punishment. If the offender becomes sick to the point of vomit, the fast is to last seven days; if he vomits the host, forty days; if dogs lick up the vomit containing the host, a hundred days. Stealing food is specified as an offense requiring a forty-day fast.

In subsequent sections of Cummean's code, fornication, avarice, anger, dejection, languor, vainglory, pride, petty cases, misdemeanors of boys, and mishandling the host are all defined as sins of greater or lesser extent, and punishments are prescribed both for the seriousness of the sin and the status of the offender. Under petty cases there is a provision that one should go without supper if he does not do his day's work. Under mishandling the host we find seven days of penance prescribed for accidentally dropping the consecrated elements, fifty lashings prescribed for a priest who stammers over the Sunday prayer for the first time, a hundred strokes for the second time, and a special fast if he does it a third time.

A section on dejection contains the following provisions, though it is hard to see how the penalties prescribed will have much effect in overcoming the ill-pleasure of those upon whom they are laid:

1. He who long harbors bitterness in his heart shall be healed by a joyful countenance and a glad heart.
2. But if he does not quickly lay this aside, he shall correct himself by fasting according to the decision of a priest.
3. But if he returns to it, he shall be sent away until, on bread and water, he willingly and gladly acknowledges his fault.[5]

The penalties found in these medieval handbooks, including discomforting postures, self-flagellation, reduced diet, short-term fasts, long days on bread and water, and even exile for the most serious offenses, seem harsh by modern standards of discipline. Perhaps they are less severe by seventh-century standards. They were designed, of course, to enable men to fulfill the Gospel in moral terms, with severe requirements for monks and priests; modified requirements for laymen. The temper of the penitentials, despite the harshness, is pastoral and preventive. The threat of penance is intended to keep people from having to perform it.

Many of these provisions found their way into the life of the medieval church and remained characteristic of its morality for many centuries. In an old Irish penitential dated around 800 A.D., which is 150 years later than the Code of Cummean, we see many of the same provisions that Cummean advanced. The old Irish penitential begins with a discussion of gluttony, including prohibitions against the eating of dead animal flesh and getting drunk on wine. The provisions against drunkenness seem to be lifted almost intact from the Code of Cummean:

Anyone who drinks beer till he is tipsy in spite of the prohibition of Christ and the Apostles, if he be in orders, does forty days' penance.

If he be in lawful wedlock, seven days. If anyone out of hospitality constrains his fellow to get tipsy, he who causes his tipsiness does the like penance. If it is through enmity that he does it, he who causes the tipsiness does penance as if he were a homicide. If his tipsiness does not hinder him [from his duties] except that he is unable to chant the Psalms, or say Mass, or such-like, he keeps a fast therefor.

Anyone who commits a theft of meat or drink from his brother while tipsy keeps a fast therefor, as well as the punishment for tipsiness. If he commit a theft without the brethren's [knowledge], it is three fasts or a fortnight's strict penance.[6]

In a second section this same penitential goes on to discuss the sin of luxury, which is really a transgression against women. The provision in this respect specifies three and a half years on bread and water, with a fast in every week of the time for priests who have fallen short. In addition priests are denied feather cushions and good beds, and are required to keep on the same shirt except for stitching, washing, or cleansing. Bishops are required to undergo twelve years, laymen three years, of similar conditions. In other sections the penitential severely discourages both fault-finding and mischief-making. It provides penalties for inflicting various modes of death: accidental death or homicide draws one and a half years' fast; murder is punished by exile; attempted suicide and abortion, three and a half years' fast.

There is a similarity in form between many of the provisions in these penitential handbooks and the casuistical codes of Exodus. Both represent the elaboration of prescriptive moral injunctions into codes which specify penalties for transgressions. The prohibitions in each, against murder, against stealing, etc. are similar. Perhaps the medieval handbooks put more attention upon sins of the mind and heart, sins like anger, pride, and even loss of zeal, than do the Covenant Codes of Exodus. Moreover, these code moralities eclipse the central motivation for ethics, which lies in a relational response to God. The rigid ethical and moralistic temper has drowned the religious exuberance. Not all Catholic morality is to be characterized as rigidly codified, even in the Middle Ages. But codification exists alongside some of the great rational schemes of deliberative ethics. Prescriptive and deliberative elements have existed together in Catholic life in almost every period. They continue to exist together in contemporary Catholic teaching and practice, as in the well-known text on moral theology by Henry Davis.

The first volume of Davis's work is quite abstract and philosophical, dealing with the nature and function of human acts, the role and function of different kinds of law, the species of sin, and the theological understanding of virtue. The second volume, entitled "Precepts," deals with the Ten Commandments and the content of the church's legislation on general moral questions. Prescriptive materials are secondary to the deliberative statement of general principles, but they do enter into modern Roman Catholic ethics. The third and fourth volumes of Davis deal with the sacraments. In volume three the time and conditions of their correct performance are given, and rules are set forth for conducting the sacrament of penance with its related indulgences and censures. Here the material is very specific, offering detailed guidance for the priest. The guidance offered in Davis is more sophisticated than that found in the medieval handbooks of penance, but even so it exhibits something of the same codified quality. Here, for example, is a provision for assigning censure to those who make relics:

> Those incur this excommunication who manufacture or knowingly sell, distribute or expose for public veneration false relics. The relics concerned are those of the Saints or Beatified, and even relics that are small, and all things commonly called relics, such as the instruments of their sufferings or penances. The censure is not incurred by one who exposes these relics unless it is his duty or privilege to expose relics. Public exposition is here meant, not exposition in a private oratory.[7]

The fourth volume deals with extreme unction, holy orders, marriage, the clerical state, the religious state, and the duties of lay people. Here the codification is most obvious, especially in the definitions of the rights and obligations that attend entrance into the clerical or religious vocations. Again, to use an example, we see the careful prescriptive character of Catholic regulations in the rule of enclosure for the male religious. A similar rule covers the female religious.

> In the case of male Regulars, the enclosure may not be entered by women of any age, class, or condition, under any pretext whatever, with the exception of the wives of those who actually exercise supreme rule in a nation and their retinue. This permission has been extended to include the wives, with retinue, of the Governors of the individual states of the United States of America. Females who illegitimately violate the enclosure are excommunicated if they have reached the age of puberty; Religious who contrary to the canons introduce or admit females of any age within the enclosure are also excommunicated.[8]

The study and mastery of moral theology, and the canon law which governs the life of the church, is a full-time occupation for many Catholic scholars. Catholics today are debating the value of such prescriptive guidance. The relational approach to moral issues has made some headway in Catholic circles, especially in the thinking of men like Karl Rahner, Bernard Haring, and Josef Fuchs. In response to this trend, still quite limited, we find other Catholic writers reaffirming the importance of prescriptive obligation, often by criticizing situational ethics as "anti-obligational."

For example, a contemporary textbook of moral theology puts the criticism of relational morality in these blunt terms:

> Another phase of anti-obligationism is its frequent carping at the legalism of moral theology. By legalism is meant principally casuistry. This is not the place to defend the legitimate and indispensable uses of casuistry, especially in the preparation of confessors, or to point out once more the errors and excesses in which casuistry has been involved in the history of the Church. But it is surprising that this characteristi-cally Protestant repudiation of "legalism" in morals should be so com-mon in the countries where Anglo-Saxon law holds sway. We live by case-law in these countries, and law students learn their profession by the case-system, which is casuistry pure and simple. But the phrase "case law" and "judicial precedent" have a very acceptable and re-spectable ring to them, while "casuistry," which is the same thing, has a very bad name indeed, and is brushed off like a disreputable relation.
>
> Law is law, whether it is the law of God, or the law of the land, or the law of a correctly-formed conscience. The essential unity of this threefold law has been lost sight of in modern times, owing largely to the Kantian divorce of the moral from the juridical order. The critics of legalism in morality are at times, apparently, taken in unwittingly by this philosophical error. Catholics who complain that generations of juristic theologians have made of morality a mere province of the law may need to be reminded that legal obligations are ultimately and *per se* moral obligations, and that conversely, moral obligations are legal obligations, that is, have their source in divine law, whether it be the eternal law of nature, or the law of God's rev-elation in the Old Testament, or the law of the gospel.
>
> The law of the gospel contains commandments which are of obli-gation, and counsels which are not. To abolish the counsels is one extreme, to belittle the commandments is the other. And while a morality of precepts without counsels is conceivable, a morality of counsels without precepts is not. It is a dangerous thing, therefore, to decry a morality of duty, of law, and of obligation, because in the last analysis there is no other.[9]

Prescription in Protestant Life

The use of law to prescribe the kinds of behavior which help toward salvation may be compatible in theory with the soteriology of Roman Catholicism, in which grace operates "not without works." But it also appears with surprising frequency in Protestantism, even though the doc-trine of "by grace alone" (*sola gratia*) might seem to deter such a develop-ment. It is impossible to ignore the fact that Protestantism has fostered various forms of legalism in which law-embraced-as-response to the Gospel has become law-embraced-to-obtain-a-reward.

Puritanism was an ethically serious form of Protestant Christianity based upon the deep conviction that God is the absolute sovereign of all life and that it is man's duty to make the world and its powers serve the rule of God. The sovereign God places men under staunch and binding orders to obey his revealed will as made known in the Bible. The Bible is to be studied, followed, and obeyed—both in its definition of the church's life and in the details of its moral precepts. In this sense the Bible was a law book of the Puritan, defining duties to God and neighbor and showing how the whole of society is to be brought under God's will. Duty, conscience, sobriety—these were the hallmarks of Puritan devotion to God.

Puritanism was indebted to Calvin for its sense of the divine sovereignty of God and its assumption that God's will comes to man in terms of a requirement for obedience. But much Puritan morality attempted to define Christian behavior with the sort of precision that emerges as codified pre-scription. The Puritan casuistries of Richard Baxter and Jeremy Taylor, which were produced a century after Calvin lived, evidence the same stress upon law found in the writings of Calvin. Both Baxter and Taylor wrote guidebooks for daily behavior and for special circumstances. In-deed, one can find similarities between the moral teaching of certain Puri-tan writers and the prescriptive legislative details of the Pharisees. Both worked from the common thrust to bring all human life under the influ-ence of God's will. Leaving little to chance or whim, the Pharisees and Puritans exhibited in different contexts a common tendency to spell out in precise detail the implications of scriptural law for the life of faithful man. They supported an earnest morality that kept the ethical life a visible demonstration to all the world of allegiance to God. We can accuse the Puritans of certain mistakes, but we cannot impugn their motives nor deny the rigor of their convictions.

Richard Baxter was concerned that faith should result in obedience. In his treatise on *The Right Method for a Settled Peace of Conscience and Spiritual Comfort*[10] Baxter inveighed against the kind of faith which is not accompanied by moral devotion, sacrifice, and discipline. In the work en-titled *A Christian Directory* he warned the reader:

> Take heed that you receive not a doctrine of libertinism as from the Gospel; nor conceive of Christ as an encourager of sin: nor pretend free grace for your carnal security or sloth; for this is to set up an-other Gospel, and another Christ, or rather the doctrine and works of the devil against Christ and the Gospel, and to turn the grace of God into wantonness.[11]

But while Baxter stressed the role of obedience he also made a place for moderation and the prudent middle course in the exercise of that obedi-ence. The obedience was to be cheerfully rendered, not dragged out as from a recalcitrant mule. Moral obedience is service to God, designed to glorify his sovereignty. To this end Baxter proposed many sets of direc-

PRESCRIPTIVE CODES IN THE CHRISTIAN TRADITION

tions: fifteen directions for reaching quiet and comforting trust in God; twenty, for procuring holiness; eighteen, for thankfulness; ten, for glorifying God; thirty-six, for guarding against unbelief, etc. These sets of directions admonished the believer to embrace true godliness. They were directed toward the cultivation of profound attitudes of spiritual depth as well as to proper behavior. But they were set forth as corollaries of the law. In refuting the position of the antinomians, Baxter declared, "if there be no law, there is no governor or government, no duty, no sin, no judgment, no punishment, no reward."[12]

According to Baxter, men are not to make the duty of obedience burdensome by manufacturing rules of their own devising. The requirements of the Holy Scriptures suffice. Yet authority does play a role in helping men to know their duty. Speaking of the clergyman's role as moral teacher, he declared:

> Some ministers are loath to tell people of their duty . . . lest it should confirm the world in their malicious conceit, that we should be masters of men's consciences, and would lord it over them. This is as much folly and cruelty as if the master and pilot of the ship should let the mariners govern the ship by the major vote, and run all on shelves, and drown themselves and him, and all for fear of being thought lordly and tyrannical, in taking the government of the ship upon himself, and telling the mariners that it is their duty to obey him.[13]

The Puritan welcomed the Gospel law to which he was so deeply committed. It was not a burden to him but a joy. Baxter said that if the rule of cheerful obedience were followed it "would do wonders on the souls of poor Christians, in dispelling all their fears and troubles, and helping not only to a settled peace, but to live in the most comfortable state that can be expected upon earth."[14] The Puritan felt that the riches and glory of this world should be acquired and used, provided they were dedicated to God's glory. He read the biblical strictures against wealth as warnings against glory and conceit in the use of goods, not a prohibition of possessions. Thus he brought all men under the rubric rather than a select few who took special vows of poverty.

The Puritans stood in the Calvinistic heritage, with its emphasis upon salvation by faith, but in later Puritanism the clear priority of grace was eclipsed. Moralism tended to become a way of salvation as well as a means for expressing gratitude. In the *Essays To Do Good* of Cotton Mather we read:

> In the first place, it must be taken for granted that the end for which we perform good works is *not* to provide the matter of our justification before God: indeed, no good works can be done till we are justified. . . .
>
> Nevertheless . . . you are to look upon it as a glorious truth of the

Gospel, that the moral law (which prescribes good works) must, by every Christian alive, be the *rule* of his life. "Do we make void the law through faith? God forbid: yea, we establish the law." The rule by which we are to glorify God is given in that law of good works which we *enjoy* (I will so express it) in the ten commandments.[15]

Saying the same thing in different words, Mather continued:

We are not under the law as a *covenant of works:* our own exactness in performing good works is not now the condition of entering into life; wo be to us if it were. But still, the *covenant of grace* holds us to it as our *duty;* and if we are in the covenant of grace, we shall make it our study to perform those good works which were once the condition of entering into life. "Every law of religion still remains."[16]

Unfortunately Puritanism stands in the public eye as the symbol of a narrow and restrictive morality which limited men in the pursuit of pleasure, but it is easy to overdraw this picture and to misunderstand the Puritan temper as negative toward pleasure rather than dedicated to scripture. The popular view of Puritan morality stems in part from its attitude toward practices such as lascivious dancing. In 1684 Increase Mather found himself engaged in a long discussion at a ministers' conference concerning the legitimacy of dancing. A thirty-page essay was the outgrowth, with the imposing title: *An Arrow against Profane and Promiscuous Dancing. Drawn out of a Quiver of the Scriptures.* Near the beginning of this article Mather declares:

Concerning the Controversy about *Dancing,* the Question is not, whether all *Dancing* be in itself sinful. It is granted, that *Pyrrhical or Polemical Saltation:* i.e. when men vault in their Armour, to shew their strength and activity, may be of use. Nor is the question, whether a sober and grave *Dancing* of Men with Men, or of Women with Women, be not allowable; we make no doubt of that, where it may be done without offence, in due season, and with moderation. The Prince of Philosophers has observed truly, that *Dancing* or *Leaping,* is a natural expression of joy: So that there is no more Sin in it, than in laughter, or any outward expression of inward Rejoycing.

But our question is concerning *Gynecandrical Dancing,* or that which is commonly called *Mixt or Promiscuous Dancing,* viz. of Men and Women (be they elder or younger persons) together: Now this we affirm to be utterly unlawful, and that it cannot be tollerated in such a place as *New-England,* without great Sin. And that it may appear, that we are not transported by Affection without Judgment, let the following Arguments be weighed in the Ballance of the Sanctuary.

Arg. I. *That which the Scripture condemns is sinful.* None but atheists will deny this *Proposition:* But the Scripture condemns *Promiscuous Dancing.* This Assumption is proved, I. *From the Seventh*

Commandment. It is an Eternal Truth to be observed in expounding the Commandments, that whenever any sin is forbidden, not only the highest acts of that sin, but all degrees thereof, and all occasions leading thereto are prohibited. Now we cannot find one Orthodox and Judicious Divine, that writeth on the Commandments, but mentions *Promiscuous Dancing,* as a breach of the seventh Commandment, as being an occasion, and an incentive to that which is evil in the sight of God. Yea, this is so manifest as that the *Assembly* in the *larger Catechism,* do expressly take notice of *Dancings* as a violation of the Commandments.[17]

We should divest ourselves of the natural and normal inclination to shudder at the content of these remarks long enough to examine them. They begin by appeal to biblical law, but they state a codified application of that law. Not the commandment itself, but an implication drawn from the commandment furnishes the content of the prescription. This is the beginning of a code morality, in which technical secondary prescriptions are set forth in the name of biblical authority. In 1820 a tract was published, over three hundred pages long, with this imposing title:

A Treatise
concerning

The Sanctification
of the
Lord's Day.
wherein
The Morality of the Sabbath
or the
Perpetual Obligation of the Fourth Commandment
Is Maintained Against Adversaries;
and the
Religious Observation of the Lord's Day, or First
Day of the Week, as Our Christian Sabbath, Is
Strongly Proved by Scripture Arguments
Containing also
Many Special Directions and Advices
For the better performing of the most necessary and comprehensive
duty of
Sabbath-sanctification.

To which are added
(By Way of Appendix)
Meditations for the Sabbath-Day
Proper for Families[18]

Puritan sabbatarianism began as a serious effort to abide by the fourth commandment. It became a detailed, rigorous process of amplification designed to indicate all prohibitions and to specify punishments for breach of the Sabbath rest. In most places needless travel was banned. One person was reprimanded for writing letters on the Sabbath "too early in the evening." In 1677 two separate couples each paid a forty shilling fine for the offense of choosing the Sabbath for a quarrel. It was not unusual for an author to take many pages to provide the "Many Special Directions and Advices" which attended the proper observance of the Sabbath rest.

Quaker morality was an extension of the Puritan method to different issues. The Puritans were usually involved in the performance of official roles as rulers and governors of states and had to make certain compromises with biblical attitudes toward the use of force. The Quakers, as a minority sect, were able to apply a rigorous reading of the Gospel law to matters the Puritans did not take as proscribed, such as participation in war. Like the Puritans, however, the Quakers had their antiliturgical bias and were bitterly (and even violently, at first) opposed to all kinds of formal worship practices. They were even critical of the Puritan kind of worship and turned to silent group meditation.

There were six general areas in which the Quakers, basing their attitude upon a reading of the biblical law, were opposed to having their members exercise a role in society. Quakers were not to (a) take oaths, (b) use special titles, (c) tip hats to superiors, or kneel before them, (d) participate in war, (e) use superfluities in apparel, or (f) engage in games, sports, plays, or comedies as a form of recreation. Robert Barclay introduced this list of prohibited acts, in his *Apology for the True Christian Divinity*, with the following statement of the necessity for the specification of prohibitions observed by the Quaker:

> . . . there are some singular things, which most of all our adversaries plead for the lawfulness of, and allow themselves in, as no ways inconsistent with the Christian religion, which we have found to be no ways lawful unto us, and have been commanded of the Lord to lay them aside; though the doing thereof hath occasioned no small sufferings and buffetings, and hath procured us much hatred and malice from the world. And because the nature of these things is such, that they do upon the very sight distinguish us, and make us known, so that we cannot hide ourselves from any, without proving unfaithful to our testimony; our trials and exercises have here-through proved the more numerous and difficult, as will after appear.[19]

An even greater codification occurred in the Shaker colonies, where behavior was regulated to the minutest detail. *The Millennial Laws* or *Gospel Statutes and Ordinances* recorded in the Shaker colony at New Lebanon in 1821 and revised in October of 1845 provided an extensive set of regulations governing the life of the member of the Shaker sect. Not since the medieval penitentials had the religious life been so carefully regulated. Even before the *Millennial Laws* were recorded, the life of the Shaker was governed by a series of prescriptions that declared certain things "contrary to order." A list from 1821 noted eighty-one proscribed practices, arranged in nine categories. The *Millennial Laws* were divided into three parts with a total of thirty-three sections, each of which contained as many as thirty-one rules. They set forth in great detail the organization of the society and the life of its individual members. The section of miscellaneous orders shows quite clearly how many different kinds of provisions were set into a religious code. Serious wrongs were proscribed, such as turning away the poor who ask alms, taking tools without permission or returning them broken without indemnity. Annoying and disrupting behavior was outlawed, such as wrestling, scuffling, or beating, holding lengthy conversations in the street, secreting communications from the group, and drinking ardent spirits. Matters of plain economy were mentioned, and women were forbidden to wash in the morning until they could do so without burning up candles to see. One of the most interesting provisions declares, "It is not allowable to redrill a hole in a rock while it is charged for blasting."[20] It is a very religious community indeed that writes a safety maxim into its codification of divine laws!

The *Millennial Laws* of the Shakers are noteworthy in that they simply prohibit actions and do not assign a specific punishment for each wrong. As compared with many detailed moral codes this failure to specify punishments is quite striking, and sets the Shaker laws in sharp contrast to the medieval penitentials. Undoubtedly the Shaker communities exercised discipline and assigned punishments for wrong-doing, but apparently they did so administratively rather than under the rubrics of codified law.

There are significant differences between the examples of prescriptive codification mentioned in this chapter as illustrations of an extensive process within the life of the church. Some of the codes mentioned are rigid and detailed; others more general and flexible; some are designed to control the life of a special community apart from the world; others, to provide the basis of a God-fearing life for all men in the world. Some draw their content from the Bible; others are derived from cultural conditions at the time of their promulgation. It may not be fair to paint the more flexible and humane codes with the same brush that tars the rigid and superficial codes. Aversion to codes can never cancel the fact that Christian groups have used prescriptive definitions of behavior in good faith to govern their members and defended such use as a corollary of the Christian Gospel.

7

Modified Forms of Prescription

Code moralities are frequently rigid, but prescriptive norms can be set forth in more flexible ways. For instance, casuistries are prescriptive in form, but produce definitions of behavior that take account of particular circumstances. Moralities of imitation, which ask very specifically how one follows a leader, often include aspects of response that border on a relational ethic. These two forms of modified prescription deserve a careful look, not only because they have appeared with some regularity in the Christian tradition, but because they belie the contention that prescription is necessarily brittle and inflexible.

Casuistries as Definitions of Behavior Related to Circumstance

Kenneth Kirk believed that Christian morality should begin with a high devotional aspiration which he called "the vision of God." This embodies man's conception of his highest attainment and reflects his overarching commitment to what he deems most valuable. But this high level of personal experience and faith seeks translation into the particular acts of moral discipline. The request for specific guidance can give rise to the formalism and legalism of codes, yet it need not do so. Furthermore, Kirk felt that such guidance must be provided to those who seek it. The simple and devout Christian who asks his pastor, "What must I do to be a Christian?" should not be turned away with a discourse against the form of the question. Rather he should be given the guidance which he seeks from his question, and given it in specific terms. While recognizing that this process is open to abuse, and while sympathetic to those who would throw out prescription altogether in order to create an ethic of free and spontaneous response, Kirk noted:

> "Surely," it may be said, "Christianity is not regulated but spontaneous; not legalised but free; not a code, but the living of a life dedicated to God and penetrated by His grace? What else is the message of Christ,

the promise of the Spirit? What other meaning can we attach to S. Paul's great indictment of the law?"

From this point of view *any* tendency to live the moral life by rule, to anticipate or solve its problems by casuistry, to bring its natural impulsive growth under the control of law and reason, must appear the merest ethical pedantry—a reversion to the ideal of the scribes and Pharisees which it was Christ's first mission to attack. The modern mind is perhaps partisan in this matter. It welcomes spontaneity, and rejects suggestions of discipline and regulation. Yet it would be absurd to maintain that the ideal of ordered self-discipline has *no* place in the Christian life; a study of the development of Christian thought about ethics may well help us nearer to an understanding of the true place of this element—an element which in perverted instances we call "formalist"—in the determination of conduct.[1]

Kirk accepted a place for prescription but criticized formalism and code morality. He was especially critical of formalistic thinking in which ethics is made a means for obtaining rewards or escaping punishments. Such bargaining lacks the vision of God that is essential to a meaningful Christian life. But discipline exercised under the experience of aspiration is different from a formalized scheme of works-righteousness. The first is necessary to a profound Christian life; the second, a betrayal of the Christian moral impulse.

It is only natural that formalism should at first have proved a cause of moral advance. As a means of personal discipline it is not merely unexceptionable, but of the highest value, provided always that—true to the New Testament demand—it is kept in subordination to the living experience of the living God which is the heart of Christianity. Further, codification of principles goes hand in hand with corporate discipline; and even corporate discipline is an agency for good as long as it is exercised for pastoral and remedial purposes—to strengthen, that is to say, and to cooperate with, the personal self-discipline of the individual. [But] . . . If it is employed not *pastorally* but *penally*— not to strengthen the weak and restore·the falling, but to exclude them, the moral code, however carefully and truthfully expressed, becomes an instrument of tyranny which dragoons the many into purely outward observance, and breaks the heart of the spiritual genius who needs freedom from restraint to realize the gifts which God has given him.[2]

Kirk has been one of the most articulate modern exponents of a Christian casuistry, that is, of an approach to moral teaching in which the implications of high moral standards are related to the specific situations encountered by the individual. His important book on casuistry, *Conscience and Its Problems*, represents one of the most thoroughgoing efforts to revive the practice of setting forth moral prescriptions in relation to circumstance. In the introductory portion of this book, Kirk discussed the need for the church of the time to provide its members with more specific guidance concerning the nature of moral duty. To fill this need, he felt the church to be

> . . . driven back to the need for a sane casuistry; for the first duty of casuistry (assuming ourselves to be in sure possession of the general principles of morality) is to determine the lines along which the advance from the general to the particular can best be made. To make the advance is also its duty; but it is a secondary duty which can only be successfully performed as the first is successfully completed. Rules of procedure must come before actual procedure itself, even though they cannot finally be tested except in the crucible of procedure. The Anglicanism of the 17th century was fully aware of this fact; Sanderson, Taylor, Hall (and, it may be mentioned, Richard Baxter as well) moved so securely among the difficult problems of their time for no other reason than that they were employing the soundest principles of medieval casuistry. It is one of the curiosities of history, to which we shall have to devote a moment's passing attention, that with the dawn of the 18th century not Anglicanism alone, but all the Reformed Churches, lost their grasp upon these time-honored rules of procedure. To that fact (whatever its cause or causes may have been) may be attributed, in part at least, the steady and ever-increasing failure of these societies to guide their members in the recurring particular problems of the Christian life in any manner which the ordinary man could appreciate; and from that moment dates the supersession of "moral theology" in the Reformed Churches by a "Christian ethics" which contents itself with the statement of general principles and evades the problem of their detailed application.[3]

Kirk's definition of casuistry places it on the borderline between the deliberative and the prescriptive motifs, for casuistry can represent a deliberative process of relating general principles to specific cases or an elaboration of prescriptive guidance. It acknowledges that standards of good conduct must be applied in shifting circumstances, and that definitions of morality that seem altogether permanent are frequently more valuable if expressed in one manner under one set of conditions and in another manner under another set of conditions. General demands may be set forth in a code; or they may be set forth as general principles; but regardless of the form in which they originally appear casuistry relates them to the specific conditions of life.

Some casuistry represents a fixed and legalistic process which shares the binding features of the original code, even when it seeks to make that code applicable to new circumstances. When elaboration and amplification spell out the implications of a code, endless details accrue in the thrust toward precision and certainty. This detailed prescriptiveness gives a supposed certainty and structure to the moral imperative, even under changing circumstances, but to the outsider it may look quite foolish as it makes big moral points of little contingent factors. Thus, the Pharisees, taking the code of Moses requiring the Sabbath to be a day of rest on which no healing was done, permitted vinegar to be used to cure a sore throat, under certain conditions. Swallowing the vinegar classified it as a drink, which was permissible; gargling it classified it as a medication, which was not.

Other casuistry actually lowers the moral standard as it relates the moral law to the variant factors of life. Jesuit casuistry permitted equivocation under certain conditions. It allowed men to follow either of two courses of action for which authority could be given without seeking to determine which action was the most adequate representation of the original ideal or norm. To moral rigorists this approach seems to undercut the moral impulse and to destroy confidence in casuistry as a legitimate form of moral guidance. But from another perspective it can be argued that it serves the cause of freedom. What professor does not permit his wife to tell callers he is "not at home" when some assignment must be completed for a deadline? Do not ministers, even those who are critical of Jesuits, protect professional secrets by equivocal answers to brash questions? Given a Latin conception of law, with its impulse to all-inclusive obedience, Jesuit probabilism can serve to protect liberty and other humane values.

Casuistry is a varied and widespread phenomenon in Christian ethics which arises from the effort to form a bridge between general norms and specific situations. There seems to be an increasing awareness of its significance and values despite the abuses which sometimes attend its use. It is dangerous to regard all casuistry as ethically undesirable. Paul Lehmann, surely no advocate of prescriptive forms of the moral standard, has nevertheless found merit in both Roman and Anglican forms of moral theology in which casuistry appears. Commenting upon the moral theology of Father Henry Davis, he says, "Plainly the approach to behavior in terms of such a structured combination of principle, precept, and principal parts of an act is versatile, viable, and comprehensive."[4]

Casuistries need critical evaluation and scrutiny, not superficial dismissal. Casuistry at the hands of some Jesuit confessors was different from casuistry at the hands of the Caroline theologians. Casuistries which are exercised as means of lowering demands differ from those which are exercised so as to provide faithful men with guidance in difficult circumstances. This is so true of the work of a man like Jeremy Taylor, with a passion "for holy living and holy dying," that it becomes almost necessary to shift the category for understanding Taylor from prescriptive to relational ethics.

The British writer, Jeremy Bentham, whose extensive treatments of jurisprudence, ethics, and related subjects did much to simplify court procedures in several countries, illustrates the casuistical enterprise in its most general and abstract form—as a branch of the philosophical approach to ethical matters. But his works give a clue to the values that are found in casuistry as a method and are not altogether divorced from considerations that derive from specifically Christian norms. In 1817 he wrote a tract against the use of oaths, attacking the ceremony in which oaths were used in Oxford and Cambridge Universities, as well as elsewhere, and seeking to prove that their use entailed the open and persevering contempt of moral and religious principle. The norm was taken from Matthew 5:34; but Bentham's detailed discussion of the reasons for abandoning the oath involved many considerations, including the ways in which the oath weakened the efficiency of the laws, enslaved the consciences of jurymen, furnished pretense for misrule, and even corrupted national morals. In one of the sections dealing with this question Bentham appealed to the idea that the practice of receiving judicial oaths is contrary to the precepts of Jesus. The discussion of the question is long and involved, but the specification for the circumstances of England was clear. The main body of the tract concluded with this clear assertion that moral considerations depend upon circumstances:

> Of the institution here in question, at the time of its creation, the effects may—upon the balance, as hath been seen—have been either good or bad—it is scarce possible to say which. But, those times having been long since passed, the question *now* is—not whether it shall be *set on foot*, but whether it shall be *preserved:* the use *now* made of it— the support *still* given to it—these are the subjects which call for consideration in this our time.[5]

In another discussion, published one year prior to the tract on oaths, Bentham defended the practice of usury.[6] In discussing usury Bentham felt the circumstances of the time required the abandonment of a moral prescription set forth in the Bible, whereas in his criticism of oaths he was reinforcing the obvious content of biblical injunctions. Bentham's treatment of morals and legislation was a thorough statement of all the implications of the principle of pleasure as a guide to morality, and shows many features of the deliberative motif. But the several places at which Bentham addressed himself to specific questions of how punishments should fit crimes and how codes should be drawn up indicates that even the deliberative approach to moral questions may come to prescriptive considerations.

Recent discussions of Christian ethics have frequently eclipsed moral theology, so that, as Kirk held, casuistry has been neglected in many writings and attacked in others. But casuistry has not been unchampioned. Several contemporary theologians have attempted to create a casuistry that is genuinely flexible yet spells out the content of the ethical demand. In setting forth a flexible idea of casuistry, use has been made of the idea of compromise. Speaking of these matters, W. Norman Pittenger has said,

To become a Christian is not to be given a simple solution of one's difficulties. It is, in certain ways, to be given even more problems that must be solved . . . and [the Christian] must still live in a secular environment. If he fails to come to some kind of terms with that environment, he will simply destroy himself. If he accepts it completely, he will deny his Christian profession. Hence he must try to compromise.

Both the word and the idea of "compromise" are very much disliked by many of our contemporary religious writers. Yet in some degree everyone does compromise; if life is to be a possibility at all, one must do so. The real danger in compromise comes if and when it is indulged in without understanding and without principle. . . . the Christian Church itself through its theologians and moralists can be of enormous help to the practicing Christian. . . . It can work out, for this time and for tomorrow, what we may flatly describe as a "casuistry" by which life will be possible for the ordinary Christian man or woman.[7]

I once made use of the concept of casuistry in working out a view of the Christian ethic which takes account of the demands of conscience and the need to compromise.[8] The use of the term *casuistry* received surprisingly little criticism, even in a day when prescriptive moral norms were under attack from a number of quarters. I may have allowed for enough compromise to satisfy the most insistent contextualists, or merely have been stating their arguments in other language. Joseph Fletcher has argued that I did not set forth a casuistry in the classical sense, but a neocasuistry that is too ready to grant the particularities of existential situations to qualify as an attempt at prescription. Fletcher complains that casuistry should not be identified with compromise, which is what is done by many who take the neocasuist approach. "Doubt and perplexity about obligation are not necessarily compromise, and even the old casuistry was not motivated merely by a desire to cut corners or water the milk."[9] Perhaps Fletcher's criticism is a matter of words, for he goes on to say that "Moralists like Long and Bonhoeffer are in any case clear about the heart of the matter—the absoluteness of the Word and the relativity of the deed. For the Christian conscience the total context of decision, the whole situation, is always 'circumstances under the law of love.'"[10]

F. Ernest Johnson was probably right when he noted that there

is an unfortunate confusion over what is known as "casuistry." Protestants are always distrustful of it because it looks to them like an oversimplified and convenient scheme of settling important issues which may have unusual and peculiar features, by applying ready-to-hand rules.[11]

But Johnson went on to declare his own support for a valid casuistical approach to the ethical enterprise, when he declared that a casuistry that is really a "case" approach to ethical problems has as much to be said for it as a similar approach in law or medicine. It may even be said that the goal of a valid ethical system is the rendering of consistent and viable value judgments that are at once in line with empirical facts and in harmony with the most authentic norms that man's reason and inspired imagination have been able to construct.[12]

In chapter five we discussed the various interpretations of Jesus which found his teaching compatible with law. But even as convinced an interpreter as C. H. Dodd recognized that the teachings of Jesus cannot be translated directly into actions in the same way as can the teachings of Paul. John Knox explores this quality in the teaching of Jesus even further, declaring the impossibility of any adequate fulfillment of the New Testament ethic. The Christian, argues Knox, must therefore stand in a tradition of ethical wisdom, embodied in the teaching of the church, which gives him guidance and support. "We have often been blind," he declares, "not only to the necessity of a Christian casuistry, but also to our necessary dependence upon a tradition of casuistry."[13]

One of the best-known and most successful attempts to spell out the relationship of Christian ethical demands to the specific situations in which they must be applied is found in the suggested use of "middle axioms." The term was first used by J. H. Oldham in 1937, who stated the concept in this way:

. . . as between purely general statements of the ethical demands of the gospel and the decisions that have to be made in concrete situations, there is need for what may be described as middle axioms. It is these that give relevance and point to the Christian ethic. They are attempts to define the directions in which, in a particular state of society, Christian faith must express itself. They are not binding for all time, but are provisional definitions of the type of behavior required of Christians at a given period and in given circumstances.[14]

John Bennett has made use of middle axioms for defining the relationship between the ultimate Christian norm and the kinds of action that must be taken in society. Because Bennett's discussion is found in a book on social action some of what he says about middle axioms may be taken as more relevant to strategies than to norms. However, they really function as the norms which guide strategies, norms which are helpful because they are changing, flexible, and subject to revision in light of circumstances. They guide actions by indicating the kinds of behavior which are actually important in particular circumstances.

While the Christian may understand love as either a general principle, if he sees the ethical question deliberatively, or as an ultimate rule of life, if he sees the ethical question prescriptively, he may use middle axioms to suggest the concrete demands of love in particular circumstances. Regardless of which motif he uses for the ultimate category, he uses the prescriptive motif when he adopts middle axioms for the secondary specification of desired behavior. Today, for example, a middle axiom would call for the elimination of segregation based upon racial distinctions. A hundred years or more ago the middle axiom appropriate to the American situation involved a call for the elimination of slavery. Middle axioms may or may not specify the means by which the goals they call for are to be obtained, though strategic considerations may help to determine what middle axioms are feasible for given times and situations. Bennett speaks of them as goals which "are not absolute and all-inclusive . . . but the next steps that our own generation must take."[15]

Middle axioms may call for actions which are distinctly different from actions called for in scripture or traditional church law. They are time bound; they are good for the era in which they are set forth. To expect that the New Testament would deal with the need for a civil rights bill or a law seeking to extend open occupancy rights to all groups is to lack historical perspective, but no more so than to think the New Testament supports slavery because it tacitly acknowledges its existence. Middle axioms bring the ultimate norm into contact with the empirical realities of the present—sometimes by finding new imperatives; at other times by finding that accustomed practices have outworn their validity.

Middle axioms are often formulated by Christian groups meeting as official bodies, whether in denominational gatherings or ecumenical bodies. Such bodies often deliver social pronouncements, many of which call for achievements which are in advance of the culture, even at times in advance of the thinking of many members of the churches themselves. These pronouncements frequently set forth specific and practical guidance. They are often controversial because they call for specific changes that some members of society are not ready to accept. For example, in 1908 the Federal Council of Churches of Christ in America adopted a number of resolutions on the problems created by modern industry. There was a long paragraph calling for certain standards of justice in American life. This series of goals came to be called the Social Creed of the Churches. Many of the goals which seemed advanced in 1908 are now taken for granted as minimal standards of justice in our national life, but in 1908 they had prophetic impact. The Creed ran as follows:

> To us it seems that the churches must stand—
> For equal rights and for complete justice for all men in all stations of life.
> For the right of all men to the opportunity for self-maintenance, a right ever to be wisely and strongly safeguarded against encroachments of every kind.

For the right of workers to some protection against the hardships often resulting from the swift crisis of industrial change.

For the principle of conciliation and arbitration in industrial dissensions.

For the protection of the worker from dangerous machinery, occupational disease, injuries, and mortality.

For the abolition of child labor.

For such regulation of the conditions of toil for women as shall safeguard the physical and moral health of the community.

For the suppression of the "sweating system."

For the gradual and reasonable reduction of the hours of labor to the lowest practicable point, and for that degree of leisure for all which is a condition of the highest human life.

For a release from employment one day in seven.

For a living wage as a minimum in every industry, and for the highest wage that each industry can afford.

For the most equitable division of the products of industry that can ultimately be devised.

For suitable provision for the old age of the workers and for those incapacitated by injury.

For the abatement of poverty.[16]

There is very little in this statement about methods for achieving these ends. It deals with goals rather than strategies. It is specific but not codified. It enunciates principles of a very concrete and specific nature—concrete and specific enough to have been controversial at the time of their first enunciation. It belongs to the prescriptive motif even though it cannot be entirely divorced from certain aspects of the deliberative motif. While such a pronouncement is the work of social prophets rather than philosophical idealists, it would be accepted by the latter as well grounded in a conception of the rationally good. General middle-axioms of this sort stand on the borderline between the prescriptive motif and philosophical idealism of a deliberative nature. It is also possible to stand on the borderline between prescriptive ethical guidance and the relational motif. We shall now turn to a variety of ethical writings which, although basically in the prescriptive category, are also highly relational.

The Imitation of Christ: Prescription Informed by Relation

Religiously devout people frequently try to follow the life pattern of the founder of their faith. The idea of "following Jesus" has, for example, been perennially practiced in the Christian tradition. The attempted imitation of a leader is both prescriptive and relational. It is prescriptive in the sense that it looks with great care at the specific behavior of the leader, to note precisely how he lived and what he did. It considers *how* to act in terms of the actual behavior seen in the life of the leader. But the attempted imitation of a leader is relational because the inspiration to undertake ethical duty depends upon the devotional attachment felt for the leader, who inspires as well as guides the response of the believer. Herman C. Waetjen has perceived this twofold aspect of the *imitatio Christi* as found in the New Testament:

> It would appear then that the imitation of Christ is indeed a biblical theme which finds its implicit and explicit interpretation in the variety of christologies presented in the New Testament. These christologies not only disclose that Jesus is Lord in whom I am raised into a new history and a new being. They also summon me to an emulation of the one who is the Pioneer as well as the Perfector of my faith.[17]

Any discussion of the emulation of Christ uncovers the most complex questions concerning the interpretation of New Testament writings. In the idea of following Jesus preached in youth groups and at Christian Endeavour meetings during the first half of this century, the process was obviously oversimplified: simply read the Bible, learn what Jesus was like, and go out to do likewise. But by now we have learned that great technical problems arise in reading the Bible in order to know what Jesus was like. We have run through the quest for the historical Jesus, radical doubts concerning the quest, and have even come to a new quest. The effort to follow Jesus as advocated in Protestant liberalism sought to make the ethical decision reliable apart from the uncertainties introduced by theology. It declared in effect: "It's not who Jesus was, but what Jesus did that serves as our touchstone." Alas, it seems just as difficult to know what Jesus did as it does to know who he was, and the two questions are all rolled up into one in the New Testament sources themselves!

Waetjen's article therefore raises important questions. He sees that the imitation theme is an important aspect of the New Testament record. Paul urges his followers to imitate him just as he imitates Christ. The same theme is sounded in the first two Gospels and in Luke-Acts. The theme of the *imitatio Christi*, undeniably present in the New Testament writings, is clothed with all the christological dogma basic to the Christian proclamation. All that needs saying about the significance, role, and being of Christ needs saying prior to any true concept of an *imitatio Christi*. Of this fact Rudolph Bultmann, Ernst Fuchs, and Gerhard Ebeling have all helped to make us aware. But the importance of the emulation of Christ as a guide for Christian behavior, while it cannot be oversimplified, cannot be expunged from the New Testament record. As Waetjens says, ". . . Paul does present a picture of Jesus just as the evangelists do, not for faith but for the Christian life which follows faith. And it is for this faith-life, the life of following Jesus that an *imitatio Christi* is involved in the christology of Paul and other New Testament authors."[18]

The *imitatio Christi* has provided a powerful ethical image many times in Christian history. It appears, for example, in connection with Christian mysticism and in movements which have been influenced by the mystical tradition. Western mysticism has always been voluntaristic and frequently associated with monasticism and obedience to the Rule. But it has also been concerned to call men to a true and inward obedience, insisting that conformity to rules without an experience of the new life which is created by a relationship to God is not sufficient. The identification of the self with God that is the high goal of the mystic has been achieved by voluntary submission to the will of God.

The relationship of the mystical approach and the *imitatio Christi* is unmistakably evident in the counsel on the spiritual life presented by Thomas à Kempis. *The Imitation of Christ* ranks as one of the truly popular writings of Western Christendom. It sprung from the experiences of the Brethren of the Common Life, a modified monastic order founded in the fourteenth century. It has even been seriously suggested that the present work consists of the edited diaries of the founder of the group, taken over and edited by Thomas, rather than being originally composed at his hand.

In this work the aim of the true Christian is defined in terms of an obedience to Christ patterned after the model of his life and work. Christianity consists of conformity to the example of Christ, even to the humility and self-effacement which is exemplified in the way of the Cross. There is a hint of works-righteousness in this treatise: on the judgment day one will answer for what he has done, not what he has thought, read, or simply believed. Knowledge about God without fear of God is useless; the Christian will cheerfully submit to the church authorities as a way to achieve reconciliation with God and spiritual peace.

While much of the book reads like an admonition to discipleship rather than like a law code, if one lists the various attributes mentioned in it as marks of the disciple, he will acquire a sizable list: removal from the world, the shunning of honors and riches, humility, perfection, cultivation of the pure spirit, diligent labor, care not to enjoy one's own wit, obedience to law, maintaining peace with others, discipline in rooting out vice, patience with tribulations, renunciation of attachments, care for meditation, keeping silence, preparation for the next life, courage in face of labor and difficulty—all of these are mentioned in just the first part. These precepts are general rather than specific, but they do describe a kind of behavior which results from the imitation of Christ. The following passage, consisting of a dialogue between Christ and a disciple, is a fair sample of the style and flavor of the writing:

> [Christ]: If thou wilt enter into life: keep the commandments. If thou wilt know the truth: believe Me. If thou wilt be perfect: sell all. If thou wilt be My disciple: deny thyself. If thou wilt have a blessed life: despise this life present. If thou wilt be exalted in heaven: humble

thyself in the world. If thou wilt reign with Me: carry the Cross with Me. For only the servants of the Cross: find the way of blessedness and true light.

[Disciple]: O Lord Jesus forasmuch as Thy life was poor and despised by the world: grant me grace to imitate Thee though with the world's contempt. For the servant is not greater than his Lord: nor the disciple above his Master. Let Thy servant be trained in Thy life: for therein is my salvation, and true holiness. Whatsoever I read or hear besides it: gives me not full refreshment or delight.[19]

John Wesley selected portions of this work and published them under the title *The Christian Pattern*. Much that is vital and compelling in Wesley's own evangelical outlook accords with the approach taken in *The Imitation of Christ*. The Christian should love God diligently, in an unreserved manner, holding nothing back, shunning the temptations of the world and its vanities. If we follow Beach and Niebuhr in suggesting that the ethic of Wesley consists of a combination of Puritanism, the sectarian ideal of perfect scriptural holiness, and the pietism typified by the Moravians,[20] the combination of prescriptive and relational elements in Wesley's thinking becomes undeniable.

Wesley agreed with the Reformation that salvation is by grace, not by works, but he consistently refused to adopt the formula *sola fide*. Consequently he always made more place for the importance of works as the fruits of the Christian's response than did most reformed theologians, particularly those in the Lutheran tradition. For Wesley, the law served as the pattern by which Christians fulfill their duty to God. He took no exception to its use in specifying proper Christian behavior and even delivered thirteen discourses on the Sermon on the Mount in which the teachings of Jesus were interpreted in terms of precepts to be followed. In the main, both in Wesley and in the movement which he fathered, the emphasis upon individual perfection and obedience to the precepts of Christ have been obviously more prescriptive in nature than relational. A legalism, perhaps, but not a harsh or brittle legalism, and never one that in theory has failed to acknowledge the importance of grace in the life of the believer.

The borderline between prescription and relation is vividly evident in the thinking of Søren Kierkegaard. Some of his most noteworthy writings treat ethics in the relational motif and have become the touchstones for many subsequent developments in Protestant theology which belong without any question to this way of thinking. But other aspects of his writings treat ethics according to prescriptive patterns of thought, with the imitation of Christ conceived in the most rigorous and demanding of terms. Kierkegaard is, therefore, something of a dialectical figure, whose thinking can be understood in either of two patterns.

His study of Abraham's intended sacrifice of Isaac set forth in his work *Fear and Trembling* surely will please the person who would support a relationist point of view by appeal to Kierkegaard. Obedience to the immediate divine demand, symbolized by Abraham's willingness to abrogate categorical standards in order to obey God's command to sacrifice his son, certainly symbolizes the concept of God's utter sovereignty and man's duty to obey. This "teleological suspension of the ethical" illustrates one very radical form of relational ethic, in which the relation to God as known in the immediate situation transcends the normal content of moral prescription. As a moving spirit of existentialism Kierkegaard has been crucial in underpinning much contemporary theology and the relationism in ethics that has accompanied it. He has been cited as both the hero of the piece[21] and the villain.[22]

But Kierkegaard wrote other things that sound rigorously prescriptive in tone and that stand squarely in the tradition of the *imitatio Christi* and its call for the rejection of the world by the Christian in order to follow Christ. In *Training in Christianity* he made a sharp distinction between the mere admirer of Christ who looks on at a distance and sings praises to his name, and the follower who seeks to resemble him. In *Purity of Heart* he stripped away all the barriers standing between the believer and his utter, total abandon to God's will, but his strictures in this book fall surely as hard upon the false use of prescriptive morality as upon a failure to be totally devoted to God. In *Works of Love* duty and obligation are touchstones in a discussion that emphasizes both the fruits or outward measures and the inner spirit of behavior. Take, for example, these two paragraphs appearing in conjunction in the early part of the work:

> Hence *how* the word is spoken, and above all *how* it is meant, hence *how* the act is performed: this is the decisive thing in determining and in recognizing love by its fruits. But here again the point is that there is nothing, no "thus," about which it can unconditionally be said that it unconditionally proves the presence of love, or that it unconditionally proves that love is not present.
>
> And yet it is certain that love must be known by its fruits. But the sacred words of our text are not uttered for the purpose of encouraging us to occupy ourselves in judging one another; they are, on the contrary, spoken admonishingly to the individual (to you, my hearer, and to me), in order to encourage him not to permit his love to become unfruitful, but to work so that it *may* be known by its fruits, whether others do recognize it or not.[23]

There can be little doubt that the ethics of the imperative stares at the reader with stark solemnity from many pages of Kierkegaard's writings. Kierkegaard did not hesitate to use the idea of a command that stands in sharpest contrast with the earthly and may, even must, result in choosing

God as against the world. Kierkegaard dwelt at great length upon the ways in which love is the fulfillment of the law. "There is not," he wrote, "one provision of the law, not a single one, which love wishes to abolish."[24]

In an essay entitled "Kierkegaard's Dialectic of Imitation," Marie Thulstrup shows how fully Kierkegaard came to accept the idea of the imitation of Christ despite his traditional Protestant inclination to think of the Christian life in terms of grace. Kierkegaard carefully avoided making the imitation of Christ a means of obtaining merit, but he was equally careful to preserve the full rigor of the high demand which he felt to be carried by this concept of discipleship. Kierkegaard saw the Christian life in terms of an inward suffering which meant dying to the world. The imitation must be authentic, not mere copy, and involve a true identity between the Christian and Christ. Kierkegaard also understood that only a few men will achieve the truly authentic variety of imitation and conceded the value of the copy-type for beginners. Christ must be presented as the pattern since that way, provided the demand is now lowered, men come to realize their helplessness and need of grace.

The clue to Kierkegaard's attitude lies in the phrase "provided the demand is now lowered." Kierkegaard spent much of his effort presenting the demand in its uncompromising rigor. To do this he relied upon a serious presentation of the *imitatio Christi* as this is found in the Synoptic Gospels. Of this emphasis Thulstrup suggests:

> The New Testament Christianity with which Kierkegaard supports his demand is therefore the testimony of the Synoptic Gospels. It is based upon Christ's utterances themselves, upon *logia*, not upon the testimony of the apostles. "God is love, and God wills to be loved; this is the Christianity of the New Testament"—but this reciprocal love, which has to do with intensity, not extensity, is the basis of all the sufferings of the imitator, according to Kierkegaard, and it leads unmistakably to martyrdom; it is the Christian's destiny. Because of the distinction Kierkegaard maintains between the Gospels, which he stresses, and the Epistles, which he relegates to a subordinate position, he is able to maintain that the New Testament emphasizes the imitation of Christ more than the efficacy of Christ's saving death. Becoming a sacrifice follows logically from imitation.[25]

Kierkegaard knew about the importance of faith, about the meaning of infinite resignation to the divine will, and about the teleological suspension of the ethical. Consequently, he stood closer to the relational motif than to the deliberative and showed little patience with philosophical generalities. Even so, the prescriptive aspect of his approach can be denied only at the risk of doing violence to the inner dynamic of his own position. According to Kierkegaard, a man can be a Christian only if he perseveres in the rigorous renunciation of the world portrayed in the Gospels. But no man can follow Christ as pattern, since Christ is qualitatively different from normal men. Hence the prescriptive demand forces the relational trust in which "a man learns to recognize his helplessness and thereby is led to pray for grace."[26]

It is important to distinguish between an engendering reality that is used simply as a sanction for a norm and one which determines the content of the norm. It is one thing to say to a child, for example, "You should not steal cookies from the bakery store because your father is working hard to support you." It is another thing to say to him, "You should behave in a manner befitting the fact that your father is struggling to provide you with the necessities of life." There is an element of response in both statements, but in the first statement the response is co-joined with a prescriptive element that is absent from the second statement. The first statement might be interpreted as either a prescriptive ethic or a relational ethic depending upon whether it is understood primarily as a prohibition of stealing or as a call to respect the father. The second statement, which contains no description of what constitutes an appropriate response, must be interpreted relationally.

Section C: The Relational Motif in Christian Ethics

8

The Relational Motif and the Bible

In relational ethics the direction of action is shaped by the sense of excitement or gratitude which arises from a live, dynamic, and compelling encounter with the source of moral guidance. When a leader or a group proves attractive and exciting or when an event induces a profound sense of indebtedness or appeal, men are frequently given new motives for their actions and new insights concerning the scope of their obligations. Speaking of the redemptive deed which is central to Christian ethics as understood in relational terms, Joseph Sittler declares:

> God's deed does not simply call, or present a pattern in front of, or evoke, or demonstrate. It *engenders;* that is, it brings into existence lives bred by its originative character. Only terms which denote a quasi-biological-organic relationship are adequate to elaborate in terms of ethics what is declared of the reality of the Christian God in his work for man's situation.[1]

In describing Hebrew ethics James Muilenburg shows how the morality of the Old Testament sprang from a response to the Exodus as the centrally meaningful event. But Muilenburg acknowledges that a prescriptive element accompanies the response, in as much as the Hebrew man is told *what* is required of him. Hebrew morality differs radically from the abstract deliberation of moral philosophy, but it involves prescriptive aspects such as laws and codes. Hence, while the sanction of Hebrew morality is relational, its form tends to be prescriptive.

> If by ethics we mean the theory or science of right conduct, the principles of morality, or the systematic analysis of "the good," then it is clear that we shall look in vain in the pages of the Old Testament for such formulations. For here we find no unified and coherent body of ethical principles, no autonomous values or ideals which one can possess and make one's own, no norms which have independent status in and of themselves. . . . Rather, [the Hebrew man] knew that he had been addressed, that he had been told what was required of

him; and he knew perfectly well when and where he had been told, what the demands were which were incumbent upon him, and Who it was Who had exacted of him such demands. . . .[2]

The idea of following the example of Christ has frequently appeared in the Christian tradition. This is not an idea confined to the early twentieth century when Charles M. Sheldon gave it such a popular thrust. Luther spoke of being "a Christ to our neighbor" and Calvin urged his followers to let their lives "express Christ." To the extent that this idea is understood as requiring certain acts which are either observed in the Lord's behavior or demanded by his teaching, it is prescriptive. But if the implication is that the Christian should act in a manner which respects and honors (rather than imitates) his Lord, a much greater flexibility is implied and the relational form of the norm becomes decisive.

The Nature of Relational Norms

H. Richard Niebuhr developed what may be the most reflective and extensive theoretical conception of the third motif. According to Niebuhr, there are three basic approaches to the making of ethical judgments:

> . . . purposiveness seeks to answer the question: "What shall I do?" by raising as prior the question: "What is my goal, ideal, or telos?" Deontology tries to answer the moral query by asking, first of all: "What is the law and what is the first law of my life?" Responsibility, however, proceeds in every moment of decision and choice to inquire: "What is going on?" If we use value terms then the differences among the three approaches may be indicated by the terms, the *good,* the *right,* and the *fitting;* for teleology is concerned always with the highest good to which it subordinates the right; consistent deontology is concerned with the right, no matter what may happen to our goods; but for the ethics of responsibility the *fitting* action, the one that fits into a total interaction as response and as anticipation of further response, is alone conducive to the good and alone is right.[3]

In the determination of what is fitting, the person or group for whom, or in respect to whom, it is fitting must be given foremost account. In the same vein Nels Ferré insists, "Ethical obligation is a social event. Ethical response has social reference. . . . Ethics is thus *through and through relational,* man with men in and through nature."[4] Paul Lehmann declares, "A koinonia *ethic is concerned with relations and functions, not with principles and precepts.*[5]

Many relationalists feel that ethical thinking is so often identified with ideals and precepts that extensive disavowals must be made before men are prepared to understand or accept the radical implications of ethics approached in terms of relation and context. There is a real sense in which ethics in the relational motif ceases to be ethics in the normal sense of the word. Instead of setting forth a norm to which men must aspire, it understands an ethos in which they live. Ethics involves a style of life from which naturally flow certain responses appropriate to that style, rather than a process of analysis and prescription. As one author put it, "The ultimate Christian conception is not that a man *should know how to bear himself* in any crisis of experience, and should act out his knowledge, but that he should bear himself rightly *without thinking about it*—almost as if he could not help it."[6] Walter Lowrie once complained that all efforts to attach to Christianity a system of morals, an ethical theory, have come from philosophical minds which do not understand the distinctive quality of a Christian "way of life." According to Lowrie, we can learn from the Bible how we ought to behave, not only in formally ethical situations but in all aspects of Christian existence. He coined the phrase, "celestial etiquette," to refer to this style of life, including ceremonial aspects, to which the Christian is called.[7]

The idea of an ethos or an etiquette is frequently understood to supersede the analytical and prescriptive approaches. Thus Dietrich Bonhoeffer argued that the sense of an ethos, the participation in a style of life, rules out other ways of formulating the ethical norms. He declared,

> It is not by ideals and programmes or by conscience, duty, responsibility and virtue that reality can be confronted and overcome, but simply and solely by the perfect love of God. Here again it is not by a general idea of love that this is achieved, but by the really *lived* love of God in Jesus Christ.[8]

In a work written in 1923, Anders Nygren attempted a methodological study of theological ethics in relation to philosophical procedure.[9] Nygren prepared the way for a philosophical inquiry into ethical systems in which descriptions of alternatives and generalizations about the function of the alternatives are possible without granting to the philosophical reason the right to pass autonomous judgment upon the ground motifs of different individual systems in their particularity. In looking at the various ethical categories encountered by philosophical scrutiny of the field, he identified "purposive ethics, legalistic ethics, and dispositional ethics." These categories are not dissimilar to those proposed in this discussion. In setting forth his understanding of Christian ethics, Nygren felt that the ground motif of the Christian ethos required its interpretation within the dispositional category, and hence we find Nygren within the relational motif, at least with respect to his understanding of Christianity.

In his discussion of the nature of the relational approach to ethics, H. Richard Niebuhr observed that "the use of this image in the field of ethics is *not yet* considerable."[10] This observation may be quite right as far as it refers to formal abstract discourse about ethical theory. But is it right to assume that the relational mode of decision-making is a new phenomenon? Have not men often used this process for making decisions without describing it in formal terms? Moreover, is it correct to imply that this approach to ethics is rare? Do not many men determine their choices in this manner without describing their process of choice in theoretical terms? How does the relational approach differ, except in degree of sophistication, from organizational morality, in which the ethical question becomes "Whom am I trying to please?" By such a question the ethical investigation is transposed from one in which the inherent quality of an act is examined to one in which a judgment is derived in regard to some observer whose favor (or disfavor) is strongly desired. Such an approach determines the nature of an action, not by a measure of rightness or wrong-ness derived from rational deliberation or from comparison to a code, but in terms of the peer group to whom allegiance is given, or the leader who is devotedly served.

Obviously, spokesmen for relational ethics are not defending what usually goes under the rubric of organizational morality. They would make a distinction between heteronomy and theonomy. The first of these terms was employed by Kant to indicate moral choices which are based upon emotion, desire, pleasure, or submission to an external authority; the second has been employed by Tillich to indicate a situation in which a believer stands freely, yet authentically and devotedly, under God. Most organizational morality is heteronomously controlled. It is submissive, scheming, rootless. But the relational ethics of which Niebuhr speaks are ethics of fidelity and bondage, not mere caprice. They are related to a God who transcends the temporal relationships between individuals.

> . . . these social theories of the moral life as responsible are neither just to the empirical facts nor consistent with their fundamental idea if they stop such analysis at the point of reference to the ethos, or the judging actions of a closed society to which a man responds in all his responses to his companions. These societies are not more self-contained than are the individuals that refer to them; these moral languages in which social judgments are enshrined are no more self-elucidating than are languages about nature. The societies that judge or in which we judge ourselves are self-transcending societies. And the process of self-transcendence or of references to the third beyond each third does not come to rest until the total community of being has been involved.[11]

Another term that is sometimes used to describe the kind of ethical decision-making involved in the relational pattern is *relativistic*. This term usually implies a view that standards differ from culture to culture and that any discussion of the intrinsically valid or permanently good is un-justified. In a very profound sense ethical choice made in the relational context is relative—relative to the situation and context. This, so its advocates claim, is a mark of strength. It means that moral judgments take into account the genuine needs of the immediate situation. But the term *relativistic* is frequently associated with a scheming, cynical, and conniv-ing disregard for considerations of the right. The relational motif describes ethical procedures which are sober and well-intentioned. To use the term *relativistic* to describe relational forms of ethical norms might breed confusion.

Nevertheless, as long as contextual ethics proposes to derive ethical norms from the particular considerations that arise in the process of con-crete decision-making, it is bound to have a relativistic ingredient in its very nature. Relationalists do not shy from the implications of relativism with the appearance of dismay frequently shown by men who use other ways of formulating the ethical norm. In fact, Paul Lehmann argues that many ethical choices are ambiguous and hence very close to being relativ-istic. Ethics of principles are inadequate because they cannot deal with the possibility that some decisions might be right in one situation, wrong in another. They cannot cope with the fact that men of equally sound intention and dedicated loyalty often come to different conclusions about what ought to be done about certain matters, such as Christian participa-tion in warfare. "In a dynamic situation such as this," writes Lehmann, "there is never any *one right action*."[12] The Christian community may need to say "yes" and "no" at nearly the same time. By doing so, it points up the fact that human ethical decisions do not neatly separate the good from the evil, but reflect the messy stuff of everyday life. The literature defending the relational motif is often anxious to demonstrate the am-biguous character of ethical choice as part of its denial of a fixed norm.

Another phrase used to describe ethics in the relational motif is *situa-tional*. This term is used both in secular philosophical discussions and in avowedly Christian contexts. The command of God may supersede the demand that is implied by a generalized norm, even though it need not do so. Among those who declare that the command of God is totally free of any bondage to principle or prior rubric, Dietrich Bonhoeffer has been one of the most articulate spokesmen; his description of God's command runs as follows:

> God's commandment is the speech of God to man. Both in its con-tents and in its form it is concrete speech to the concrete man. God's commandment leaves man no room for application or interpretation. It leaves room only for obedience or disobedience. God's command-ment cannot be found and known in detachment from time and place; it can only be heard in a local and temporal context. If God's com-

mandment is not clear, definite and concrete to the last detail, then it is not God's commandment.[13]

Not only does Bonhoeffer's formulation prepare for the possibility that ethical norms can vary from situation to situation, but it also leaves the formulation of the ethical judgment in a highly individualistic relationship. Any man may be free to claim a "clear, definite, and concrete" command from God. While the "clear, definite, and concrete" command of God may be made known to individuals, it may also impel them to social responsibility and even heroism. It does not imply that the believer who finds his norm through a radically vertical relationship to God shuns all responsibility to the world. Rather, it means that this responsibility may be differently defined for different individuals according to circumstances. If we apply the term *individualistic* to this way of formulating norms, we must think of it as the opposite of *universalized* rather than as the opposite of *social*.

The relational motif is sometimes set forth by using a distinction between imperative and indicative ethics. Ethics in the imperative devises norms and extols men to attain them; ethics in the indicative announces an event that has taken or is taking place in men's lives and trusts them to respond to it. Richard Niebuhr put the indicative approach in this way: "Responsibility affirms: 'God is acting in all actions upon you. So respond to all actions upon you as to respond to his action.' "[14] Paul Lehmann observes that the primary ethical question is not " 'What *ought* I to do?' but 'What *am* I to do?' "[15] The action of the living God shapes "what I *am* to do."

This action of the living God is indicated in some ethical thinking by a single act; in other ethical outlooks by a continuing series of events. Hebraism relates itself to a dramatic event of overwhelming significance when it refers to the Exodus from Egypt as the mighty action of God which engenders a response. In some Christian ethics the redeeming action of Christ's obedience, death, and resurrection becomes the central focus. But in other forms of Christian relationalism the entire sweep of God's action in history calls forth men's response. The central and specific events, such as the Exodus or the Christ drama, are taken as but single facets in a series of divine actions. Lehmann regards the community, or *koinonia*, which has been called into being by the Christ event, as the locus of the ongoing activity of God. In Niebuhr's thinking all human experiences are taken as possible avenues of God's activity. No special event is accorded exclusive claim. In either case, that of the single focus or that of the continuing context of all experience, the indicative mood is used to formulate ethical norms on the basis of what has been done or is being done rather than what ought to be done.

The question of the relationship of Christian ethics to the ethics of other major religious and philosophical traditions is debated very sharply within the group of men who use the relational motif. In many discussions of relational ethics from the Christian perspective much time is taken to show that, apart from the Christian faith, ethics of this sort is impossible or useless. The representatives of the relational point of view include the strongest advocates of the utter uniqueness of the biblical and Christian point of view to be found in the contemporary theological scene. Thus N. H. G. Robinson declares that the claim of Christ is "not just *a* moral claim alongside other moral claims, it is *the* moral claim."[16] On the other hand, other writers within this group see their delineation of an ethic of response and relationship as valid, not merely for setting forth a Christian ethic in professed uniqueness, but as a valid way in which to think about ethics in general. Those of this second persuasion would accept the possibility that ethics can be relationally understood apart from a specific Christian context. As an example of this perspective we find H. Richard Niebuhr declaring with respect to his conception of responsive ethics:

> The object of the inquiry is not, as in the case of Christian ethics, simply the Christian life but rather human moral life in general. It is at this point that I part company with many theologians who tend to deal with the Christian life as though it were somehow discontinuous with other modes of human existence.[17]

The relational motif should not be understood as a monolith within which there is no variation. It cannot be understood as a totally unique moral method which eschews dialogue with other ways of formulating the ethical norm. To be sure, some exponents of a relational way of formulating the ethical norm make a strenuous effort to declare themselves radically different from other points of view. Some of the strongest polemics in contemporary Christian ethical discourse come from the pens of the contextualists as they declare deliberative morality to be an essentially human enterprise and prescriptive morality to be an abortive form of religious ethics. But in the long history of Christian reflection the relational motif has appeared in a variety of expressions, some of them irenic rather than polemical. We shall endeavor to explore both the unity and diversity in this way of formulating ethical norms in light of the Gospel, beginning with the exegetical derivation of this type of ethic from biblical materials.

Biblical Ethics as the Ethics of Response

The term *principles* has been employed to interpret biblical ethics in deliberative terms, and the term *law* has been used to cast biblical ethics into prescriptive categories. But biblical ethics can also be interpreted in relational terms. From the New Testament the saving work of Jesus Christ is presented as the deed that engenders moral response; from the Old Testament the mighty action of God in bringing his people from Egyptian bondage is taken as a clue to a unique moral relationship between God and his people.

Many writers who understand biblical ethics in relational terms take pains to show that deliberative and prescriptive morality are foreign to biblical faith. Speaking of the effort to derive an absolute norm from the Old Testament, Gerhard von Rad has declared,

> . . . no matter how urgently it was sought, no satisfactory answer to this question of an absolute norm could be found in the Old Testament. The reason was that the question itself was a wrong one, and in consequence the statements in the Old Testament simply could not be brought into harmony with this way of thinking. It was H. Cremer who recognized the impossibility of applying this way of thinking to Biblical thought, and succeeded in breaking through to a completely different way of thinking which has so far been rightly accepted as proven, in its basic thesis at least. As we now see, the mistake lay in seeking and presupposing an absolute ideal ethical norm, since ancient Israel did not in fact measure a line of conduct or an act by an ideal norm, but by the specific relationship in which the partner had at the time to prove himself true.[18]

Quoting Cremer's *Biblisch-theologisches Wörterbuch*, von Rad goes on:

> "Every relationship brings with it certain claims upon conduct, and the satisfaction of these claims, which issue from the relationship and in which alone the relationship can persist, is described by our term צדק [righteousness]." The way in which it is used shows that "צדק is out and out a term denoting relationship and that it does this in the sense of referring to a real relationship between two parties . . . and not to the relationship of an object under consideration to an idea." To some extent, therefore, the specific relationship in which the agent finds himself is itself the norm.[19]

According to von Rad this ethical approach judges a man's life, or the nation's life, "wholly from the point of view of faithfulness to a relationship."[20] The Old Testament concept of righteousness cannot, consequently, be understood in forensic terms. "In particular, conduct loyal to a relationship includes far more than mere correctness or legality, that is, righteousness in our sense of the word."[21] The righteousness which Yahweh granted to Israel is a righteousness known and experienced in relationship. Von Rad credits Pedersen with having clarified the fundamental difference between this view and all idealistic and humanistic ideas.

Th. C. Vriezen[22] has argued that all religious morality is fundamentally determined by the relationship between God and man. Consequently the morality of the Old Testament must be understood as quite different from an autonomous ethic which relies upon human reason for the determination of the moral norm. The ethic of the Old Testament derives from the nature of the divine being, but also springs from the experience of a special community that has been called into existence by that diety. While the formulations of Vriezen are less evidently concerned than those of von Rad to set Old Testament ethics in sharp contrast to a prescriptive methodology, they exclude the deliberative approach of moral philosophy with almost as much rigor. Moreover, they indicate that the relational element must be acknowledged as part of any biblical morality.

Walther Eichrodt is not sure that Old Testament ethics can be entirely characterized in any one category. He draws a distinction between the prophetic and the priestly understanding of morality. The prophets knew the Mosaic heritage, but they also knew that the official cultus had obscured some of its living reality. Hence, the prophets referred less often to the Mosaic heritage than they might have done had the Torah, as understood in their day, represented a more valid portrayal of the ethical relationship of the nation to its God. Speaking of the covenant, Eichrodt observes:

> This conception had long become too fixed as a description of a relationship established once for all, a statutory institution, and so no longer did justice to the *vital personal quality of the divine-human relationship*. And this, for the prophets, was the thing that mattered. For them election was only the beginning of permanent intercourse, the reality of which derived from constant fresh decisions for God—a lasting association committing man to obedient attention to a divine will ever calling him to new tasks. For priest and people, on the other hand, election was a matter of firmly established ordinances, placed at man's disposal, and which in certain circumstances might even support man against God.[23]

Von Rad, Vriezen, and Eichrodt are not discussing the relationship of God to his people merely as an impulse prompting Israel to follow the law, but are declaring that this relationship is decisive as a source of moral guidance. No prescriptive content drawn from law is allowed to intrude as the formalized criterion of a good relationship.

What is true of Old Testament studies is equally true of discussions of the New Testament. In a previous chapter, reference was made to interpretations of Jesus and Paul in terms of law. In relational views the teachings of Jesus and the theology of Paul are set forth in contrast with law. For example, T. W. Manson rejects the very Matthean sources upon which Dodd seems to depend for his interpretations. He holds the interpretation of Christ's teaching in terms of law to be perverted and false to the spirit of Jesus. Manson finds the community important in the molding of ethical decisions and describes the New Testament community of the church in much the same way that Vriezen describes the Old Testament community of the covenant. In summarizing his treatment Manson emphasizes these central themes:

> The first is that the ethic we are dealing with is the ethic of a kingdom: the ethic of a society with a leader and ruler; and the primary quality of the ethic is that it comes from the ruler himself, who is the interpreter and exemplifier of it. This holds if we think in terms of the kingdom of God, in which God himself gives the rules of life and exemplifies them; "you are to be holy as God is holy; perfect as he is perfect; merciful as he is merciful." It still holds if we think of it in terms of a messianic kingdom. It is the Messiah whose life and death exemplifies and interprets the ideal which is summed up in the commandment "Love as I have loved you." In the last resort the Christian ethic inevitably comes back to Christ himself. It is from him that it derives its content, its form and its authority. Its force is most likely to be felt by those who belong to the community which he founded and maintains, the community which belongs to him. And the power to carry it into effect is most likely to be found in living association with that community and with its head.[24]

Joseph Sittler has stated the case as colorfully and as radically as any commentator who holds that the teaching of Jesus is antithetical to law. In describing the Sermon on the Mount, Sittler says,

> Here, as in every teaching, parable, miracle of Jesus, is disclosed a faith active in love which cracks all rabbinical patterns, transcends every statutory solidification of duty, breaks out of all systematic schematizations of the good—and out of the living, perceptive, restorative passion of faith enfolds in its embrace the fluctuant, incalculable, novel emergents of human life.[25]

Sittler argues that the teachings of Jesus embarrass every effort to make principles or legislative provisions the vehicle of his message. Instead, the insights of Christ come in "gull-like swoops" or emerge as "lightning flashes" picking up a detail here and another there, examining it momentarily so as to set forth a paradigm for the nature of love, and then moving on to another instance and another illustrative detail. In suggesting that the teachings of Jesus cannot be reduced to a manageable code Sittler notes that Jesus dealt with ethical matters in a completely different way than either moral reasoning or specific law.

The same issues that occur regarding the teachings of Jesus occur regarding the theology of Paul. He declared his independence from Jewish legalism in terms so vigorous that he quickly created an antinomian development among a group of his followers. In Galatians we find Paul seeking to counteract the effects which his break with the law had produced among certain of his followers. These antinomians had taken Paul's teaching as an excuse for license. Paul, of course, felt that the relationship of the Christian to his Lord demands a free, responsible, and concerned acceptance of the obligations that are hardened by law into rigid and external requirements. Apparently his followers more readily grasped what Paul rejected than what he affirmed, and thus behaved in a manner that Paul neither expected nor condoned. The loss of moral impulse can also occur when the negative side of a relational ethic is heard before its positive impulse is understood. John Knox doubts that Paul has an adequate theoretical foundation for his affirmation of moral demands on the one hand and his rejection of law's importance on the other. Knox asks,

> What ground is there for ethical obligation, once one is in Christ?
> Paul nowhere convincingly answers this question—and his raising it several times would seem to show that he was troubled by it. His answer—most fully set forth in Romans 6—takes the form of a demonstration that the believer *will* be righteous, not of an explanation of why he *ought* to be: since he has the Spirit, he will manifest the fruits of the Spirit. In the practical sections of his letters, to be sure, Paul shows himself not only aware that Christians actually often did not observe the law of Christ, but also ready to insist that they are obligated to do so. But Paul has no persuasive *theoretical* basis for this insistence.[26]

In another place Knox says, "Paul's doctrine of justification has in itself the seeds of antinomianism and Paul's critics, or perhaps heretical followers, were not being merely perverse in saying so."[27]

Joseph Sittler suggests that Paul is talking the language of faith, not the language of law. The language of faith is relational, not imperative. It is a language which is constantly engendered, continuously elicited, that presupposes an intimate relationship between two persons. Because Saint Paul understood this relationship between Christ and the Christian to override all else, Sittler holds that Paul was not so much saying law is wrong as that law is useless. To set moral imperatives before sinful men, men who do not have the relationship of faith, will never induce them to do good and may even tempt them to transgress. To enunciate moral law to the new man in Christ is to engage in the superfluous, since the new man in Christ will already interiorize its requirements by virtue of his faith and free response.

According to this view, Saint Paul must be understood in the reference of faith rather than in the reference of morality. Faith is relational and organic, binding the believer to an object of trust that informs all his actions and shapes all his outlooks. While others argue the pros and cons of law, Paul subordinates the issue, confounding those who would relate him to rabbinical legalism as well as those who would make him out to be an antinomian. Paul has respect for the law and its requirements—he even calls it a pedagogue; but he also rejects the law as a way to obtain righteousness. With this transformation of the ethical question, the categories of the discussion are shifted. In the place of the right, the commanded, and the prescribed, appear categories such as response, faith, and "for me to live is Christ." In his effort to rule out legalism because it blocks the life of faith, Paul attacked the law; in his effort to rule out license because it distorts the response of faith, he affirmed the place of obedience. Paul considered the place of law ambiguously because he took it to be secondary to the great and crucial issue of man's relationship to God, a relationship which includes the commandment to love God and neighbor but which is not adequately understood in moral terms alone.

A realization that Christians have read the Bible in different ways should come as no surprise, though sometimes it is supposed that the moral and ethical implication of the scriptural materials are easier to grasp than theological implications of the biblical record. Christian ethics cannot escape the hermaneutical question but neither can it dare claim to solve it. Paul Lehmann is right in observing that "a recognition of the hermaneutical problem shatters an apparently ingrained habit of Christians of beginning with the New Testament, or with the Bible, as though that were obvious."[28] Even when the biblical story is considered seriously and critically men come to different decisions regarding how it should be read as a source of ethical insight.

9

Response to the Divine Initiative

Saint Augustine developed one of the first great post-biblical statements of the relational motif. For Augustine the fundamental problem of morality was the solicitation of a response to follow the right; determination of good conduct was considered a secondary and somewhat less important matter. The problem of moral conduct resides in the will, which must be captured and led to do the good. The will can only do the good when it is in the service of God, because only then is the motive as well as the content of the action meaningfully related to the true good, which is in God.

Augustine neither abrogated nor absolutized the law. He simply placed attention upon another matter—the intent and devotion of the will. True obedience to the law can only come when man's sinful will has been redirected. Indeed, it is even possible to have a false obedience to the law in which the sinful man follows the requirements of the law for the wrong reasons. The heart of the ethical question, therefore, lies not in the determination of right action as contrasted with wrong action but in the creation of a right attitude and experience in the heart of the believer. This new attitude makes possible a service to God that includes obedience to the law and, when the situation calls for it, even action at variance with the law. For Augustine the ethical problem was a problem of the relationship to God under which conformity to a standard may or may not be a crucial matter. This is how Augustine stated the priority of love for God:

> If, then, to those who love God all things issue in good, and if, as no one doubts, the chief or perfect good is not only to be loved, but to be loved so that nothing shall be loved better, as is expressed in the words, "With all thy soul, with all thy heart, and with all thy mind," who, I ask, will not at once conclude, when these things are all settled and most surely believed, that our chief good which we must hasten to arrive at in preference to all other things is nothing else than God?[1]

Men who are drawn to God by love for God (*caritas*) will in turn love the created world, their neighbor, and even themselves. Self-love has a permissible role to play, providing it is a secondary and derivative role. Self-love becomes a legitimate possibility only if one has primary regard for God and uses this self-regard under the impulses and directives that are born from service to Him. If the mind's attention, or the will's devotion, departs from the first and central allegiance, wretchedness and folly will result. But if the Christian man is totally engrossed in a God-directed love he will find his true end.

> The farther, then, the mind departs from God, not in space, but in affection and lust after things below Him, the more it is filled with folly and wretchedness. So by love it returns to God—a love which places it not along with God, but under Him. And the more ardor and eagerness there is in this, the happier and more elevated will the mind be, and with God as sole governor it will be in perfect liberty. Hence it must know that it is a creature. It must believe what is the truth—that its Creator remains ever possessed of the inviolable and immutable nature of truth and wisdom, and must confess, even in view of the errors from which it desires deliverance, that it is liable to folly and falsehood. But then again, it must take care that it be not separated by the love of the other creature, that is, of this visible world, from the love of God Himself, which sanctifies it in order that it may abide most happy. No other creature, then—for we are ourselves a creature—separates us from the love of God which is in Christ Jesus our Lord.[2]

Augustine related the four classical virtues to the response of the man who is faithful to God. Each virtue was reinterpreted to become a form of the love for God. The virtue is first defined, then reinterpreted:

> . . . temperance is love giving itself entirely to that which is loved; fortitude is love readily bearing all things for the sake of the loved object; justice is love serving only the loved object, and therefore ruling rightly; prudence is love distinguishing with sagacity between what hinders it and what helps it. The object of this love is not anything, but only God, the chief good, the highest wisdom, the perfect harmony. So we may express the definition thus: that temperance is love keeping itself entire and incorrupt for God; fortitude is love bearing everything readily for the sake of God; justice is love serving God only, and therefore ruling well all else, as subject to man; prudence is love making a right distinction between what helps it towards God and what might hinder it.[3]

Augustine did with the virtues what Paul did with the law; made them of derivative and secondary significance when redefined by the Christian faith in terms of a relationship to God. *Temperance* became, in Augustine's view, love for God which restrains the passions, preserves men from getting entangled in moral fogs or snared by misleading passions, and keeps them on the right course of action. Augustine felt that only when men are unconditionally committed to God are they able to control their passions and behavior in such a way as to be worthy exemplars of moral virtue. Similarly, by *fortitude*, Augustine had in mind that which inflames men with love and devotion to God so that they will be able to suffer even the loss of earth or earthly things because their trust is in Him. Men of fortitude will not even be afraid of death. They will say, "If God be for us who can be against us?" Augustine cited both Old and New Testament examples of men whose courage came from their love and devotion to God. By *justice* Augustine meant the making of all judgments in relationship to God, thereby avoiding conflicting claims. The love of God enables the Christian to rule lightly all lesser and derivative matters and to weigh properly between the conflicting claims of secondary loyalties. *Prudence* becomes the capacity wisely to determine what helps and what hinders the self in maintaining its relationship to God. This includes the development of a sense of what ought to be desired and what ought to be avoided if the love of God is to show itself in moral behavior. It is the love of God and not rational good sense which sets straight the value structure of the obedient man, and thus helps him to conduct his life wisely. Even happiness—which comes from devotion of the self to God—has a place in Christian experience.

Augustine's understanding of the ethical norm is sometimes described by the phrase, echoed by Luther and even at times taken to summarize Paul: "Love God and do as you please." The central thesis is better caught in the wording: "Love God *and then* do as you please." True love for God, the singular absorption of the heart and will in the service of the almighty and righteous Creator of the universe, elicits moral goodness and grace. The man who is fully and completely devoted in this manner will not need to worry about the kind of moral actions he desires to take. His desires will be dominated by the grace that springs from his faithful relationship to God. Loving God, such a man will please to do only what is right. Morality constitutes a fitting and appropriate response to the relationship between the Christian believer and God.

Augustine's understanding of Christian morality suffered an eclipse after his death. Only small groups and peripheral thinkers espoused his theological ideas until they appeared again in the work of Martin Luther. Luther was convinced that good works flow from the renewed and rededicated person who has been freed from bondage to sin through the justifying love of God. He followed Augustine in placing the fundamental ethical problem in the will rather than in the intellect. Hence, the greatest need of man is not to know the good, but to experience a forgiveness to which he can respond so as to draw him beyond his self-concern into a life of joyful service. To explain the difference between morality performed in the situation of love and morality performed in the situation of fear Luther drew upon the human example of the relationship between man and woman.

> When a man and a woman love and are pleased with each other, and thoroughly believe in their love, who teaches them how they are to behave, what they are to do, leave undone, say, not say, think? Confidence alone teaches them all this, and more. They make no difference in works: they do the great, the long, the much, as gladly as the small, the short, the little, and vice versa; and that too with joyful, peaceful, confident hearts, and each is a free companion of the other. But where there is a doubt, search is made for what is best; then a distinction of works is imagined whereby a man may win favor; and yet he goes about it with a heavy heart, and great disrelish; he is, as it were, taken captive, more than half in despair, and often makes a fool of himself.
>
> So a Christian who lives in this confidence toward God, knows all things, can do all things, undertakes all things that are to be done, and does everything cheerfully and freely; not that he may gather many merits and good works, but because it is a pleasure for him to please God thereby, and he serves God purely for nothing, content that his service pleases God. On the other hand, he who is not at one with God, or doubts, hunts and worries in what way he may do enough and with many works move God.[4]

The Christian man is given freedom through the experience of justification, but his freedom is a freedom for obligation and service, not a freedom from duty and responsibility. Like Paul, Luther set forth his practical affirmations of duty in somewhat paradoxical terms. Near the beginning of his *Treatise on Christian Liberty* this paradox is set forth in very famous words:

> A Christian man is a perfectly free lord of all, subject to none. A Christian man is a perfectly dutiful servant of all, subject to all.[5]

The relationships between freedom and obligation, faith and works, release from the law and obligation to responsibility remain paradoxical in Luther. All strongly justificationist theologies are paradoxical in their understanding of these relationships, but seldom has any thinker so succinctly phrased this paradox as Martin Luther did in the words just cited.

Luther had to fight against the misinterpretation of his understanding. He made categorical denials that the doctrine of justification by faith can be used as an excuse for release from ethical obligation:

> Although, as I have said, a man is abundantly justified by faith inwardly, in his spirit, and so has all that he ought to have, except in so

far as this faith and riches must grow from day to day even unto the future life: yet he remains in this mortal life on earth, and in this life he must needs govern his own body and have dealings with men. Here the works begin; here a man cannot take his ease; here he must, indeed, take care to discipline his body by fastings, watchings, labors and other reasonable discipline, and to make it subject to the spirit so that it will obey and conform to the inward man and to faith, and not revolt against faith and hinder the inward man, as it is the body's nature to do if it be not held in check. For the inward man, who by faith is created in the likeness of God, is both joyful and happy because of Christ in Whom so many benefits are conferred upon him, and therefore it is his one occupation to serve God joyfully and for naught, in love that is not constrained.[6]

The dialectical relationship between freedom and bondage is also reflected in Luther's discussions of moral obligation. Faith is central, because by faith the very inner being of a man is set right, so that the fruit of his life is good. Faith insures that the heart will be right, as well as the acts. The disposition of the heart determines whether or not acts are valid expressions of devotion to God or fraudulent exercises performed for wrong motives. Faith so controls and directs the heart of the true believer as to issue in appropriate works, but the converse is not true:

For as works do not make a man a believer, so also they do not make him righteous. But as faith makes a man a believer and righteous, so faith also does good works. Since, then, works justify no one, and a man must be righteous before he does a good work, it is very evident that it is faith alone which, because of the pure mercy of God through Christ and in His Word, worthily and sufficiently justifies and saves the person, and a Christian man has no need of any work or of any law in order to be saved, since through faith he is free from every law and does all that he does out of pure liberty and freely, seeking neither benefit nor salvation, since he already abounds in all things and is saved through the grace of God because of his faith, and now seeks only to please God.[7]

Luther's ethic makes it possible for the Christian man to respond in liberty to the demands of the situation in which he finds himself and to relate creatively to the problems that arise. Stressing this aspect of Luther's thought, George W. Forell has observed:

Luther refused to recognize any permanent and unalterable ethical standards if these existed in a religious vacuum. The ethical standards of the pagan philosophers he considered "lies" and "godless fables." All ethical standards are meaningful only in life. They are good if they serve to reveal God; they are evil if they hide God from men. Actions, faculties, beings, and standards are good or evil according to the function which they fulfill in helping or hindering the establishment of the saving relationship between God and man.[8]

While Luther eschewed ethical systems and stressed ethical relationships, substituting the question "Whom are you supposed to love?" in place of the query "What are you supposed to do?," he nevertheless had much to say about the duty of the Christian man to his neighbor. Luther felt that faith must become effectual through love, resulting in services cheerfully rendered. Even as Christ became a dutiful servant of all men, so the Christian must become "a Christ to his neighbor." "I will therefore," he wrote, "give myself as a Christ to my neighbor, just as Christ offered Himself to me; I will do nothing in this life except what I see is necessary, profitable, and salutary to my neighbor, since through faith I have an abundance of all good things in Christ."[9]

Luther was sufficiently free to speak not only of the limits of the law but of its possible use. He admitted that there are many laws of church and of state which are useful as guidance when faith is weak or unheeded. They would be unnecessary if all men had complete faith. They are useful because faith is still incomplete and partial in the present state of the church. Accordingly, Luther had much to say about the Ten Commandments. They stand as the measure of our sin and wickedness, prompting confession of sin. The Ten Commandments also provide a guide for action, but in a very special sense. In his *Brief Explanation of the Ten Commandments, the Creed, and the Lord's Prayer* (1520), Luther even set forth a detailed list of transgressions of each commandment, nearly like a code. He also set forth a list of fulfillments for the Commandments, each of which reflects a sense of love in the relationship between God and man. Luther suggested that the Ten Commandments furnish a sufficient guide for the faithful man—he need look to no other source of ethical judgment —but also a guide which is beyond the power of man himself to fulfill. Consequently, the Commandments convict men of their failures and show them afresh the need of God's grace.

The *Treatise on Good Works* contains a more extended discussion of the Commandments and their place in the Christian life. In the discussion of each commandment Luther shows how it deepens and enriches the believer's sense of an appropriate response to God's grace. Luther even found the Commandments helpful to those of weak faith, who cling to them as means of good works. Luther counseled his followers to help such men, not to despise them, to treat them as a physician treats a sick soul, and to wean them from reliance upon works by a slow, careful process in which they continue to adhere to the Commandments until they are ready for the full freedom of the Christian life. In the full freedom of the Christian life the Commandments play a role, not as obligatory laws, but as a means whereby every relationship of the believer to God is explored and richly appropriated. Here, as in most of his writings, Luther was more concerned to set forth the experiences which a relational approach includes than he was to explore what relationalism rules out. He explored the meaning of grace more consistently than he condemned the role of law, though both elements are woven together in every facet of his thought. What the love of God is to the ethics of Augustine the experience of grace is to the ethics of Luther, but the centrality of response and of relation is surely as evident in the one as in the other.

The great American theologian Jonathan Edwards addressed himself to a different situation and used a quite different idiom than Augustine or Luther, but the structure of his thought shows much the same approach to Christian moral impulse. Near the end of the second chapter of *The Nature of True Virtue*, a chapter in which Edwards has carefully argued that a "benevolent propensity of heart to being in general, and a temper or disposition to love God supremely, are in effect the same thing,"[10] he sets forth his position with both a positive declaration and a negative refutation of its alternatives. The positive declaration reads thus:

> . . . a truly virtuous mind, being as it were under the sovereign dominion of love to God, above all things, seeks the glory of God, and makes this his supreme, governing, and ultimate end. This consists in the expression of God's perfections in their proper effects, the manifestation of God's glory to created understandings, the communications of the infinite fulness of God to the creature—the creature's highest esteem of God, love to, and joy in him—and in the proper exercises and expressions of these. And so far as a virtuous mind exercises true virtue in benevolence to created beings, it chiefly seeks the good of the creature; consisting in its knowledge or view of God's glory and beauty, its union with God, conformity and love to him, and joy in him. And that disposition of heart, that consent, union, or propensity of mind to being in general, which appears chiefly in such exercises, is *virtue*, truly so called; or in other words, true *grace* and real *holiness*. And no other disposition or affection but this is of the nature of virtue.[11]

The negative refutation, which follows immediately as a corollary, and which is aimed at efforts to find more autonomous grounds for ethical decision, declares:

> . . . those schemes of religion or moral philosophy which—however well in some respects they may treat of benevolence to mankind and other virtues depending on it, yet—have not a supreme regard to God, and love to him laid as the foundation, and all other virtues handled in a connection with this, and in subordination to it, are not true schemes of philosophy, but are fundamentally and essentially de-

fective. And whatever other benevolence or generosity towards mankind, and other virtues, or moral qualifications which go by that name, any are possessed of, that are not attended with a love to God which is altogether above them, and to which they are subordinate, and on which they are dependent, there is nothing of the nature of true virtue or religion in them. And it may be asserted in general, that nothing is of the nature of true virtue, in which God is not the first and the last; or which, with regard to their exercises in general, have not their first foundation and source in apprehensions of God's supreme dignity and glory, and in answerable esteem and love of him, and have not respect to God as the supreme end.[12]

Edwards belonged to that theological tradition which sees faith as a state of being, a disposition of the entire will, a matter of total selfhood. It is not merely consent to certain propositions or a set of abstract ideas whose truth value is accepted, but a total orientation of life. For this reason true virtue springs from a selfhood in which there is a propensity toward and involvement with God. The "religious affections" involving love for, and joy in, God are the source of both faith and morals. Edwards sided with those thinkers in his time who, for different reasons and on different grounds, identified morality with the sentiments and the will. But Edwards broadened his conception of the sentiments in such a way as to transcend any purely emotive subjectivism. The moral sense is, like the sense of beauty, rooted in deep appreciation, cultivated by subtle training, expressive of the heart. Unless the heart, the whole selfhood of a man, is right, men's actions will not be right; unless the selfhood is related to God it will not be truly virtuous. Choice and disposition are the central aspects of Edwards' view of the moral situation, rather than abstract knowledge of the good or begrudging acquiescence to a standard. In fact, man is not free to follow a course of action which is at variance with his disposition and inclinations. He follows what to him is "the apparent good."

Edwards set the ethics of true virtue, in which God is the central object of devotion, in contrast with the ethics of natural attainment. These constitute two moralities, in paradoxical tension with each other. There is a penultimate place for the secondary or natural morality. But only when the movement is from total being and universal benevolence as known in God, from the infinite to the finite, are the secondary values kept in proper context. For this reason, the primary ethical task is to restore the relationship between God and man which sets the other relationships of life into proper place. Without this proper focus for the religious affections Christian morality is impossible. God must be the object of love, the very ground of its appearance, because He is the very Being of being. Similarly, both beauty and moral excellency are rooted in God, who is the seat of both. ". . . [A]ll beauty to be found throughout the whole creation, is but the reflection of the diffused beams of that Being who hath an infinite fulness of brightness and glory."[13]

In his work *A Treatise Concerning Religious Affections*, Edwards examined twelve signs of true religion. These signs are engendered by the relationship of God to the believer; they are consequently "spiritual, supernatural, and divine." The eighth sign is the spirit of love, expressed in meekness and forgiveness as exemplified by Christ. There is more than a hint of the *imitatio dei* in this section of Edwards' work:

> Christ is full of grace; and Christians all receive of his fullness, and grace for grace: i.e. there is grace in Christians answering to grace in Christ, such an answerableness as there is between the wax and the seal; there is character for character: such kind of graces, such a spirit and temper, the same things that belong to Christ's character, belong to theirs. That disposition wherein Christ's character does in a special manner consist, therein does his image in a special manner consist. Christians that shine by reflecting the light of the Sun of Righteousness, do shine with the same sort of brightness, the same mild, sweet and pleasant beams. These lamps of the spiritual temple, that are enkindled by fire from heaven, burn with the same sort of flame. The branch is of the same nature with the stock and root, has the same sap, and bears the same sort of fruit. The members have the same kind of life with the head. It would be strange if Christians should not be of the same temper and spirit that Christ is of; when they are his flesh and his bone, yea are one spirit, and live so, that it is not they that live, but Christ that lives in them.[14]

The twelfth sign is Christian practice. This section is of singular importance for understanding Edwards' position, for here he deals with the content of Christian behavior. The section begins with the observation that religious affections "have that influence and power upon him who is the subject of 'em, that they cause that a practice, which is universally conformed to, and directed by Christian rules, should be the practice and business of his life."[15] Edwards simply assumed that Christian practice is directed by Christian rules. Nowhere did he take up the case against rules or against laws as a necessary corollary of his position. He spoke of the importance of obedience, as Calvin did before him. He talked about practice (what Luther would have called works) as the sign by which we know that grace is operative in the life of the believer.

Edwards does not attack rules or obedience to a code. He clearly finds the locus of Christian morality in another place, but he does not flay the law. His discussion is also remarkable for the fact that he does not spell out any law for the Christian. To be sure he presents a general picture of the life which signifies a holiness appropriate to the love known in Christ, but there is little effort to spell out the details, to set up explicit standards by which the good life is measured in contrast with the unholy life. The nearest thing to a specification of behavior comes in his effort to show that virtue must be positive, and that the true Christian cannot be obedient in merely negative terms.

> A man therefore can't be said to be universally obedient, and of a Christian conversation, only because he is no thief, nor oppressor, nor fraudulent person, nor drunkard, nor tavern-haunter, nor whoremaster, nor rioter, nor nightwalker, nor unclean, nor profane in his language, nor slanderer, nor liar, nor furious, nor malicious, nor reviler: he is falsely said to be of a conversation that becomes the gospel, who goes thus far and no farther; but in order to this, it is necessary that he should also be of a serious, religious, devout, humble, meek, forgiving, peaceful, respectful, condescending, benevolent, merciful, charitable and beneficent walk and conversation. Without such things as these, he don't obey the laws of Christ, and laws that he and his apostles did abundantly insist on, as of greatest importance and necessity.[16]

Edwards did not write in the biblical idiom even though he was well acquainted with biblical materials. He used categories that were familiar to philosophers, but he never argued for the autonomy of reason in the determination of ethical standards. Without engaging in polemics against philosophy, he transformed its use by pressing toward a view of human life described in terms of true piety. Such piety consists of a deep, abiding, sober, and unstinting service of God. It is rooted in gratitude for the benefits that God has shown to man. Thus Edwards declared that "unless we will be Atheists, we must allow that true virtue does primarily and most essentially consist in a supreme love to God; and that where this is wanting, there can be no true virtue."[17] Such a love for God as Edwards described is no mere shift of intellectual opinion from unbelief to belief; it is no mere addition of a religious concern to the other concerns which compete for men's attention. It is a fundamental reorientation of the total personality resulting in a new selfhood, with new goals, new drives, and new loyalties. Response and relation are key realities in this conception of the ethical life.

Contemporary discussions of Christian love as a response to the divine initiative have been greatly influenced by a study of the doctrine of Christian love, entitled *Agape and Eros*, by Anders Nygren, the Swedish bishop of Lund. In this three-volume study Nygren compared two theories of love, one rooted in Greek backgrounds and the other in the Christian tradition. According to Nygren, these two ideas of love are radically different from each other, even antithetical. By bringing the idea of Agape, or self-giving love, into a situation dominated by Eros, or self-regarding love, Christianity brought a fundamental revolution to human thinking about both religion and morality. Nygren suggested that the consequences of this revolution were not really appreciated and appropriated by the Christian community until the time of the Reformation.

It is important to understand the sharp distinction which Nygren drew between Agape and Eros, but equally important not to oversimplify or to vulgarize the distinction. Eros, which is frequently defined as "self-regarding" love must not be taken simply as earthly and sensual. Plato exemplified Eros in its thrust toward heavenly vision, a vision involving even the idea of deliverance from the purely sensual. Eros thrusts upwards to the divine, but it does so acquisitively, egocentrically, anxiously. It appears in Aristotle as well as Plato, in the neo-Platonists, and in the Greek mystery religions. "Eros is an appetite, a yearning desire, which is aroused by the attractive qualities of its object; and in Eros-love man seeks God in order to satisfy his spiritual hunger by the possession and enjoyment of the Divine perfections."[18]

Agape, on the other hand, begins in God and moves downward toward man. It transvaluates both Jewish legal piety and Hellenistic morality because it holds that God loves sinners as well as those who fulfill the law. It runs counter to the Eros-dominated piety of Greek religion because the very idea of a god who pours out himself in love for lower creatures contradicts the idea of gods who in their perfection live above the changing flux of human existence. All the dimensions of God's love, neighborly love, love for God, and self-love are transformed in Agape.

Nygren devised a tabular listing of the distinctions between the two forms of love as follows:

Eros is acquisitive desire and longing.	Agape is sacrificial giving.
Eros is an upward movement.	Agape comes down.
Eros is man's way to God.	Agape is God's way to man.
Eros is man's effort: it assumes that man's salvation is his own work.	Agape is God's grace: salvation is the work of Divine love.
Eros is egocentric love, a form of self-assertion of the highest, noblest, sublimist kind.	Agape is unselfish love, it "seeketh not its own," it gives itself away.
Eros seeks to gain its life, a life divine, immortalised.	Agape lives the life of God, therefore dares to "lose it."
Eros is the will to get and possess which depends on want and need.	Agape is freedom in giving, which depends on wealth and plenty.
Eros is primarily *man's* love; God is the *object* of Eros. Even when it is attributed to God, Eros is patterned on human love.	Agape is primarily *God's* love; God *is* Agape. Even when it is attributed to man, Agape is patterned on Divine love.

Eros is determined by the quality, the beauty and worth, of its object; it is not spontaneous but "evoked," "motivated."	Agape is sovereign in relation to its object, and is directed to both "the evil and the good"; it is spontaneous, "overflowing, "unmotivated."
Eros *recognizes value in* its object —and loves it.	Agape loves—and *creates value in* its object.[19]

The concept of Christian love set forth by Nygren is a concept in which God's grace plays the decisive and initiating role:

> For Agape it is precisely God's love, God's Agape, that is both the criterion and the source of all that can be called Christian love. This Divine love, of which the distinctive feature is freedom in giving, has its direct continuation in Christian neighbourly love, which having received everything freely from God is prepared also to give freely. Here, therefore, we have no need to try to make room for neighbourly love, nor to find any external motivation for it. It is God's own Agape which seeks to make its way out into the world through the Christian as its channel.[20]

In Nygren's view of the transformation wrought by Agape, fellowship with God is central; fellowship with the neighbor is derivative. Ethical standards come not from abstract inquiry into the nature of the good, but from the relationship of the believer to God—a relationship that provides both motivation and judgment in the determination of the ethical norm. Nygren felt that Augustine had diluted the radical character of Agape in his concept of *caritas,* which held sway over Western Christendom for several centuries, because he permitted self-love to be a part of Christian virtue. Luther, who knew that Christian love was rooted fully in God and in no other source, understood Agape in fresh terms. Speaking of Luther's views, Nygren said:

> He is perfectly aware that the love he has described is no human love. "For such love is not a natural art, nor grown in our garden." Christian love is not produced by us, but has come to us from heaven. The subject of Christian love is not man, but God Himself, yet in such a way that the Divine love employs man as its instrument and organ. The Christian is set between God and his neighbour. In faith he receives God's love, in love he passes it on to his neighbour. Christian love is, so to speak, the extension of God's love. The Christian is not an independent centre of power alongside of God. The love which he can give is only that which he has received from God. Christian love is through and through a Divine work.[21]

Siding with Luther, Nygren has argued that Christian faith declares no goodness to be valid apart from the relationship to God which is the central experience of the Christian life. No autonomy, as in Kant, which determines goodness apart from God; no *caritas*, as in Augustine, with its admixture of human self-love; no natural human love, even when caught up in divine love, as in Edwards, can qualify as Christian love, or Agape. This purest conception of Christian love is presented by Nygren as the "ground motif" of Christianity itself. Apart from the relationship of man to God— a relationship both initiated and preserved by God's grace—no goodness is possible in Christian terms.

In writing *Agape and Eros* Nygren functioned as an interpreter of the fundamental character of the Christian ethical motif, seeking to understand and explain it. Nygren's own understanding of ethical method as a whole is not encompassed by his study of the Agape motif in Christian ethics in particular. An earlier work *Filosofisk och kristen etik* (1923) shows that Nygren himself must not be clamped into the relational mold without remainder. Even so, Nygren drew such a sharp distinction between Agape and Eros that many scholars have found his treatment of Greek morality most unfair and his study basically polemical. The most extensive instance of such a criticism has appeared in the work of a Jesuit theologian, M. C. D'Arcy, who argued that these two forms of love cannot be clearly and radically separated from each other. Indeed, D'Arcy questioned the division of love into merely two forms, suggesting that it may have several expressions. Moreover, he held that there must be a capacity in man to love properly on his own if the love of God is to make contact with man at all. Nygren tends to efface the role of such love in his view of Agape as the pure form of the divine initiative. Self-love and love for God are, for D'Arcy as they were for Jonathan Edwards, interrelated. They correct each other.

> In human affairs . . . the self-regarding love, which stands for reason and judgement and watches over and commands progress in self-perfection, must ever be active and even take precedence over the love of self-effacement. We have to say, what doth it profit to save the whole world and suffer the loss of our souls? . . . Our first duty is to belong to Him from whom comes our existent self, but what seems to be the most obvious and pressing duty is to direct the steps of our own advance aright, to struggle for existence and growth and be what our inward monitor tells us we ought to be.[22]

Nygren's conception of the radically selfless character of Agape has also been criticized by J. Burnaby in *Amor Dei*[23] and by Paul Tillich in *Love, Power, and Justice*.[24]

Nygren's views have been challenged by friendly followers as well as by outright critics. Nels Ferré, who has done much to make the thinking of the Lundensian school of theology known in America, has complained that Nygren leaves aside the order of creation in relating Agape to the order of redemption. The order of creation includes many kinds of natural love, structures of justice, and points of contact with other human experiences. Ferré argues that grace, which belongs to the realm of redemption, does not destroy the human dimensions of experience, but fulfills and elevates them. Eros, no less than Agape, is a divine creation; otherwise it would not be present in human society. Erotic types of love are considered detrimental only to the extent that they become a cloak for selfishness, when they cause the self to make all other values subservient to its own concerns. Such a perversion of Eros springs from the human inclination to sin rather than from an inherent fault in one form of love.

Ferré also points out that Agape is subject to its own forms of perversion. When a person's love becomes so outpouring that he seeks to "force fellowship" or when it leads to a kind of utter selflessness that is anxious to impose itself upon others, corruptions creep in. The gushing type of reformer, concerned for everybody else, does not epitomize the best in Christian ethics. The inquisitor, who declares himself responsible for preserving unbelievers from their own false convictions, hardly demonstrates the value of a love that supposes itself to be entirely outgoing. Like D'Arcy, Ferré proposes that Christian love be understood in terms of a balance or synthesis between Eros and Agape, a balance for which he suggested the term *Philia*, or covenant love.

> It is conditional love depending upon what the other contracting partner does. It is not unconditional, like Agape. It is neither simply outpouring nor intaking love. It expects both to get and to give, both to give and to get. It is the kind of self-love and other-love which fulfills the law and the prophets, but which cannot constitute the heart of the Gospel. Philia is an attempt to balance Agape and Eros. It starts with the self and with others on the basis of justice, of equality. Nomos, law, or right relation, underlies it.[25]

Covenant love makes society possible because it includes a place for law and for the relationship of justice. But it is no less a relational concept than Agape. Three quotations set forth the relational aspect of Ferré's thought with unmistakable clarity:

> ... there can be no pure society except in faith. Faith is the response of man's depth to God's depth. Faith is the releasing of the image of God in man from its bondage to man's sin, fearfulness and pride, and the joining of it to its Source. Faith is not over and against love, but in and by love. ... Faith is the yielding of the entire self to God's will for freedom and faithfulness in fellowship.[26]

> To open up to God is to surrender without qualification to the only One who is trustworthy beyond our fullest thought or imagination. We do not want to curb and to confine this relationship to any

institutional connections, to any confession of historic creeds, to any kind of moralism of life or worship—we want only the reality itself to be the standard. Where God in Christ is, there is genuinely out-going concern, rooted in trust in the Trustworthy. . . .[27]

Ethics is situational and relational, finding its specific reality within its specific context.[28]

Ferré believes that Christian ethics can only spring from the committed and dedicated mind, from the believing heart that stands in humility before God. A genuine faith is essential to a valid ethic. While Ferré criticizes Nygren for failing to do justice to the created order and the structures of society, he criticizes other theologians, like Reinhold Niebuhr and John Bennett, for their failure to portray a "distinctive dimension of Christian ethical concern." This distinctive dimension consists of confidence in the power of God at work in the lives of those who stand in relationship to Him. The emphasis the realists place upon the social, historical, and polit-ical factors in the human situation ignores the role of God and discounts the power of the Holy Spirit. It truncates the realm of Christian action by regarding only naturalistic means of action as worthy of serious considera-tion. According to Ferré, a relational ethic can expect creative results from the power of the divine at work in the lives of men and need not limit its considerations to what can be expected of normal human decisions in a world of merely natural forces.

Ferré deals with the significance of the Holy Spirit for Christian action, but his conception of action as a relationship to the Holy Spirit also in-volves a feeling that faith in God is necessary to perceive that nature of true society defined and intended by God. Faith is therefore important for both motivation and guidance. The Christian norms of faith, hope, and love are relational in the sense that they are understood only when de-rived from response to the love of God for the world which he seeks to redeem. We derive our knowledge of the nature of love by relating to God, who is Agape. In God we understand the basic nature of true reality and the ways through which the world may relate itself to its true destiny.

Relational forms of Christian ethical thinking can employ many vocabu-laries. Each vocabulary sets forth the relational motif in a subtly different form. Joseph Sittler speaks of the "engendering deed." The work of Christ and the Old Testament portrayal of God's concern for Israel both reveal God's "will-to-restoration" for man, the action of Him who "assaults man" in holy love. The life of man and the life of God are so organically related that nothing but misunderstanding can arise by treating them separately from each other. The "engendering" deed is crucial. God is himself active in the process of decision and response about ethical mat-ters. The response is not a human decision elicited by a higher and independent love of God, but is something in which God is himself involved. The Christian ethical life is bound up, therefore, with the work and deed of God. "The kingdom of God is not a plan, or a program, or a concept, or an idea. It is a force within whose grip every man is caught; a grip never loosened, but rather having its ultimacy illustrated by every moral achievement and approximate obedience."[29]

Sittler is talking about a state or condition of life, not about a group of opinions or even a mere decision of the will. The Christian man is a new being, made new by the response engendered by the action of God in the life of the believer. Consequently, the Christian life can never be meaningful apart from God. It hinders the priority of this relation to speak of love as a principle or as a norm. Only when the love of God becomes an operative reality of existence itself rather than an ethical abstraction dare we speak of the truly Christian life. This understanding of the wholly organic nature of Christian love and the new situation of faith rules out any abstract conception of love that is developed by moral reasoning. It also rules out any codified effort to specify the content of love. All codes bind the will of God and do not require His continued and necessary relationship to every particular act. Nothing that appears in the ethical realm as a human value—love, justice, or other ideal—is valid unless it is related organically in both origin and continued relation to the divine love of God which is active in human history.

Within this scheme every moral ideal is reinterpreted in relational terms. The Commandments become a guide to the proper relationship of man to God. God makes and preserves the structural orders of marriage, property, human integrity, and human life—not as values in themselves, but as expressions of his will. The idea of justice, by itself abstract and detached, is replaced by the biblical idea of righteousness.

> . . . the biblical term *righteousness* is grounded precisely in a postulate that justice need not propose. Righteousness is a term used to designate human life sprung from, determined by, and accountable to the life of God. It is a thoroughly theonomous term. That is why, although faith-active-in-love ought to relate itself to all in human life which seeks justice, this faith can never account for itself nor be at rest with the achievements of justice.[30]

> The Hebrew term translated *righteousness* . . . means to be right, vitally related to one's source, to live in such a way as to affirm and celebrate the God from whom one has his life. That is why, in the Bible, men are called to be righteous only on the ground that God is righteous. Men are not called to an ideal, or threatened with failure to match an elevated standard of abstract goodness. They are called rather to be what they are, live their true life, realize their being in

their existence, and work out their relationships on earth in organic continuity with their relationship to the Creator.[31]

Sittler's presentation weaves together two emphases that belong to the relational motif but which are not always present together in an individual thinker. On the one hand it speaks in vivid terms of the "engendering deed," the action of God which brings into existence the motive and content of Christian behavior. It speaks of the resurrection as a sign of victory and as a present force which shapes and impels the behavior of Christians. On the other hand, Sittler's discussion takes issue with the deliberative interpretations of Christian ethics which have shaped Christian thought from the time of Harnack but which, according to Sittler, have failed to understand the engendering and relational character of the Christian experience of Christ. Sittler, therefore, joins with a host of voices in contemporary theological ethics who present the contextual character of the Christian norm as a form of response to God's active love in the lives of men.

10

Guidance from Command or Context

The relational motif is complex and varied. It can include the imitation of Christ which has been explored as a borderline expression of prescription. It surely includes belief in the engendering of an appropriate response in the faithful life of the believer. It may also include reliance upon the guidance which comes from the immediate command of God made known to faith in a particular time and place or the guidance which comes from a community of devotion or the context of particular situations.

Response to God's Commands

Exploring the implications of justification by faith for the moral life, Brunner argued that Christian morality is a matter of response to God's will as made known in each concrete situation through the authority of the Holy Spirit. A command from God is heard in each situation with a compelling clarity to the man of faith. So unique is each situation in which the command is given that men "cannot know beforehand the content of the Command. . . . [They] can only receive it afresh each time through the voice of the Spirit."[1]

Faith is central in this view of ethics. The will of God cannot be known apart from the situation of faith. No moral principle, no statement of law, no deliberation of the reason, can encompass the will of God. We may get intimations from the law and from analysis of the ways in which God's will has frequently made itself known to men in previous situations, and thus arrive at penultimate truths concerning Christian obligation—but no such insights can be permitted to define the content of God's will or to require that it be subservient to any structure of law or reason.

> The Good is simply what *God* wills that we should do, not that which we would do on the basis of a principle of love. God wills to do something quite definite and particular through us, here and now,

something which no other person could do at any other time. Just as the commandment of love is absolutely universal so also it is absolutely individual. But just as it is absolutely individual so also it is absolutely devoid of all caprice. "I will guide thee with Mine eye." No one can experience this "moment" save I myself. The Divine command is made known to us "in the secret place." Therefore it is impossible for us to know it beforehand; to wish to know it beforehand—legalism—is an infringement of the divine honour. The fact that the holiness of God must be remembered when we dwell on His love means that we cannot have His love at our disposal, that it cannot ever be perceived as a universal principle, but only in the act in which He speaks to us Himself; even in His love He remains our *Master* and Lord. But He is our "Lord" in the sense that He tells us Himself what it means to "love," here and now.[2]

In this formulation the ethical impulse is entirely dependent upon God's self-revelation of his will. "Not even an Apostle can tell you what you ought to do; God Himself is the only One who can tell you this."[3] Moreover, we can tell nothing in advance concerning the nature of God's will: "By itself ethics can decide nothing beforehand; *nothing at all*."[4] ". . . God is always bidding us do some particular thing, something which cannot be done at any other time, something quite new."[5] "The particular decision is not anticipated; it cannot be 'looked up' in the ethical law-book."[6] These categorical statements of God's freedom to make the content of his command new and fitting for each situation presuppose the utter sovereignty of God, a sovereignty that extends even to the determination of the right and the good. Man's duty is always to God, regardless of its content.

While the divine command is never subject to a requirement extrinsic to God Himself, it has the semblance of continuity and law, which the Christian can employ for penultimate guidance.

It is, of course, true that the Law, that which can be ascertained beforehand, the prescription, the "division" of the land of the future, also has a place in the Christian ethic. . . . We are not Antinomians because we do not wish to be legalists; on the contrary, it will be our duty to guard the inheritance which we have received from Zwingli and Calvin by the careful consideration of this indispensable function of the law over against a fanatical Antinomianism, a danger which actually threatened Luther himself, and since that time has been a still greater danger to a certain kind of Lutheranism. But certainly we shall have much more to say—and especially within a *Christian ethic!*—about the temporary significance of the Law, a significance which ought to be carefully restricted from many different points of view.[7]

The penultimate guidance found in the law is not to be treated lightly, even though it must always be qualified. The law is binding upon the

Christian in a secondary sort of way. "The believer finds himself involved in a curious situation: from obedience to God he has to obey the *Lex*, in spite of the fact that the latter does not express what God Himself wills."[8]

The secondary role of law in the thought of Brunner is difficult to correlate with his strong emphasis upon the uniqueness of the divine command for each particular person and circumstance. In dealing with the Sermon on the Mount, for example, Brunner had this to say:

> The Sermon on the Mount interpreted as law, and the system of ethics which is designed in accordance with this law, is of the very highest significance for the conduct of one who in faith is seeking to do the will of God—but it is not "Christian ethics."[9]

Of civil law Brunner made this observation:

> The law is always powerful according to its threefold function: as the word of discipline, repentance, and guidance. And the law which guides is the same as the civil law radically interpreted from the point of view of love, just as the civil law can only exercise its function of maintaining order, and its pedagogical function, because at the same time it is connected with the commandment of love. Thus the law exercises us at the same time in discipline, humility, and joyful childlike obedience.[10]

In his theoretical discussions of the nature of Christian ethics Brunner seemed to take the law away. When he talked about the nature of moral decision he seemed to readmit the law, though not as an instance of "Christian" guidance. Brunner criticized casuistical applications of the law, but his own use of the orders of creation as means for arriving at ethical decisions exhibits some of the very things he complained about in the casuists.

In some respects the unique command of God, subject to no structural necessity, and the guiding, or regulative, function of law come together in Brunner's concept of the "orders" of creation. These orders will be of interest to us in regard to the institutional motif, but they also are important in Brunner's thinking about the formulation of the ethical norm. While one can say nothing certain in advance about the nature of God's command, one can write about the kind of moral judgments which are implied by the orders of creation. Brunner was aware that there is always a tension between the command and the order. While we cannot in theory know the content of the command we do know the kind of general things which God is likely to command because in the orders of creation we have a glimpse of the nature of God.

> The Divine Command is not a law which hovers above our actual existence without any connexion with it; it is the command of the

God who has created our actual existence. We are not called to do something for our neighbor which is remote from and alien to his existence, but so far as we can, in what we do to him, we are to fulfill that which God means for us in this particular created order. . . .

. . . it is our duty to preserve and develop the life of our neighbour, so far as this is possible to us, according to our knowledge of the processes which maintain and enhance life; and it is our duty to serve him "in his existence as a human being," and in his "growth as a human being"—according to our knowledge of the rules which govern this existence and the growth of human life.[11]

Interpreters have differed in their estimate of Brunner's position. Many have assigned Brunner to the relational category. W. Alvin Pitcher has declared Brunner's ethics to be the ethics of the indicative rather than the imperative.[12] On the other hand, certain observers have doubted the adequacy of Brunner's break with the categories of law and imperative obligation. Hence Paul Lehmann rejects the view that Brunner belongs to the ethics of the indicative and assigns him to the imperative school. Richard Niebuhr could not bring himself to think of Brunner in relational terms and felt he overly stressed the categories of legal obligation.

There can be no doubt that Brunner declared conduct to be measured solely in terms of man's relationship to God. God acts in and through the man of faith. The man of faith enjoys a new relationship to God, expressed in terms of justification by faith and involving a quality of life rather than adherence to an external standard or an abstract norm. In this respect Brunner's treatment of ethics set forth in *The Divine Imperative* should be read in terms of his thought about revelation and faith set forth in *Revelation and Reason*.[13] Just as there is no propositional revelation, no autonomous reason prior to faith, so likewise there is no legalistic standard, no autonomous moral imperative. Faith makes the believer into a new being with new capacities for response. Only this new man can safely use law in the penultimate sense.

Brunner pioneered the contemporary effort to restate the relational features of Christian ethics as understood in the Reformation heritage. He excluded moral philosophy and codified law as legitimate channels for Christian morality. But he carried to the relational motif—and this is the root of much difficulty—terms like *command* and *law* which are common to the very kinds of ethic he rejected. Hence Brunner's ethics can be characterized as ethics of creation, stressing the orders, or as ethics of obligation. Despite all this, Brunner must be interpreted as a relational thinker and his ethic judged in that light.

Continental theology produced many contemporaries of Brunner who used somewhat different categories for stating the same basic understandings. In contrast to Brunner's heavy use of creation, Friedrich Gogarten has relied upon the category of redemption. In contrast to Brunner's emphasis upon obligation, Karl Barth has placed more weight upon freedom. But these differences pale alongside the similarities among these men. They all posit the importance of revelation and vehemently reject the validity of autonomous moral deliberation; they all derive the content of the moral norm from the will of God and somewhere in their discussion use the idea of command in connection with that will; they all stand in the Reformation heritage in which justification by faith is a central concept.

Karl Barth has scattered his observations about ethics in several places, nowhere devoting an entire work to a systematic treatment of Christian ethics. His *Church Dogmatics* concentrates most heavily upon ethical matters in volumes II/2, and III/4, but Barth insists that these volumes only discuss the ethical implications of the particular doctrinal matters central to the immediately related parts of the *Dogmatics* and that each subsequent doctrinal discussion will be followed by appropriate ethical observations. Thus he very clearly subordinates ethics to dogmatics.

Perhaps the most succinct statement about the nature of the ethical norm, as this is shaped and determined by the understanding of grace and response central to the Gospel, was prepared as an essay in the book *The Word of God and the Word of Man*, written by Barth in 1922. In this essay he declared:

> Since there is such a thing as forgiveness (which is always forgiveness of *sin!*), there is such a thing as human conduct which is justified. There is an *obedience unto salvation* which begins when we come down from our high places, from our High Place—as the moralists would apparently conceive it—and declare a thoroughgoing religious and moral disarmament. There is an effective *brotherly love* which provides a "service" different from the Christian charity with which we are familiar; it begins with our forgiving our debtors—with empty hands!— as we also are forgiven. And if there is forgiveness, there are *worse* and *better* goals: there is such a thing as conscious choice and the establishment of a definite habit for the better. There is such a thing as co-operation in the tasks of industry, science, art, politics, and even religion; *civilization* possesses its own true dignity, not as the very order of creation made manifest but as a *witness*, a quite earthly *reflection*, of a lost and hidden order—and as such it is seen neither to call for nor to be capable of sustaining any special sacredness. In brief, there is such a thing as the *possibility*—and *possibility* here means *necessity*—of saying Yes both to the ethical question and to its *answers*—and in a way not sicklied o'er with doubt and pessimism.[14]

Barth identifies himself with Paul, Luther, Calvin, and Søren Kierkegaard. These all, Barth believes, understood the paradoxical relationship of grace and response in the Christian life. But Barth is no mere parrot of other men's formulations. His own understanding of the Christian life revolves about three points: (a) man himself cannot answer the ethical question, (b) Christ does, and (c) when Christ does, the ethical dimensions of truly human existence are both authenticated and made possible without the distortions that are inevitable when the ethical question is answered by man alone. Each of these key propositions deserves separate elaboration.

Man cannot himself answer the ethical question: Logic can only investigate how things actually are, not what they ought to be. Science deals with secondary causes, with factors of contingent and external significance; not even the historical sciences can provide normative guidance. External consideration of the nature of the ethical norm is inadequate because the ethical question is fundamentally one in which man sees himself as he is seen, with every act of his life weighed in the balance. Thus, scrutiny of conduct precipitates a crisis. By asking the ethical question, man threatens to annihilate himself. The way is then prepared for grace to enter.

> In order to let him realize his own relation to him in its positive significance, that is, as love, forgiveness, life, mercy, *grace*, God waits only—if God may be said to wait—for the submissiveness which gives to him the glory due unto his name, for the penitence in which man makes an unconditional surrender, for the *desperatio fiducialis*, the confident despair in which man joyfully gives himself up for lost— joyfully, because he knows what it means to be lost in this way. The ethical question not only casts a dark shadow upon what we do in life, but lets through, at the very point where it is *darkest*, a new light.[15]

Barth takes issue with Kant, and even more with Fichte, for treating ethics as a self-authenticating aspect of human life. Whereas those who stress the autonomy of ethics take man's ability to distinguish good from evil as the glorious mark of his superiority to the animals, Barth declares this capacity to be the cause of man's separation from God. He is critical of those who have implied that ethics is an easier and self-evident foundation for the Gospel than dogma. He insists that the Epistle to the Romans describes human life with more realism than do the ideals of the Sermon on the Mount. ". . . [W]e are faced with a need and placed before questions which make us think that the difficult asseverations of the Christian dogma of the old style correspond far more closely to the actual situation than does our predecessors' confident assertion that 'following Jesus' is a simple task."[16]

Barth then holds forth Jesus Christ as the solution to the ethical question, not because he provides a moral example in the fashion of the human prototype, but because he cuts through the human form of the ethical question to show men the dynamic implications of God's grace at work in their lives. This makes him at once both the premise and the conclusion of the ethical enterprise. The breaking in from above of the salvation known and effected by Jesus Christ remakes the human situation, including its ethical dimensions. Charles West has described the consequences of Barth's outlook. Speaking of the situations given to man by God as the channels of response and responsibility, West says,

> These groupings, traditions, loyalties in which man is born are God's gifts, his dispensation (*Fügung*) for and in which man is responsible —not to the gifts!—but to God in his covenant in Christ. As an object of God's gracious election man is free over against these conditions of his existence—a pilgrim on the earth. There is not even a general commandment: *"Thou shalt speak thy mother tongue."*
> The significance of this position should not be underestimated. Barth here is giving not only a caution, but also a charter, to free, responsible, and (in a general sense unbound to any philosophical system) empirical ethical thinking in the whole field of ethics, guided only by a determination, as realistic and scientific as may be, of the social conditions at hand, and a Biblical, Christ-centered understanding of the needs of the fellow man.[17]

In Volume II/2, Barth sets forth law as a form of the Gospel, showing that the Ten Commandments are rooted in the experience of Israel's release from Egypt. In this section Barth repeats his contention that the ethical implications of God's grace at work in Jesus Christ cannot be vindicated by the criteria of a general human ethics. However, much that is found in general ethics is useful when kept in subservience to the ethics of grace. In Jesus Christ all that is humanly valid is already present, but the movement is always from that which is present in Christ toward that which man is elected to become, and not (as in Kant) from man toward God.

Law is placed in subservience to the Gospel, not simply as a penultimate matter without significant transformation, but as the very reality within which grace becomes manifest. Speaking of God's command in relationship to law, Barth wrote:

> It is true, of course, that this command also says: Do this and do not do that. But in the mouth of God this means something different. Do this—not because an outer or inner voice now requires this of you, not because it must be so in virtue of any necessity rooted in the nature and structure of the cosmos or of man, but: Do this, because in so doing you may and will again live of and by My grace. Do this, because in so doing you may make it true that your rejection has been rejected in the death of Jesus on the cross, that for His sake your sin has been forgiven. Do this, because in Jesus Christ you have been born anew in the image of God. Do it in the freedom to which you have been chosen and called, because in this freedom you may do this, and can do only this. For this, and not for any other reason, do it. You may do it. And: Do not do this—not because you again hear an outer or inner voice which seeks to make it doubtful or dreadful for you, not because there is any power in heaven or on earth to prevent or

spoil or for some reason forbid it. No, but: Do not do this, because it would be a continuation of the fall of Adam, because it would not correspond to the grace addressed to you but contradict it, because you would have to do it as the captive which you certainly are not, because you, the free man, are exempted from the necessity of doing it—really exempted by the fact that you have been made righteous and glorious in the resurrection of Jesus Christ, that you have actually been cut off by Him from this very possibility. This is how the command of God speaks.[18]

All that Barth says in relation to the command of God, about its personal and spiritual nature, about its releasing powers, about the permissions it bestows rather than the actions it precludes, about its joyful features—all this clearly places Barth in a relational motif. In Volume III/4 his emphasis upon freedom—the freedom which the command of God (unlike other commands) bestows upon the man of faith—can hardly be interpreted except in relational terms. Even though, like Brunner, Barth uses terms like *law* and *command*, he means something quite different from the traditional connotations of these ideas and especially something quite different from the meanings attached to them by men like Henry and Murray. Had Barth used different terms to convey his meaning he might have avoided some of the criticism he has shared with Brunner for not having thoroughly turned his back upon prescription.

The writings of Dietrich Bonhoeffer reflect a Barthian influence yet formulate issues with their own originality. They have attracted considerable interest in recent years, an interest prompted in part from the fact that Bonhoeffer was a heroic figure in the German resistance movement under Hitler and in part because his writings give a striking and vivid statement of Christian faith rooted intensely in a relationship to God.

The starting point for Bonhoeffer's understanding of Christian ethics is the deliverance of sinners by the power of God at work in Jesus Christ. In the early part of his *Ethics* Bonhoeffer made repeated use of the Latin phrase *Ecco homo*, or "Behold the man!" Christ is the man in whom the world was reconciled to God. No abyss of evil is beyond the power of Christ. In Christ we behold the evidence that God loves the world as it is, not the world as it might be. The guilt of mankind is borne and taken away by Christ through grief and pain, a Christ who conquers the evil of the world by the power of his resurrection.

The good news that God has become a man and has conquered over sin and death is resisted by both the wicked and the righteous individual. The wicked man is tempted to lord it over other men, to scorn the concerns of his fellow human beings. He despises the claim that God himself is at work in human affairs. The good man also succumbs to the temptation to be a despiser. He withdraws in disgust from the base realities that engulf mankind. His upright and respectable contempt for mankind, however, is not less sinful than the contempt shown by the tyrant who would control and lord it over others, exploiting them for his own purposes. But "in the face of God's becoming man the good man's contemptuous attitude cannot be maintained, any more than can the tyrant's. The despiser of men despises what God has loved. Indeed he despises even the figure of the God who has become man."[19] Even an "honestly intended philanthropism" which tries to avoid the errors of these two extremes ends by despising the real man God has loved, for it is afraid to face and acknowledge the dire condition of man—the condition which God has met in the work of Jesus Christ.

Ethics, therefore, begins with surrender. Only when men experience "formation" (we would say "conformation") to the fullness of manhood in Christ, is a new stance created which overcomes the corruptions springing from ethics pursued as a human enterprise. Speaking of this total surrender, for which Bonhoeffer used the term *discipleship,* he wrote:

> This is not achieved by dint of efforts "to become like Jesus," which is the way in which we usually interpret it. It is achieved only when the form of Jesus Christ itself works upon us in such a manner that it moulds our form in its own likeness (Gal. 4.19). Christ remains the only giver of forms. It is not Christian men who shape the world with their ideas, but it is Christ who shapes men in conformity with Himself.[20]

Discipleship is costly; it demands immediate and total obedience; it is a gift. Discipleship involves personal confrontation and loyalty; it also results in a molding of the loyal person to the wishes, desires, and image of the Master. This is done, however, not as men seek to follow and imitate Christ, but as Christ works in and through them by his power. The starting point of Christian ethics is this power of God's grace in Jesus Christ. The Christian "must from the outset discard as irrelevant two questions which impel him to concern himself with the problem of ethics, 'How can I be good?' and 'How can I do good?'; and instead of these he must ask the utterly and totally different question 'What is the will of God?' "[21] Programs as well as ideals and the abstract search for a knowledge of good and evil are also suspect.

Because the will of God is reserved to the freedom of God himself, it is not possible to know beforehand what God will desire at any given moment. Therefore, one must rely upon a continual awareness of what God wills at each new time. This is known by faith, not by postulating general principles or insights.

> The knowledge of good and evil seems to be the aim of all ethical reflection. The first task of Christian ethics is to invalidate this knowledge. In launching this attack on the underlying assumptions of all

other ethics Christian ethics stands so completely alone that it becomes questionable whether there is any purpose in speaking of Christian ethics at all.[22]

> Unlike the ethical, the commandment of God is not a summary of all ethical propositions in the most general terms. It is not the universally valid and timeless in contrast to the historical and temporal. It is not principle, as distinct from the application of principle. It is not the abstract as opposed to the concrete, or the indefinite as opposed to the definite. If it were anything of the kind it would have ceased to be *God's* commandment, for on each occasion it would then have been left to us to deduce the definite from the indefinite, the application from the principle and the temporal from the timeless. This would mean that precisely at the crucial juncture the decisive factor would no longer be the commandment, but our understanding, our interpretation and our application. The commandment of God would once again be replaced by our own choice.[23]

This commandment of God gives rise to no law, to no code, to no body of ethical teachings for perennial human guidance. Apart from the situation in which the command is given, in which the clear, irrefutable, and unquestionable guidance of God is acknowledged, ethical precepts have no place. We have moved logically away from the normal features of prescriptive law. Bonhoeffer agreed with Barth and Brunner in treating justification *sola fide* as the last and final ground of ethical decision. He even talked about the penultimate importance of the law. But the gulf he left between the ultimate and the penultimate, between the command and the law, is far greater than that supposed by Brunner. With Bonhoeffer we are moving toward a situational ethic.

Many of the themes and issues noted in Brunner, Barth, and Bonhoeffer also appear in Rudolph Bultmann in a slightly different vocabulary. The key term in this new vocabulary is *radical obedience*. It sets the demands and expectations of God in opposition to a general theory of value ethics. Obedience is rooted in the proclamation of the Word as this makes known the will of God for the moment at hand. Bultmann argues that the Kingdom of God has broken into the human situation and rendered it radically new. Men must live now as if the final judgment is at hand, calling for the very radical sort of decision which the New Testament sets forth eschatologically in its doctrine of the end. The Kingdom of God, the reality of which Bultmann presupposes in his call for radical obedience, "is that *eschatological* deliverance which ends everything earthly."[24] Because the Kingdom alters the situation of man, even though it is ultimately future in orientation, it nevertheless decisively determines the present. The Kingdom is not a human goal toward which men move in the creation of value; it is a divine act which confronts men with the need to decide for or against obedience to the divine will. The ethical life of the Christian is shaped by his response to the divine command.

Bultmann shares with Brunner, Barth, and Bonhoeffer the conviction that God's will is totally free, cannot be subsumed under the categories of human values, and confronts men with an imperative which demands obedient response. He has showed how this orientation was an essential feature of Old Testament life, a way of understanding the human situation to which Jesus was basically loyal. Jewish obedience involved knowledge of God's will—not the search for, nor grasp of, a human system of values. It derived its significance from the relation presupposed in the act of obedience, without which there was no value. In suggesting that the ethics of Jesus was essentially similar to the ethics of Judaism, Bultmann makes this observation:

> The obedience for which Jesus asks is easy, because it frees a man from dependence on a formal authority, and therefore frees him also from the judgment of the men whose profession it is to explain this authority. Such obedience is easy, because it depends on the judgment and responsibility of the one concerned. Of course from another angle it is all the more difficult. For to the weak man it is a relief to have the judgment of good and evil and all *responsibility* taken away from him. And *this* burden is just what Jesus puts upon men; he teaches men to see themselves as called to *decision*—decision between good and evil, decision for God's will or for their own will.
>
> The liberation which Jesus brings does not consist in teaching man to recognize the good as the law of his own human nature, in preaching autonomy in the modern sense. *The good is the will of God, not the self-realization of humanity, not man's endowment.* The divergence of Jesus from Judaism is in thinking out the idea of obedience radically to the end, not in setting it aside. His ethic also is strictly opposed to every humanistic ethic and value ethic; it is an ethic of obedience.[25]

The obedience of which Bultmann writes must be understood in relationship to the will of God. It is a response, in concrete and particular circumstances, to the divine word as made known to the man of faith in the situation or moment in which he finds himself. It involves the entire selfhood of the obedient man and cannot be the mere performance of predefined duty. While the obedient man may bring to his decision an awareness of standards known from the past, these must be questioned as all else is questioned in the moment of decision. The immediately, or radically, obedient man has no standards apart from his openness to God's will for him at a given time. This openness consists of trusting faith, never of certain assurance. It uses the givenness of the situation in which man finds himself, but only as the touchstone from which—or to which—the will of God is related.

. . . obedience will always take place as *decision* between concrete possibilities. However, decision means the choice to hear *one* command as the divine requirement out of the multitude of voices of concrete commands. These are *as such* never divine demands, and man can never be *certain* whether he has heard rightly. Thus Luther's *pecca fortiter, sed crede fortius* holds true.[26]

The man of faith in the situation of radical obedience is a new sort of creature. His whole being should be involved in what he is doing. His obedience must come from a fully surrendered selfhood rather than from an external compulsion to conform to rules. The fully obedient man must be prepared for the newness in the demand of the moment, since no general ethic either of value or of law can embody the will of God for this moment. Apart from the relationship which obedience entails—an existential relationship of man to God—the ethical enterprise is something other than a Christian reality. There is really no Christian ethic unless God has so acted as to make it possible for the man of faith to become radically obedient—a possibility which entails the creation of an entirely new being, a new creature reborn in Jesus Christ.

The use of terms like *law, command, divine rule,* and *obedience* in the formulations of Brunner, Barth, Bonhoeffer, and Bultmann is apt to convey implications which belong to prescriptive rather than relational understandings. The thinking of these four has greatly affected the entire contemporary discussion of Christian ethics. It has given rise to new, and perhaps more daring, statements of the significance of particular circumstances and occasions for the determination of ethical norms. The terms *situationalism* and *contextualism* have come into more frequent use, replacing terms like *law, command,* and *obedience* for describing man's relationship to God. In these more daring ways of stating the Christian norm a heavy stress is given to the guidance that can be drawn from the community of faith (the church) or from the situation and its possibilities (the context). In either case, however, the church and the context are understood as the results of God's action in history, and the moral norms drawn in response to them are ultimately expressions of faith in Him.

Guidance from Community and Context

Paul Lehmann was one of the first American theologians to advocate Christian ethics based upon the guidance drawn from community and context. In an essay published in 1953[27] Lehmann set forth his views of a *koinonia ethic,* acknowledging with great interest Brunner's effort to set forth an evangelical ethics based on the classical Reformation understanding of the Christian faith. He commended Brunner's starting point, but then declared that Brunner turned a wrong corner when he employed terms such as the command of God and the threefold use of the law. Of this fateful mistake Lehmann said,

> . . . this means that Brunner has slipped with the successors of the Reformers, even with the Reformers themselves, into that fateful retreat from the sovereign priority of grace into the traditional and deadly ordering of the ethical life *from* the law *to* the gospel. This is not good; for this means that Brunner's ethics is primarily an ethics of obligation rather than of free response (despite all that he says about responsibility as freedom-in-response). When the will of God regarded as demand overshadows the will of God regarded as gift; when obligation overshadows freedom in "unconditional obedience," then the will of God tends to be detached from its concrete context in the redemptive activity of God, and to be welded instead to the sterile and abstract uniformity of the divine law. In a word, the content of Christian ethics is, as the translator of Brunner's book rightly puts it, "the Divine Imperative." But an ethic, based upon the self-revelation of God in Jesus Christ, is more concerned about "the Divine Indicative" than it is about "the Divine Imperative." The primary question is not, "What does God command?" The primary question is "What does God do?"[28]

According to Lehmann, we must begin with the question, "What is God doing?" Therefore Christian ethics is indicative rather than imperative. The Christian will engage in disciplined reflection upon the question, "What am I to do in light of what God has done and is doing?" He will answer this question as he confronts the shifting and changing demands of each concrete situation in which he finds himself.

> The basic answer to the definitive question of Christian ethics is *the will of God*. But how we arrive at this answer is not self-evident. And when we have arrived at this answer, it is not self-evident what the will of·God is. The definitive question of Christian ethics, therefore, immediately raises two subsidiary questions: How do I know that I am to do the will of God, and, what is the will of God which I am to do?[29]

Lehmann suggests that the answers to both subsidiary questions are given through the existing Christian fellowship, or *koinonia*. (Hence the term sometimes applied to his outlook, "*koinonia* ethic.") The *koinonia* is the fellowship which has been "called into being by God." While related to the church, the *koinonia* is not to be equated with the empirical church as such. The *koinonia* works together with Jesus Christ as its Lord. In it men find the meaning of the Gospel and the purpose of life. The fellowship provides the ethical guidance; it is the structure of loyalty to which the Christian is committed. It does not furnish a set of unchanging principles, but a living community of felt responsibility. Its guidance is concrete, particular, dependent upon what is available in its present life, and related to the facts of each particular case. Apart from knowledge of the particular circumstances related to each case little guidance is possible. The guidance from the *koinonia* is, therefore, contextual. "When ethical reflection is pursued in the context of the Christian *koinonia*, the method and materials of ethics acquire a concrete and contextual character. *A koinonia ethic is concerned with relations and functions, not with principles and precepts.*"[30]

Since the *koinonia* is the result of God's activity, set forth indicatively rather than imperatively, it is closely related to the biblical drama and is concerned to proclaim the mighty acts of God's love as expressed in both the covenant with Israel and the creation of the church as the new Israel. Morality becomes a communal rather than an individual matter. In the community men come to see the will of God that they are to do, not only as a group but as individuals within the group. When the understandings of God's will which have come from the group in the past, such as the double commandment of love for God and love of neighbor, become abstract imperatives, replacing the indicative known in the fact that God has established a beachhead of forgiveness in the world, they cease to have significant Christian meaning. Reconciliation rather than moral exhortation is the key mood of Christian response; maturity rather than correctness is the truest achievement of the Christian man of faith. While reconciliation and maturity are best prompted by the indicative declaration of what God is doing,

> The "ought" factor cannot be ignored in ethical theory. But the "ought" factor is not the primary ethical reality. The primary ethical reality is the human factor, the *human* indicative, in every situation involving the interrelationships and decisions of men. In the *koinonia* something is already going on, namely, what God is doing in the situation out of which the ethical question and concern arise to fashion circumstance and behavior according to his will.[31]

As a relationalist, of which he is a special type, Lehmann excludes the deliberative and prescriptive approaches. He does so, however, only after an appreciative appraisal of moral philosophy, which is deliberative, and moral theology, which is casuistical. In an extensive analysis Lehmann concludes that moral philosophy cannot take adequate account of the predicament of man, a predicament in which knowledge of the good does not necessarily result in the inclination to follow the good. Moral theology does raise the problem of conscience and seeks to deal with motivation and impulse. However, a deeper investigation shows that conscience is trained and determined by a context, such as found in the *koinonia*. Without such a context, moral theology proves quite as inadequate in creating the impulse to moral behavior as does moral philosophy.

Contextualism, which is attracting much current attention, has appeared in variant forms. Joseph Fletcher[32] makes many of the points emphasized by Lehmann, but he makes a place for Christian love as a central, ultimate, and intrinsically valid norm, a procedure which stands in some contrast with Lehmann's observation that "A *koinonia* ethic, therefore, defines the will of God as forgiveness and justice and reconciliation, rather than as love."[33] Whereas Lehmann rejects moral philosophy and its casuistry, Fletcher is willing to include casuistry, or neo-casuistry, within a contextualist approach. When such a casuistry is case-focused and concretely oriented, Fletcher considers it a ready handmaiden to a situational ethic. The only condition Fletcher imposes is that love alone be the constitutive principle and that the casuistical decision be clearly understood to have only regulative significance.

Fletcher sets the classical approach in contrast to what he takes to be the new approach in Christian ethics:

> . . . in the past Christian moralists have first elaborated the ideals of the faith (Christian ethics), then they have formulated some "middle axioms" or working principles tailored to take account of the relativities of life and man's imperfections (moral theology), and finally they have tried to "apply" their prefabricated rules to life by imposing them from above life and before the event (casuistry).
>
> But now, in this method defended here, we turn that process hindsideto; we start with the situation empirically and inductively in all its contextual particularity, then we attempt to hammer out a few tentative working principles "generally" valid, and only in the end, in an even more open way, do we refer in fear and trembling to the ideal. And of the ideal itself we see but one principle, a monolithic norm or standard against which every other principle has to be checked in the concrete situation. The one judge is "agapeic" love.[34]

Gordon D. Kaufman has explored the several contexts in which decisions are made: they are made within a metaphysical context, in which the relationship between man and the ultimate reality with which he deals is important; they are made in a sociological context, in which the church and the world help to shape the nature of decision; they are made in personal-biographical contexts, unique for each individual. Kaufman carefully avoids making any one of these contexts the only legitimate or significant source of guidance, though he interprets the functions of all three in contextualist terms. In commenting upon the meaning of the ethical task, Kaufman has this to say:

> Man's proper role in life is here assigned him by God; human life finds its true meaning so far as it is a fulfillment of the purposes of God. But since [in the Bible] God is conceived as living and personal—and not as the impersonal structure of nature, as in naturalism—it is not possible to define laws of conduct or right action (corresponding to

laws of nature) which hold once and for all. Rather, right action here will simply be living-as-a-person-in-community with God, on the one hand, and one's fellow men, on the other. To live in community, it should be evident, involves much more than merely following out some pattern of absolute values or ideals or laws which have once for all been laid down as norms of conduct. To live in community is to live in *responsiveness* to the other persons in the community, to listen when they speak and to answer honestly and relevantly and significantly, to minister to their needs and to allow them to minister to yours. In short, it is to be a living and responsive *thou* to their *I*'s.

From this point of view the task of ethics is not the isolating of some ultimate standard of right and wrong, then insisting on conformity to that standard. Rather, the concern here is to be responsive to the voice of the living God as he confronts and speaks to us in every moment, to live as human persons before this supreme Person, that is, to act creatively and freely in every moment in response to his will for that moment. In short, it is to enter into community with God and his other creatures, or to use the biblical symbol, it is to participate in the kingdom of God.[35]

Kaufman's discussion is of special interest because it argues a contextualist position from within basic allegiance to the Mennonite tradition. It opens the possibility of a Christian pacifist witness taken on contextualist grounds; it seeks to interpret the role of the Mennonite witness in a contrasting manner to the prescriptive understanding of biblical law often present in sectarian movements.

Albert Terrill Rasmussen, writing with a major interest in the decision-forming function of the community, and the ways in which the Christian should exert his influence in community, has declared,

We repeat that love is social and relational at its very heart—it is a gift that no man can create. Community, at the deepest levels, is the instrument of its generation and transmission. Christians receive love as they become parts one of another in the one body in Christ. Then and only then can they even begin to love God and serve Him, love their neighbor in some measure of self-forgetfulness, and seek his good.[36]

Because love is "social and relational" Rasmussen feels that each Christian decision must be made in light of the concrete particulars that surround it. Each decision is made as a unique instance and present factors demand fresh consideration. It involves unique encounter.

Divine ethical guidance is available to the Christian, not in the form of literal Biblical directives of ideal solutions, but in the action of God Himself upon us and upon the situation. We do not carry ready-made directives with us into a decisional situation except as a self orientated to Christ and with a sensitive responsiveness to God developed in Christian community. On the contrary, we must first plunge into the situation in confronting its pressures and its cross claims and then be prepared to respond to God and the restraints and possibilities that He opens before us. This does not mean that a Christian goes into a situation with no principles, no categories, and no memories. Without these he could not understand the situation or respond significantly. He carries with him his whole self with its present perspectives, its cherished values, its definitions of right and wrong.[37]

Alexander Miller took the idea of the *koinonia* as a cumulative inheritance of understanding. This cumulative resource is helpful in decision-making, argued Miller, even though it does not prescribe specific commands. Here is Miller's own description of Christian decision-making:

Christian ethics differ from idealistic ethics in that the absolute is an absolute loyalty and not an absolute principle, while the Christian calculation differs from typical pragmatism in that, while there is always a hidden absolute in pragmatism, an unadmitted presupposition about what is good for man, in the Christian scheme the calculation is grounded in a very precise understanding of what is good for man, determined by the revelation of God in Christ. "Live life, then," says St. Paul, "not as men who do not know the meaning and purpose of life but as those who do."[38]

In discussing the relationship of faith and the ethical question, Clyde A. Holbrook suggests that the man of faith first asks what God is doing to sustain and redeem the situation in which he finds himself at a given and particular time. Having arrived at some glimpse of the divine initiative, the man of faith then asks what he, or his group, should do. Hence, the man of faith asks,

"What ought and can be done here and now which, at least in some fragmentary fashion, will be both a response to the divine sustenance, judgment, and redemption and the concrete need before me?" This is to say that a man of faith, in gratitude, puts himself responsibly and sensitively at the disposal of God's will for a situation, to the limits of his reason, imagination, and courage. He does not presume to read off in advance what God wills in detail, nor does he assume that he will be miraculously safeguarded from errors of discrimination. He does not cast into an artificially wooden scheme the ambiguous particulars of a morally problematic situation. But he does hold himself alert and responsive to what God lays upon him through his neighbor's need. He has mercy, because God is merciful to him. He forgives, because he lives in forgiveness. He seeks justice, because God's judgment upon him is just. He loves, because God first loved us. Thus the indicative gives the foundation of moral attitudes and actions by arousing in us gratitude, but the specific needs determine the structure and relevant content of our acts.[39]

James Gustafson has had a good deal to say about Christian ethics as a contextualist response to situations. He has insisted that the church must act where it finds itself in the world. Gustafson assumes contextualism, not only as a theological position, but as a working premise for keen social analysis.

> Christian social ethics must analyze social action in the sociological sense. The possibility of effective moral action in society depends upon careful analysis of the social process and system. The moralist must know the patterns of personal and institutional interrelationships within which he seeks to develop purposive change. . . .
>
> Social action in the intentional moral sense must be grounded in knowledge of how decisions are made in the centers of social power. Effective moral action depends upon astute and accurate analysis of the social system in general and of the problem situation in particular.[40]

Jan Milič Lochman of the Comenius Protestant Theological Seminary in Prague has developed a treatment of contextualist ethics related to the problems of living as Christians under a Communist-dominated state.[41] He emphasizes the importance of the historical situation in which ethical decision must be made and the legitimacy of taking into account the limitations implicit in certain situations. In a formal sense Lochman's argument sounds like that of many contextualists, but it has its own nuances which spring from the situation out of which he writes.

We cannot be exhaustive. The examples chosen illustrate a tendency rather than describe a movement in detail. The contemporary discussion is broad and full, but it is not clear that any works of profoundly enduring significance have emerged from it. There are bound to be new and helpful explorations of these themes from men of many theological traditions and geographical locations but it is not clear that the future of Christian ethics will be dominated entirely by this approach. The criticism of relational and contextualist ethics has begun, and can be expected to mount in degree as contextualist and situational forms of Christian ethics become increasingly well known and the problems which they pose, as well as the contributions they make, are recognized with greater clarity.

This concludes the discussion of norms and their formulation. In the next part of the book attention will be directed toward the implementation of ethical decisions. There are those who would question the distinction between norms and strategies upon which this analysis is built. Such an objection would be fair and just if the division were so presented as to suggest a temporal sequence through which all Christians move, determining first their ideals and then applying them. In many situations norms arise from the process of acting; sometimes actions are taken and are then scrutinized in the light of normative questions. But it is difficult to talk about both elements at once, and these matters are most easily discussed when they are separated for the purpose of analysis. In distinguishing between the formulation of norms and the implementation of decisions, we are not requiring assent to that particular view of their interrelationship which always regards the latter as subsequent and subservient to the former. We are simply dividing into two segments the discussion of matters which often run together in the actualities of life.

III
The Implementation of Ethical Decisions

Section A: The Institutional Motif in Christian Ethics

II

Law, Order, and the Catholic Tradition

Discussions of Christian social policy have been dominated for years by formulations made by Ernst Troeltsch. He drew a contrast between a church-type and a sect-type of social policy. The church-type "takes up into its own life the secular institutions, groups, and values which have arisen out of the relative Natural Law,"[1] whereas, the sect-type takes its outlook "purely from the Gospel and from the Law of Christ [and holds that] the Christian character and holiness of this ideal should be proved by the unity reigning within the group and by the practical behaviour of the individual members, and not by objective institutional guarantees."[2] While it has not figured as largely in the discussions, Troeltsch also wrote of a third type, the mystical, which concentrates upon the vertical relationship of the individual to God. This does not produce a social policy since "mysticism lays no stress at all upon the relation between individuals, but only upon the relations between the soul and God."[3]

Troeltsch confessed that the purity of his historical types had been seriously qualified by modern developments. "The days of the pure Church-type within our present civilization are numbered,"[4] he wrote, thinking perhaps of twentieth-century tendencies which alloyed the church pattern with aspects of the sect temper and even of mystical individualism. The careful American reader who turns to Troeltsch's exhaustive list of distinctions between the church and the sect[5] will find himself hard put to take either category as the adequate description of an American denomination.

Troeltsch's main distinction between the church and the sect distinguishes between those who relate to the culture, using it for the accomplishment of Christian ends, and those who separate themselves from the culture because they deem it corrupting. It focuses attention on the contrast between a modification of the norms of the Gospel through the use of a relative natural law and a stringent obedience to the requirements of the Gospel as presented by the New Testament. The problem of compromise versus withdrawal, basic in Troeltsch's categories, remains perennial in matters surrounding the implementation of Christian norms, but this polarity cannot be used for the analysis of contemporary possibilities without reservations and modifications. Indeed, it may even obscure basic differences in ways of embracing the world throughout Christian history.

Troeltsch's church-type should be divided so as to show a distinct difference between an embrace of culture in terms of structures of justice and order and an embrace of culture in terms of the exercise of power and influence. In one understanding of Christian strategy in the world, institutional features are uppermost. Acceptance of authority and the legal procedures of due process are felt to promise the greatest resource for exercising social responsibility. In another understanding the exercise of power and influence is deemed vital, and Christians feel concerned about the push and pull of conflicting vitalities rather than about the legally defined relationships which preserve law and order. Words like democracy, the state, politics, and even the family are understood differently when viewed as structures of justice and order than when conceived as arenas of conflict in which balances of power result in tolerable harmonies.

On the other hand, the processes which Troeltsch described separately under the sect-type and the mystical-type have tended to converge and can be spoken of together as examples of an intentional motif. In this pattern for implementing Christian decision, special communities of dedication and renewal are created, communities which practice withdrawal from the world, either for the sake of gathering strength to return and minister to it or for the sake of preserving the high visibility of their own moral accomplishments. Such communities have taken many forms but have been present in practically every era of Christian history.

Structures of Justice and Order: The Institutional Motif

Any thinker may rightly be interpreted in terms of the institutional motif if: (a) the importance he attaches to the organizational control of power is greater than the importance he attaches to power as the means by which organization is maintained; (b) he counsels obedience to existing authority because the authority commands intrinsic respect, not merely because it can coerce subservience; (c) he believes that holding an "office" or "role" calls for actions which are different from what the individual would perform acting by himself in bondage to the Gospel ethic of love; or (d) he considers given existing orders, such as the state, to be created by God for the expression of Christian concern even though ambiguity and sin are involved in the use of such orders in order to attain particular objectives.

In the beginning of the third book of *The Divine Imperative* Emil Brunner turned his attention from the nature of the Divine Command to the spheres of existing reality in which the Command is to be carried out. Brunner spoke of "the particular spheres of life within which we are to act," and asserted that they are given to men from the divine will which governs the world. He continued:

> Each of these spheres of life, with its "orders," presents itself to us first of all as a definite way of common life, as a form of social organization; it is our task to discover the meaning of this existing reality, and this means, to find the meaning of community. The third book deals with the following questions: What is real "community" within each of these social "orders"? Thus, what is the Creator's intention for these orders? What does it mean to live within them in love, as an individual? And how ought love to express itself within them?[6]

The given realities of which Brunner spoke are institutions of human organization normally found within the communal life of man. They should not be conceived in purely governmental or narrowly political terms, since the "orders" or institutions of which Brunner spoke are much broader in scope and purpose than any political symbol can represent. They include such things as the biological distinctions between man and woman, which result in the institution of marriage; the elementary needs of men for minimal subsistence and their quest for the more affluent society, which bring forth economic institutions; and the dimensions of community and personal enrichment, which are served by cultural institutions.

There are many words pointing to the realities to which Brunner refers. Brunner, of course, preferred the term *orders* and his usage is justified even by the English phrases "the economic order," "the political order," and, much less often, "the sexual and cultural orders." Other men, inspired by Augustine, employ the term *city*, or *polis*, but this gives an overly political flavor to what is implied and thereby introduces a greater degree of the coercive element than would be characteristic of such cultural realities as family, schools, and concert halls. Other theologians have used terms like *mandates* and *spheres* to denote the world and its procedures, the culture and its resources, within which they feel Christians should be willing to institutionalize their decisions.

What essential features characterize institutions? One quality is concreteness. An institution has a form to which one can point, saying, "Here are its characteristic and essential structures. This is how it stands. Here is how it works." It is not quite adequate to use the term *tangible* in this connection, for the concrete character of an institution is not its physical extension. One cannot touch a social institution in the same way one can handle a piece of fruit, but surely the reality of a constitutional order, the given features of sexual differentiation, the actualities of economic process, and the fruits of cultural attainments are concretely evident—observable, real, and enduring. We can tell when they are present, when absent. We can see them at work as well as notice the consequences flowing from them. They endure beyond the temporal constituency which composes them at any particular moment; the institutions of the presidency can survive the assassination of one incumbent; a monarchy can change hands; a constitutional government endures even though political parties take turns as dominant agents of its operation.

An institution involves a system of control, often specifying the possible ways in which actions can be undertaken, decisions reached, ends sought. It embodies accepted channels of action, limits of authority, and checks upon those who would exceed the bounds. Different behavioral responsibilities and possibilities are open to the adult than to the child; different functions in marriage for the woman than for the man. Similarly, there are different possibilities open to citizens of a constitutional democracy than are open to citizens of a totalitarian dictatorship or to members of an outlawed revolutionary group. Social change and social controls are functionally different in situations of institutional stability than they are in situations in which there is no accepted procedure to which the majority of men loyally repair.

Not only is an institution concrete, but it is also basically communal, always involving more than one person in its operation. The most intimate social institution is the family, which is consummated around the conjugal features of the sexual relationship and the intimate responsibilities for the rearing of children which are born as a consequence of this relationship. Similarly, the corporate features of the state, cultural attainments in the arts and sciences, and the functioning of economic processes depend upon groups. Even proponents of rugged individualism in economics speak of a social system within which the individual may struggle to attain his goals. Without the market even the staunchest advocate of free competition would be unable to justify his theory of the price system. Hence, believing as he does in the role of the orders, Brunner observed, "we regard life in community, and not the life of the individual, as the concrete realization of the moral ideal."[7]

The individual does not dictate to the institution the conditions under which he can choose to relate himself to it. In some cases the individual cannot even choose whether or not to belong, but finds himself automatically included in the communities of which he is a part. In other cases he finds that, having chosen, he cannot easily and readily break away from his accepted obligations. An individual does not choose his ancestry or his ethnic identification. He has very little to say about the economic order under which he lives or the state to which he is forced by circumstance to render allegiance. To be sure, he can work to change the economic order; he can work to change the state—in some instances. He can seek to find another means of livelihood, but it will seldom be supported by an entirely different set of economic processes. He can seek to become a citizen of another state, but the more likely that a state permits voluntary defection the more likely it is to be a state to which allegiance is desirable. Moreover, while men can change their allegiance in some cases from one institution to another, once they relate themselves to a particular institution they are bound to work with given elements within it. As Sidney Cave observed,

> Some choices we can make, but we did not choose the family into which we were born, the economic order of our time and place, nor the nature of the State to which we owe allegiance. These communities belong to the "givenness" of life. They are anterior to our power of choice; we do not begin as individuals, and then become the voluntary members of communities. We belong to family and nation before we have any individual life, and our personalities develop in environments which are not of our making. We are born not "man," but either male or female.[8]

It is important to avoid a doctrinaire conception of this givenness of institutions. Each institution must be scrutinized as a separate case. There is more inevitability about the given features of manhood and woman-hood than about the nature of vocational choice or the form of the political order. The degree to which particular institutions are rigid and inflexibile varies from case to case, even in the same sort of institution. Theological systems can easily err by overly emphasizing the ordained and given quality of the orders. They have consequently often abetted the perpetuation of institutions that not only could have been, but should have been, changed. On the other hand, radical religious impulses have fostered contempt and even disregard for these realities. This occurred, for example, in some of the individuals espousing the left wing of evan-gelical enthusiasm. It occurs today in those occasional individuals whose radical idealism leads them to demand a perfection not possible in existing institutions.

Some institutions are more "given" than others. Some are created by social decisions consciously made by a group of individuals; others seem to exist prior to the individuals who belong to them. In commenting upon these matters Werner Elert has judiciously balanced the permanent and the temporary, the given and the fabricated, aspects of institutions in the following description of their role in the affairs of men:

> The orders of life are of either permanent or temporary validity. The relationship that results from an occasional encounter often belongs in the latter category. The good Samaritan and his protégé

were brought into a relationship that continued from the moment the Samaritan noticed the victim until they parted. Lasting orders may be entered by the deliberate choice of the participants, for instance in a marriage or a business partnership. Other orders claim us without our explicit consent—our race, our national background, our citizenship. Nation and state occupy a special place in this connection because their existence exceeds the life span of the individual. They call for a sense of communal responsibility besides the responsibility which one individual has for another. We designate orders of this kind "communities" (*Verbände*). A community comes into existence when a number of individuals decide to band themselves together for some definite purpose. The character of such a community depends upon the purposes of its members. Such an organization can be chronologically limited. A community may also be in existence before an individual is born into it and continue after his death. It is then no longer subject to the decisions which an individual makes with regard to it.[9]

Not only are "orders" or "institutions" concrete (but not tangible), given (but not unchangeable), but they are also related in a peculiar way to the problem of values. We could uncover a host of difficulties by describing them as functionally neutral with respect to values, but properly interpreted the phrase does contain an element of truth. As a class or a genus, institutions do not necessarily embody particular values, even though individual institutions may lend their support to particular goals. The category of the state, for example, taken as a genus may well be said to be functionally neutral with respect to values, but any particular state may very well exercise strong dominion within its sphere of influence for or against particular ends. The word *ambiguous* is better, since it expresses more directly the possibility of either good or evil consequences, the possibility of both positive and negative implications, even at the same time.

Theological terms like *orders, mandates,* or *institutions* cannot be equated with the sociological term *structures*. Translation by substitution is impossible. Institutions have both structural and functional features. Hence we will be talking about both structural and functional realities when discussing the institutional motif. But despite the differences in terminology there are some correlations between the categories of theologians and those of social scientists. In his textbook on sociology R. M. McIver[10] discusses many of the issues dealt with in this analysis. Under the general heading of the organization and function of social structures, he investigates the nature of community and speaks of what he calls the institutional complex. He treats the family in a chapter by itself, followed by a chapter dealing with "The Great Associations," which are concerned with political, economic, and cultural institutions, with the church included among the cultural associations. If one compares this division of the material to that of several books in Christian ethics which use the term *orders* (or its equivalent), the similarity in categories becomes striking. In Bonhoeffer we meet these "mandates": labor, marriage, government, and the church. In Brunner the "orders" include: marriage, labor, government, culture, and the church. In Sidney Cave: marriage, industry, the state, and (in an epilogue) the church. Clinton Gardner, who also uses the concept of orders for the discussion of basic problems in the application of Christian norms speaks of sex and marriage, love and justice, economics, politics, and race. The latter category, which is paralleled in McIver by a chapter on class and caste, would seem to appear more often in American writings. Whatever the differences in the ways in which the realities are grouped or in the ways in which they are interpreted by these various writers, the same kinds of reality are chosen for discussion.

Even the most conservative views of the orders—which picture them as the precondition of human relationships under law—cannot be understood simply as static views of social reality. The interplay between the structural and the functional elements in the concept of "orders" is reflected even in a passage from Emil Brunner which emphasizes the conserving function of the orderly structure.

> Since the one thing that matters is that the orders should be *real* forces for the preservation of order, and therefore unceasingly operative, man's first duty—even as a Christian—is the obedient acceptance and preservation of the present, existing order—however imperfect, rough and "loveless" it may be. For, at the moment, this order is the only dam which prevents the irruption of the forces of chaos, because it alone is a *real* order. The only kind of order which would be better than the present one would be an order which could replace it immediately, without any break in continuity.[11]

The functional nature of institutional reality is presupposed in Paul Ramsey's argument that private property is subject to judgment in terms of the uses to which it is put in relationship to the needs of the neighbor. Private property placed in use for the public service, such as an inn or restaurant, must particularly be treated in terms of its function. "The definition of such property right should itself contain an indissoluble and *unavoidable* connection between my ownership and the good of all men who in time come to that spot with needs I have so used my property as to be able to provide for."[12]

The meaning of the institutional motif may be made more vivid, perhaps, through the use of a case study in the implementation of Christian charity, drawn from an account of the East Harlem Protestant Parish.

> An old man was struck down by a coal truck that was trying to beat the signal lights. Don Benedict saw the accident. His first impulse was

to pick up the bleeding man, put him in a cab and drive at once to the hospital. That would have made him literally a Good Samaritan. But he knew that such action was illegal. The law stated that injured people might not be removed. The only thing to do was to try and make him comfortable, to call an ambulance, and to keep the crowd back. Fifteen minutes went by. Thirty minutes passed. When an hour had gone the man had ceased to moan. After an hour and thirty-seven minutes the ambulance arrived. The man died on the way to the hospital.[13]

It is one thing to be a Good Samaritan in rural Palestine, in the terms of the relatively simple biblical imagery of helping a dying man to the local inn and providing for his care until recovery. It is another thing to become the Good Samaritan within the structural and legal tangles of a complex city. To be sure, the ambulance might have arrived much sooner, and its skillful ministrations might have saved a life which inept attention would have jeopardized. The law is written, in part, to discourage well-intentioned but unskilled people from doing harm to those they seek to help. While in this case the institutional complex was a cumbersome obstruction to charity, it is conceivable that in other cases it would become a definite asset, the very channel of the necessary care.

Following the tragic event in which the bleeding man died because the ambulance service was slow, the Group Ministry of the East Harlem Parish reconsidered their responsibilities for the implementation of Christian charity. They devised a campaign to obtain better police protection for their area, designed to prevent coal trucks from crashing the signal lights. They might also have pressured for better ambulance service, even for repeal of the law forbidding spontaneous and personal assistance for injured people. All such efforts, but especially the first two, would have expressed different ways of institutionalizing the meeting of human need. Moreover, the effort to obtain better police protection was based upon an acceptance of the remedial possibilities within the political structures of the city. Had the ministers advocated the creation of a vigilante group to police the area inadequately protected by city forces, they would have resorted to another pattern for implementing their concerns. They would also have adopted another pattern had the tragic experience with the city ambulance caused them to remove themselves to an agrarian context in which the rural imagery of the original parable of the Good Samaritan could be applied more directly and in kind. To be sure, in seeking better police protection a campaign of political pressure was employed, but the fundamental conviction which informed such a campaign was a hope for the proper functioning of institutionalized protection. These ministers stood in a long tradition of Christian willingness to turn to institutional safeguards as an implementation of Christian moral impulse.

Institutionalism in the Catholic Tradition

Saint Augustine is one of the first major Christian thinkers to create a theological underpinning for a Christian concern about the world and its institutions. He wrote approximately a century after the recognition of the Christian church by the Emperor Constantine, as the political disintegration of the Roman Empire raised new questions about the value of the alliance between Christianity and the Empire—an alliance which emerged as a consequence of that recognition. He wrote as a theologian, with sweeping inquiry into fundamental problems surrounding the relationship of faith to reason, of freedom to grace, of worldly vitalities to divine providence. Many different understandings of the Christian faith, and particularly understandings about the relationship of the Christian to his ethical duty in respect to the world, cite the thinking of Augustine as the acknowledged source of inspiration. Recalling that Whitehead felt Western philosophy to be a series of footnotes to Plato, Daniel D. Williams has remarked that "theology in Western Christianity has been a series of footnotes to Augustine."[14]

The influence of Augustine has been both widespread and varied. His thinking about the two cities, the city of this world and the city of God, greatly influenced institutional and organizational features of the great medieval synthesis and its theory of the two swords. His political thinking has inspired contemporary Christian "realists" who see political responsibility in terms of power and influence and who urge Christians to accept the duties of citizenship in the harsh realities of a coercive world. His thinking about sex may have had a not inconsiderable influence in the development of Western monasticism, which provides a Roman Catholic expression of the separatist motif. Indeed, a good deal of Christian thinking about ethical issues (but certainly not all of it!) may well be considered in terms of the contrasts between several readings of St. Augustine. It is important, therefore, that we review Augustine's thought in relationship to the implementation of ethical decisions. We may characterize its main thrusts, explore its implications, and show why it has—by its own ambiguities—inspired different readings of its implications. We shall be particularly interested in the institutional and operational motifs as these appeal to Augustine as mentor.

The most important, but not the only, work for understanding Augustine's outlook toward the Christian's response to the world is his City of God. Augustine's thinking is based upon the contrast between two cities. One of these is the city of this world, based upon love of man for himself, finding satisfactions in its own achievements, ruled by princes who love their possession of power, delighting in its own strength, possessed of human wisdom and pride, and doomed to eventual extinction. The other city is the heavenly one, based upon the love of man for God, finding its glory in obedient service to God, duly worshiping its Creator, and permanently enduring as a company of holy angels as well as holy men.[15] The two cities have been described as the temporal stage versus the eternal abode. Moreover, in the world the two cities are intermeshed and interacting, so that the Christian must sojourn in the one while his ultimate loyalty is rooted in the other. The burden of citizenship in the earthly city is a consequence of sin; the promise of healing within the heavenly city is the expression of grace. The pagan man knows only the first, with its trials and heartaches; the Christian knows both.

It is because the Christian knows both the promise of the heavenly city and the harsh, yet necessary, realities of the earthly city, that he must come to grips with the tension between these two realities. Domestic peace, insured by the just rule of the earthly father, is a prototype for the rule of the civic order: ". . . the well-ordered concord of domestic obedience and domestic rule has a relation to the well-ordered concord of civic obedience and civic rule."[16] Just as the father must use correction by word or blow, so society may use punishments and correction to insure civic harmony. Christians share in the life of these orders; but there is a difference between the Christian and the pagan embrace of the earthly city.

> . . . the families which do not live by faith seek their peace in the earthly advantages of this life; while the families which live by faith look for those eternal blessings which are promised, and use as pilgrims such advantages of time and of earth as do not fascinate and divert them from God, but rather aid them to endure with greater ease, and to keep down the number of those burdens of the corruptible body which weigh upon the soul. Thus the things necessary for this mortal life are used by both kinds of men and families alike, but each has its own peculiar and widely different aim in using them. The earthly city, which does not live by faith, seeks an earthly peace, and the end it proposes, in the well-ordered concord of civic obedience and rule, is the combination of men's wills to attain the things which are helpful to this life. The heavenly city, or rather the part of it which sojourns on earth and lives by faith, makes use of this peace only because it must, until this mortal condition which necessitates it shall pass away. Consequently, so long as it lives like a captive and a stranger in the earthly city, though it has already received the promise of redemption, and the gift of the Spirit as the earnest of it, it makes no scruple to obey the laws of the earthly city, whereby the things necessary for the maintenance of this mortal life are administered; and thus, as this life is common to both cities, so there is a harmony between them in regard to what belongs to it.[17]

Augustine discussed these two cities in an extensive historical context. The first three books of the treatise look at the fall of Rome and explain why the Christians cannot be held responsible for this turn of events; the next six books examine the fundamental philosophical differences between ancient paganism and the Christian faith, between Greek Platonism and the transformation wrought by Christian faith upon the categories of the philosophers. With the eleventh book we come to the primary argument, still however, in heavy theological terrain. Augustine traced the conflict of the two cities from Creation itself. The earthly city has its origin in the Fall, which was rooted in human disobedience. Subsequent tensions between the two cities result in the drama of creation within which God is working out his purposes. Augustine used several chapters (from fifteen through eighteen) to deal with the history of the relationship of the two cities from Cain and Abel through the work of Jesus Christ. With the beginning of the nineteenth book we are introduced to the more concentrated discussion of the purposes which are served by these two cities. The final three books deal with the end of history, or eschatology, in terms of which the tension between the two cities comes finally to a resolution.

While it is necessary to interpret *The City of God* as a whole, any more detailed grasp of its myriad generalities must be left to other studies. We must inquire only about one basic issue: How did Augustine view the civic world which he commended to the Christian community as a necessary place of temporary abode and to which he looked for the implementation of many (but not all) aspects of Christian decision? We have already indicated that he saw the earthly city in terms of the family pattern, with domestic harmony the prototype for civic harmony. We have also suggested that the Christian is concerned in a penultimate sense with the harmony of the civic order, even though he has the vision of a higher harmony in the heavenly order. We might have mentioned Augustine's willing use of the civil state for the punishment of the Donatist heretics. Moreover, in his controversy with the Donatists—who felt the state to be utterly diabolical—he had several things to say about the role of kings and the service to God that is to be rendered through their office.

It is, therefore, possible to find in Augustine most of the necessary foundations upon which to build an institutional motif. Augustine frequently affirmed the inevitability of a commonwealth in the conduct of human affairs. He would have united families into states, even states into a family of states. Augustine frequently argued that Christians should accept the civic order, even the responsibility for conducting the necessary wars upon which it depends for its continued existence. In a letter to Marcellius he wrote:

> Let those who say that the doctrine of Christ is incompatible with the State's well-being, give us an army composed of soldiers such as the doctrine of Christ requires them to be; let them give us such

subjects, such husbands and wives, such parents and children, such masters and servants, such kings, such judges—in fine, even such tax-payers and tax-gatherers—as the Christian religion has taught that men should be, and then let them dare to say that it is adverse to the State's well-being; yet rather let them no longer hesitate to confess that this doctrine, if it were obeyed, would be the salvation of every commonwealth.[18]

Figgis listed several features of Augustine's thought on political matters which can only be interpreted in terms of the institutional motif. He claims that Augustine clearly called for the organized state, that he saw law as the consequence of consent rather than as the expression of mere force, that he claimed justice to be a necessary ingredient within the accomplishments of any state which has internal legitimacy. But Figgis also pointed out several places at which Augustine's political outlook qualified the institutional motif. Not only is the *civitas terrena* clearly accorded a secondary place, being the accomplishment of the reprobate, but Augustine's assessment of all existing governments and empires was bluntly realistic about the basis upon which they maintained order. In speaking of the order which characterizes the earthly city, Augustine had this to say:

> . . . the earthly city, which shall not be everlasting (for it will no longer be a city when it has been committed to the extreme penalty), has its good in this world, and rejoices in it with such joy as such things can afford. But as this is not a good which can discharge its devotees of all distresses, this city is often divided against itself by litigations, wars, quarrels, and such victories as are either life-destroying or short-lived. For each part of it that arms against another part of it seeks to triumph over the nations though itself in bondage to vice. If, when it has conquered, it is inflated with pride, its victory is life-destroying; but if it turns its thoughts upon the common casualties of our mortal condition, and is rather anxious concerning the disasters that may befall it than elated with the successes already achieved, this victory, though of a higher kind, is still only short-lived; for it cannot abidingly rule over those whom it has victoriously subjugated. But the things which this city desires cannot justly be said to be evil, for it is itself, in its own kind, better than all other human good. For it desires earthly peace for the sake of enjoying earthly goods, and it makes war in order to attain this peace; since, if it has conquered, and there remains no one to resist it, it enjoys a peace which it had not while there were opposing parties who contested for the enjoyment of those things which were too small to satisfy both. This peace is purchased by toilsome wars; it is obtained by what they style a glorious victory. Now, when victory remains with the party which had the juster cause, who hesitates to congratulate the victor,

and style it a desirable peace? These things, then, are good things, and without doubt the gifts of God. But if they neglect the better things of the heavenly city, which are secured by eternal victory and peace never-ending, and so inordinately covet these present good things that they believe them to be the only desirable things, or love them better than those things which are believed to be better—if this be so, then it is necessary that misery follow and ever increase.[19]

Augustine was aware of the realities of power and influence in the political life of the world. He called attention, not only to the structures of justice and order which institutionalists acknowledge, but to the exercise of power and influence which operationalists feel to be important.

Theologians who think institutionally as well as those who think operationally view Augustine as the source of their inspiration. It is clear enough that elements of Augustine seem to justify the institutional motif in some matters, the operational in others. It is also clear that Augustine's thought has influenced both approaches in subsequent Christian social outlooks. Does his thought contain the ambivalence, or does our question breed difficulties?

In exploring this question we must acknowledge several factors. Augustine was so concerned to work out a Christian rationale for the embrace of the world that he was less concerned for the consistent evaluation of that world. Edward R. Hardy, Jr.,[20] finds certain ambiguities in Augustine related to this question. One such ambiguity involves Augustine's analysis of human society. Whereas the categories of his two-fold contrast are clear—the heavenly city of love for God set against the earthly city of love for man, of bliss against misery, of goodness against wickedness, etc.—Augustine's actual evaluation of existing society is ambiguous. It shares features of both motifs. Hence, it must be embraced yet criticized. When Augustine spoke of certain aspects of society he saw one side of the ambiguity; when he spoke of other aspects he saw the other side. Hardy is more impressed with the institutional features that inhere in Augustine's thought, but he admits that Augustine's categories contain a harshness which might give credence to another point of view. If Hardy is right, then Augustine's ambiguities give rise to the problem before us.

Another way to deal with this question would be to examine Augustine's treatment of a specific issue. He considered at length the relationship of the civil judge to the problem that arises when it is necessary to obtain evidence by means of torture. Torture of the innocent witness is obviously wrong, yet Augustine made a place for it as a part of the institutional process of justice.

> . . . the wise judge does these things, not with any intention of doing harm, but because his ignorance compels him, and because human

society claims him as a judge. But though we therefore acquit the judge of malice, we must none the less condemn human life as miserable. And if he is compelled to torture and punish the innocent because his office and his ignorance constrain him, is he a happy as well as a guiltless man? Surely it were proof of more profound considerateness and finer feeling were he to recognize the misery of these necessities, and shrink from his own implication in that misery; and had he any piety about him, he would cry to God, "From my necessities deliver Thou me."[21]

An institutionalist could interpret this passage as a clear statement of the necessity of office, of the need for the judge to pursue his work in accordance with the requirements laid upon him by the job. The operational motif, however, is potentially evident in the assumption that the judge's office cannot accomplish its purposes without the coercive element of torture, which is therefore justified. Augustine simply rolled both elements into such a unified ball that it becomes impossible to find in his thinking any definitive answer to the question upon which the distinction between institutional and operational motifs depends: Is power the ground of the office or the office the justification of the power?

Perhaps another consideration which points to the existence of ambiguity in Augustine is the historical evidence that Roman Catholicism has built both ways from his thinking. There is an institutionalist tradition in medieval Catholicism, culminating scholastically in the thinking of St. Thomas; there is also an operational reality, evidenced in the use of ecclesiastical power to impose its will upon the culture. The latter view has been given theoretical formulation in the teaching about the "two swords." Augustine alone cannot be held responsible for all the diversity in the church, nor dare we suggest rigorous causal connections in this regard. The double development in Roman Catholicism is another indicator of the essential ambiguity in Augustine's thought concerning the comparison of the institutional and operational motifs.

If there is ambiguity in Augustine there is little, if any, in Thomas Aquinas. Thomas exhibited the institutional motif in a highly cogent form. The doctrine of natural law was used to construct a uniform social philosophy, in which the institutional element was basic. In question 90 in the *Summa Theologiae* we find an extended discussion of the place of law in the governing of human affairs. Thomas began by affirming the teleological purpose of law, which he found rooted in human reason. The law serves the common good. In this it may either be directed by the whole people whose common good is at stake or by a vice-regent who has the good of the whole people on his mind. Accordingly, Thomas concluded, "Law is nothing else than an ordinance of reason for the common good, promulgated by him who has the care of the community."[22]

This discussion of law involves both issues that relate to the formulation of norms and issues that relate to the implementation of decisions. Laws sometimes function as norms, but they also result in the creation of institutions and the determination of strategies. There is a clear relationship between the idea of law and the functioning of institutions.

> . . . a law is nothing else than a dictate of reason in the ruler by whom his subjects are governed. Now the virtue of any being that is a subject consists of its being well subordinated to that by which it is regulated; and thus we see that the virtue of the irascible and concupiscible powers consists in their being obedient to reason. In the same way, *the virtue of every subject consists in his being well subjected to his ruler,* as the Philosopher says.[23]

At this point Thomas considered the relations of eternal law to natural law, of natural law to human law. The purpose of human law is to guide and train man in the attainment of virtue. Again, the Church Father quoted the Philosopher to justify the contention that such training is necessary in order to perfect the virtue in man that is eclipsed by sloth and proneness to vice. Human laws are just only if they can be derived from the natural law; no human law can have the force of law if not in harmony with the rational dictates of the natural law. Thomas quoted Isidore to the effect that law must be "founded on reason," and that it should "foster religion, be helpful to discipline, and further the common welfare."[24]

In examining the nature of human law, Thomas detailed how the human law should be framed for the common good of all rather than the private good of a few; how the law must prohibit the gross vices but cannot hope to eliminate all evils, and how the law must engender the common virtues but cannot hope to support all the virtues which each faithful man should strive for personally. The law binds the conscience when it is just, i.e. in accordance with the natural law. Hence men are subject to law when the law is just, and when subjection to the law results in the serving of the common good.

> Since, then, the lawgiver cannot have in view every single case, he shapes the law according to what happens most frequently, by directing his attention to the common good. Hence, if a case arise wherein the observance of that law would be injurious to the general welfare, it should not be observed.[25]

When unjust laws are enacted, they may be resisted and then changed. ". . . [H]uman law is rightly changed in so far as such change is conducive to the common welfare."[26]

It is obvious that such a clear vision of the rational, properly enacted, and creatively important place for legislation in the conduct of human affairs cannot but demand the institutions by which such human laws are made and enforced. Beginning with the family, with the father as the head, the ascending levels of law rise upwards to the community, with the king as the head. The state is necessary for the fulfillment of the divine purposes which intend order and welfare to be the lot of man.

In Augustine the city of this world enjoys a peace and harmony which are less than perfect, composed of great ambiguity, and destined for eventual extinction. In Thomas the institutions that govern human life are rationally meaningful structures. Thomas granted that they should be overthrown when they are not just, but he also allowed for the possibility —even probability—that most of the institutions will be reasonably just. The peace of the earthly city, rather than consisting of a tolerable harmony built with imperfect devices for the curbing of fallen human nature, tends rather to be a proper harmony of life reflecting the divine harmony of creation and serving the needs of man. Rather than ambiguous necessities, law and order are creative possibilities; rather than curbs against sin necessitated by the Fall, they are the means by which men organize the common good in conformity to the patterns of divine creation. This is not a blind conservatism which takes every existing order as the reflection of the divine intention. Thomas had ample theoretical room for the rights of rebellion and the necessities of change. But every change must justify itself in terms of its greater service to the common good. Indeed, since the binding power of the law is diminished by change, "human law should never be changed, unless, in some way or other, the common welfare be compensated according to the extent of the harm done in this respect."[27]

The feudal structure of medieval society, with its differentiation of function, its inequality of status, its obedience to the light of supposed natural law, and its eventual subservience to the divine hierarchy were naturally supported by this understanding. There was little inner thrust for change, little theological ferment by which the pretensions of worldly rulers were brought under scrutiny, little sense of tension between the theoretical perfection of the heavenly city and the harsh realities of the earthly one. Alden D. Kelley suggests that this view "is a rationalistic understanding of society and is on the whole oblivious to the nonrational, even irrational, elements in men and society."[28]

The influence of Thomas has been crucial in Roman Catholic teaching, even though many church practices have relied upon the exercise of power or influence. Consider the encyclical of Pope John XXIII entitled *Pacem in Terris*. A broad and subtle document, it has many implications but is expressly instructive regarding the importance of law as a means for implementing ethical decisions. The Introduction provides a general discussion of the place of order in human affairs. Not only is order defended, but those who deny its necessity are specifically criticized.

Peace on earth, which men of every era have most eagerly yearned for, can be firmly established only if the order laid down by God is dutifully observed.

The progress of learning and the invention of technology clearly show that, both in living things and in the forces of nature, an astonishing order reigns, and they also bear witness to the greatness of man, who can understand that order and create suitable instruments to harness those forces of nature and use them to his benefit. . . .

How strongly does the turmoil of individual men and peoples contrast with the perfect order of the universe! It is as if the relationships which bind them together could be controlled only by force. But if the Creator of the world has imprinted in man's heart an order which his conscience reveals to him and enjoins him to obey: "They show the work of the Law written in their hearts. Their conscience bears witness to them" (Romans 2:15).

And how could it be otherwise? For whatever God has made shows forth His infinite wisdom, and it is manifested more clearly in things which have greater perfection. (Cf. Psalm 18:8-11.)

But fickleness of opinion often produces this error, that many think the relationships between men and States can be governed by the same laws as the forces and irrational elements of the universe, whereas the laws governing them are of quite a different kind and are to be sought elsewhere, namely, where the Father of all things wrote them, that is, in the nature of man.

By these laws men are most admirably taught, first of all how they should conduct their mutual dealings among themselves, then how the relationships between the citizens and the public authorities of each State should be regulated, then how States should deal with one another, and finally how, on the one hand individual men and States, and on the other hand the community of all peoples, should act toward each other, the establishment of such a world community of peoples being urgently demanded by the requirements of universal common good.[29]

The Thomistic elements in this passage are evident, even in the language, but the problems to which it is addressed are modern. Part One of the encyclical lays down the proposition that everyman is a person with rights and duties. The rights of persons are listed as follows: to have life and a worthy standard of living; to cultivate moral and cultural values with freedom guaranteed for the expression of opinions; to worship God according to conscience; to choose whether to marry or follow a religious (celibate) vocation; to work in healthy conditions for a just wage and to hold private property under socially responsible conditions; to meet, assemble, move freely, emigrate or immigrate; and to take an active part in human affairs.

The argument then emphasizes the interplay between rights and duties. Every human right has a corresponding obligation, and men are required to recognize and observe their mutual rights and duties if society is to function properly. Moreover, any political order is beneficial when it is founded upon truth, justice, charity, and freedom. Hence, in the final analysis the political order is a spiritual reality, grounded in the order of God. The encyclical declares that "any human society that is established on relations of force must be regarded as inhuman. . . ."[30] This statement clearly makes order prior to power, and implies that any other priority is basically wrong.

In Part Two of the document the relationship between individual citizens and public officials is examined. Civil authority is taught to be from God, and rulers exercise authority under His Providence. When, and only when, they do so are they to be obeyed:

> Those, therefore, who have authority in the State may oblige men in conscience only if their authority is intrinsically related with the authority of God and shares in it.
> By this principle the dignity of the citizens is protected. When, in fact, men obey their rulers, it is not at all as men that they obey them. Through their obedience it is God, the provident Creator of all things, Whom they reverence, since he has decreed that men's dealings with one another should be regulated by an order which He Himself has established.[31]

The encyclical goes on to declare that men have a right to choose who shall rule them, what form of government they shall live under, and how the authority that comes from God is to be exercised over them. "It is thus clear," says the encyclical, "that the doctrine which We have set forth is fully consonant with any truly democratic regime."[32] So long as the public authority promotes the common good, enables all members of the community to share that good, is constitutionally structured so as to protect citizens from the arbitrary exercise of undefined power, and permits citizens to participate in the process of government, it is a legitimate public authority. The government is secondary to the moral order. The pope declares it impossible to accept any view which finds the source of civic rights and duties and the constitutional structure of authority in "the mere will of human beings, individually or collectively."[33] In the economic sphere, for example, the state must seek to expand individual freedom rather than to curtail it and to protect the personal rights of each and every individual.

Parts Three and Four concern relations between states, which are also declared to be under the requirements of the moral order. All political communities are of equal natural dignity (just as are all men), hence relationships between them must be established on truth. There must be justice in interpolitical relations, with means for settling disputes by lawful due process. Justice also entails rights for ethnic minorities, fair treatment of political refugees, cessation of the arms race, and the right of economically underdeveloped countries to attain a more adequate standard of living. Since economic interdependence is already upon us, political interdependence must also come.

> Today the universal common good poses problems of worldwide dimensions which cannot be adequately tackled or solved except by the efforts of public authorities endowed with a breadth of powers, structure and means of the same proportions: that is, of public authorities which are in a position to operate in an effective manner on a worldwide basis. The moral order itself, therefore, demands that such a form of public authority be established.[34]

Such an authority should be set up by common accord, not imposed by force. The pope saw value in the United Nations as it stood but implied the wish for the extension of its authority.

Part Five of the encyclical ended with exhortations of a pastoral nature urging Roman Catholics to take part in public life.

The encyclical was greeted with enthusiasm by many readers, particularly those who did not stop to ask how the ends for which it called are to be brought about. Michael Novak saw the encyclical as bringing into official acceptance many ideas which have been unofficially advocated by Catholic writers such as Emmanuel Mounier, Jacques Maritain, Gabriel Marcel, and Teilhard de Chardin.[35] Other observers saw the document as ruling out power politics and cold-war tactics. It is not clear that the traditional teaching of the just war is abrogated by the argument, though Howard Schomer has argued that it certainly requires a radical overhauling of the concept.[36]

Other observers have suggested that the document, for all its values, has not sufficiently faced the problem of power in the affairs of men. Will Herberg suggests that its plea for world community in institutional terms cannot be converted into policy as simply as the encyclical implies, that it looks too quickly to ultimates and forgets the problems in the immediates.[37] Paul Ramsey complains that the encyclical lacks a due appreciation of the extent to which force must be used to sustain order.[38] Ramsey is appreciative of the importance of institutions and when he takes issue with the Pope's encyclical it is a criticism that comes from a sympathetic source.

Perhaps John XXIII emphasized the place of institutions to the eclipse of power. Perhaps he took the Aristotelian and Thomistic understandings of reason as a self-authenticating and self-sustaining foundation for institutions and stressed them more than the Augustinian sense of ambiguity and the role of power in the creation and sustenance of political order. He may have done this to counter tendencies in our day to put the emphasis the other way around. The institutionalist is always concerned about the structural authority which controls and governs power and never thinks of its use apart from such safeguards.

12

The Institutional Motif in Classical Protestantism

Classical Protestantism has generally relied upon structures of justice and order for governing the affairs of men. In the Lutheran heritage these structures have been understood apart from the work of salvation and redemption and embraced as the "left hand" work of God. In the Calvinistic tradition they have been seen as positive instruments for enforcing holiness of life within a commonwealth of faith.

Realms and Orders: The Lutheran Heritage

Luther was not a scholastic theologian, shaping every statement with careful attention to its consistency with his whole point of view. He was not a systematizer but a reformer. He wrote in the flush of excitement and was given to sharp, even unbridled, utterances. R. H. Tawney may have overstated the case, but he certainly had reasons to declare, "Luther's utterances on social morality are the occasional explosions of a capricious volcano . . . and it is idle to scan them for a coherent and consistent doctrine."[1]

According to Luther the Christian turns to certain "orders of creation" for the expression of his social responsibility.

> God has appointed three social classes [*drei Stände*] to which he has given the command not to let sins go unpunished. The first is that of the parents, who should maintain strict discipline in their house when ruling the domestics and the children. The second is the government, for the officers of the state bear the sword for the purpose of coercing the obstinate and remiss by means of their power of discipline. The third is that of the church, which governs by the Word. By this threefold authority God has protected the human race against the devil, the flesh, and the world, to the end that offenses may not increase but may be cut off.[2]

In other places Luther added a fourth order, "the calling," to the three orders mentioned above. The Christian man thus finds himself in four institutional structures, the family, the state, his daily job, and the church. Through these structures he carries out his duty to God.

These "orders" are part of God's creative design. They are part of the life of all men, not merely the life of Christians, but this does not mean that Christians are any less obligated than non-Christians to use them as the channels through which they express their responsibilities to God and to the neighbor. It means rather that these "secular" realities, created by God both as the channels of service and as restraints against sin, stand alongside the "sacred" aspect of life known in the Gospel. Hence there are two realms, the secular realm of institutions and the spiritual realm of faith, both of which are divinely instituted and required for the Christian man. Even the church has its secular side, as an institutional reality, along with its spiritual functions as the locus of the Word.

Luther did not expect the orders to become Christianized, but neither did he wish them to be severe merely for the sake of harshness. William A. Mueller criticizes Troeltsch for seeming to equate Luther with Machiavelli and quotes Karl Holl to substantiate the view that Luther's concept of the state included welfare functions as well as disciplinary purposes. In summarizing his judgment, Mueller writes as follows:

> Thus, while Luther enjoins strictest obedience to the orders of secular authority (as also to all other orders such as matrimony, parents, teachers) as being divinely ordained, he does not, as some have maintained—we are thinking of Figgis and others—exalt civil power over spiritual authorities. How else could he have spoken of the worldly realm as "the kingdom of the left hand"? Nor is the state, to him, an end in itself as Machiavelli had taught and as some modern nations assume and practice! True it is that Luther taught that as the *Obrigkeit* wields the sword against the wicked it becomes a tool of God's wrath. But God's wrath is not an end in itself either but rather and ultimately a means of God's mercy.[3]

Perhaps the most illuminating part of Luther's teaching for the understanding of the institutional motif is found in his discussion of the difference between a Christian's responsibilities as an individual and a Christian's responsibilities as an official. Whereas the Christian acting as an individual follows the ethic of love, offering his other cheek, surrendering his cloak, and generally giving of himself unstintingly in the service of a needy neighbor, the Christian acting as an official must be governed by considerations of justice. This is not to dodge his responsibility but to translate it. The judge who as an individual might feel forgiving toward an offender must as an official mete out the sentence called for by the law. By requiring such a sentence the judge stands as the champion of order and justice, the very epitome of the divinely ordained means for preserving society from the onslaught of wickedness. The judge neither enjoys his role nor carries it out with remorse; he simply acts according to the duties imposed upon him by his station in life. The duties that inhere in the task of the soldier, the father, and other offices are to be carried out in the same spirit of duty —a duty institutionally defined and administered.

Werner Elert noted that Luther's choice of the judge has been unfortunate, since it emphasizes the punitive features of public office. Elert observed that public officials with more positive functions, such as the ration board administrator, face the same decisions in their exercise of public office. Elert argued that a ration board administrator must refuse the request of the first mother who asks for an adequate supply of food for her hungry children, despite his personal desire to give her all she needs, in order to provide the next mothers who are in line with their fair share. "Precisely for love's sake he will be entirely impartial and thus act also in accordance with the law."[4]

Luther saw each of the orders primarily as an effective instrument for curbing sin. Even family life is interpreted as a means by which the sensual urges of man are kept in check. The labor which is necessary in the economic order serves the needs of punishment and discipline. In the case of the state the necessary task of restraining sin may require the prince to go to war, even though no Christian acting as an individual would be right in doing so.

> Every lord and prince is bound to protect his people and get peace for them. That is his office; it is for that that he has the sword (Romans xiii). This should be for him a matter of conscience and he should so depend upon it as to know that this work is right in the eyes of God and is commanded by Him. I am not now teaching what Christians are to do; for your rule does not concern us Christians, but we are rendering you a service and telling you what you are to do before God, in your office of ruling. A Christian is a person to himself; he believes for himself and for no one else. But a lord and prince is not a person to himself, but to others; he has to serve them, that is, protect and defend them. To be sure it were good if he were a Christian besides and believed in God; then he would be happy; but it is not princely to be a Christian and therefore few princes can be Christians, as they say, "A Prince is a rare bird in heaven." Now even if they are not Christians, nevertheless they ought to do what is right and good according to God's outward ordinance. He will have this of them.[5]

According to Luther, war can be justified only when institutionalized. It must be fought in the fear of God; inferiors must fight at the command of rulers; rulers must put down uprisings (many of Luther's most vehement statements about the role of rulers were uttered in the context of the Peasant's War); the war must be fought in a right cause (Luther counseled objection to participating in an unjust cause); and it must not be undertaken for the sake of the soldier's own glory.

Despite his pessimistic judgment about the qualities of princes and their rule, Luther remained convinced that princes are to be obeyed because they exercise their role as a consequence of God's decree. In this way Luther acknowledged the role of power in the conduct of human affairs, but he understood power as institutionally sanctioned. He found in the existing authority the symbol of divinely ordained order, even when abused. Because he felt that the orders served both as expressions of God's rule and as dikes against sin, and because he saw the element of sin to be a necessary aspect of the actual orders themselves, Luther was prepared to tolerate in existing structures a greater degree of ambiguity than he would have accepted had he demanded of the orders a more direct expression of Christian standards.

The orders are governed by natural law interpreted according to the use of reason. Whatever strictures Luther delivered against the use of reason to attain spiritual truth (and thus to contest the revealed Word) he did not apply to the use of reason in the governance of the orders. George Forell has said, "According to Luther the natural orders are reasonable orders and have to be interpreted by reason. As a matter of fact, politics and economics are the fields where it is not only proper but imperative to use reason."[6] Luther could be practical about the orders, especially when his thinking was not influenced by immediate existential anxiety about their contribution to the welfare of his reformation. He posited in theory the place for change even though he seldom effected it because of his confidence in the eschatological ending of the age and because, by and large, it was to his interest to accept the existing power of the German princes. Moreover, by seeing the orders in terms of the reason, distinct in kind from the realm of the spiritual controlled by faith, Luther was preserved from the errors which can arise when a particular historical institution is seen as a direct (rather than indirect) expression of the Gospel. He certainly did not equate particular social programs with the Gospel even when he understood them as related to the divine ordaining of life in the curbing of sin.

While Luther spoke of the difference between what the Christian might do as an individual and what he might do as an official in any of the orders, he felt it is the calling of all Christians to act as officials whenever they are required to do so. They are not to search for the purity which might be associated, as by the separatist, with purely private responsibility. Indeed, since the family involves the dimensions of official responsibility, how indeed could anyone find purity in the separation of himself from the orders? To live in two realms under one compulsion, as does the Christian who participates in both the spiritual government of the Word and in the temporal government of the world, is not to announce that one state is more blessed than the other—to be sought for its own sake. It is to move from one realm to another, seeking to use the second for the fruitful implementation of ethical decisions inspired by the first. That corruptions and difficulties appear in practice does not cancel the legitimacy of the intention to serve God by restraining evil (and by promoting peace) in the orders which He has created.

The main contours of Luther's thought have shaped the outlook of many individuals, not only in the Lutheran but in related traditions of classical Protestantism. For example, Emil Brunner argued that God, as Creator, presents to us the situations of life within which we are to work. We must accept these before we can do anything toward changing them. Our neighbor is given to us by the will of God. His whole being is our sacred responsibility because he confronts us in the orders of life. Our course of action is dictated by the actualities of the concrete situations in which we find our neighbors. "Here we see not merely particular spheres of life *within* which we are to act, but orders in accordance with which we have to act, because in them, even if only in a fragmentary and indirect way, God's Will meets us."[7]

Brunner's list of the natural forms of community begins with the community of the family, based upon the sexual impulse. It includes the community of work, arising from the need to earn a living. It culminates in the state, which is the greatest form of community, setting standards for the others. But Brunner also spoke of two other communities. That of culture, based upon intellectual impulses, and that of the visible institutional church, arising from faith. The last two communities are more amorphous than the first three. The first four can exist apart from faith, being expressions of the created nature of man. Faith is necessary to understand these orders fully, but they are present without its prior work.

> Faith finds these forms of community already present, or rather the believer finds himself and others placed within this framework. Therefore he has to come to some kind of understanding with them. How he is to do this constitutes the most difficult problem of Christian ethics, precisely because they are so foreign to the nature of faith, and because they are based upon a standard of law which is totally different from that which is known by faith.[8]

Brunner followed Luther's argument concerning the given quality of the orders and concerning the distinctive implications for behavior that are implicit in the concept of an office. In exercising his office the Christian has both a primary duty and a secondary duty. Brunner's discussion of the office in relation to personal relationships was rent by the tension he acknowledged between the demands of the office in terms of the orders and the demands of personal relationships which he found in love. He began with the duties inherent in the office and pointed out that the Christian

> must, as it were, first of all forget all he ever knew about the meaning of love, in order that he may help to protect and to further the life of these "orders" themselves in accordance with their own logic. . . . Our "official duty" is "harsh," objectively technical: the human relation which it requires to men is external: its method is that of the forcible control of the masses, indeed it seems to be wholly opposed to love. To carry it through it needs the use of force, possibly of physical force, even to the point of taking human life.
>
> But it is no use groaning over this state of affairs, nor have we any right to refuse to do our "official duty" because things are so. If such action is necessary, in order to preserve the "dyke" which protects our present civilization, we must simply accept the fact, for love's sake. I must behave differently to my neighbour in my capacity as a judge, a policeman, a bank official, a schoolmaster, etc., from the way in which I would behave towards him in a "private" relationship—as man to man.[9]

But Brunner did not leave the matter with this flat, unequivocal, officialism, and went on to argue for Christian responsibility in personal relationships, provided the exercise of such personal concerns is compatible with the maintenance of the established orders. Indeed, Brunner ended the chapter with the wistful and unexplored observation that the very loss of the personal relationships of life may explain in part why the dikes of civilization are in such a precarious position in the contemporary world.

In his thinking about political matters Brunner also developed the kind of dialectic which has just been illustrated with regard to the office. He began with the necessity of the state:

> There has never been a human society without something which resembles the State, and without some kind of legal coercion, and in this historical world there never will be a human society without these orders, since sin makes both necessary. But without doubt there are states which are better or worse than others, there are legal codes which are better or worse than others. The forms assumed by the State and by the systems of legislation may vary, but their fundamental structure is always the same.[10]

Brunner exhibited many conservative tendencies in his theories about the state. Not only did he argue for the necessity of inequality based upon differentiation of function—condemning enlightenment views of equality as misleading—but he made statements about the power of the state which seem at first reading to be flat assertions of Machiavellianism. He said at one place, "The fundamental character of the State is not right but might. Even the despotic State is a State, but it only possesses a "right" as a by-product and in an uncertain sense."[11] At another place he said, "The essence of the state is not justice but power. Even the unjust state is still a state, but the impotent state ceases to be a state."[12]

Brunner also developed a theory of transition and even of revolution. "Adaptation to the existing order . . . is the *first* point in the Christian ethic," he writes, "but it is never the *last* point."[13] Since the existing order is broken by sin it may be considered transitional. The Christian may therefore legitimately seek something new, through it and for it. God does not honor the preservation of the orders *per se*, but only their use and utilization. The orders, which are fallen through sin, are to be perfected and redeemed. Brunner criticized those who hold (as do some in the Lutheran tradition) that the "orders" are not subject to the command of Jesus Christ, but only to the "reason." He acknowledged that there are some orders which ought to be overthrown. Nevertheless, he remarked, "The legalism of those who uphold the existing order is bad; but the lawlessness of fanatics is worse. . . ."[14]

Brunner's plea, even in regard to the revolutionary possibility suggested above, was for new and better institutions in place of unsatisfactory ones. Man never leaves the "orders," even though in certain circumstances he may need to resist and to change existing ones.

> . . . in view of the world as it is—the environment in which our neighbour lives—the will of God does not merely tell us to adapt ourselves, to accept, but also to resist, to protest, not to be "conformed to this world." The kind of apologetic which is characteristic of a certain conservatism, by which, with the aid of the idea of Providence, the existing "order" at any given time is justified as that which is willed by God, and every form of criticism and desire to change conditions is suppressed as "godless rebellion," as disobedience to orders willed by God, can only arise out of a condition in which faith has been badly distorted. Without a living, painful conscious-ness of the appalling contrast between the world which God wills and the world as it now is, genuine faith cannot be imagined. The spirit which sighs for release from the oppression of the present "order" forms a necessary part of obedience to the Divine Command.[15]

In the writings of Dietrich Bonhoeffer we find a more careful theo-logical rationale for the changes that Brunner affirmed to be possible. Bonhoeffer wrote in the Lutheran tradition, not in slavish obedience to its premises, but nevertheless in conversation with its conceptual frameworks. Instead of "orders" he used the term "mandates"; instead of "office," "deputyship." The resultant understandings are significantly different, even though they belong without question within the institutional motif.

The most significant shift revealed in Bonhoeffer's *Ethics* is the movement of the "orders" from the realm of reason and natural law to the realm of Christocentric command:

> The commandment of God is not to be found anywhere and everywhere. It is not to be found in theoretical speculation or in private inspiration, nor yet in historical forces or sublime ideals. It is to be found only where it presents itself. The commandment of God can be spoken only where God Himself gives the warrant for it, and only in so far as God gives the warrant for it can the commandment of God legitimately be performed. The commandment of God is not to be found where there are historical forces, powerful ideas and convincing perceptions. It is to be found where there are the divine mandates which are founded upon the revelation of Christ. Such mandates are the Church, marriage and the family, culture and government.[16]

A mandate is a "concrete divine commission which has its foundation in the revelation of Christ."[17] It involves the idea of an institution—but purged of the conservative overtones associated with "the pseudo-Lutheran Christ who exists solely for the purpose of sanctioning the facts as they are."[18] It involves the idea of an estate, but it must not be allowed to be colored by the idea of privilege associated with that concept today. A mandate involves the idea of an official duty, but does not carry the secular or bureaucratic implications of the term *office*. Bonhoeffer was concerned to emphasize that the mandates are introduced into the world from above, as divine commissions related to the will of Christ and not merely as divine creations which have been corrupted by the Fall and left to the canons of natural reason for guidance.

Bonhoeffer, like Brunner, acknowledged the reality of defined roles of superiority and inferiority in the social order, but he recast the concept. He warned against the dangers that are implicit when superiority is defined from below, as when a man claims his rank and presumes upon it. When this happens,

> ... the relation between superior and inferior is reversed or confused, [and] there arises between them the most intense hostility, mistrust, deceit and envy. And in this atmosphere, too, purely personal abuse of superiority and inferiority flourishes as never before. In the horror which is aroused by the violence of this rebellion the fact that there was ever the possibility of a genuine institutional order established from above can only appear as a miracle, and so, in reality, it is. The genuine order of superior and inferior draws its life from belief in the commission from "above," belief in the "Lord of lords."[19]

George Forell has interpreted Bonhoeffer's ethics as a rediscovery of the true Luther vis-à-vis the pseudo-Lutheran statements of the two realms in which the dialectical relationship between the realms has been lost. "Bonhoeffer sees the unity [between the reality of God and the reality of the world] in the way in which the secular and the Christian elements prevent one another from assuming any kind of static independence in their relation to each other. They are polemically related and thus bear witness to their common reality, their unity in the reality of Christ."[20]

A fuller exposition of Bonhoeffer's thought would explore these matters in several themes; we can look briefly at only one. In elaborating his thinking about the role of the state, Bonhoeffer exhibited the skill of a highly gifted theologian who threads his way between many potential difficulties. He began by making a distinction between the *state*, which involves the rulers and those ruled, and the *government*, which refers only to the rulers. The term *state* means an ordered community, whereas the term *government* represents the power which creates and maintains order. Government, which is necessary in any form of society or in any state, is divinely established to exercise dominion. Bonhoeffer rejected ideals (whether classical, medieval, or modern) which view the state as a human creation, as a social contract, rather than as a divine mandate. He rejected them because within such views the power which is of necessity exercised by the state in preserving order is no longer under divine control.

> Whenever the basis of the state is sought in the created nature of man, the concept of government is broken up and is then reconstructed from below, even when this is not at all intended. Whenever the state becomes the executor of all the vital and cultural activities of man, it forfeits its own proper dignity, its specific authority as government.[21]

Bonhoeffer made a place for government as well as for its control. He recognized its necessity without ignoring the possible corruptions which inhere in its false use. He did not flinch from the need to exercise power— symbolized by the sword—yet he balanced power with justice and declared that men exercise their roles as public officials only under the mandate from above. Government protects the righteous as well as restrains the unrighteous. Bonhoeffer observed that two ideas existed in tension in the Reformation. One idea underscores the state as an instrument of power but fails to make a sufficient place for the concept of justice by which the exercise of power is judged. The other idea thinks of the state in terms of justice—as the instrument of law and order—and fails to see the element of power in all civil authority. Bonhoeffer advanced a view which seeks to hold these two ideas in tension—a view that acknowledges the necessity of state power without having to make the excessive assertions about state power which have been cited from Brunner.

Bonhoeffer traced the state to the mandate given it by Jesus Christ, a

mandate which assures that the state will be understood as derived from "above" rather than from "below." Because the state is derived from "above," it commands obedience but also stands under controls. Cast into the christological categories of Bonhoeffer, the control "from above" is elaborated as follows: Christ, as the mediator of creation is responsible for the formation of government; without Him, it would not exist; its purpose is therefore to serve him by maintaining order; He is the Lord of government, Whose service government neglects at its peril; His atonement acts to redeem government, which can only be sustained by the brave acceptance of the guilt which goes with the exercise of rule. In all his discussion of these matters Bonhoeffer considered the relationship of the Christian to the state as a penultimate rather than an ultimate relationship, a fact which George Forell takes as the critical difference between the political theory of Barth and that of Bonhoeffer.

Bonhoeffer wrestled with the problem of Christian obedience to government. The general case calls for obedience, but there are exceptional cases.

> In the exercise of the mission of the government the demand for obedience is unconditional and qualitatively total; it extends both to conscience and to bodily life. Belief, conscience and bodily life are subject to an obligation of obedience with respect to the divine commission of government. A doubt can arise only when the contents and the extent of the commission of government become questionable. The Christian is neither obliged nor able to examine the rightfulness of the demand of government in each particular case. His duty of obedience is binding on him until government directly compels him to offend against the divine commandment, that is to say, until government openly denies its divine commission and thereby forfeits its claim. In cases of doubt obedience is required; for the Christian does not bear the responsibility of government.[22]

Many subsequent thinkers have been inspired by the "two realms" theory; we have introduced only the thought of two Continental theologians whose outlook is very similar to that of Luther yet whose differences illustrate the problems which arise in the development of Christian responsibility by the use of this pattern. Nils Ehrenstrom, Albert Hyma, Gustaf Aulen, Eivind Berggrav, Gerhard Ebeling, and Edgar M. Carlson are but a few whose works discuss the complex issues involved in the Lutheran approach.

Magistrate and Commonwealth: The Calvinistic Heritage

Calvin rejected the thinking both of those who saw in the princes a substitute for the divine rule and of those who felt that the freedom of the

Gospel does away with the need for civil government. He thus rejected Renaissance tendencies to glorify the state and Anabaptist tendencies to reject it. Of the passages devoted to the two positions that are rejected, those against the anarchists are far the longer and the stronger, for Calvin contended that only by the use of government can the wickedness of men be kept in check.

Like Luther, Calvin emphasized the duty of the individual citizen to obey, even to suffer martyrdom if necessary, rather than to engage in revolution. Christians are therefore to accord the magistrates obedience, even when the rulers are less than just. Calvin pointed out that the magistrates may legitimately use force in the exercise of their rule and resort to war in order to preserve the peace of their kingdoms, providing they can do so without "giving vent to their passions even in the slightest degree."[23]

There were two points at which Calvin's reasoning diverged from that of Luther. Calvin made a more specific provision for the overthrow of tyranny. While as an individual the Christian is admonished to obedience, Calvin was convinced that it is up to the magistrates of the people, acting in an official capacity, to resist the tyrannical actions of willful kings.

> . . . I am so far from forbidding them to withstand, in accordance with their duty, the fierce licentiousness of kings, that, if they wink at kings who violently fall upon and assault the lowly common folk, I declare that their dissimulation involves nefarious perfidy, because they dishonestly betray the freedom of the people, of which they know that they have been appointed protectors by God's ordinance.[24]

Likewise, Calvin brought the protection of morals and religion under the sovereignty of the magistrates, so that civil government is responsible even for the tranquillity of the church and the restraint of theological heresy.

Calvin's two modifications of Luther's reasoning have very profound, yet somewhat conflicting, consequences. In the first we find the seeds of a democratic development which were to germinate in Puritan Protestantism and eventuate in modern democracy. Scholars like A. D. Lindsay,[25] John T. McNeill,[26] and James H. Nichols[27] have argued that in Calvin we have the possibilities of democratic ideals. But in the second modification, in which the state is made responsible for the control of religious as well as political matters, we have the possibility of a revitalized medievalism or an even stricter theocracy. Arguing from the implications of this perspective, Rudolf Sohm[28] and Arthur C. McGiffert[29] have argued that Calvin perpetuated the medieval situation of ecclesiastical domination.

Calvin obviously did not believe in the separation of church and state. Much that went on in Geneva is distasteful when measured with the perspectives of an outlook informed by Renaissance humanism. Geneva was a theocracy rather than an example of democratic freedom. But Calvin did understand the potential role of elected magistrates in the government of the state and elected elders in the government of the church. His ideas provided springboards for later Calvinists, like John Knox and the French Huguenots, as well as American colonial Calvinists, to develop powerful arguments against tyranny.

Similarly, Calvin's thinking about the state as an instrument of education, social welfare, the cultivation of sound morals, and the control of religious beliefs, enabled him to view the state in a more positive sense than Luther did. John C. Bennett has suggested that Calvin's thinking about the state was closer to the medieval Catholic position than Luther's. Bennett finds this to be a commendable factor in Calvin's thinking about and use of the state for serving human needs, and notes, "What Calvin says about man's capacity for political order and about his understanding of the moral law is quite remarkable."[30]

The outlook of Calvin was transmitted through the heritage of the Puritans. It appeared clearly in the life of the American colonies, especially in New England, where the Puritan experiment in the creation of the holy commonwealth was free to make its way unmolested—at least for a time. The Puritans were concerned to apply religion to the whole of life and were perhaps the last Protestant group to try to do so on a total scale. In order to accomplish this end the Puritans turned to institutions—to the creation of a commonwealth based upon scriptural law and covenant community.

In 1645 Governor John Winthrop delivered a speech on liberty to the General Court of Massachusetts, which sets forth the theory of the Puritan commonwealth. In it Winthrop suggested that the magistrates, being called to their office by the people, nevertheless derive their authority from God, in accordance with Whose laws they ought to rule. By obedience to the duly constituted authority, the people enjoy civil liberty. Winthrop's oration concerning the nature of this liberty runs as follows:

> The other kind of liberty I call civil or federal, it may also be termed moral, in reference to the covenant between God and man, in the moral law, and the politic covenants and constitutions, amongst men themselves. This liberty is the proper end and object of authority, and cannot subsist without it; and it is a liberty to that only which is good, just, and honest. This liberty you are to stand for, with the hazard (not only of your goods, but) of your lives, if need be. Whatsoever crosseth this, is not authority, but a distemper thereof. This liberty is maintained and exercised in a way of subjection to authority; it is of the same kind of liberty wherewith Christ hath made us free. The woman's own choice makes such a man her husband; yet being

so chosen, he is her lord, and she is to be subject to him, yet in a way of liberty, not of bondage; and a true wife accounts her subjection her honor and freedom, and would not think her condition safe and free, but in her subjection to her husband's authority. Such is the liberty of the church under the authority of Christ. . . .[31]

The theory of the state and of society which lies behind Winthrop's oration is solidly Calvinistic in nature and completely institutional. The Puritan commonwealth is a civil government, justified as the necessary restraint for human sin, resting upon a supposed loyalty to the law of God as revealed in scripture, fundamentally in harmony with the outlooks upon civil authority prevalent in that part of the Western world influenced by the Calvinist heritage.

Puritans did not think the state was merely an umpire, standing on the side lines of a contest, limited to checking egregious fouls, but otherwise allowing men free play according to their abilities and the breaks of the game. . . . The state to them was an active instrument of leadership, discipline, and, wherever necessary, of coercion; it legislated over any and all aspects of human behavior. . . . There was no idea of the equality of all men. There was no questioning that men who would not serve the purposes of the society should be whipped into line. The objectives were clear and unmistakable; any one's disinclination to dedicate himself to them was obviously so much recalcitrancy and depravity. The government of Massachusetts, and of Connecticut as well, was a dictatorship and never pretended to be anything else; it was a dictatorship, not of a single tyrant, or of an economic class, or of a political faction, but of the holy and regenerate.[32]

This view was not, of course, unchallenged even in its own day. Roger Williams and Thomas Jefferson had other ideas concerning the nature of the civil order. Their influence was felt in the formation of the new nation. But while the ideas of Jefferson and Williams were different, they were sufficiently a part of the pattern to enable the rapprochement necessary in the creation of American constitutional government. There is a variation within the features of the institutions to which these different men were loyal, but no fundamental disagreement about the need for institutional structuring of the life of the nation.

The Anglicans who were involved in this process could cite their own authorities, especially in the person of Richard Hooker, whose famous work *The Laws of Ecclesiastical Polity* emphasizes in its own way the need for institutional form in the church's life and in human life in general. Hooker was fighting the idea, prevalent in his day, that the church as a spiritual group does not need the structural features of institutional order, just as Calvin was fighting against the anarchism of the left wing. The first book of *The Laws* sketches in broad strokes the general place of law in the governing of human society. Hooker spoke of both the divine and the natural law, arguing that man by his very rational nature is able to devise and accept those lawful structures which constitute the ordered state of government. The ordered life of the church is of the same character as the ordered life of man under law. Both are necessary within the economy of God.

To mention Hooker in the same section with the Puritans is to cite the antagonists in a very bitter feud. Some aspects of Hooker's work were a direct refutation of Puritan thinking and a vindication of the Anglican structure of the church. Yet both acknowledged the institutional motif, even though they quarreled bitterly about how the institutional should be defined. Moreover, there is not a little evidence that Hooker was deeply moved by Calvin. He said at one point that Calvin was "incomparably the wisest man that ever the French church did enjoy"[33] and of the church structure in Geneva he wrote: "This device I see not how the wisest at that time living could have bettered, if we duly consider what the present estate of Geneva did then require."[34] Hooker was not seeking to imitate the Genevan experiment in the England of his day, but his appreciation of Calvin and the legitimacy he granted to Calvin's structure for the church in Geneva seem beyond question. Whether Calvin, transplanted to the England of Hooker's experience, would have joined Hooker in support of bishops and in defense of the Anglican establishment against the Puritan protest is much more conjectural.

Hooker's view of government, however, is more rationalistic than Calvin's. Just as Calvin laid more stress upon considerations of reason than Luther did, so Hooker did even more so than Calvin. Hooker found the natural laws of order which underlie the formulation of the just state to be discussed and affirmed in scripture, but his final source of judgment is in the reason. Laws are good and just when they spring from first causes and principles grounded in the human reason. Hooker described the entire purpose of his first book of *The Laws* as the effort to show men why "just and reasonable laws are of so great force, of such great use in the world. . . ."[35] The first book of the treatise ends with these words:

> Wherefore that here we may briefly end, of law there can be no less acknowledged, than that her seat is the bosom of God, her voice the harmony of the world, all things in heaven and earth do her homage, the very least as feeling her care, and the greatest as not exempted from her power, both angels and men and creatures of what condition soever, though each in different sort and manner, yet all with uniform consent, admiring her as the mother of their peace and joy.[36]

In opposing the tyranny of kings and princes, Hooker developed a theory of popular sovereignty. He held that society itself is the source of law, not a prince or potentate. This earned him the enmity of the Puritan, Richard Baxter, whose opposition to despotic kings was no less strong than that of Hooker's, but whose trust of popular sovereignty was a great deal less certain. The commonwealth of Baxter was to be ruled by God-fearing men, not by all sorts and conditions of humanity. But for Hooker: "Laws they are not therefore which public approbation hath not made so."[37] The exact form of government seemed to Hooker to be a matter of little concern as long as the government does not serve special privilege and as long as the content of enacted law is consistent with that of natural law. Hooker even looked to the rule of law in international affairs:

> The strength and virtue of that law is such that no particular nation can lawfully prejudice the same by any their several laws and ordinances more than a man, by his private resolutions, the law of the whole commonwealth or state wherein he liveth. For as civil law, being the act of a whole body politic, doth therefore overrule each several part of the same body, so there is no reason that any one commonwealth of itself should, to the prejudice of another, annihilate that whereupon the whole world hath agreed.[38]

It is obvious that Calvin's thinking has inspired such a diversity of subsequent developments that only an intensive study could scratch the surface of the historical consequences. The tremendous changes within the Calvinistic heritage also account for the fact that recent and contemporary expressions of the Calvinistic impulse are not as similar to their original source as recent and contemporary expressions of the Lutheran impulse. More translation has occurred, and one must search more perceptively for Calvinistic elements in the current scene even though they are just as prevalent, if not more so.

In conservative Dutch Calvinism, under the influence of Abraham Kuyper, the concept of "sphere-sovereignty" arose. A recent spokesman for this outlook is Herman Dooyeweerd, Professor of Jurisprudence at the Free University of Amsterdam, which Kuyper founded.[39] According to this concept human life is organized in spheres such as the family, the labor union, the municipality, the nation-state. Each of these spheres is rightfully sovereign to itself, yet each is subject to the majesty of God, from which its authority is derived. Since each sphere is sovereign in itself, they do not conflict, each being dutifully loyal to the Word of God as the governing principle of its existence. This view of societal relations usually presupposes a strong prescriptive theory of biblical revelation.

In an essay entitled "Church and State"[40] Karl Barth takes a very positive attitude toward Calvin's treatise on political authority as found in the last book of *The Institutes*. This provides a clue to Barth's own thinking, which has often baffled contemporary interpreters. Barth cannot, by his own disclaimers, be placed within the Lutheran tradition as represented by Brunner. He cannot even be equated with Bonhoeffer, though each has a christological emphasis. Despite the fact that Barth criticizes all the Reformers for basing obedience to the state upon a legalistic reading of the scriptures rather than the freedom of the Gospel, his own institutionalism is rooted in the Reformation tradition and particularly in its Calvinistic expression.

Barth flatly declares the need for the civil community, or "Kings." But Barth also declares that Christians must not absolutize the state or pattern the life of the Christian community after it. Existing order is necessarily tyrannical; it cannot be order unless it can enforce its decrees. But rather than to suggest that Christians ought therefore to revolt, Barth suggests that Christians ought therefore to submit. By submitting to existing orders Christians deprive the orders of their tyranny, since freely given obedience is not coerced. Barth applies this curious logic to the church, society, positive law, families, and cultural institutions, as well as to the state.

Barth has so much to say about the place of freedom in the Christian response to the orders that some observers have been led to suppose he abrogates the institutional element. But Barth's freedom is always freedom from the orders conceived in institutional terms; it is never the grounds for thinking of society in a different motif. Barth's insistence upon freedom guards against the sanctification of any existing order and insures that Christians will always be able to judge the situation in which they find themselves.

Christians will judge what is appropriate for the orders by drawing analogies from the church and the kingdom of God. Applying this process to the state, Barth develops an interesting set of conclusions. Because God became a neighbor to man, treating him with compassion, the state is constrained to treat all men as human beings and not as impersonal tools. Because God's justifying act is for all men, the state will protect all and can expect all men to be submissive to it. Because Jesus came to save the lost, the state must concern itself with the protection of the weaker members of society. Because the church is a fellowship of the freely called, the state will safeguard the freedom of its citizens to live in the several orders, such as family, art, science, etc. Because Christ is the head of a corporate body, individualism and collectivism are transcended. Because of a single faith and a single baptism the state must accord equal opportunity to all adult citizens, including women. Because there is a variety of gifts and tasks in the church, a system of checks and balances between legislative, executive, and judicial powers is called for in the state. Because Christ is the light of the world there is no place for secret policies and secret diplomacy in the conduct of government. Because the church is nourished by the Word, the state must maintain free speech. Since service is the hallmark of membership in the church, the exercise of political rule is to be considered a form of service. Since the church is ecumenical, all purely nationalistic self-interest is qualified. Because God's anger lasts only for a moment, but his mercy is enduring, the state will use violent coercion only as a last resort for the temporary accomplishment of some objective.

Barth's conclusions about these matters may be legitimate and proper. We can be thankful that he did not use other analogies to draw opposite conclusions in defense of tyranny, absolute property rights, or the conclusions of the radical right wing. Few interpreters are convinced by the method by which Barth arrives at his judgments, even when they agree on other grounds with the political conclusions he reaches.

For all this attempted derivation of political theory from christological considerations, Barth carefully avoids making the state into a branch of the church. The church does not seek to make over the state into its own image. "Its desire is not that human politics should cross the politics of God, but that they should proceed, however distantly, on parallel lines."[41] The kingdom of God is a paradigm for politics, but not a program. The pagan state, which is ignorant of the kingdom until led to it by the church, can never be remade into the kingdom. "The State would be disavowing its own purpose if it were to act as though its task was to become the Kingdom of God."[42] Some of Barth's comments about the function of the state sound like reiterations of conservative Lutheranism. "However much human error and human tyranny may be involved in it, the State is not a product of sin but one of the constants of the divine Providence and government of the world in its action against human sin. . . ."[43] "No appeal can be made to the Word or Spirit of God in the running of its affairs."[44] "The State can assume the face and character of Pilate. Even then, however, it still acts in the power which God has given it. . . ."[45]

Barth explores these issues in many ways, coming at them first from one side and then from the other. The steady pattern in which assertion and qualification are kept in continual balance is no mere instance of accidental inconsistency. It is the very quality of the system, a system in which Barth refuses either to affirm the idea of the holy state or the secular state, or to reject them. The way of analogy precludes both identity and separation of these two realms. He refuses to be caught either with the medieval pattern or with the Lutheran dualism. He can wink at every form of human political order yet embrace whatever one he chooses. His embrace of a liberal type of democratic welfarism is supported by elaborate reasons of haphazard derivation, but by this very process Barth witnesses to the radical character of the freedom which he finds in the Gospel. The conclusions that Barth has drawn by analogy to the Gospel have been something of an enigma to his friends. He has shifted his loyalties throughout his career, not always by carefully considered forethought. He resisted Hitler on the grounds that Hitler created a "Pilate state." He has less clearly been able to oppose the Communist regimes of eastern Europe. He has blasted

American life for its subordination of the human to the technical, yet in his later political theory he has found a democratic order involving the separation of legislative, executive, and judicial functions to represent the form of the civil community most analogous to the prototype of the kingdom of God.

The method of analogy (or *Gleichnis*), by which Barth starts with the nature of the redemptive community as known in Jesus Christ and moves by inference to those features of the civil community which can be compared to it, has led Barth to many differing conclusions during his career. This shift has been evaluated in different ways by those who have commented upon his thinking. Will Herberg and Charles West both feel that the early theological positivism of Barth has changed for the better and that an Olympian aloofness from political involvement has been overcome. Others, like George Forell, speaking critically rather than appreciatively of this shift, regard Barth's later writings as abortive efforts "to derive the political credo of social-democratic liberalism from the structure of the kingdom of God."[46]

In discussing the role of power in relation to law, despite occasional sentences in which he slips into what seems to be an affirmation of power as the final arbiter of human events, Barth affirms the necessity of having power under law. He draws a distinction between "*potestas* . . . the power that follows and serves the law"; and "*potentia* . . . the power that precedes the law, that masters and bends and breaks the law. . . ."[47] The first type of power marks the good state; it is to power-under-law that Christian political theory leads us.

Barth's use of the institutional motif can also be traced with respect to other aspects of human life. Barth uses the concept of orders, or "spheres" in his discussion of norms as well as implementations. The long discussion which opens the *Church Dogmatics*, Volume III, Part 4, is important in this respect. Barth's discussion of community, and especially his discussion of community in marriage, illustrates this process. He sees marriage in terms of its relationship to the sexual differentiation between man and woman. Each has a unique role to play. There is priority and posterity; subordination and superordination. But just as one is tempted to feel the discussion runs in the same groove with that of Brunner, Barth begins to apply his concept of freedom to the institution of marriage. It is not universally demanded of all. It is not a purely natural commandment, but a highly special divine calling. Those personal features which involve the creation of the "lasting" life companionship of two people in covenant are emphasized rather than the stark duty of fidelity for which Brunner called. The dimension of love is important between the partners who choose to covenant with one another. Marriage can be consummated fully in many ways. It may sometimes need to be dissolved.

In this view, grounded in a framework set forth in sections 41 and 45 of Volume III, Part 1, creation and covenant are held together, each standing for an important aspect of the human situation yet neither being sufficient to furnish an interpretive framework by itself. The category of creation points to much that is traditionally associated with the use of the term *orders*, with their fixed, static, and given qualities. The concept of covenant supplies the necessary corrective. Covenant stands for the dynamic element that gives internal meaning as well as external forms to the institutions of society. It stands for the dynamic element by which God as the redeemer can change the present forms of creation. Pentecost—which reverses Babel—can place men into new cultural spheres. Whereas the "orders" are commonly related to creation alone, for Barth the "spheres" are related to both creation and covenant.

Freedom and flexibility are thus introduced into the institutional motif without abandoning it. The pseudo-Lutheran conception of the orders is transcended without releasing the Christian from the institutional spheres within which he must hear and obey the comand of God. Both the givenness and the tentativeness of the spheres (or dispositions) is borne in mind.

> If [the Christian] hears the command of God here and now, then always by the same God he is disposed to be in company with some and not at first with others in the spheres of language, locality and history, thus finding himself at a particular place in the sphere of near and distant neighbours. If he hears the command obediently, this includes the fact that he regards, honours and accepts this disposition. To do this is part of his obedience in so far as he is summoned to obedience in this situation. Yet he does not obey the disposition. He obeys the command of God. This is not identical with the disposition. And the disposition itself does not contain any imperative. We cannot learn from it what is right and what is wrong. It is simply the concrete presupposition under which he must hear the command and will and do the right.[48]

The institutional motif is not bound parochially to any single church tradition. Just as Hooker embraced it as well as Calvin and Luther, so William Temple joined Bonhoeffer, Barth, and Brunner as a spokesman for this motif and its affirmation of the natural orders of community. Temple emphasized the impartiality of justice and the role of the official. "The State officer cannot know the prisoner in such a way as really to determine the treatment allotted to him in the light of what is best for his spiritual welfare."[49] The state may use coercion even though it is wrong for the individual to do so. Although the Christian's ultimate loyalty is to God, his secondary loyalty is to the state, and this secondary loyalty is to be rendered except when resistance and objection to the state are demanded by Christian integrity.

The other orders of creation also figured in Temple's thinking. "The family is so deeply grounded in nature and the nation in history that anyone who believes in God as Creator and as Providence is bound to regard both as part of the divine plan for human life."[50] Likewise, the church, the guild, the trade union, and the educational institution all have a role to play in the Christian life. While the Christian accepts the givenness of these institutions, he also suggests the directions in which they must move if they are to serve morally justifiable ends. He will insist that political organizations, for example, serve the cause of freedom, but leave to the politician the decisions as to how such an end shall be attained.

Brunner's formulation of the institutional motif differs from the same theme in the thinking of Barth and Bonhoeffer. Anglican forms of institutionalism differ from the Lutheran forms. But despite the differences, these outlooks seem remarkably alike when set in contrast to other forms of the institutional motif or to the operational and intentional approaches to the implementation of ethical decision.

13

Institutionalism Antithetical to Power

Ernst Troeltsch once complained that beginning with the eighteenth century "the social philosophy of the Christian community [like the state church] . . . suffered an undeniable disintegration, through its dependence upon continually changing conditions."[1] Troeltsch had seen enough, even in the last third of the nineteenth century, to justify his observation that significant changes were occurring within the Christian understanding of social issues. If only Troeltsch (who died in 1923) had lived to see the middle third of the twentieth century! He might have despaired of characterizing trends in social thought, not only in the Continental situation dominated by theologians like Schleiermacher and Ritschl, but in the American situation as well, where the diversity and complexity was even more evident.

Several thinkers, some of them associated with the social gospel, developed an alternative form of the institutional motif in which the role of power was either minimized or denied. These thinkers adopted an evolutionary metaphysic for the interpretation of society and understood human history in terms of a progressive thrust toward a social order dominated by love. In the final half of the nineteenth century the Darwinian theory of evolution had become, not only a well-accepted scientific hypothesis, but a powerful metaphysical image. Many Christians found inspiration in the idea of a progressive development toward higher forms of social harmony. They related this image to the theological conception of God's action within the world and found it helpful in affirming the creative possibilities of human life. They believed God to be at work in the institutions of society to accomplish his purposes and to further the establishment of His kingdom within the human orders. This outlook was most articulated by men like Washington Gladden, Lyman Abbott, George D. Herron, and Walter Rauschenbusch, but it was a pervasive influence in large segments of American Protestantism.

The turn of the century was a time of general optimism about society and its possibilities, which affected the thinking of theologians. Consider, for example, Newman Smyth's understanding of Christian possibilities for society: "The kingdom of organized love has begun on earth, but it is far from completion."[2] He believed that human moral development had moved from a prehistoric stage, to a legal epoch, to the Christian era of the Incarnation. In the first stage, tooth and claw were dominant; in the second, the sanctions of law; in the third, love will reign. The reign of love will include social aspects; an individual ethic is inadequate to embody the meaning of Christian responsibility. "Perfect virtue is to be measured on the plane of a perfect social good."[3]

Smyth's hopes for progressive realization of the Christian ideal in society led him to suppose that conflict would be eventually transformed. He did not expect to eliminate conflict, which he deemed an essential aspect of human life, but he did feel that conflict should be altered so as to divest it of its destructive features. Thus he declared: "Bows and arrows, gunpowder and muskets, artillery of tremendous destructive power, and torpedoes capable of making the earth quake, or even the weapons now in use of industrial warfare, such as strikes, boycotts, or trusts, are none of them, necessarily, indispensable means either of economic progress or of the conquest of moral ideals for supremacy over evil."[4] But the elimination of violence and coercion would not mean the elimination of conflict itself. When spiritualized, conflict can become a legitimate part of the kingdom of God.

Smyth argued that Christian ideals should be realized through the method of cooperation, which has become increasingly important in the progress of civilization. "The history of civilization indicates already an immense gain of the action of the principle of coöperation over the action of the principle of competition."[5] The method of conflict is then described as the method of sacrifice; the method of cooperation as the method of service. "These two words, sacrifice and service, denote the Christian method of seeking the answer to the Lord's prayer, 'Thy Kingdom come.' "[6] Finally, the Christian will seek to embrace the material world in an increasingly spiritual way. Only when the Christian brings the material things of the natural order under the spirit, and completely masters them for the purposes of Jesus, will the kingdom arrive.

In a chapter entitled "The Spheres in Which the Christian Ideal Is To Be Realized,"[7] Smyth discussed the family, the state, the church, and "intermediate social spheres." While he chose essentially the same social realities that have been encountered in other institutionalists, it is his interpretation of these spheres which becomes of decisive significance for understanding his perspective. Each of them is understood in its creative contribution to the positive attainment of the good. The family becomes the institution in which the Christian ideal of love is expressed. It is to be reverenced and protected for its positive redemptive significance. It gives light and warmth to the social whole. Similarly, Smyth looked at the state, not as a necessary dike against sin, but as the positive channel for expressing that essential unity which is already present among men. "The state, as the consequence and formal expression of this human relationship, is always derivative, not primary."[8] Smyth rejected both the social contract theory, which does not make sufficient place for the given human community that precedes the making of any contract, and the views which see the state as deriving its being directly from God. The state arises out of human community

> as the organization of the social human relations, and the authoritative expression of the rights and duties which are involved in these objective human relations of men to one another, deriving its sanctions from their truth, and having worth in so far as it realizes harmoniously these relations. The state is thus to be conceived of as organized society, whose authority is the authority of the whole over its parts, and whose function it is to secure the harmony of all the constituent parts in an outward order of social life. The authority of the state, therefore, is derived immediately from the moral value of the social relations which it organizes.[9]

This view of the state distinguishes it from both the theory of absolute sovereignty found in Hobbes and the liberalism found in Locke. It furnishes a rationale upon which the true functions and limits of the state's authority can be determined. The state is legitimate only when it functions to conserve and extend the values of natural human community, not when it destroys them. Smyth advocated the use of legislation to seek those ends "which experience may prove to be conducive to the good of the whole, while not destructive of the primary individual relations and functions of human life and activity."[10]

After examining the extent to which the state exhibits a moral quality and the thorny question as to the ways the state should have religious aims, Smyth concluded:

> The task of ethicizing and Christianizing all civil institutions is the practical politics of Christian faith. Politics is more in Christian ethics than it was, or could have been, in Aristotle's discussion of the forms of government, or even in Plato's dream of the republic. For we are called by the existing status of governments, as well as by the voice of their history, and the hopes of their future, to consider what civil institutions and what laws shall best answer the Christian possibilities of the life of a people, and bring to clearer and happier actualization the idea of the Christian society which goes before our civilization. It is not merely some ideal form of possible human government,

whether of constitutional monarchy or democracy, but it is the ideal of a Christian society to be realized on earth, which is the large, inspiring idea of the progress of the Christian nations. Each state in the Christian world, under the influence of Christian ideas, as it strives however imperfectly to realize in its sphere the Christian life of the people, is compelled to go beyond and beneath all formal questions concerning its institutions, and to seek to steep its laws in Christian ethics. And beyond the ethicizing of individual states, and the reception by them of the baptism of the Spirit of Christian history, the further problem remains of Christianizing the relations of the nations to one another, or the Christian ethicization of international law.[11]

One of Smyth's contemporaries, George D. Herron, posed the antithesis between the institutional and the coercive in even sharper terms. He called for the reconstruction of society in accordance with the standards of Jesus. This transformation involved the overthrow of capitalism and the institution of a democratic socialism. It was to come about through sacrifice, not coercion. Indeed, coercion had no place in Herron's scheme of things; the new order was to be established by evolution, not revolution.

Herron became a national figure; he toured America setting forth his views. A collection of his speeches is found in his book *The Christian State: A Political Vision of Christ*. Herron was convinced that above all human institutions there is a divine order or government. "The end of institutions is to progressively apprehend and interpret the laws of this government, and increasingly apply its forces to the more perfect organization of human life."[12] When human institutions ignore this divine order, they fail in their appointed task. Institutions which are attentive to this divine order will bring harmony to human life.

> It is the mission of the state to discover this centre and accomplish this unity of man. The state is the only organ through which the people can act as one man in the pursuit of righteousness; the only organ through which the people can act together in the organization and perfection of their common life in justice. The state can have no other meaning than the interpretation and execution of the mind of God toward the people. It must be the organized faith of the people; the manifestation of the highest right of which the people have knowledge in common; the organ of their common consciousness of God. It is ordained to be the visible institution of the unseen government of the world.[13]

Herron carried this line of reasoning to its logical end. The state becomes the "realized religion of the people."[14] It replaces the church. Through the state the Christian implements his moral ideal. There is just a hint of the coercive role of the state in the observation that it will take away the right of the exploiter to defraud his fellowmen, but the overwhelming features of the state are positive in character:

> The Christian economic state would take away the liberty to oppress and defraud, but give the liberty to work, to have faith, and to do justice. The real property rights of the people, the preservation of the home, and the perpetuity of the family, have their future dependence in the association of rights under the guardianship of the state as the social organ of a Christian democracy. Such a mutual surrender and investiture of rights, instead of endangering the individual and the family, would be the freedom of the individual to develop the highest personal life, and the security of the family from the invasion of want and oppression. The collection of rights and interests in the state as the organ of the Christian economy of the people, would remove life from the sphere of chance to that of a moral social certainty, and give opportunity for that free individual development which is the true end of civilization.[15]

It would hardly seem possible to be more hopeful concerning the good that can come from a social structure! Coupled with Herron's idea that society must be based upon cooperation, do away with warring self-interests, and institutionalize the spirit of sacrifice, the quotation seems strange reading in terms of much that has already been cited as Christian expressions of the institutional motif. But such is the theme, repeated many times in the speeches of Herron:

> If the state would be saved from the wrath of the rising social passion, it must believe on Christ as its Lord, and translate his sacrifice into its laws. Our institutions must become the organized expression of Christ's law of love, if the state is to obey the coming social conscience that is to command great moral revolutions in political thought and action. For society is the organized sacrifice of the people.[16]

It is important to look at this variation of the institutional motif, not because it comands extensive adherence today, but because it represents a divorce of the coercive from the institutional. The institution sustains itself because it commands the respect and allegiance of the people rather than because it has the ultimate sanction of power. Institutions become the visible expressions of love rather than structures of order for holding evil in check.

Walter Rauschenbusch is probably the best-known spokesman for the social gospel. Rauschenbusch argued for a socially alert Christianity prepared to rectify the injustices of the economic order in his day. His thinking ranged over a broad field. His books included a work on the place of prayer in relationship to social issues as well as a wide-gauge theological system related to his main concern. The most relevant treatment of his understanding of social order is found in the central portion of his book entitled *Christianizing the Social Order*. Rejecting the notions that the state should make pious overtures to the headship of Christ, or that religiosity should be required as a compulsory duty, Rauschenbusch nevertheless spoke of making the state a channel of specifically Christian objectives: "Christianizing the social order means bringing it into harmony with the ethical convictions which we identify with Christ."[17] This means to humanize the social order, until "the moral sense of humanity shall be put in control and shall be allowed to reshape the institutions of social life."[18]

Rauschenbusch rejected a perfectionist understanding of this program. "As long as men are flesh and blood the world can be neither sinless nor painless."[19] He observed that "Every child is born a kicking little egotist and has to learn by its own mistakes and sins to coördinate itself with the social life of every successive group which it enters."[20] These acknowledgments of human sin seem to carry Rauschenbusch away from Herron's high hopes for a society without coercion. They hint of the classical view that the state is a protection against evil. Rauschenbusch even declared: "A Christian social order makes bad men do good things."[21] But this hint of the classical pessimism is overshadowed by Rauschenbusch's hope for the successful embodiment of Christian values in a changing and maturing society.

According to Rauschenbusch, four aspects of the social order result in the progressive achievement of positive social values. Beginning with the family, the harsh patriarchal system of family life has been replaced by a system which embodies a far greater degree of love. In the early stages of human development, the family acted as a restraint upon sin. "This despotic family organization contained very large ingredients of good. It furnished the weak protection against enslavement and death. It coerced the savage to work, sweated the idleness out of him, and made his labor more productive by forcing him into coöperation with others."[22] But this function is no longer necessary in the family. As the patriarchal pattern has changed, not only the wife and children, but the father himself have come to share love.

> Thus the constitutional structure of the family has passed through an ethical transformation by slow historical processes. The despotism of the man, fortified by law, custom, and economic possession, has passed into approximate equality between husband and wife. The children have become the free companions of their parents, and selfish parental authority has come under the law of unselfish service. Economic exploitation by the head of the family has been superseded by economic coöperation and a satisfactory communism of the family equipment. Based on equal rights, bound together by love and respect

for individuality, governed under the law of mutual helpfulness, the family to-day furnishes the natural habitation for a Christian life and fellowship. There is no conflict of the Christian spirit with the accepted laws of family life; only with the transgressions of those laws. We can therefore say that the family has been assimilated to Christianity. As an institution it has been christianized.[23]

A similar process has taken place in the life of the church, which started as a coercive despotism and ended as a free fellowship. "Like the family, the Church was christianized by unlearning despotism and exploitation, and coming under the law of love and service."[24] Similarly, education, which moved from an aristocratic privilege and coercive pedagogy to a more open and nearly universal process, shows the progressive attainment of Christian values in the social order. Lastly, the state, which is a fourth great social order, has undergone this process. "The fundamental redemption of the State took place when special privilege was thrust out of the constitution and theory of our government and it was based on the principle of personal liberty and equal rights."[25]

These great transformations all suggest that the spirit of Christ can change social institutions. Rauschenbusch, convinced of the progress made in other realms, then turned to the economic order, in which he felt tooth and claw still ruled. "Business life is the unregenerate section of our social order."[26] He made numerous suggestions for bringing this aspect of human life under the same transformation he believed to have taken place in the other four orders. Rauschenbusch hoped that force would not have to be used to accomplish this result. He counseled peaceful means as much as possible. Unlike some spokesmen for the social gospel he was not a theoretical pacifist. He understood that force is a part of life, especially as used by employer groups in subjugating their employees. He counseled against resort to counterforce as a short-cut to achieve justice, but he declared:

> I do not hold that the use of force against oppression can always be condemned as wrong. Americans are estopped from denying the right of revolution, for our nation was founded by revolutionary methods, employed too by a minority of the population for class purposes. The test of brute strength is the *ultima ratio* when all higher arguments have proved vain. The great Roman historian [Livy] expressed the general conviction of nations: "War is just for those for whom it is necessary, and arms are holy for those to whom no hope is left except in arms.[27]

This concession to the use of force for settling controversy when all else fails does not consider force to be a centrally necessary feature of all social order. It is a last resort rather than a continuing responsibility; a concession to the failure of institutions rather than the essential mark of their function.

Ideally force can be minimized as men establish the kind of society in which justice and order are based upon the consent of the governed and the willing acknowledgment of social responsibility.

While no contemporary thinker would subscribe to the statements of Herron, and perhaps not even to those of Rauschenbusch, the influence of these men is still evident in a good deal of the contemporary liberal Protestant approach to social issues. Walter G. Muelder's view of the responsible society belongs very much within the social gospel tradition. His thinking has certainly been tempered by the criticisms made of the social gospel, but his categories and his confidences rest within the assumptional patterns of the movement. Muelder considers five institutions basic to culture: the family, education, politics, economics, and religion. The significance of his thinking, however, lies not in its choice of institutions, but in its understanding of their function. He begins his discussion with the family by acknowledging that there is a world-wide crisis with respect to family life. The traditional patterns are disintegrating and cannot be taken for granted. We need to look at the several forces in the modern world which affect the family situation, including such items as the growing autonomy of women, the increasing depersonalization of all human relationships, and the changing nature of religious sanctions for the basic values of family life. Many of these changes can be welcomed because they overcome a rigid, authoritarian patriarchalism with an experience by which God's own being and love can be understood. In the family, *eros* is transformed to *agape*. The ideal family is an order without coercion.

Muelder's discussion of family life within the institutional motif differs from Brunner's discussion of family life under the orders. Both hold that discipline is necessary to good order in the family, but whereas Brunner feels discipline must keep human passions from going wild, Muelder feels that the purpose of discipline is to deepen the roots of responsible life. In Brunner the patriarchal pattern is affirmed because it embodies authority. In Muelder the patriarchal pattern is willingly acknowledged to be a thing of the past. The family is interpreted as a positive channel for the expression of love—not a sentimental love, but the rigorous love of self-giving fidelity. "Christian marriage is a permanent partnership in moral development and the joyous sharing of love and companionship between the parents and with the children who are brought into the family."[28] Responsible planning, the creation of emotional maturity, the filling of social and psychological needs of the partners and children, and the mixing of kindness with discipline are all vitally important in the most creative use of this institution. The family also fulfills a basic educational function, which if poorly done cannot be easily overcome by other social experiences.

A similar reshaping of the institutional motif occurs in Muelder's discussion of the state. Muelder, in contrast with Herron, acknowledges the role of power in the operation of government. But, in contrast to thinkers assigned to the operational motif, he finds the authority and power of the state always subordinate to its institutional status. His three theses are stated as follows: "(1) that responsible states can be developed (and do exist to a degree), (2) that the state properly understood is an association which can be made responsible to God and the people, and (3) that the people need to learn how to use the state and all other forms of political organization to express social responsibility."[29] Muelder rejects theories of the state which reduce it to power alone, or to class struggle. He also rejects any effort to subordinate the state to ecclesiastical domination. In summary, he declares:

> One of the crying needs of the nation is for a return to the understanding of the moral and social foundations of law and politics, the strengthening of its roots by moral renewal in all social groups from the family to the state, and a rebirth of the sense of the vocation of politics as a sacred religious and moral duty on the part of churchmen and others.[30]

In fulfilling its function, the state must concern itself with economic affairs. It must seek to abolish poverty, hold unscrupulous practices in check, and maintain moral scrutiny over the use of all property which can be used as expressions of social power. Even though Muelder approves of governmental action in economic affairs, his outlook differs from Herron's idealistic socialism, in which governmental operation of the economic order was the means to express Christian ethical concern directly. Muelder is concerned that economic factors be dealt with by government in a constructive effort to serve the common good, but he is not advocating a doctrinaire socialism as the means to attain this result. Muelder thus keeps a pragmatic flexibility within his institutionalism, acknowledges the problems of power without embracing a view of *realpolitik*, and emphasizes the importance of democracy and freedom as the hallmarks of a healthy social system.

The following quotations underscore the continual emphasis which places Muelder so firmly in the institutional motif with the liberal overtones of the social gospel tradition. "An overemphasis on the idea of power and the negative function of the state in using physical force inhibits creative thought on how the state, conceived as a limited but responsible association, can be constructively developed as a servant of justice and freedom, perhaps even of love."[31] "True political power is the contradictory of power politics."[32] ". . . [I]t is probably the case that a positive conviction for democracy would never be generated out of a purely negative approach to man and the state."[33] "The conception of the state must be constructive, critical, and realistic with a demand for constant review of its functions and limits."[34]

All institutionalists are concerned that order shall be prior to power. Order must be built upon respect for the law: "Law, if it is to control power," writes a modern institutionalist, "may not be defined merely as the will of him who holds the power, but must rest on fundamental principles of justice, acceptable to the human heart at its best."[35] Some institutionalists carry their concern for the priority of law to a point where they hope to do away with the need for power, but this is by no means a universal conclusion. Nor is the institutionalist position shared by all students of human society. Those who reverse the priority, acknowledging the need for power to establish order, present another major motif in Christian social thinking.

14

Theological Justifications of Power and Influence

The institutional and operational motifs are built upon contrasting analyses of man's social life. In one, law, order, and due process are acknowledged and cherished; in the other, emphasis is placed upon the power configurations of society and the political maneuverings by which laws are enacted and decisions made. In the one, law enforcement is the function of an "office" and the policeman's role is one of authority; in the other, law enforcement is seen as a matter of dominion and the policeman is deemed effective because he possesses superior power.

Many theologians interpret the world about us, not as a structure of "orders," but as a "sea of influences" or as a "conflict of vitalities." They hold that power plays a crucial and inescapable role in the world. Speaking from this perspective, William L. Miller defines politics as "the fight for power wherever it is." Politics involves "the struggle over these decisions on which people differ, by groups. It is the conflict over the ability to make the decisions—that is, over power."[1]

Whereas institutionalists approach international affairs with a desire for international law and are frequently anxious to create an institutionalized authority to transcend the nationalistic divisions of autonomous states, those who think in operational terms feel that international relations can only be affected by the exercise of power and influence. They see channels of diplomatic pressure and the threat in large war potentials as the only meaningful instruments for dealing with international problems. These two approaches can make a difference in judging the importance of international organization. Noting that many people believe the United Nations is a good thing simply because it furnishes a new level of organizational structure, Kenneth W. Thompson has observed:

> It can, of course, be argued that local and particular interests are absorbed and disappear within the programs of the United Nations. This, in fact, is the prevailing view of moderns who insist that foreign policies must be humanitarian in character. In all this we are reminded

of research trends in the 1930's in international studies when American scholars preferred to view every international movement as good, and all national efforts as bad. Where the League of Nations and National Socialism were concerned, this distinction was in general quite plausible. If the examples had been the Communist International and the legitimate aspirations for national security of, say, England or the United States, the dichotomy between good internationalism and bad nationalism would have been seen to be fallacious. Indeed, scholars since the war have conceived of international institutions essentially in terms of international politics, which is to say, they have studied the United Nations in terms of the respective claims for national security by the member states. International organizations provide the framework within which nations strive to harmonize their independent purposes, and United Nations policies are essentially the resultant of the policies of its members.[2]

When viewed from one perspective, political organizations look like structures of justice and order; when viewed from another perspective, they are considered operations of power. An institutionalist, like Walter Muelder, places the priority on the order:

> Political order is more a matter of integration than of domination. Force alone is never enough to hold a group together. In all constituted government behind any show or organization of force lies authority. Authority always includes the idea of legitimate power, and authority is responsibe to the underlying social structure. The force which government exercises, and in the state the monopoly of violence is granted the government, is but an instrument of authority, vindicating the demands of an order that force never alone creates.[3]

Reinhold Niebuhr, speaking of the same interplay between power and authority in political life, argues the other way around. Denying that the democratic principle of self-rule provides a substitute for the role of force in sustaining a nation, he writes:

> The fact that the authority of all governments rests upon both force and prestige also belies the theory of a radical difference between new and old forms of nations and empires. The cohesion of the American national community presumably was established by the rational consent of the thirteen colonies, who wisely formed a single nation. But while the Civil War is studied in all our history books it has not struck the imagination of the nation that in a crisis force was necessary, and was used, to preserve the unity of the nation.[4]

Significant differences in the social thought of these two men flow from this contrast. In discussing the possibilities and nature of world community, Muelder clearly hopes that international law can be progressively established, even though this is difficult. "To accomplish an effective legal order above the states and achieve an international law with binding force for peace are both complex and difficult. . . ."[5] "[But] The importance of good law is not diminished by the obstacles to achieving it. . . ."[6] Niebuhr, on the other hand, declares, "The idea of unifying the world community through world law is so illusory that it has intrigued only the most abstract idealists and a discussion of such proposals would be irrelevant."[7] The difference between Muelder and Niebuhr involves even their attitudes toward the role of science. Muelder declares, "The scientific spirit and discipline is a peacemaker among warring claimants regarding fact."[8] Niebuhr, in contrast, asserts, "The sober facts about the communities of men and the corresponding necessity of balancing every power with a countervailing power, and of allowing freedom to place every center of power and of ideology under review, were not discovered by an objective science."[9] Regarding the family as the prototype of the state, Muelder can say, "Through the idea of government the political order has continuity with the family,"[10] whereas Niebuhr is led to observe, ". . . every form of dominion, except possibly the first dominion of fatherhood, contains an embarrassment to the moral consciousness of man."[11]

Those who think in institutional terms look upon the same realities as those who think in operational terms, but they come to different evaluations of what is going on within them. For example, justice is understood differently by those who see it as the consequence of carefully defined processes which are adhered to by common consent under a system of constitutional safeguards and those who see it as a balance of power between conflicting interests. The law court is the obvious symbol of the first concept of justice; the successful picket line, an obvious symbol of the second. While few serious Christian thinkers would settle for one of these to the complete exclusion of the other, almost every thinker tends to emphasize the pre-eminence of one and to regard its use as more effective than the use of the other.

Those who think in operational categories may argue that even the law court functions like the picket line, as a theater for the play of influence. Lawyers are successful when they can persuade juries on emotional grounds to decide for their clients. In some places the cultural ethos makes an impartial trial impossible, even under constitutional procedures. A sober analysis cannot escape the conclusion, so it is argued, that factors of power and influence are far more crucial than structures of justice and order.

The foregoing distinctions illustrate two ways of interpreting the nature of political and social events. They have theoretical counterparts in political theory. Alden Kelley speaks of a distinction between two traditions in political thought: on the one hand, the idealistic-rationalistic tradition; on the other, the romantic-vitalistic movement. The former stems from

Aristotle and holds that it is natural and necessary to have a governing principle in order for men to live together in society. In this tradition a great deal of effort is expended in the search for the most adequate rational principle which can serve this function. In contrast, the latter view feels that nonrational, even irrational elements hold society together. Whereas the former view is found in Aristotle, Aquinas, a number of papal encyclicals, and T. S. Eliot, the latter is found in Spencer, Bentham, Mill, and Marx. Kelley's sympathies are with the romantic-vitalistic movement. He pleads for a grasp of these issues which is informed by the knowledge of the *shape*, rather than the theory of politics, its actualities rather than its theoretical possibilities. But Kelley also notes that Christianity has traditionally been wedded to the idealistic-rationalistic tradition and agrees with Reinhold Niebuhr, to whom he ascribes the judgment that while "Christianity properly understood actually had more in common with the romantic-vitalistic philosophies, it appeared to be wedded to a rationalistic optimism."[12]

Roger Shinn has found a similar difference in two types of socialism—Marxist and utopian.[13] Marxist socialism takes seriously the class struggle, with its elements of coercion in the determination of social conditions prior to the successful consummation of the revolution. Utopian socialism believes in cooperation and is often coupled with pacifist assumptions and trust in the possibility of mutual decisions obtained by peaceful means. Moreover, utopian socialists have high hopes for what comes from the rearrangement of institutional features when economic processes are guided by the common will of the people through democratic decision, whereas Marxism actually looks forward to the day when the state as an institution will wither away.

Any discussion of power should take into account various conceptions of power. According to the Machiavellian outlook, conflicting forces battle in deadly conflict with each other, using every means at their command to win a position of superiority. Beguilement as well as tooth and claw may mark the process, but in either event the conflict stands unmitigated and raw. The victor gets the spoils regardless of the justice involved, since justice is a function of strength. The strong exercise dominion over the weak. This view of power has seldom, if ever, become the basis of a Christian view.

Another understanding of power views it as the necessary means for insuring adherence to morality and justice under law. In this view power is felt to flow from the authority of institutions, and such power is held to be different from the power which is exercised, for example, in the effort to become a constituted authority. If the Machiavellian approach can be described as power without authority, this approach may be defined as power as the expression of authority. Obviously, to the extent that authority is given the priority, this view belongs to the institutional motif.

In a third view of these matters, power is taken as the means to establish authority. Power is felt to be the ultimate sanction for law and order. Authority without power is helpless, and power must be supposed before any meaningful order can be presumed. In this view, the constituted authority is held to be dependent upon the command of superior power. This third view is basic to the operational motif.

Let us consider the difference between these views in practical and illustrative terms, using the common traffic ticket as an example. When a motorist pulls over to the curb at the sound of a siren, shows his license to a uniformed officer, accepts a traffic summons, and appears of his own (reasonably) free will at traffic court, his action may be interpreted in two ways. The institutionalist will maintain that the motorist understands the ticket as a symbol of just and orderly procedure which he accepts, that the motorist respects the officer as an agent of justice, and that he is willing to acknowledge his wrong in relation to an established measure of guilt. In this case the motorist responds to the summons in the knowledge that court is a duly created instrument of justice. The operationalist, on the other hand, will argue that the motorist acts from motives of fear, knowing that greater punishment is in store for those who resist arrest, try to escape, or hold courts in contempt than is in store for those who come voluntarily. The officer and the court can function only because they hold a monopoly of power in the situation. To be sure, the dignity of the law is never independent of its ability to coerce obedience, but coercion that enforces constituted authority works quite differently than coercion that threatens life or limb merely because of its power.

The enduring and stable features of an institution outlast the personnel belonging to it at a given historical moment. A power configuration, however, is more dependent upon the individuals who rally behind its program at any particular time. It tends to be *ad hoc* rather than given, to depend upon specific goals it wishes to accomplish rather than to occupy a permanent place in the created order of things. Power groups sometimes decompose after they have served a specific purpose or attained a specific objective, whereas the orders tend to endure despite changes in programs and directions of policy. The state endures longer than the political party, and it endures even through changes in the controlling party. Hence, institutions tend to appear stable, dignified, and proper. They call for citizenship. Operational configurations, on the other hand, tend to look transient, sinister, and dedicated to achieving ends that are tainted with the self-interest of their members. They call for partisanship.

Both the created orders and operational configurations are part of the world. Any effort to implement ethical impulses without compromise with the world will reject both patterns. While the world is differently understood in institutional terms than it is understood in operational terms, it is accepted in either case as a necessary, yet sin-filled, reality within which the Christian is obligated to work. Hence, Emil Brunner, as a representative of the institutional motif, had this to say about the nature of the state:

> Every State represents human sin on the large scale; in history, in the growth of every State the most brutal, anti-divine forces have taken a share, to an extent unheard of in the individual life, save in that of some prominent criminals. In the State we human beings see our own sin magnified a thousand times. The State is the product of collective sin. . . .
> This, however, still does not lead us to the deepest view of the paradoxical nature of the State; without this daemonic, violent power of compulsion we cannot imagine how any unity of a people could have come into existence, and without this power of compulsion the State cannot fulfill its divinely appointed purpose in and for society. It is the State which creates the legal system, without which human civilization could be unthinkable.[14]

Joseph Sittler, speaking about political life from a perspective that emphasizes its operational features, makes this realistic appraisal of the political process:

> While most Christians today, to be sure, would admit that the Gospel is relevant to the realm of politics, they turn in revulsion from the actual operation of political parties and the devious devices required for the formation of practical policies. To involve themselves in jockeying, trading, calculation, compromise, baby kissing, and boodle-splitting requires a rough handling of ethical "principles."[15]

All power and influence depend upon the effective use of sanctions. Sanctions may be positive, offering rewards and enticements; they may be negative, threatening deprivations or harm. It is possible to classify sanctions according to the following categories: emotive sanctions, involving the power of example, etiquette, caste, class, "ways of life," prestige appeals, and the need for group identity; economic sanctions, including the capacity to aid or hinder gain, to impose boycotts, to control acquisition and consumption; political sanctions, including the power to use the caucus and ballot, the right to lobby, the threat to intimidate and destroy; and ecclesiastical sanctions, including excommunication and the ban, prophetic judgment and censure, the fear of losing an eternal reward, and the power of criticism publicly pronounced from the pulpit or privately administered in the confessional. But are not these sanctions grouped according to the very "orders" set forth within the institutional motif while at the same time they view social processes in a different light?

Reinhold Niebuhr has developed one of the most thorough and extensive systems of Christian thinking in which power and influence are given acknowledged priority over structures of justice and order. While Niebuhr acknowledges the place of structures, he practically always points to the factors of power necessary to establish or maintain such structures operative in sinful society, applying this analysis to political, economic, and cultural realms. His thinking was born in part from his struggles on behalf of justice during the unionization of the auto industry while he was a Detroit pastor, and it was nurtured to fruition by his role in calling American churchmen from pacifist isolationism to the acceptance of responsibility for the defense of the Western world against the threat from Hitler.

Niebuhr has always taken into account the power factors that operate in the economic realm. He has therefore held that in order to achieve economic justice, political measures of a coercive nature must be employed in the correction of the market: "Justice in a technical society requires that the centralization of power inherent in the industrial process be matched by collective social power."[16] Niebuhr finds collective organization of workers into labor unions one possible form of collective power; political intervention in the economic field another possible form of economic power. He sets down this general thesis:

> ... any unregulated enterprise or relationship in human life will tend to produce more inequality than is morally justified or scarcely acceptable. This tendency is due to a simple fact. If there are no restraints upon human desires, any center of power in human society will be inclined to appropriate more privilege to itself than its social function requires. Therefore, no matter how inexact are the equalities and inequalities which emerge from a political interference with a market economy, they are probably closer to the requirements of justice than those of a completely unregulated economy. They have been established, not by nice calculations of "natural law," but by tensions and contests of power which are a legitimate part of a democratic society. They serve the general ends of justice because the equality of political power (inherent in the rights of universal suffrage) has been used to level undue inequalities in the economic sphere.[17]

Niebuhr is afraid of any unchecked power, from whatever source it is derived. This prompts him to criticize a laissez-faire doctrine that would allow economic organization to go unchecked. It also enables him to criticize the Marxist hope for a social order in which the coercive power of the state is presumed first to be just and then to wither away. It furnishes the grounds on which he takes issue with those who prefer voluntary controls rather than coercive action by the state within the economic order. Niebuhr grants that in an ideal social organization men would work together harmoniously without compulsion, but he argues that even the family finds it necessary to employ coercion to maintain its harmony. Moreover,

> an uncoerced equilibrium is something short of a real society, not only because any *ad hoc* balance of power is inadequate for the attainment of justice, but also because there is an incipient chaos in an uncoerced equilibrium. A tension of competing interests may quickly degenerate into an anarchy of conflicting interests. That is why a community must avail itself of coercion to establish a minimal order.[18]

Niebuhr's views have developed not only in relationship to economic matters but in his understanding of international affairs. He fought very hard around 1940 for involvement in the defense of Western Europe. He faced widespread pacifism in the church which had made common cause with isolationism in the country as a whole. But even before urging active military involvement Niebuhr was writing about the contributions which resort to arms might make to the defense of Western political democracy. At the end of an article published in *The Christian Century* for December 18, 1940, he threw down the gauntlet in these terms:

> No matter how they twist and turn, the protagonists of a political, rather than a religious, pacifism end with the acceptance and justification of, and connivance with, tyranny. They proclaim that slavery is better than war. I beg leave to doubt it and to challenge the whole system of sentimentalized Christianity that prompts good men to arrive at this perverse conclusion. This system must be challenged not only in this tragic hour of the world's history, lest we deliver the last ramparts of civilization into the hands of the new barbarians. It must be challenged in peace and in war because its analysis of human nature and human history is fundamentally false.[19]

According to Niebuhr, international affairs must be premised upon a realistic estimate of human actions. Christians only fool themselves when they suppose that peace and reconciliation can be effected by a moral suasion that divorces itself from coercive elements. This illusion was bred by those forms of the social gospel which underestimated the role of coercion in the management of human affairs and which too easily pictured love as a simple historical possibility.

Niebuhr's thought has too often been caricatured. He does not make a fetish of coercion. He does not glorify it nor rely upon it to accomplish permanently satisfying results. He does not espouse Machiavellianism in the effort to escape sentimentalism. He criticizes men like Augustine, Hobbes, and Marx even while he is indebted to aspects of their thinking. If persuasive rather than coercive techniques can be used to achieve justice, Niebuhr is pleased, but he is not fooled into thinking that power can ever be entirely eliminated from man's corporate life.

The subtlety of Niebuhr's thinking is well illustrated by his book *Moral*

Man and Immoral Society. In chapter eight he writes about the contribution that political force makes to the achievement of justice. Much that he says in this chapter is written in the time-bound context of the date it was prepared and reflects Niebuhr's early socialistic tendencies. However, the thesis is essentially the same one which appears in later writings, that power is a prerequisite for achieving justice and order. Then the reasoning shifts, and the succeeding chapter deals with the problems of preserving moral values in politics. Without contradicting the previous chapter, Niebuhr shows how the contributions of morality are essential to the health of a social order. The moralist does not control the struggles which emerge in the fight for justice in any easy or simple way, yet the fight for justice must not proceed entirely free of the judgments made by the moralist. "Moral reason," observes Niebuhr, "must learn how to make coercion its ally without running the risk of a Pyrrhic victory in which the ally exploits and negates the triumph."[20]

In comparison with the language and concepts used by traditional Christian thinkers, or by men like Barth, Brunner, and Bonhoeffer, to describe the orders or mandates, Niebuhr's language in his book *The Structure of Nations and Empires* seems essentially naturalistic. God may laugh at the rise and fall of nations and empires which grow pretentious in their use of power, but He does not have very much to do with the processes by which they come into being. A nation may command obedience because it marshals superior influence, but it cannot claim that its authority should be obeyed because it is divinely instituted. Perhaps it is because of the way he speaks of God's action that Niebuhr's political thinking has been more influential outside of the Christian community than has been the thinking of men who appeal to theistic and christological factors in describing the nature of the state.

Niebuhr's argument was written against the background of the cold war, in which two powerful nations have been pitted against each other. Niebuhr finds each nation and its allies proof of the fact that nationalistic power cannot be brought under constitutional controls merely by the resolution to do so. He believes that Wilson failed to set up an effective League of Nations following the First World War because he failed to make a sufficient place for the power to support it. Eisenhower followed Wilson's steps ideologically after the Second World War, but because American power was so great the nation assumed the responsibilities commensurate with its power despite the inadequacies in the theories for doing so. Niebuhr does not rule out the possible institutionalization of power in the international realm, but he does insist that any successful institutionalization is dependent upon favorable conditions in the power situation.

Niebuhr assumes that his readers will have little difficulty recognizing the priority of coercive force in totalitarian governments and traditional communities. He takes the importance of coercion in international affairs as almost self-evident. But he also contends that many of the same factors are at work in democratic societies, though in transformed ways. Granting that forces of natural cohesion have a greater place than the coercive power of centralized authority, he declares that "none of these cohesive forces, which may be described as 'horizontal,' obviate the necessity of the vertical force of cohesion inherent in a central authority."[21] Democratic nations function with many of the same elements of power and influence, constituting a cohesive bond, which are at work in traditional aristocracies.

> The prestige of a democratic government is clearly only partly derived from the idea that it speaks with the "consent of the governed." It must fashion equilibria of social and political power which will impress the people with its capacity to preserve order and to extend justice. If it fails in this purpose generally, if it operates only with the confused notion of Rousseau's "general will," it will either lose the tacit consent of the whole people, haunted by the fear of anarchy, or it will lose the confidence of a section of the people, which feels itself particularly defrauded of justice."[22]

This argument is pursued at length and with rigor, yet is generally tempered by a pragmatic common sense. Niebuhr looks to the balances of power which exist in the complexities of all social arenas to prevent a single locus of power from gaining total authority or dominion. He observes that "the most unambiguous relation of dominion to community is established in a free integral community in which checks are placed upon the dominion within the community, and in which every subordinate power is balanced by some other power."[23] In maintaining their dominion the leaders of the community must persuade the people that they act for their good, or for a larger universal good supported by the community. They may do this by using either secular or religious sanctions, but in either instance their case must have sufficient cogency to render it plausible. It will seldom, if ever, be as cogent as they pretend it to be, for the rulers of this world can seldom see the antinomies and contradictions which attend their own attempts to maintain order. "The truth about a political order is told by those who stand historically and ideologically outside it."[24]

Niebuhr feels that Augustine, whom he regards as one of the most realistic and perceptive thinkers in history, was able to give a realistic account of the realities of the city of this world precisely because his ultimate loyalty was with the heavenly city. However, Augustine's account of the heavenly city erred precisely because he was so loyal to it, for no known historical reality has exhibited the attributes Augustine attached to the heavenly city. Since Augustine stood outside the earthly city we may take his realistic analysis of the city of this world, pointing as it does to the moral ambiguities and balances of power which rule in the earthly affairs of men, to be more accurate than the analyses provided by idealists whose involvements with the earthly city have resulted in bland and sentimental analyses of its political processes.

> Augustine was, by general consent, the first great "realist" in western history. He deserves this distinction because his picture of social reality in his *civitas dei* gives an adequate account of the social factions, tensions, and competitions which we know to be well-nigh universal on every level of community; while the classical age conceived the order and justice of its *polis* to be a comparatively simple achievement, which would be accomplished when reason had brought all subrational forces under its dominion.[25]

Augustine derived his political realism from biblical rather than philosophical categories. It was rooted in an astute understanding of self-love, or pride, as the basic and sinful nature of man. It perceived clearly that all aspects of human community, including the family, are foci of tensions, competitions of interest, seats of conflict. Niebuhr obviously finds Augustine's operational side to be more crucial than his institutional aspects.

No observer can doubt Niebuhr's emphasis upon the role of power in human affairs. But it is equally important to note that he can criticize a political cynicism that is blind to the novel and creative elements in the institutionalization of power at the same time he can criticize idealisms which fail to take power with sufficient realism. Niebuhr can look upon world government as illusory when proposed as the way to solve the dilemmas of present world divisions—no government is possible until the divisions are basically healed—yet he can also welcome every constructive accomplishment in the international order which has contributed to the furthering of interchange and world community. Niebuhr's varied, complex, dialectical, and often intensely practical wrestling with the issues of love and justice, freedom and necessity, realism and idealism, sin and grace, possibility with impossibility, and many other antinomies which are held in creative tension rather than solved in scholastic balance, enables him to meet problems with a responsive good sense which more doctrinaire thinkers could not muster.

In terms of his interests, assumptions, consistent emphases, and overwhelming preoccupations Niebuhr presents one of the most thoughtful and persistent expressions of the operational motif within the modern theological scene. His influence upon other contemporary thinkers has been enormous.

15

Contrasting Views of Power and Influence

Much contemporary theological thinking about social policy is concerned with questions about how power is to be understood and the ways it should be employed. This concern is evident in both advocates of coercive power and defenders of nonviolence as a social strategy.

Political Realism in Recent Protestant Thinking

Kenneth W. Thompson is one of many contemporary Christian thinkers who is concerned that Christians should take account of power and self-interest in the political realm. He finds Walter Lippmann, who speaks without reference to Christian theology, conscious of the same factors that Augustine and Niebuhr have acknowledged. In contrast, pronouncements of church officials tend to be buoyantly optimistic about translating Christian ideals into political strategies. To emphasize the contrast between political realism and religiously prompted idealism, Thompson compares two testimonies given before Congress on behalf of technical assistance: one, given by a representative of the State Department; the other, by a representative of the then Federal Council of Churches. Both supported the program, but whereas the representative of the State Department argued the bill's importance almost completely in political terms, declaring it to be necessary to keep India from becoming a Communist state, the representative of the churches argued on humanitarian lines and expressed the hope that the technical assistance programs would "be kept totally independent of considerations of military or defense policy."[1] Expressing a clear preference for the testimony of George Allen from the State Department to that of Walter Van Kirk from the Federal Council of Churches, Thompson observes:

> If we are less forthright [about our self-interest] we shall only invite
> the resentment, disdain, and rebuke of the Indians, who will point to
> the dross of self-interest that joins inextricably with the gold of

moral purpose in every foreign policy. The best we can do, Mr. Allen advises, is to identify and consolidate our interests with those of India. Indeed, the highest ethical standard for nations may be the mutuality of their national interests and purposes. India, with a subcontinent to exploit and develop, shares with us the need for an era of economic growth, international peace and security. Thus it must be said that the relevant political ethic for the diplomatist requires, to begin with, an awareness that the texture of interstate relations is comprised of multiple national interests, with their military, political, economic, and moral components, which clash in conflict or are resolved in consensus and agreement. In politics, interest or power and morality can rarely be conceived of in isolation; and ethical judgments must be made not in the abstract but in relation to the contingent realities of the particular situation. Moral principles in their pure form seldom intrude on the political but are modified in light of the facts of interest and power.[2]

In his book *Christian Ethics and the Dilemmas of Foreign Policy*[3] Thompson urges the realistic balancing of political factors in a tolerable harmony of self-interests. He rejects three other ways of viewing international affairs: the moralistic view that would guide every action on idealistic grounds, the cynical conclusion that all international life is a battle for the spoils, and a "reformist apocalyptical" approach which looks forward to a change in the character of international life. Christians, he argues, must accept the fact that they cannot cure everything, should beware of enunciating absolute principles rather than pragmatic possibilities, and should buckle down to the long haul in which international affairs are accepted as continually unfinished business. We must learn to live with successive crises but contribute to their amelioration by divesting ourselves of vested interests and self-righteous postures.

The subtle yet important differences which can appear in basically similar points of view show up if we compare the writings of Ernest W. Lefever to those of Kenneth Thompson. Theologically trained, Lefever has devoted most of his career to government affairs and to thinking about the religious and ethical implications of politics and foreign policy. In a small essay entitled "Politics—Who Gets What, When, and How," Lefever defines politics in terms of power and policy. Politics is the use of power to advance certain goals. He quotes Hans Morgenthau, admitting that this may put the matter a bit strongly: "Let us face bravely the lust for power and power politics in all their threatening ugliness as the inevitable elements of human life in a political society."[4] But while he holds that power is crucial to political life, Lefever argues that policy is just as crucial. While politics is "who gets what, when, and how," it is also "what he does with it." Politicians are distinguished from one another by what they propose to do with the power they hold. God is very much concerned about the policies supported by different groups. He cares, as he did in the days of the Hebrew prophets, what policies are adopted. Because God cares about policies, the Christian must also come to care and use his influence to see that policies are adopted which are compatible with God's concern about justice and mercy for his children. A "nonpolitical" approach to politics, which is especially prevalent among Protestant citizens, cannot cope with political processes:

> Protestants generally approach politics from a nonpolitical point of view. What do we mean by this? We mean that they fail to recognize politics as essentially a struggle for power in the interests of an over-all program for dealing with the major issues confronting us. We tend to flee power and call it evil. This leads to political apathy and irresponsibility. As Christians we must accept power as neither good nor bad in itself, but as a gift from God to be used for the advancement of his purposes in the world.[5]

In general, according to Lefever's diagnosis, Protestant statements from church bodies tend to be too vague and idealistic, and to call for changes which involve the abolition of power rather than its redirection. Some Protestantism of past decades was successful in opposing child labor and in advocating social security, but too often its interests have been petty and moralistic, calling for prohibitions of alcohol and gambling, supporting candidates with "clean" lives, and judging matters in overly personal terms. Too many church-goers decry bribes and personal use of influence but ignore the greater corruptions in which large power blocs use legislation to protect their private interests.

Protestants should learn to be politically responsible. This means that they "must accept the fact of power, the priority of issues over personalities, and the creative role of compromise and conflict."[6] It also means that they should exert their influence through the political party of their choice, since the political party is the most effective instrument for exercising power. Lefever feels that effectiveness is greatest in the major parties and argues that third or splinter parties only jeopardize the success of the major parties by subtracting the most critical bloc of votes in close elections. Those who vote for the candidates of a splinter party only throw the plurality in the major contest to the side they would least like to see win.

The necessity and role of power in the implementation of Christian decision are described in greater depth in Lefever's book *Ethics and United States Foreign Policy*. In the preface he acknowledges his indebtedness to a number of thinkers who belong to the "realist" school, including Reinhold Niebuhr, Hans J. Morgenthau, William T. R. Fox, Walter Lippmann, George F. Kennan, and Kenneth W. Thompson. Very early in the book Lefever sets forth his program:

> This book is a modest attempt to deal with [the problem of United States foreign policy]. The writer is convinced that there is widespread and profound confusion among religious and political leaders regarding the relation of ethics to international politics, that religion is often a source of confusion rather than understanding, and that efforts to apply morality to foreign policy frequently end in disaster. Much of this confusion flows from a misunderstanding of what international politics is on the one hand and what ethics, especially Judaeo-Christian ethics, is on the other. Many Americans do not understand the role of power in foreign policy. "Power politics" and ethics are often thought of as mutually exclusive and morally incompatible poles or political alternatives. The writer believes there is no foreign policy, however noble, which does not include "power politics," or, however cynical, which does not include moral considerations.[7]

In stressing the twin foci of power and morality, Lefever levels sharper criticism at the religious people who would shun power than at those who neglect morality. In fact, he finds that national aims, goals, purposes, and policies are usually defined in terms of some end. The danger in foreign policies does not lie with purposeless power but with the religious disavowal of power which undercuts the legitimate pursuit of pragmatic diplomatic negotiation on behalf of just goals. The religious condemnation of "power politics," the religious idealism which calls for attainments far beyond the realm of the possible, and the impulse to undertake crusades, all receive Lefever's censure. He feels that the errors which have sprung from religious idealism could be corrected by a serious attention to biblical religion, in which the declaration of what *is*, as well as the vision of what *ought to be*, preserves a healthy realism. In contrast,

> The morally-concerned reformer and the political idealist often become, in their zeal, so preoccupied with the imperatives of human responsibility that they ignore the givenness of human existence. Ignorance of the limits and possibilities of man and history has often led to utopian crusades which have ended in disaster. The long road from Versailles to Pearl Harbor and beyond is cluttered with the whitened bones of crusades that failed—the League of Nations, peace through economic planning, the Kellogg-Briand Pact, and peace through the renunciation of war, to name but a few. These crusades, in which American religious leaders invested so much energy and devotion, failed not for lack of good intentions or enthusiasm but because the crusaders tended to believe that morally desirable goals were, for the mere fact of their desirability, politically possible. They misread current history because they failed to understand the tragedies and contingencies of the whole realm of history. They misunderstood history because they did not understand the limits and possibilities of human nature.[8]

Thompson and Lefever deal with many of the same themes, make many of the same observations, and call for remarkably similar approaches to the same problems. They both criticize prevailing notions among Protestants as to the moral foundations of national action. But there are differences in emphasis. In criticizing the religious idealists, Lefever tends to focus his attention on their failure to acknowledge the role of power in the conduct of foreign policy. Thompson centers his criticism of religious leadership upon its failure to acknowledge the place of national interest in the conduct of policy. In considering the thought of Hans Morgenthau, Thompson concentrates on those aspects of his thinking which point beyond the analysis of power; Lefever finds the power theory to be congenial as expressed. Thompson feels very strongly about the need for humility in place of a moral self-righteousness; Lefever is more evidently concerned for responsibility as an alternative to power weakness.

Political realism has expressed itself, not only in terms of international affairs, but in terms of hard-headed admonitions to Christians to be concerned about domestic politics. Many books, mostly written since the 1950's, have been addressed to laymen and designed to inculcate a concern about political affairs. Not all such books have contributed to the deepening of theological insight, but they deserve consideration because they witness to a prevailing preoccupation of a large segment of contemporary Christian thinkers.

In William Muehl's *Politics for Christians* we have a polemic against false understandings of political action extant in many Protestant circles, coupled with suggestions for becoming more effective within the political process. Major criticisms are aimed at the moralistic individualism which is often mixed with religion. Because religious men cherish virtues in the individual, they tend to vote for men whose personal qualities appeal to their sense of propriety rather than for men who advocate politics which Christians ought to support. The average American misunderstands the democratic process by believing it to be healthiest when it is free of tensions and struggles. He renders his political witness weak because he shuns the very manipulations by which it can be expressed. He feels that good politics depends upon having good people in office, yet paradoxically he also feels that good people will not expose themselves to the compromises involved in seeking and holding office. He takes many issues, such as school levies and reform movements, "out of politics" by supporting them on a "nonpartisan" basis, thus perpetuating the myth that anything really worthwhile lies outside the political arena.

Much of Muehl's book consists of practical advice to the reader on how to get involved constructively in local political action. Such involvement is rooted in a Christian understanding of the mutual bondage of each man to his fellow man.

The Christian faith as understood by the Protestant theologian does not furnish a spiritual rationalization for rugged individualism. It teaches us, rather, that men were created together and are judged in their relationships, that every man is a priest, not for himself alone but for all other men, that every human association can be the means of grace.[9]

Christian faith, properly understood, undercuts the moralistic distinctions between "good guys" and "bad guys" which bedevil pietistic politics. All men are infected with self-interest and make decisions in terms of their self-interest. Only when this self-interest comes against the self-interest of others does it awake to its own deception and make allowances for its own tendencies to overestimate its importance.

If every man's perception of "the good" is corrupt, then no man can be said to be "right thinking" in the sense that he is able to transcend self-interest and respond fully to objective righteousness. God's will does not speak through the words or deeds of any one man or group. It is made manifest in the creative relationships which modify and chastise, balance and correct, the presumption and error of the individual.[10]

The Christian in politics must come to grips with the presence of power and use power for attainment of the ends he seeks to serve. Power cannot be wished away. If the Christian does not use it, other men will take it for their purposes. Justice must be the hallmark of effective political decision-making; love by itself becomes sentimental or paternalistic. Democracy involves the "pulling, hauling, bargaining" processes by which the diverse and conflicting elements in a community are brought together. Conflicts are normal in a healthy democracy, which finds fair and effective means of handling them. The mechanisms of politics, including the machine, the party boss, the bloc vote, and the peddling of influence (all those things which "nice" people often abhor), must be employed for the formulation and implementation of policy. "If we really accept the significance of *what* is done in politics, we shall be compelled to measure our own sincerity, in part at least, by the extent to which we master the details of political procedure."[11] William Miller puts it this way, "The trouble with the politics of many Christians is not that they aren't Christian enough; it's that they aren't political enough."[12]

Francis Pickens Miller, the Presbyterian opponent of the machine politics of Virginia, has also written about Christian responsibility in the political realm. He declares the necessity of entering politics in order to implement one's Christian convictions and speaks about the arts of compromise and voter appeal. But he also notes the dangers that come from a failure to know one's moral values as well as the dangers which inhere in hanging on to them too rigidly. He finds it necessary to avoid two dangers, one that springs from moralism, the other rooted in naïve failure to relate moral ends to political judgments. His plea for a wise Christian participation in politics is the same plea set forth by Muehl, but the terms in which it is cast point to a double root of political ineptitude among Protestants, and to a twofold danger which must be kept in mind by all who enter into the political enterprise.

> Thus far, our experience in America with active Protestant Christians in politics has not been too encouraging. Unhappily, many Christians in politics tend toward one of two extremes. On the one hand, there is the kind of politically naive Protestant who swallows the rottenest political bait, hook, line, and sinker; and, on the other hand, there is the perfectionist to whom all public questions are either black or white, and who believes that the Christian must take his stand on absolutes which must be realized day after tomorrow. The perfectionist in his way discredits Christian ethics as much as the man who compromises his Christian ethics. What is wanted is an ethical sense of timing coupled with capacity to work with practical politicians without being taken in by them.[13]

The writings just discussed have a clear and specific purpose; they seek a specific result; they apply to a particular sort of ethical issue. They cannot, however, fairly be said to represent fully developed theological treatments of Christian ethics in its broadest implications. They talk about power and influence but do not use them as categories with which to construct a systematic position. They may be considered tracts more than treatises; admonitions more than investigations; perhaps even "scoldings" rather than scholarly analyses.

Alan Geyer's *Piety and Politics* seems from its title to be another exhortation written for the lay audience urging Christians to avoid the false identification of religiosity with politics and to become capable and realistic in their concerns for public policy. Actually, it is a careful study of the interplay between religious opinion and the formation of foreign policy. While Geyer does not engage in direct encounter with Lefever and Thompson, he works to modify certain formulations of the realist position which they represent. Geyer is not convinced that Christians approach political matters with an unbending moralism that renders them inept. He prefers to analyze the failure of Protestant social action in terms of an "opinion gap." This "opinion gap" has several features, including a tremendous gulf between the thinking of church leaders and the average church member, an experience of church membership which involves trivial values and nonpolitical factors, and a genuine perplexity concerning the interactions between religion and politics shared alike by "preachers, laymen, theologians, missionaries, politicians, and social scientists."[14] If this "opinion gap" is to be overcome much thought and analysis must go into a deeper recognition of the way religious values are related to politics.

Geyer avoids a picture in which the power realities are presented as something in the "outside" world which Christians embrace as a result of an understanding found in faith. He rejects the analysis which sees religion as "moralistic," secular pursuits as "realistic." He considers religion to be an important ingredient in the power complex, a source as well as reconciler of conflict. Finally, he speaks of the "institutionalization of conflict," a term which means "to subordinate [conflict] to common values and to processes of co-operation, to make it productive of human good, and to reduce its destructiveness."[15] To institutionalize conflict we must learn to ferret out self-righteousness, to beware of moral indignation, and to focus upon the true problems lying at the roots of disagreements. Maturity must replace immaturity in conflict, so that "phoney" issues and useless crusades are avoided. "National interest," which is often taken to be self-evident by the "realists," must be defined in relation to moral and spiritual values as well as pragmatic possibilities.

Contemporary pleas for Christians to take power seriously usually deal with the political realm, since domestic and international politics lend themselves to analysis in operational terms. But community and local affairs may also be understood as calling for the exercise of power and influence. According to Albert T. Rasmussen, Christians live in a "sea of influence" and must marshall counter-influences to offset the tremendous forces in our age which oppress the moral sensitivities. The practical arts of organization, investigation, discussion, decision, and action should be mastered. The churches must learn to enter power situations with the unified strength born of consensus and implemented by a keen awareness of the processes for exerting influence.

> . . . if churches are to carry weight in public opinion, they must unite to proclaim their convictions vigorously through channels that can give them a hearing. If they are going to enter the pressure struggles, they must act corporately to press for just policies, and they must send their members into their offices to use this authority in negotiating decisions with the backing of strong Christian consensus.[16]

Because he deals with the task of Christians in community and vocational realms there is less emphasis in Rasmussen's book upon military forms of coercive power than in many of the other discussions that have been mentioned. Rasmussen does not deny the place of military power; neither does he concentrate upon it as the dominant factor in the exercise of power and influence. He does not even confine his understandings of influence to political terms, though he surely makes a place for politics. His concept of influence is very broad. He speaks of good leadership in terms of its ability to exercise persuasive influence before compulsive power is necessary. He thinks of influence in terms of reconciliation as well as in terms of pressure. But his fundamental perspective is clear: he pleads for Christians to take seriously their roles in achieving moral goals through the exercise of power and influence.

Nonviolence as a Form of Power

It is natural to think of power in coercive terms because the role of military power is so evident in the world. But power has many forms, all of which are operational. Belief in nonviolence shares fully in the assumption that power and influence must be exerted to achieve certain goals, but it differs in its judgment concerning the forms of power which ought to be used.

The power of nonviolence to overcome resistance and to sway men has been long recognized even though infrequently practiced. In Romans 12:20 Paul commends the feeding of opponents as a means for heaping coals of fire upon their heads. The early Christian martyrs defended their convictions with nonviolent methods, not merely of necessity but also out of the conviction that suffering endured without rancor can bear witness to the truth in the Gospel. In the play *Murder in the Cathedral*, T. S. Eliot uses the musings of the archbishop to probe the ways in which accepted martyrdom is the ultimate means of exercising power over others. In the same vein A. J. Muste has written: "It is . . . eternally and unquestionably true that the hunted has the advantage over the hunter."[17]

Not all pacifists look to nonviolence as a means of exerting power. Many withdraw into special communities dedicated to special achievement, abdicating responsibility in political life. This type of pacifism is often called "religious pacifism" to distinguish it from types of pacifism which accept the place of power and influence provided they are exercised in nonviolent ways. But, there is another type of pacifism, within the operational motif, which generally looks to nonviolence as a strategy for achieving social results in situations where violence would only be futile. The operational pacifist, far from being convinced that structures of law and order can be sustained without sanctions, may even declare that nonviolence must be used to persuade men to do what the law cannot make them do. Martin Luther King articulates this position:

> Nonviolence can touch men where the law cannot reach them. When the law regulates behavior it plays an indirect part in molding public sentiment. The enforcement of the law is itself a form of peaceful persuasion. But the law needs help. The courts can order desegregation of the public schools. But what can be done to mitigate the fears, to disperse the hatred, violence, and irrationality gathered

around school integration, to take the initiative out of the hands of the racial demagogues, to release respect for the law? In the end, for laws to be obeyed, men must believe they are right.

Here nonviolence comes in as the ultimate form of persuasion. It is the method which seeks to implement the just law by appealing to the conscience of the great decent majority who through blindness, fear, pride, and irrationality have allowed their consciences to sleep.[18]

King's "pilgrimage to nonviolence" began with boyhood experiences of racial and economic injustice in Atlanta which prompted him to search for a method by which the patterns of segregation could be attacked. It was given a forward impulse by reading Thoreau's *Essay on Civil Disobedience*. In his theological studies King found Walter Rauschenbusch's concern for economic justice an inspiration, but he felt that Rauschenbusch was too optimistic about the processes by which reform might be attained and too ready to equate a particular program with the Christian Gospel. He rejected Marx and Lenin because of their materialism, ethical relativism, and willingness to champion temporary political totalitarianism. During his seminary days a talk by A. J. Muste kindled King's interest in pacifism, but it was a sermon by Mordecai Johnson which fanned the spark to blazing heat.

Mordecai Johnson spoke of the life and teachings of Gandhi and his nonviolent methods for resisting British rule. King was impressed by the place which Gandhi made for "Satyagraha" or soul-force. It convinced him that Gandhi had lifted the love ethic of Jesus to a social ethic of importance. King became convinced that the Gandhian method of nonviolence "was the only morally and practically sound method open to oppressed people in their struggle for freedom."[19] This method involves resistance to evil as much as does the method of violence, but employs different means. King took into account Reinhold Niebuhr's vigorous criticisms of pacifism, but failed to be swayed in his convictions by Niebuhr's strictures. In describing his continuing convictions, King writes:

> True pacifism is not unrealistic submission to evil power, as Niebuhr contends. It is rather a courageous confrontation of evil by the power of love, in the faith that it is better to be the recipient of violence than the inflicter of it, since the latter only multiplies the existence of violence and bitterness in the universe, while the former may develop a sense of shame in the opponent, and thereby bring about a transformation and change of heart.[20]

During King's youth, studies of Gandhi's method and enthusiasm for his teaching were extensive and persuasive. One of the most widely read books on the subject was Richard B. Gregg's *The Power of Non-Violence*,[21] which is a thoroughgoing study of nonviolence as a means of encountering and resisting evil. It offers specific concrete suggestions for

the use of nonviolence as a means of persuasion. It has a chapter on training and discipline. It acknowledges certain features in the training of
soldiers—discipline, neatness, devotion, endurance, and the frank recognition that conflict is an inevitable part of human experience—which ought
to be utilized in the training of nonviolent resisters. Gregg suggests that
nonviolent resistance resembles war in eight ways:

(1) in having a psychological and moral aim and effect;
(2) in being a discipline of a parallel emotion and instinct;
(3) in operating against the morale of the opponents;
(4) in principles of strategy;
(5) in being a method of settling great disputes and conflicts;
(6) in requiring courage, dynamic energy, capacity to endure fatigue
    and suffering, self-sacrifice, self-control, chivalry, action;
(7) in being positive and powerful;
(8) in affording opportunity of service for a large idea, and for
    glory.[22]

Gregg's book must be understood as a pragmatic defense of a strategic
instrument. There are some moral considerations woven into the larger
discussion of the history, methods, and preparation for use of nonviolence,
but they are very much subordinate to the considerations of a practical
nature upon which Gregg builds his case. Gregg defends nonviolence
because it is "efficient."[23] He believes it is advantageous because it can
rehabilitate men if applied to the penal system of the state. It should be
employed because it restores moral equilibrium to a society that has been
rocked by the upheavals which follow aggressive violence. Gregg interprets love as a psychological power rather than as a moral ideal. It will win
over anger, not necessarily because it is morally superior, but because
"it can be more efficiently and effectively wielded, has better aim, has
a better fulcrum or point of vantage, than anger."[24]

A similar study of nonviolence as a method was done by Krishnalal
Shridharani, who wrote out of firsthand experience with some of Gandhi's
early campaigns. He compares Satyagraha to warfare, setting it forth in
more sociological terms than those found in Gregg:

> . . . both, in the first place, are modes of social action aiming at the
> solution of social conflict and secondly that both come into being
> when and where negotiation and arbitration fall short of solving dis-
> pute. Underlying these two characteristics common to both violence
> and non-violence, is that basic assumption that certain· radical social
> changes cannot be brought about save by mass action capable of pre-
> cipitating an emotional crisis.[25]

Shridharani poses a central question: "Is Satyagraha a form of coercion?" His answer is full of semantic distinctions. Gandhi, he notes, said,
"No," because Gandhi defined coercion as that which seeks revenge and

punishment. C. M. Case, on the other hand, said, "Yes," because Satya-graha exerts pressure. Refusing to follow either, Shridharani declares of Satyagraha,

> There is an element of what, for want of a better term, we shall call *compulsion* in it, if not of coercion, since the latter implies revenge and punishment. As a matter of fact, Gandhi himself once used the very word *compel* in connection with his ideology. . . .
> Nevertheless, there being no spirit of punishment or revenge, *compulsion* does not achieve the extent of *coercion*. It stops with affecting what Gandhi calls "a change of heart," and the consequent "redress of the wrong." As a result, the opponent is not vanquished, but victory comes to both sides. Satyagraha, therefore, does not entail the vicious circle of defeat and revenge, and settles the question once and for all by an amicable agreement.[26]

The methodological studies of nonviolence, represented here by the writings of Gregg and Shridharani, were read with enthusiastic approval by many Christian pacifists. Some went a great deal further than either Gregg or Shridharani in declaring nonviolent direct action to be morally (and not merely pragmatically) preferable to violence as a form of political pressure. Indeed, as in the case of A. J. Muste, the moral and spiritual justification for nonviolence becomes even more important than the pragmatic justification. Nonviolence would be morally required even if it did not succeed, since nonviolence and love go closely together. "All the greatest religious teachers and saints, as we have pointed out, are in some form expounders of nonviolence or nonresistance as the meth-odology of love in both personal and social relationships."[27] Muste inter-prets Jesus as a convinced adherent of nonviolence, convinced he must adhere to it on principle regardless of the outcome. Reviewing the temptation in the garden of Gethsemane, which Muste believes to have involved Jesus in the urge to abandon his trust in nonviolence, he remarks: "Whatever might betide, in the face of utter failure and the imminent triumph of the satanic powers, he would not relinquish that conviction, deny this God of love."[28]

The moral defense of nonviolence differs from the pragmatic defense, though they frequently are made together. Martin Luther King weaves both elements together in his discussions of the method. King believes nonviolence to be a method by which the morally strong can resist evil, while bringing opponents into eventual fellowship. It breaks the chain of hate, enhances the chances of reconciliation, and changes the feelings and actions of men. King feels that nonviolence comes very close to embody-ing the Christian ideal of *agape*, the tough-minded, other-directed, love described by the New Testament.

Advocates of nonviolence as a pragmatic instrument point to Gandhi's success and to the Norwegian resistance to Nazi occupation. Its detractors would argue that it has succeeded only in special cases when used against relatively gentle or humanitarian foes, or when used as a holding operation until more significant release has come from military help. Paul Ricoeur has argued that nonviolence is an artificial method which does not take into account the fact that violence forms the very character of human history. Consequently, Ricoeur argues, the pacifist who advocates nonviolent resistance "summons history to something other than what history naturally signifies."[29] While nonviolence may work in some cases as "a symbolic gesture, a limited and rare historical success,"[30] it cannot become a substitute for violence in the making of history because it is essentially a negative response to the perennial form of historical action. Nonviolence succeeds because it negates violence and would lose its tactical value if there were no orders from violent men to contradict. It depends upon the continued practice of violence to exercise its techniques of noncooperation and nonretaliatory refusal.

Ricoeur does not expect the advocates of nonviolence to agree with him, since their very position would be undermined by the admission that it depended upon the continued practice of violence by other men. Whereas Ricoeur, speaking as an historian, sees a place for creative encounter between violence and nonviolence, the first representing the structure of political history and the second a conscientious protest against that structure, such a view

> can only be a view of the historian. For a man who lives and acts, there is neither compromise nor synthesis, but a choice. The intolerance of any mixture is the very soul of non-violence; if faith is not total, it denies itself. If non-violence is the vocation of a few, it must appear to them as the duty of all; for someone who lives it and no longer merely looks at it, non-violence aims to be the whole of action; its will is to construct history.[31]

Religious pacifists, who believe in nonresistance as contrasted with nonviolent resistance, will not accept the methods of Gandhi as proper expressions of the love ethic of the Gospel. This position has been argued at some length by Guy Franklin Hershberger in *War, Peace, and Nonresistance*,[32] who quotes from Reinhold Niebuhr to clinch his argument. Niebuhr, of course, writes from another perspective, but his strictures against Gregg are like those of Hershberger:

> There is not the slightest support in Scripture for this doctrine of non-violence [which allows one to resist evil provided the resistance does not involve the destruction of life or property]. Nothing could be plainer than that the ethic uncompromisingly enjoins non-resistance and not non-violent resistance. Furthermore, it is obvious that the dis-

tinction between violent and non-violent resistance is not an absolute distinction. If it is made absolute, we arrive at the morally absurd position of giving moral preference to the non-violent power which Doctor Goebbels wields over the type of power wielded by a general. This absurdity is really derived from the modern (and yet probably very ancient and very Platonic) heresy of regarding the "physical" as evil and the "spiritual" as good. The *reductio ad absurdum* of this position is achieved in a book which has become something of a text-book for modern pacifists, Richard Gregg's *The Power of Non-Violence*. In this book non-violent resistance is commended as the best method of defeating your foe, particularly as the best method of breaking his morale. It is suggested that Christ ended his life on the Cross because he had not completely mastered the technique of non-violence, and must for this reason be regarded as a guide who is inferior to Gandhi, but whose significance lies in initiating a movement which culminates in Gandhi.[33]

While Niebuhr and Hershberger are agreed in the view that nonviolence cannot qualify as an expression of the love ethic of the Gospel, they use this insight in very different ways. Niebuhr evaluates nonviolent action in the same terms as responsible use of coercive power and therefore objects to any claim of moral superiority for nonviolence. Both uses of power are seen by Niebuhr as contradictions of the impossible possibility of Christian love. Niebuhr's criticism is therefore made from within the operational motif. Hershberger, on the other hand, sees both violent and nonviolent action as impossible for the true Christian. His ethic of nonresistance would require another strategy altogether, a strategy that must be discussed below as an expression of the intentional motif.

16

The Ecclesiastical Uses of Power

Not only do Christians often use the power and influence of the world to effect social change but they frequently make the church itself an instrument of power. Such power can be exercised through specifically ecclesiastical sanctions, or it can result when the church is used as a special political unit. Indeed, many people look upon the history of the church, particularly in the Middle Ages, as the history of the arrogant use of power. Popes sought to subjugate rulers, as did Pope Gregory VII, who made Henry IV of Germany stand barefooted in the snow on the high Alps of Italy begging readmission to the church. Gregory had embarked upon a rigorous policy designed to keep the control of the church in papal hands. Among the policies that Gregory employed to accomplish his ends was a prohibition of lay investiture, denying to secular rulers the right to share in the creation of bishops and other church officials. When Henry IV challenged the papal wishes and appointed an archbishop of Milan, Gregory excommunicated him. Accompanying the decree of excommunication were decrees removing Henry from temporary authority over Germany and Italy and releasing his subjects from their oaths of allegiance.

The right of the pope to release subjects from pledges of political fidelity to an emperor was based upon an assumption of papal supremacy. It was justified in terms of the doctrine of the "two swords," according to which temporal and spiritual authority exist side by side, with the supremacy of the spiritual authority to rule in all cases of conflict. The very choice of terms—"two swords"—is indicative of a subtle theological and flagrant political process at work. The "two cities" of Augustine became temporalized, defined by power, and set into potential opposition to each other. The processes reserved by Augustine for maintaining peace in the city of this world had been adopted for maintaining the supremacy of the papal power both in the church and over the temporal order.

When Henry's political followers found themselves released from bondage to his rule, the king's political status was threatened. Though Henry initially issued a blasting criticism of the pope, within a year he was begging for readmission to the church in order to stave off a threatened rebellion in his political dominion. By securing readmission he not only thwarted the rebellion but kept himself in a position to carry on subtle subversions against the papal claims. It remained for the first in line of Henry's successors and the fourth in line of Gregory's successors to settle at least theoretically, the thorny issues raised by this contest between admittedly temporal and supposedly spiritual power. When Emperor Henry V and Pope Calixtus II signed the Concordat of Worms in 1122 a genuine compromise was made, giving the church equal power with the temporal authority, albeit overcast with the somewhat special prestige of the spiritual. In Italy the emperor was present at the investiture of bishops and touched them with the royal scepter as the symbol of temporal power bestowed, but this symbolic act was not always performed in other countries in Europe, even when ecclesiastical blessings were given at the crowning of political rulers.

Considerations of power were involved in this controversy between the pope and the emperor. Each leader was maneuvering for supremacy. Pope Gregory justified his action on theological grounds in a document addressed as a prayer to the Apostle Peter. The document read in part:

> Especially to me, as thy representative, has been committed, and to me by thy grace has been given by God the power of binding and loosing in heaven and on earth. Relying, then, on this belief, for the honor and defense of thy Church and in the name of God Almighty, the Father, the Son and the Holy Ghost, through thy power and authority, I withdraw the government of the whole kingdom of the Germans and of Italy from Henry the King, son of Henry the Emperor. For he has risen up against thy Church with unheard of arrogance. And I absolve all Christians from the bond of the oath which they have made to him or shall make. And I forbid anyone to serve him as King.[1]

Gregory based his case for papal supremacy upon several considerations. The general councils had called the Roman Church and not the Empire the universal mother. Constantine, in his role as emperor at the Council of Nicaea, understood the bishops "as gods and decreed that they should not be subject to his judgment but that he should be dependent upon their will. . . ."[2] Throughout European history, kings had sometimes been excommunicated by pontiffs. As guardians of spiritual life the ecclesiastical officials held themselves to be superior to political rulers, who must depend upon priests for the salvation of their souls. "Who," Gregory asked bluntly, "in his last hour (what layman, not to speak of priests), has ever implored the aid of an earthly king for the salvation of his soul?"[3] Noting that only the pontiff has the power to make the priests to whom all men turn, Gregory offered this advice to kings and emperors:

> For we know that earthly glory and the cares of this world usually tempt men to pride, especially those in authority. So that they neglect humility and seek their own glory, desiring to lord it over their brethren. Therefore it is of especial advantage for emperors and kings, when their minds tend to be puffed up and to delight in their own glory, to discover a way of humbling themselves, and to realize that what causes their complacency is the thing which should be feared above all else. Let them, therefore, diligently consider how perilous and how much to be feared is the royal or imperial dignity. For very few are saved of those who enjoy it. . . .[4]

This was no tongue-in-cheek statement. Gregory was strongly convinced that history showed very few kings to be righteous and very few popes to be otherwise! Consequently, kings are to be subservient to popes as children are to obey their parents. By doing so they shall ensure their own reward as well as maintain the docility of their kingdoms.

Gregory VII was not the only pope to seek papal supremacy over secular authority. The history of the medieval ages might well be construed as a history of the conflict between two swords. In ethical terms it saw the emergence of coercive strategies designed to ensure obedience to the church. In the movement from excommunication, to interdict, to Inquisition, the use of power became ever more obvious. Excommunication was effective as long as the affected individual felt membership in the church to be necessary to his salvation. It was also effective if a large group of subjects felt the king's membership in the church to be a necessary precondition for sound rule. But when kings arose who did not care whether they remained in the church or not, the interdict came to be used in place of excommunication. An interdict banned the ministrations of the church, not only to the king himself but to the subjects of his realm. Even if the king was indifferent concerning his soul, the subjects often cared about their own and put pressure on the king to submit to the pope in order to get the interdict removed from the country. The Inquisition, which came even later, was a court to judge heresy. It was used against baptized persons who had lost their faith or were espousing false doctrines. It was not employed as a means of converting non-Christians to the faith. But, while the Inquisition began as a means of preserving the purity of the faith, it also became an instrument for cementing the power of the church. It employed direct coercion against the heretic, including the possible use of torture to exact confessions during an inquiry.

Ecclesiastical use of power can take place without detailed theological justification for its use. When such justifications arise they often appear after the fact and are frequently made in the most pretentious terms by those whose ability to maintain the claims of the church's authority has been most seriously eroded. Take, for example, the bull promulgated by Boniface VIII in 1302. The bull followed a series of controversial incidents between the pope and King Philip the Fair of France. The kings of France and England had taxed the clergy of their lands to meet the expenses of a war, and Boniface had issued a papal bull, *Clericis laicos*, which forbade the payment of such taxes on pain of excommunication. Philip had retaliated by forbidding the export of money from France without the permission of the king, a move which threatened papal revenues and the stability of the Italian bank system.

With this background, Philip had arrested Bernard Saisset, a papal nunciary and refused to release him in response to the orders of Boniface. The first States-General, meeting in 1302, sustained the action of the king, and the pope answered with the famous bull *Unam Sanctam*, which not only declared the single supremacy of the Roman Church but the supremacy of her power over that of secular authority. The bull read in part:

> And we learn from the words of the Gospel that in this Church and in her power are two swords, the spiritual and the temporal. For when the apostles said, "Behold, here" (that is, in the Church, since it was the apostles who spoke) "are two swords"—the Lord did not reply, "It is too much," but "It is enough." Truly he who denies that the temporal sword is in the power of Peter, misunderstands the words of the Lord, "Put up thy sword into the sheath." Both are in the power of the Church, the spiritual sword and the material. But the latter is to be used for the Church, the former by her; the former by the priest, the latter by kings and captains but at the will and by the permission of the priest. The one sword, then, should be under the other, and temporal authority subject to spiritual. For when the apostle says "there is no power but of God, and the powers that be are ordained of God" they would not be so ordained were not one sword made subject to the other. . . .[5]

The claims made in the bull were not fully substantiated by the events that followed its pronouncement. Philip arranged the capture of the pope, which occurred just as the pope was to proclaim Philip's excommunication. While Boniface was later released by his friends, he died shortly thereafter, and subsequent popes were unable to match papal claims with papal power. The papacy entered the degrading period of the Avignon schism.

Another way of describing the shift in church practice from the institutional to the operational pattern is to observe the decline of the idea of the just war, which had been decisive in Christian thinking from Augustine's time to about the beginning of the eleventh century, in face of the rising ethic of the crusade. The theory of the just war makes it possible to judge the use of force by certain measures of propriety and legitimacy. It institutionalizes conflict by setting bounds upon the use of coercion. But in the war ethic of the crusade, believer is set against infidel. Any and all actions used against the enemies of the faith are considered legitimate. The duty and necessity of crushing evil is considered more important than holding coercive techniques under critical judgment.

It is easy for modern man, and particularly those of secular persuasion, to regard ecclesiastical uses of power with grave misgivings. But these reactions are not entirely justified. Modern men, both religious and secular, have developed the war ethic of the crusade into the ideology of the total war. Such war has ceased to be institutionalized. It is a brute conflict in which the shrewdest manipulation and most extravagant exercise of power is presumed to win and those who call for restraint are regarded as traitors. Perhaps the recent conduct of limited wars for specific objectives fought under self-imposed restraints which respect noncombatant immunity and keep military operations proportionate to the goals being sought are bringing back important aspects of the just war.

Moreover, it is easy for Protestants, in viewing the events and declarations of Roman Catholic history, to assume that their heritage is free of such corruptions, particularly in a free land that is religiously pluralistic. But Protestant attempts to maintain the power of the church have also produced coercive oppression. Moreover, contemporary Protestant practices render no assurance that the exercise of power and influence is a matter of past history.

Many contemporary studies, prompted perhaps by the theoretical recognition of the role of power in human affairs, have scrutinized the life of the contemporary Christian community to show the role played by churches in the power processes of community life. Liston Pope did a pioneering study of such factors in his book *Millhands and Preachers*, which looked at the role of the churches and their leaders in Gaston County, North Carolina, during and following a bitter textile strike against the Loray mills in 1929. In order to comment upon the churches and their roles during the strike itself, Pope studied the whole power configuration of the community and reached the conclusion that the churches were basically allies of the mills.

> To sum up, for emphasis, in statements too sharply put: in the cultural crisis of 1929 Gastonia ministers revealed that their economic ethicways were products of the economic system in which they lived, with no serious modification by any transcendent economic or religious standard. They were willing to allow the power of religious institutions to be used against those who challenged this economic system, and themselves assisted in such use. At no important point

did they stand in opposition to the prevailing economic arrangements or to drastic methods employed for their preservation. In no significant respect was their role productive of change in economic life. By and large, they contributed unqualified and effective sanction to their economic culture, insofar as their words and deeds make it possible to judge.[6]

In much the same tradition Kenneth W. Underwood made a detailed study of the interrelations between Catholic and Protestant power in Holyoke, Massachusetts. While he has been careful not to generalize from his study of a single New England city to a general theory of ecclesiastical power, he has shown how power and influence can be used in local situations. Underwood focused on the so-called Sanger incident. In October of 1940 Margaret Sanger was invited by the Mother's Health Council to speak on the matter of birth control and in favor of a petition to the legislature of the state on behalf of a law permitting doctors to prescribe contraceptive techniques to married couples when a matter of life or of health is involved. The admitted position of the speaker was at well-known variance with the conviction of the Roman Catholic Church on this issue and did involve the plea to change the law of the state. A problem arose as to where to find a hall. Turned down by one Congregational church, the group was given initial permission to hold the meeting in another Congregational church. Shortly, the pastor of the "mother" Roman Catholic parish in the city organized forces to prevent Mrs. Sanger's appearance. Underwood documents in detail the various processes by which permission was later denied to hold the meeting in the Congregational church which had initially made its hall available. Finally, the Textile Workers CIO offered its building through the decision of a national officer of the Union, and the meeting was held.

Through the incident, Underwood has examined the structures of power and influence in the church life of the city. He includes historical materials, the analysis of layman culture, the organizational patterns of the two major faiths, financial issues, cultural differences, relationships of the church to centers of power, and attitudes of the major traditions to each other. In his report he sets forth a great many of the things a clergyman or active, intelligent layman ought to know about the decision-making structures of the community.

Underwood's primary theoretical concern is to analyze the thinking of the religious groups under study, but in doing so he reveals to us his own conception of Christian social responsibility, a conception that is very much informed by a view emphasizing the importance of power and influence in the decision-making process. Underwood notes that both Catholic and Protestant leaders approach politics with a similar confidence that they are making judgments about politics from the perspective of an established and assured system of natural and divine laws or ultimate ends. Neither group of leaders believes that its decisions are measured or affected by the situations in which they are to be applied. The Catholic sees his norms, generally speaking, to be derived rationally from natural law; the Protestant most often appeals to the Sermon on the Mount, or to another expression of an ultimate end. A few Protestant pastors approach political questions situationally rather than deductively, but their influence upon their fellow ministers has been small.

Neither the Catholic nor the Protestant clergymen of Holyoke accepted in theory a direct-action program in which they play the leading role. The Catholic understanding is well expressed by the Catholic Action program, which emphasizes "indirect" forms of action. Such a program

> represents the culmination of a long process of transforming the direct political power of the medieval papacy into a form of influence relevant to modern times. The Catholic church is aware that modern democratic governments are controlled by the people, not by "princes" or "kings." Politics is prevented from "touching the altar" in most Western nations not by bulls of excommunication or religious disciplining of top leaders but by the influence of the educational program of the church upon rank and file citizenry and upon many leader groups in the society. The church leaders believe they are sufficiently realistic to recognize that future influence in politics depends not so much upon establishing church power at the pinnacle of government, as upon achieving wide popular support of church beliefs.[7]

The Protestant understanding is, in Underwood's judgment, less articulate and less effective. He observes that many Protestant pastors are little concerned about power as an instrument of political action. Indeed they even seem to shy away from its use. Their social projects tend to be humanitarian rather than political. This comparison is necessary, not only because the Catholics often have the politically oriented ward politicians in their parishes, but because the Protestant clergy tend to issue general pronouncements through the newspapers rather than to mount a determined onslaught against the decision makers. In summarizing the Protestant tendencies observed in his study, Underwood writes:

> The Protestant ministers make no claim to having a formulated theory of "indirect" power for church action, but they make the same distinctions the Catholics do between appropriate "non-political" methods of the church and non-appropriate partisan methods. However, they are much more given than the Catholics to moralizing about their approach, to identifying the other faith group with "political" methods. The Protestants claim that Catholics "use power and coercion while the Protestants use moral suasion." Most Protestant clergy say they "are suspicious of religious leaders who talk about

power." (The Catholic priests know where power resides but talk little in terms of "power" or "coercion.") They are anxious to see good done in politics but lack concrete knowledge of the relevant alternatives of action available to them. They are eager to counsel laymen on religious and ethical problems in politics, but they rarely know the party affiliation of their leading laymen or the extent of their political activity.[8]

Underwood clearly emphasizes the importance of power and influence in the decision-making process. He is critical of a bland idealism, which he finds more prevalent in Protestantism than in Catholicism, which projects a "hero-type" of pious, good-natured, independence as the ideal sort of citizen. Such a projection, he holds, breeds a confusion which generates the expectation that men can overcome the tough realities of an ambiguous world of power and institutional rigidity. He sympathizes with the city politicians who seem to prefer a context in which decisions might be made in terms of political factors alone, without having to be concerned about their religious significance in moralistic terms.

Underwood has written about Protestant practice on the local level, comparing it with Roman Catholic practices. A study of the national level of action by church bodies has been prepared by Luke Eugene Ebersole and published under the title *Church Lobbying in the Nation's Capital.* Ebersole's book includes some historical materials dealing with religious lobbies of the past, such as the Anti-Saloon League. It deals with other lobbies that have survived since the book was written, of which Protestants and Other Americans United for Separation of Church and State is one of the better known. In addition to lobbies that represent special causes, the churches themselves maintain offices in Washington for legislative concerns. The Catholic church set up such offices in the second decade of the present century; Protestant denominations have generally done so since the Second World War. Ebersole writes:

> In the main, the methods of church lobbies are unspectacular and involve few political threats. Church lobbies are organized to perform two chief functions: to inform, advise, and persuade legislators and administrators; and to channelize information concerning legislation and governmental actions to the church public. The lobbies vary in their willingness to apply political pressure, in their willingness to admit the use of political pressure, and in their ability to use political pressure.[9]

Ebersole feels that his study is too limited to arrive at definitive judgments as to how much pressure lobbies can generate. It is, of course, a report of particular conditions rather than a theory of how Christians should operate. But it does show how particular church bodies can, and have, made use of influence as a means of seeking social objectives which they support.

Paul M. Harrison turned his attention to the inside of an ecclesiastical body. Using the functional analysis of Talcott Parsons, Robert K. Merton, and Marion J. Levy, Jr., he examined the exercise of power within the American Baptist Convention. In doing so he highlighted the difference between the theological self-understanding of a particular denomination and the empirical realities of its organizational life. Describing his approach, Harrison declares:

> For more than a century the Baptists have emphasized the freedom of the individual in all matters of faith and practice. In addition, they have insisted upon the autonomy of the local church and the freedom of the congregation to govern its own affairs apart from the direction of church councils or associations of churches. Thus in its modern expression the Baptist doctrine of the church maintains that there is no authority in church councils and that denominational officials can legally possess no power.
>
> At the same time the Baptists have formed an impressive denominational organization . . . which in important ways bears a striking resemblance to the large social structures found in the spheres of government and business. The officers of the denominational agencies have obtained a significant degree of influence over the affairs of the local churches.[10]

Behind Harrison's study there is a theological analysis which contrasts with that of Max Weber, whose work on the nature and role of authority was cast in terms primarily related to formally defined and hierarchical social organization. Weber called for understanding the ways in which leadership legitimizes its authority within a social system, and showed that this legitimatization involves tradition, law, or the charismatic qualities of the leader. Harrison suggests that Weber's understandings do not fit "the congregationally-ordered, democratic churches which emerged from the left-wing of the Calvinist movement"[11] and that a rational-pragmatic conception of authority is necessary for understanding developments in this tradition. Harrison concludes:

> . . . it is of critical importance to recognize that the presence of power is not eliminated by noble purpose. Power in a social system is shared by those who are able and willing to mobilize the political, economic, psychological, and ideological resources of the community.[12]

In his chapter "Postscript for Baptists," Harrison assesses the implications of his study for his own denomination. He suggests that local churches have the right and duty to criticize the denominational power structures but lack the means to do so. He also suggests Baptist officials have developed inordinate power precisely because the official theory of the denomination so deeply distrusts defined institutional power.

> Free Church polity is predicated on the ground that every man has the ability to know the truth and the right to proclaim it. But it is also affirmed that those who possess the instruments of power will claim a monopoly on truth and will attempt to circumscribe the right of the minority to be heard. The polity of the Free churches reflects an effort to establish an equilibrium between these contending parties. The Baptists may have been wise when they removed the bishops from their places; but when they also eliminated the ecclesiastical authority of their own associations the bishops returned in business suits to direct affairs from behind the curtain of the center stage. Since their responsibilities are prodigious their presence is acknowledged. But paradoxically, their power is unrestricted because their authority is so limited. When Baptists recognize that authority is more than a grant to power and that it also defines and therefore limits the uses of power they may sustain the proximate harmony they are seeking.[13]

Harrison is not suggesting that mere structuring of denominational affairs in institutional terms would solve the dilemma, though he seems to imply that such a structuring would be vastly preferable to the current refusal of the denomination to delegate specific (and therefore limited) powers to its board executives, thus leaving them to define their own power roles. The Baptist difficulties form an instructive comparison with Roman Catholic practices, the more so because Baptist procedures are often created by a very distinct urge to avoid the difficulties and pretensions of the Roman patterns! Rome may use power while bolstering it with formal teachings about institutional order; the Baptists discover power to rear its head even when formal institutional orders have been eschewed in order to avoid its appearance. The conclusion to be drawn, implicit in Harrison's study, is that power must be taken seriously before it can be controlled. For Rome to take the problem of power seriously would be for it to recognize that institutional authority does not always safeguard the church against the misuse of power; for the Baptists to take power seriously would be for them to recognize that refusal to sanction institutional authority does not in itself safeguard against the rise of oligarchy.

It is important to avoid the stereotypes of past judgments in commenting upon these matters. The use of ecclesiastical power to further parochial ends is not the exclusive practice of any single group. To be sure, groups which affirm, if only through some of their spokesmen, that truth does not have equal rights with error cause others to be uneasy. But their exercise of power may be no more insidious than that of groups which simply control the decision-making factors of a community by habit and accident.

Moreover, the ferment in Roman Catholic circles today about the importance of ecclesiastical freedom in a religiously pluralistic society is of great interest to all those who are concerned about these matters. H. A. Rommen, Jacques Maritain, and John Courtney Murray are among the contemporary Roman Catholics who favor religious pluralism as good, not only for democracy, but for the Roman Church itself.

Any pluralistic society would be required to grant the church the right to create a voluntary organization in which participation is limited to those willing to abide by the stipulated conditions. It would also be required to grant the church the right to teach its faithful that this or that course of conduct was contrary to the faith. The right of the church to counsel its members to refrain from seeing particular movies or reading particular books would also need to be granted, provided the church did not strive to make it impossible for other citizens to have access to them. What cannot be condoned is the church's claim to know the content of the natural law with sufficient clarity to justify the use of ecclesiastical power to affect public policy by the use of methods which short-circuit the democratic decisions of a pluralistic society, or which deny to other men the right to create voluntary societies on their terms and to enjoy the right to advocate policies stemming from another interpretation of human welfare.

It may be that church bodies in today's world which seek to exercise power and influence are dependent upon basically political forms of power belonging to the world rather than to the unique function of their own activities. Surely the power of excommunication is severely limited in a culture where loyalty to the church is potentially secondary in the public eye, and the interdict has no relevance in a pluralistic society. There is some influence in the ecclesiastical group which is willing to play upon the ethos of tolerance to quell other groups from sponsoring activities that seem an affront to its special teaching, but this too is of limited usefulness. It may well be that those who would turn to the exercise of power and influence in our day must rely mainly, as do the political realists, upon the instruments generally available in the world at large rather than upon those devices which belong to the more limited sphere of church operation.

Section C: The Intentional Motif in Christian Ethics
17
Separatism and Renewal Within the Church

The intentional motif includes monasticisms which are bound in close fidelity to the church but which believe in the importance of a life of special dedication lived in detachment from the world; it includes sectarian movements which would separate the entire church from the world by shunning the normal institutions and power realities of common life; it includes attempts to infuse new spiritual zeal and moral earnestness into the life of the church by first developing a high spiritual devotion in a core group; it includes special groups which seek religiously inspired ends outside the existing scope of the church's concerns by the inculcation of zeal and devotion. Some of these strategies are concerned about the world but in a way that would radically change the world and make it distinctively new.

Because they assume that the dedicated Christian should manifest some shining luster, some unique spirituality by which he can be differentiated from non-Christians and even from ordinary Christians, intentionalists generally seek a heroic ethic, a demanding morality, and the satisfaction attending the performance of special duties. They often look upon the situation of persecution in early Christianity as the golden age of the church's life because the risks involved in being a Christian kept out the morally uncommitted. While a chosen withdrawal cannot have the same moral meaning as an imposed persecution, the separatist would prefer it because it maintains the gulf between church and culture which marks the suffering, outcast church in a hostile world.

The intentionalist is usually concerned about devotion. He tends to be more worried by apathy than by injustice. He believes that spiritual wholeness is the prerequisite for health, even for serving the world. He tends to cultivate inner conviction before advocating outward action. He finds the company of the small dedicated group essential to the cultivation of conviction and the intensification of zeal. He cherishes the unique moral visibility of Christians, a visibility standing in contrast to the moral timidity of the world.

252

There is no term which fully describes all the different outgrowths of the impulse to moral purity which eventuate in the creation of self-defining groups. The term *withdrawn* does not adequately cover the cell groups nor even such service-centered monastic movements as the Franciscans; the term *purist* breaks down because many of the groups are uncompromising about only selected issues; the term *monastic* has special meanings in reference to vows of obedience, poverty, and chastity. The term *separatist* runs the danger of implying complete world-denial. The term *intentional*, which we have chosen, may be most useful only because its relatively infrequent use has kept it from acquiring too many prior connotations.

Ernst Troeltsch carefully explored the impulse to create special communities of intense devotion to the Gospel and distinguished the sect type of Christianity (which rejects the world) from the church type (which embraces the world). He described this difference with these words:

> The Church is that type of organization which is overwhelmingly conservative, which to a certain extent accepts the secular order, and dominates the masses; in principle, therefore, it is universal, i.e., it desires to cover the whole life of humanity. The sects, on the other hand, are comparatively small groups; they aspire after personal inward perfection, and they aim at a direct personal fellowship between the members of each group. From the very beginning, therefore, they are forced to organize themselves in small groups, and to renounce the idea of dominating the world. Their attitude towards the world, the State, and Society may be indifferent, tolerant, or hostile, since they have no desire to control and incorporate these forms of social life; on the contrary, they tend to avoid them; their aim is usually either to tolerate their presence alongside of their own body, or even to replace these social institutions by their own society.[1]

There can be no doubt that Troeltsch was correct in considering the sect to be a form of separatism. The sect undoubtedly provides one of the most evident and widespread expressions of the belief that Christians can only live in obedience to the Gospel ethic if they belong to special communities of dedication. The sect clearly develops into a sociological type which can be studied and observed with much greater clarity than a cell-group movement which continues to live within the mainstream of the church's life without making its distinct earnestness so obvious. The sociological type produced by the sect impulse appears with perennial regularity in the ongoing life of Christendom. The forms in which it appears may vary from generation to generation but the motivation is basically the same. John A. Hutchison is right in observing that

> No age of the Western world has been without sects, from the early Christian movement of the Roman Empire to Jehovah's Witnesses in

the twentieth century. In the eleventh century, Peter Waldo gave away his wealth, forsook the world, and set out upon the path of obedience to Christ, founding the Waldensian movement. The next century saw the flowering of the Cathari and Albigenses. The Franciscan movement had some of the characteristics of a sect, particularly in its early development. But at no point did it challenge the Church's authority; and for its part the Church was wise enough to reach out and embrace it. The Church was however neither wise enough nor flexible enough to follow a similar policy with the Lollards and Hussites of the fourteenth century. Sectarian groups sprang up and flourished, despite untold persecution during the age of the Reformation, as is indicated by the Anabaptists of continental Europe and the Separatists, the Levelers, the Diggers, the Quakers, and the Baptists of England. Many of their ideas and ideals as well as their adherents made the voyage across the Atlantic to America here to exert great influence on American thought and values.[2]

Hutchison suggests that the Franciscans and the sects started from very similar impulses, but that one group was accepted by the church whereas the others were persecuted. If this be so, then it is proper to suggest that monasticism and the sect share a common impulse even though they come to a different fruition. Troeltsch assigned ascetic monasticism to the church-type because it remained loyal to the established ecclesiastical structure. It is just as legitimate to assign monasticism and sectarian withdrawal to a common motif in which renewal and dedication through small groups play decisive roles. Both arise as a reaction to worldliness in the church and believe in the creation of a special community situation as a means of attaining the moral objectives of the Gospel.

Many cell groups arising inside the church have thought of themselves as called to a special degree of devotion within a special community. Even when they have hoped to renew the church by first refurbishing their own spiritual zeal, they have been motivated by many of the impulses which gave birth to monasticism. Both the monastic order and the cell group have ethical interests. They demand a higher righteousness from the members than they expect from others. In the case of monasticism this involves allegiance to a totally different sex standard and economic situation, as well as submission to authority. In the case of the cell group it usually results in the demand for a higher standard of personal discipline, including tithing and the practice of mutual criticism between the members.

Moreover, in both monasticism and the cell group, as indeed in the sects as well, the moral life is tied to a profound concern about the devotional life. Monks engage in extensive and regular liturgical worship. The members of the cell group admonish each other to cultivate the life of prayer.

Speaking of contemporary movements which have arisen in the churches of Europe to revitalize the life there, Olive Wyon says:

> In every case, this "new life" emerges from a praying group: whether it is called a "community" or a "company" or a "team." In other words, the "living water" comes from Christ himself, where two or three meet in his name—and where, as in the first community of Jerusalem, they remain steadfastly together in faith and fellowship, in sacramental life and prayer.[3]

Movements interested in the cultivation of moral rigor and spiritual vitality in their internal life may respond differently to the claims of the world. Some may retreat from the world in order to maintain their own disciplines; others, cultivate their internal disciplines in order to make themselves of greater service to the world. Western Christianity has tended to favor the group which looks outward rather than inward, but both forms have arisen in its history. Indeed, it is sometimes difficult to assign a group to one or the other category. Much Western monasticism, for example, shuns the world yet claims to serve the world in doing so. Its intercessory prayers are made for the benefit of the world and its ministrations of charity and education have been of undeniable benefit to others.

> No doubt many a monk cultivated the garden of his own soul and was content to let the outside world go to the devil. But the high-minded and authentic monk of the West was not insensitive to the need of the world he had left behind. In his worship at the altar, in his prayers of intercession, in his preservation and cultivation of Latin culture and art, in his charity and hospitality to the world's hungry and disinherited, but above all in his cultivation of purity of life, he looked not only up to heaven but down in love upon the world he had renounced.[4]

Many Christian movements which arose from the sect impulse have also rendered service to the world. The interest shown by the American Friends Service Committee in good and worthwhile projects of an humanitarian nature is well-known. The Brethren and Mennonites have engaged in many projects which have served the needs of the world. To be sure, these groups tend to serve the world with peaceful needs, to bind and heal the wounds of mankind without engaging in the struggles and the conflicts which often produce those wounds. To regard movements of intentional renewal as altogether self-cultivating is to render them a gross injustice.

Troeltsch separated the mystical and sect types of Christianity, but this distinction has been less consistently a part of subsequent discussion of these matters than his distinction between church and sect. Indeed

Troeltsch himself seems to have had some doubts about the adequacy of his own categories, for he wrote:

> In actual practice both of these religious types were constantly merging into each other. The sect aspired to the inwardness of mysticism; mysticism strove to actualize the sacred fellowship of the sect. "Enthusiasm"—the result of great excitement and of the oppressive hostility of the churches—also played its part in drawing both these groups closer together. But inconsistencies and tensions, due to the partial fusion of the two types, still remained.[5]

Any mysticism which is completely indifferent to matters of social strategy and ethical implementation tends to be carried along in the pattern of the established church with its adherence to the institutional motif. Any spiritual enthusiasm which becomes, as did Thomas Muenzer's, so driven to attain a radically revolutionary situation that it resorts to violence in order to attain it, manifests operational tendencies. Only those mysticisms which think of dedication through disciplined groups as expressions of Christian action should be identified with the intentional motif.

Revivalist movements are often interested in ethical renewal, especially in the renewal of individual devotion. They plead for individual repentance and rededication and often preach against the corporate sins of a particular age. In many of the great revivals, however, there has been a strong emphasis upon the reform of society as well as the rededication of the individual. A preacher like Jonathan Edwards was interested in both the salvation of individuals and the cleansing of town life. Timothy L. Smith has shown that revivalism in the great epochs of the past has often been concerned about the social consequences of Christian conviction.[6] Revivalism in the modern period may unwittingly support traditional and conservative strategies for dealing with social issues because it fails to take account of the social question. When revivalism has taken account of social issues, it has emphasized the significance of spiritual renewal for social reform and even given birth to perfectionist groups of a separatist character. Thus revivalism can be associated with monasticism, sectarianism, pietism and mysticism as a potential origin of the intentional impulse.

Because membership in special groups is always voluntary, dedication to their purposes is required. Active participation is expected and many intentional groups exhibit the characteristics of the mass movement. Eric Hoffer points out that in the early phase of such movements enthusiasm runs high. This phase Hoffer calls the revivalistic phase; it is marked by "the man of fanatical faith who is ready to sacrifice his life for a holy cause."[7]

> All mass movements generate in their adherents a readiness to die and a proclivity for united action; all of them, irrespective of the

doctrine they preach and the program they project, breed fanaticism, enthusiasm, fervent hope, hatred and intolerance; all of them are capable of releasing a powerful flow of activity in certain departments of life; all of them demand blind faith and singlehearted allegiance.[8]

To be sure, not all renewal groups express their enthusiasm in the forms described by Hoffer. Some of them are retiring, service motivated, and devoted to peaceful ways. Many of them are pacifist and shun the world precisely because it is marked by conflict. But most are zealous for their cause beyond the normal measures. The Quakers were hardly sedate in their beginning, nor did the Anabaptists always carry the virtue of meekness to the point of self-effacement. They demanded singlehearted allegiance. They set rigorous and demanding conditions for membership, with little place for a lingering allegiance to the world. They were often tempted to show impatience with the lesser accomplishments of ordinary Christians. In this sense they did exhibit the attitudes which Hoffer suggests.

Intentional communities of both the separatist and renewal types tend to lose zeal as they gain size or acquire maturity. They may devise strategies to counteract this tendency. Monastic communities recruit members anew in each generation and hence bring new dedication to the group on a continuing basis. Sect groups, however, sometimes abandon their spiritual and social radicalism. They frequently find that the children lack the full conviction of the founding parents. When this happens the "true believer" phase disappears and the sect is faced with difficulties. Sometimes a small minority seeks to revitalize the sect—working as a group within a group—but at other times the sect becomes similar to the established church and another group arises to carry on the radical witness of the separatist impulse. For this reason particular expressions of the separatist impulse are often transient but the pattern common to these ephemeral developments seems to be an ungoing feature of the church's life.

Church-Related Monasticism

Herbert B. Workman[9] found the impulse to renounce the world to be the essential motivation of the monastic movement. This impulse to self-surrender, also evident in the decision of the martyr, comes as a divine call. Monasticism provides a reasonable and constructive outlet for this passion. Louis Bouyer presents monasticism as "the search for God."[10] In this he follows Kenneth E. Kirk, who uses the phrase "the vision of God" to describe the spiritual quest of the monk.[11] But Kirk also speaks of monasticism as an example of moral rigorism. The moral rigor of monasticism arose in part as a protest against the laxity which plagued the church, especially after recognition by Constantine took place. Monastic life serves many functions: it provides a means for renunciation of pleasures and self-seeking by demanding poverty, obedience, and chastity; it cultivates the life of prayer and worship, hence bringing closer the vision of the divine; it binds into rigid communities those who practice its rule, thus providing a channel for the self-surrender which expresses a special acceptance of the Gospel ethic.

Many of the first monastics were solitary men, searching for peace apart from the world. The individualistic monasticism of the early years in the life of the church often produced excessive self-denial. Communal controls were instituted which channeled the monastic impulse into reasonable forms. Saint Anthony and Saint Pachomius were the two best-known leaders of third-century monasticism. Each drew around him a group of monks who followed his leadership by submitting to the discipline of a rule. In the fourth century Saint Basil the Great carried forward the development of community monasticism. His rule was patterned after the image of the Christian family and was very important in providing discipline to sustain internal order and the vision to engage in outward-reaching charity. Under Basil manual labor was made a significant part of the monastic life, and care for the sick, hungry, aged, and helpless was given a central place among the concerns of the ascetic calling.

Pachomius and Anthony depended almost entirely upon the charismatic power of their own leadership to effect their reforms of solitary (cenobite) monasticism. Basil, who also was interested in theological study as a function of the monastic life, created a community by his skill as an organizer and attractiveness as a leader. With the arrival of the fifth century the church was taking a more active interest in monasticism. Even though community disciplines had been developed within many individual monasteries, the relationships between them were still unstructured. Monasteries differed radically in the nature and severity of their rules, and monks changed monasteries frequently and without good cause. Benedict of Nursia brought the chaos into order during the first half of the sixth century, putting Western monasticism clearly under the sponsorship and control of the Roman Church.

Benedict's rule, which came to be the norm of all Western monasticism, is a moderate rule which provided for worship, work, and rest in proportions suited to the normal human being. It described the monastic life in ordered terms which excluded both extreme self-discipline and extreme laxity. Monks were to eat enough to subsist but not enough to be gluttonous; they were to sleep enough to allow their waking hours to be alert yet not enough to permit enjoying sleep for its own sake; they were to pray without letting prayer become an obsession. A proper amount of manual work was specified so as to avoid that "enemy of the soul—indolence." Not only study, but teaching, was made a part of the monastic calling—a fact of great importance for European culture as a whole. Personal cleanliness was considered important in the life of the monk, and the excesses attending individual attempts at self-punishment were curtailed.

Within the Roman Church another sort of monasticism arose which may be of even greater significance for Christian ethics than the community monasticism which sets up residential patterns under the Benedictine rule. This type of monasticism found expression in the "Canons Regular," which later became the Premonstratensian Canons. Developed to bring rigor to the life of the clergy, it expanded to a focus of missionary zeal. This type of monasticism also appeared in the coming of the Friars, inspired differently by Assisi and Dominic. The Franciscans were concerned to spread the faith by rendering service and assistance to the poor. They lived a life of simple poverty and service, implicitly challenging the search for riches in the culture of the day. The Dominicans were more concerned to deal with upper classes in terms of scholarship and learning, and their influence is felt to this day, everywhere that missions are conducted by priests who sign "O.P." after their names. Finally, we find this sort of monasticism appearing in the Society of Jesus, founded by Ignatius, trained with his *Spiritual Exercises*, and symbolic of the final subservience of the monastic impulse to the church. The Jesuits have not always enjoyed the full respect and trust of others. They have been resented by the diocesan clergy as intruders; they have been symbols in minds of others for the Inquisition. But by a strange twist of circumstance they have also come in our time to produce some of the most potent forces in the modern church favoring redefinition of its attitude toward religious pluralism and the values of democratic freedom.

Monasticism probably began within the church as a protest against uncritical embrace of the world by Christians. It provided an opportunity for some men to live a life of special dedication to the Gospel. In time, the Catholic churches made peace with monasticism as an ongoing expression of one type of Christian devotion. Monasticism became institutionalized, and came also to acknowledge the right of the church to embrace the world institutionally. The church accepted the witness of the monk as pointing to the life of heaven. The vows of poverty, chastity, and obedience were understood eschatologically, whereas the ongoing life of the church was understood incarnationally. The monk makes one witness; the church in the world, another.

Traditional Reformation theology rejected the division of witness and responsibility through which monasticism became a continuing aspect of Catholic life. The intentional impulse has consequently appeared mostly in other forms within Protestantism. But to think of monasticism as a movement confined to Roman Catholicism and Eastern Orthodoxy is increasingly impossible. Peter F. Anson[12] has shown the extent to which the monastic impulse has been and continues to be present within the Anglican communion. What is even more surprising is the appearance of monastic-like communities in the Protestant churches of Europe since the Second World War. When H. B. Workman wrote his study of monasticism, he believed that it was a dying pattern. Subsequent developments have shown him to be wrong. Not only is monasticism attracting a full quota of noviti-ates for the Roman Church, but it is appearing in Protestant communions whose own tradition has been vigorously hostile to the monastic ideal for over four centuries.

The best-known and most clearly monastic experiment in contemporary Protestantism is the Taizé Community in France, which has a sister community for women at Grandchamp, Switzerland. There is also a "third order" of clergy and laity, married and single, men and women who take less vigorous vows than the members of the community itself. They remain in their regular jobs, take an active interest in their own parishes, and witness to the same goals cherished by the mother community. The founder of the Taizé Community is Frère Roger Schutz, who considers it his special vocation to revive monasticism for Protestant purposes and to witness strongly for the eventual reunion of all Christendom. Both aims find expression in the community that he has founded. Shutz is convinced that monasticism must be open to the world in the sense of rendering witness in it and service to it. This has shaped the patterns developed at Taizé. He is also convinced that the central strength of the Christian movement is maintained by the special community of devotion, prayer, and service.

The Taizé Community prefers to speak of itself as cenobitic rather than monastic. The term implies *koinos bios*, or common life, a phrase that implies somewhat larger meanings than the word *monasticism*, which has been traditionally associated with the Gospel counsels of poverty, chastity, and obedience. Nevertheless, free to pattern their common life by any standard, the Taizé group chose a pattern entirely compatible with that of traditional monasticism. Celibacy is practiced by the professed brothers, not in negation of sex as such but because marriage is understood to involve a total claim which is incompatible with the total claim of the brother-hood. Since only one community can receive a total allegiance, the brothers make the choice for the community. They put themselves totally at its disposal, not only by renouncing marriage but by agreeing to a community of property and to obedience to the will of the order. The three conditions of belonging to the Taizé Community hardly differ from the three traditional vows required of members of monastic orders.

In governing its life together the Taizé Community acts as a council of the whole. Issues are thoroughly discussed, but the Prior makes the decisions. His role and authority are considered to stand alongside those of the brothers, and his decision-making role, *primus inter pares*, keeps the community from engaging in battles over policy. Votes are never taken since the common life would be destroyed by the introduction of political maneuvering into the life of the brotherhood. The operational means of governing human life has been explicitly rejected.

The foregoing aspects of Taizé are fully compatible with traditional Roman Catholic monasticism. Twentieth-century innovations provide for the brothers to leave each day, after the early morning office, for work in the surrounding neighborhood. They work in ordinary garb, but use a white habit during the hours spent in the chapel. The liturgy is drawn from many traditions, witnessing in its own way to the ecumenical concerns of the community. Whatever is earned by the brothers in jobs away from the house is put into a cash fund, together with contributions from the members of the third order. Brothers away from the house on special projects (*frères en mission*) are expected to maintain themselves at the same level, or just below the level, of living characteristic of the groups to which they minister. The surplus comes to the treasury, the monies of which are completely dispersed each month in order that the movement itself will live from "day to day" and not become the holder of vested riches.

The rule of Taizé is filled with a Christ-centered mysticism. The Christian life is interpreted in terms of utter abandon to Christ. It is understood as the zestful sprint and constant march in total abandon to the will of the Lord Jesus Christ. This abandon requires laying aside the cares of state, of family, of political life, of satisfactions which coddle the appetites. These are laid aside within the monastic, or cenobitic, order. Malcolm Boyd, reporting on the Taizé Community, has characterized the rule as a "superior devotional manual rather than an organizational statement."[13]

Despite its Protestant commitments, Taizé has embraced monastic patterns in the hope of renewing the life of the church and reuniting its Protestant and Catholic branches. It has, thereby, expressed in its own way the perennial concern of monasticism to renew the life of the church through the dedication of the few and the life of the world through the ministrations of the enlivened church.

Renewal Groups Within the Church

There has hardly been a period in the history of the church when some group has not been concerned to renew its life, pleading with its members —or selected groups of its members—to intensify their devotional life and purify their moral practices. The devotional has sometimes been uppermost; at other times, the moral. In almost all cases both the devotional and the ethical have been understood as common features of a renewed spiritual life.

In the early days of the church, Montanus pleaded for asceticism and rigor in protest against spiritual and moral laxity in the church at large. In drive and impulse Montanism sought to reform and revitalize the church. Montanus would have applied his rigorous demands to all members of the church, excluding those unwilling to abide by them. His influence was considerable despite growing opposition to the movement.

Tertullian of Carthage, one of the early Latin Church Fathers, died a Montanist. The thrust toward rigor is evident in all his writings. Even though he was mainly concerned with speculative doctrines, he repeatedly asserted that discipline is essential to sound doctrine. In condemning heretics, he wrote:

> I must not leave out a description of the heretics' way of life—futile, earthly, all too human, lacking in gravity, in authority, in discipline, as suits their faith. To begin with, one cannot tell who is a catechumen and who is baptized. They come in together, listen together, pray together. Even if any of the heathen arrive, they are quite willing to cast that which is holy to the dogs and their pearls (false ones!) before swine. The destruction of discipline is to them simplicity, and our attention to it they call affectation.[14]

During the Middle Ages the intentional impulse expressed itself through monastic forms, but with the dawn of the Reformation other attempts at renewal appeared. In 1670 a German Lutheran by the name of Philipp Jakob Spener gathered a small group from the church in Frankfort of which he was the pastor, meeting with them in his home for prayer and discussion of the Sunday sermon. His aim was to deepen the spiritual life of the church by intensifying the devotion and enriching the theological understanding of a small group within it. The church of Spener's day had been infiltrated and corrupted by the world. There was governmental interference with the church, controversy about theological matters, inadequacy in the clergy, and immorality and self-seeking among the members. Spener was impressed by Luther's teaching about the priesthood of all believers. In 1673 he published his *Pia Desideria*, in which he called for the creation of communities within which all Christians could minister to one another in building devotional depth and moral zeal. These groups he called the *ecclesioloe in ecclesia*, or the little church within the church. They were to be patterned along the lines of the *collegia pietatis* which had met in his house five years before.

Spener's creation of communities of renewal and rededication was a strategy for implementing Christian decisions. The moral needs of the world were to be met by those who first received an experientially centered zeal for religion apart from the world. The little group in which this starts first renews its own life and then ministers to the church; the church in turn ministers to the world without adopting its ways. Spener intended no break from Lutheranism, only its renewal. But his strict demands for simplicity and moderation in food, dress, and behavior aroused opposition from those who regarded such pleasures as harmless matters, "indifferent" in their consequences for the Christian life. Spener even rejected the enjoyment of the theater, dances, and cards. Indeed, the kind of moralistic otherworldliness popularly attributed to the Puritans was more typically the consequence of the pietist influence in Protestantism.

The method of Spener, including Bible study, the religious cultivation of the new birth, and a search for deepened theological understanding, is found in almost unbroken sequence in subsequent Protestantism. Franke, Zinzendorf, Law, and Wesley each emphasized the place of the small group in the discipline and renewal of the Christian life. They first aimed for changes in the hearts of men rather than for changes in the structures and the power relationships of the world. In Zinzendorf's community at Herrnhut there was strict discipline, designed to create a group distinctively different from the world, yet ready to go forth to change and convert it. The tension between the idea of a distinctive group within the church, unique only in devotional zeal, and the idea of a special group with distinct organization and loyalty, was never resolved. Many of the groups that sought the renewal of the whole church found themselves to be splinter segments cut off from the church. Despite Zinzendorf's reservations about radical disjunction, the Moravian group which he founded with the intention of renewing the church became a sect apart from it.

William Law intended to call the church as a whole to a new level of devotion when he wrote *A Serious Call to a Devout and Holy Life*. He wanted to renew an old rather than to create a new community, to revitalize the spiritual condition of the existing church rather than to form a new religious movement. Law urged his followers to live their Christian calling in the everyday duties of life, but to do so with a spirit and in a manner that would exhibit their special calling as Christians.

> Our blessed Saviour and his apostles are wholly taken up in doctrines that relate to *common life*. They call us to renounce the world, and differ in every *temper* and *way* of life from the spirit and way of the world. To renounce all its goods, to fear none of its evils, to reject its joys, and have no value for its happiness. To be as *new-born babes*, that are born into a new state of Things; to live as pilgrims, in spiritual watching, in holy fear, and heavenly aspiring after another life; to take up our daily cross; to deny ourselves; to profess the blessedness of mourning; to seek the blessedness of poverty of spirit; to forsake the pride and vanity of riches; to take no thought for the morrow; to live in the profoundest state of humility; to rejoice in

worldly sufferings; to reject the lust of the flesh, the lust of the eyes, and the pride of life; to bear injuries, to forgive and bless our enemies, and to love mankind as God loveth them; to give up our whole hearts and affections to God; and strive to enter thro' the strait gate into a life of eternal glory.[15]

Law took the Reformation doctrine of vocation, which calls all Christians to a service of God regardless of the kind of work in which they are engaged, and declared that such work should be performed with a unique attention to Christian virtue and in renunciation of the spirit of this world. Instead of separating monastic Christians from ordinary Christians, he separated Christians from ordinary man. Christian life became, in his view, a new, distinctive type of living marked by charity, love for enemies, the patient bearing of evil, self-denial, and humility.

> Thus it is in all the virtues and holy tempers of Christianity; they are not *ours*, unless they be the virtues and tempers of our *ordinary life*. So that Christianity is so far from leaving us to live in the common ways of life, conforming to the folly of customs, and gratifying the passions and tempers which the spirit of the world delights in. It is so far from indulging us in any of these things, that all its virtues, which it makes necessary to salvation, are only so many ways of living above, and contrary to the world in all the common actions of our life.
>
> If our common life is not a common course of *humility, self-denial, renunciation* of the world, *poverty* of spirit, and *heavenly* affection, we don't live the life of Christians.[16]

John Wesley was twenty-five years old when Law wrote his *A Serious Call to a Devout and Holy Life* and was probably influenced by it. Wesley's view of the Christian life was similar to Law's, and Wesley was equally concerned for the renewal of the life of all Christians. He drew up a "Deed of Declaration" organizing a movement to renew the life of the church. Henry Bettenson remarked of this document: "There is obviously here no intention of making Methodism anything more than a movement for spiritual revival *in* the Church of England."[17] Eleven years later, four years after Wesley's death, the Methodists formed themselves into a dissenting body. As in the case of the Moravians, the thrust toward spiritual zeal and moral perfection resulted in separation from the established church.

Under the Wesleys and George Whitefield, Methodism developed a great zeal to preach the Gospel to all sorts and conditions of men, exhorting them to live a new sort of life. Methodist circuit riders fought theological scepticism, spiritual apathy, and moral breakdown. They inveighed against the coarse savagery and illiterate barbarisms which they saw about them. Wesley's attention was directed outward toward the improvement of the culture even though he worked from a beach-head established in a group of special dedication. When his movement became independent, it acquired the characteristics of a church rather than of a sect, but a church in which zeal, individual renewal, conversion, and the drive for perfect obedience were taken as the hallmarks of the Christian life.

Eighteenth-century Methodism was complex: it had one root in the Anglican tradition, another in the pietism typified by the followers of Zinzendorf, still another in Puritanism, and yet a fourth in sectarian soil. Wesley, like William Law and Richard Baxter, accepted life in the world but required it to be lived with a different spirit and a higher morality. He expected spiritual holiness to be spread abroad in the land by those who had been so touched and disciplined by the small group as to make visible a new kind of life. Wesley's idea of Christian perfection was dominated by the image of total devotion to God and full love of neighbor. He interpreted salvation in terms of justification by faith but refused to adopt the classical Reformation formula of *sola fide* (by grace alone). Wesley was concerned with conversion but avoided such a preoccupation with the next life as to destroy proper concerns about the conditions of this one. Wesley's Methodism foreshadowed features in both revivalism and the social gospel, yet it cannot be understood as a simple prototype of either. It began with a demand for personal and group renewal, but it engendered works of charity, demands for reform, and the desire to see the Gospel brought to all men. It was to serve as the spiritual father of other movements which proposed to bring new life to the church by starting with the conversion of individuals and their spiritual reinforcement in small groups.

Unlike the sects, Methodism did not condemn the ties between church and state normative for the institutional view of Christian responsibility. Unlike operationalists it did not spend its energy in urging Christians to involve themselves in the political processes of life. However, with the passage of time, Methodism changed. Today its life has been affected by the forces affecting all the denominations. In some places it is fully enmeshed with its culture. Its theologians plead for social action in both institutional and operational terms. It lobbies, it sanctifies its share of the contemporary established order, and it raises spokesmen for the renewal of the church through fellowship groups.

The call for the renewal of the church is sounded no less strenuously in our day than it was in the time of Wesley. There is always sufficient apathy to elicit it. Moreover, the appeal of renewal is basic and perennial. Bookstores may not now sell, nor libraries circulate, many copies of William Law, but they have plenty of demand for books of more recent vintage that plead for the same recourse to holy living. Perhaps it is easier to cherish the belief that renewal will work if the book is a recent one than if the book comes from the past and works at the disadvantage inherent in the recognition that its plea, at best, had ephemeral consequences.

In 1938 four clergymen and four laymen went to the island of Iona to rebuild a monastery which had fallen into ruins. Members of the Scottish church, these men were concerned to create a life of corporate devotion and communal discipline. They gather at Iona only for the summer, returning to separate duties (mostly in parishes) on the mainland of Scotland during the major portion of the year. The movement which they founded has since grown in size. In 1962 it had 143 full and 725 associate members. A threefold rule commits the members to a common discipline of prayer and Bible study, careful use of time, and frugal use of money. Full members are on probation two years before joining the movement and must spend the summers on the island. Associate members make a semi-annual recommittal of their intentions.

Iona is an intentional community—in this respect a trifle like monastic movements—but its special rules of discipline are fully compatible with normal life. Laymen can follow the discipline as well as clergymen. Celibacy is explicitly rejected. Moreover, the members of the Iona Community participate directly in efforts to alleviate social injustice and suffering. The community thinks of itself as foreshadowing a new reformation of the church, feeling that by the twenty-first century its practice of the Christian life may be normative for all Christians. It has remained closely related to the church, within which it has remained a loyal gad-fly, rather than becoming a new movement.

According to the founder of Iona, George MacLeod, worship is the central and primary focus of the Christian life. "The worship of God comes before the service of man." In elaborating this point, MacLeod has explained:

> Certainly the healing of bodies is implied in—as it was inspired by— the Incarnation: and the problem of the unemployed, and the direction of youth organizations are primary obligations through the Incarnation. But it is our unaltered conviction that healing will not be total again, nor the unemployment problem solved, nor youth organization take its right direction: in a word, human beings will not find their Humanity again, till we put right again, and first of all, our service to God.[18]

Because worship plays such a central part in the thinking of the founder of this community, the church also plays a central part. The Iona Community works for the church's renewal, but it has no rigid formula for the pattern that such a renewal must take. T. Ralph Morton, a member of the Iona group, has written about the several renewals that have characterized the history of the church, finding values in each. He interprets the rise of monasticism as an effort to renew the church following the loss of zeal which came after the Constantinian recognition. He interperts the Reformation as a renewal of the church along the lines of the family pattern. The rise of the congregation and the missionary enterprises of the nineteenth century are likewise portrayed as patterns of renewal. Each renewal emerges when the church captures the vision of the spirit in fresh terms and is able to relate it to the everyday lives of its members.

> . . . new forms of Christian living arose through the experience, first, of individual men, and then through that of groups of men who saw a new need and heard a new call. It is only as somehow that need has been strongly felt by other men and that call has answered their hopes, that the new pattern of life has appeared intelligible to them and something creative and effective has happened in the church.[19]

According to Morton, the pattern to emerge today cannot be a copy of any of the old ones, but it must embody the essential thrust toward spiritual renewal and moral discipline found in them. Pioneering groups must arise to fill the vacuum in the spiritual life of the present church and to point the way to a new sort of social living. The church is the starting point of mission, but only when it has been renewed can it function creatively and effectively in ministering to the world. George MacLeod put the matter succinctly when he wrote, "We must become more separate and more involved."[20] The separation of the church, beginning with the pioneer group, is expressed in its renewed sense of worship and discipline. The involvement of the Christian, which flows from the renewal experienced in the church, takes political and humanitarian forms.

The community at Iona does not think of the church as an action group in the political sense. Political action is expected of its individual members who take their inspiration from the life of the worshiping community in which they are involved, but these members act as individuals when they turn to politics.

> We have said that to be baptized implies a political obligation. But that is an obligation on the *individual Christian:* the declaration of its colour is not the obligation, nor the right, of the *Church,* or of the congregation. The Church can never become a political party, nor the congregation a political cell. To become a political party is to accept the intention of taking executive power: for the church to accept executive and political power is to involve it in the use of all the rightful sanctions to maintain order, and thereby to set at nought its primary task of being a home of reconciliation whose one sufficient weapon must be love.[21]

Iona is only one of many contemporary movements, all of which are concerned to renew the life of the church by gathering small numbers into personal groupings, either in the parish itself or at locations to which men can retreat for short periods of inspiration and rededication. Among the retreat centers which have sprung up in America the following are among the best-known examples: Kirkridge, Bangor, Pennsylvania; Five Oaks, Paris, Ontario; Rolling Ridge, North Andover, Massachusetts; Shadybrook House, Mentor, Ohio; Parishfield Community, Brighton, Michigan; Pendle Hill, Wallington, Pennsylvania; and the Yokefellow Institute, Richmond, Indiana. It would be impossible to list, let alone describe in detail, the many groups that have created places for the renewal of the life of the church. The Catholic church has numerous retreat houses, many of which predate Protestant efforts. Moreover, the methods used by these groups vary considerably; some of the retreat centers have residents, devoted to full time living under a rule; others are staffed by paid professionals; others are seasonal. But they have this in common: they maintain allegiance to the churches from which their members come and to which they return.

These groups usually see the Christian life in terms of a striving for higher attainment, often in perfectionistic categories, believing that faith in Christ should make a difference in the personal life of the believer, a visible and evident change in his pattern of existence. This visible change is most likely to express itself in service to others, undertaken in a spirit of love and with a sense of brotherhood. Personal relationships are highly cherished, and the small group is heralded as the antidote to the impersonal harshness of a technological and organizational culture. Group devotions and discipline contribute to the intimacy and mutual sense of belonging.

Another function of the retreat center is education. In describing the work of the Yokefellow Institute, Samuel Emerick shows how its educational program is designed to make the average layman more articulate about his beliefs. Through readings and discussion men who attend the Yokefellow programs arrive at a deepened understanding of the Christian faith and a more conscious awareness of the gap between that faith and the normal local expression of it. When they return to church and job, they are in a position to influence the life of the world by the vision they have seen.

> The great hope which presses in upon us in our time is that the church will become a fellowship of penetration, a truly redemptive force in society. The inevitable question is, How can the salt and light and leaven of Christian truth penetrate the structures of education, industry, campus life, politics, and social life? How can these realms be brought under the lordship of Christ? The obvious answer is in the committed and informed laymen who see their occupation, their politics, their social contacts as areas in which to serve the Mind of Christ.[22]

Groups which hold to a discipline requiring a new sort of life are bound to experience tensions if they urge their members to concern themselves about affairs in the world. It is not easy to be in the world yet not of it. Those inner disciplines that support and sustain the devotional zeal of individuals and the cohesiveness of a group are difficult to pursue apart from a protected situation. Consider, for example, the rule (or style-of-life) suggested for members of the Kirkridge Community. It makes some reference to life in the world, at least to duties in the local congregation. But the obligations it lays upon its members emphasize the disciplines that set the group apart from the normal life of the world rather than those duties which catapult them into the midst of power configurations. A person is not likely to run for school board, for Congress, or for some other job in the matrix of society if he is also concerned to fulfill the following obligations:

1. *Prayer:* A minimum of one-half hour daily supplemented with family worship.
2. *Identification:* Sharing with persons who are suffering to bring them strength for new life. Practicing redemptive non-violence.
3. *Study:* At least one solid book monthly.
4. *Stewardship:* Drastic discipline of time, energy, and money so that ample and increasing margins may be available for deepest concerns.
5. *Church:* Responsibility in local congregation and in the wider Christian fellowship.
6. *Nurture Group:* Regular participation with a few others for study, prayer, and sharing.
7. *Retreat:* At least once a year; if possible monthly, for two or more hours.
8. *Support of Kirkridge:* In prayer, by inviting others to join, and with annual financial contribution.[23]

Attempts to renew the life of the church by starting with small groups for special study and discipline can also be carried on within the parish life of the local congregation. In his book *New Life in the Church*,[24] Robert A. Raines pleads for this technique. He describes the present difficulty in the church in terms of the lost sense of mission which must be renewed by a conversion or rebirth. He would preserve the sense and experience of conversion, prompted in the past by revivalism, but transform the means by which individuals are brought to such a renewal. The church should provide conditions in which God may awaken people, bring them to decision about the centrality of the Christian life, and nourish their growth in faith and discipline. Raines's strategy starts wholly and unreservedly within the church, which he would remake and renew by intensifying the Christian experiences, understandings, and dedications of its individual members. This process is to be affected by training "a hard core of committed and growing disciples who shall serve as leaven within the local church."[25]

The training of committed persons is to be done in small groups, in which prayer, sharing of personal experiences, Bible study, and the taking of Holy Communion together are central features. The study of the Bible must be centered on matters of spiritual concern; it is not to be an intellectual exercise for greater edification through grasp of subject matter. Biblical insights are central for the Christian life, as also for knowing about the Christian's relationship to the world. Speaking of a retreat during which representatives of labor and management were gathered for study and renewal, Raines recounts the following experience:

> The purpose of the retreat was to discover whether we could consider some sort of "Christian approach" to the problems of labor-management relations. The clergymen present discovered how ineffectively the church has been communicating her gospel in recent years. For these laymen had an idea of Christian faith which they summed up in the phrase "Christian principles." They kept repeating, both labor and management people, that all we need to do is apply "Christian principles" and all our problems will be solved. Finally one of the laymen was asked to write on a blackboard a list of these principles. He did so. The list included the following: sincerity, integrity, honesty, fairness, consistency, mutual understanding.[26]

In Raines's comment about this experience his separatism shines forth:

> These are all fine virtues, of course. But they are not specifically Christian principles. Any good Jew would adhere to this list and would justly resent the claim that these are "Christian" principles. Most of our nonchurched and non-Christian friends would subscribe to these principles. This is simply a list of virtues which any good citizen of a democracy would endorse, whatever faith or lack of faith he possessed. These laymen on the retreat had unconsciously boiled down Christianity to good citizenship.[27]

Because Raines believes Christians should have a different and more highly visible goodness than that found in ordinary citizens, he must search for different strategies for meeting the problems of the world. He even seems to value lightly the practice of "good citizenship" and general moral virtue because these are so greatly inferior to his vision of dedication. Moreover, he feels that lives need changing, not institutions—or to say it more fairly, changing of lives precedes any possible changing of institutions. The strategies used within the institutional and operational motifs are implicitly rejected. Raines does not mention how the representatives of labor and management who probed new depths of biblical understanding in the retreat dealt with the problems of justice and conflicting claims when they went back to work after the week-end. The implication, however, is that by opening channels of personal communication the possibility of more helpful relationships was established.

Not all attempted renewals of parish life remain this distantly connected to the realities of political concerns. Some point out that renewal of the church can come only out of the encounter with the world which arises from the struggle for justice. Thus, Robert W. Spike observed that "there is no more potent evangelistic witness in a community than the church's concern and action on behalf of justice or in the meeting of some critical human need."[28] The Iona Community has been very much involved in social action. The Kirkridge membership is often found in peace action groups. In general, when groups that are interested in spiritual renewal do manifest social concern, such concern tends to take the form of action that is in harmony with pacifist convictions. When such groups are interested in social justice they usually manifest a piety which emphasizes individual renewal rather than structural justice. The personal element is emphasized as an antidote to the depersonalization of our culture. Thus, in the words of John L. Casteel, "If our society is to be restored to health, and to humane living, ways must be found to re-create the firsthand personal relations between men that we are rapidly losing."[29]

After the Second World War a church in Washington, D.C., under the leadership of the Reverend Gordon Cosby, embarked upon an experiment which combined features of the intentional community and the parish church. Serious attainment of theological understanding and moral discipline was made a precondition of membership. Such membership has to be annually renewed and carries with it obligations with respect to the use of time, energy, and money. The tithe is considered the minimum expected contribution. A member of the Church of the Savior must prepare for joining through a long course of study, pledge himself to total commitment, accept the discipline, participate in the active fellowship of the group, and submit to mutual correction and admonition. The church, while related to ecumenical bodies, has no denominational ties, yet it carefully acknowledges the legitimacy of other churches and requires its members to pledge that should they sever ties with the Church of the Savior, they "will join some other expression of the Christian church." This parish breaks with neither the church in other expressions nor with the realities of the world, in which its members are expected to participate. It is, however, an example of the effort to implement Christian decisions by furnishing a special community of renewal and rigor which contributes to the nurture and sustenance of the Christian life and depends upon tight, internal cohesion for its effectiveness.

18

Sects, Guilds, and Causes

The intentional motif also expresses itself outside the normally established or culturally accepted church. It may do this by setting up an alternative community of faith, generally critical of the church and the world. It may also gather men together around particular programs carried out without reference, positive or negative, to the ongoing life of the churches.

The Sect as an Alternative Community of Faith

Sects reject the relative natural law by which the church accommodates to the state and society and replace it with a perfectionist reading of scriptural law. They vary in their understandings of what the rejection of the world demands but are alike in their insistence that the behavior of Christians must be different from that of other men. They usually reject the use of coercion, force, and power. Because of this the sectarian will not accept public office but seldom will he become a revolutionary. He will not take an oath, but he does not feel called to prevent others from doing so or to crusade for changes in laws which demand of others things which he himself cannot perform. The sects are marked by a strong emphasis upon lay religion and require all members to pursue a life which does not compromise with the world. They exercise strong internal discipline over their own group but disclaim any interest in exercising control over the social order in general. The sects want no part in a seignorial society in which rank and honor confer privileges and power, but they can develop rigid stratifications based upon eldership and sex differences within their own communities.

If we regard the sectarian movement as a protest, not only against the world but also against the church, then it becomes necessary to think of the sect as a phenomenon which developed after the appearance of the established church. While the early primitive Christian movement was distinctively different from the world, it is not generally spoken of as a sect movement. Only protests against the worldly church, such as appeared in the Montanist and Donatist movements are properly referred to as sects. Many sects arose in protest against the medieval establishment. Ever since, the sects have generally been identified with Protestant Christianity, even though they have often been as critical of classical Reformation traditions of church-state identification as they have been of Catholic patterns. The Waldensians, Lollards, and Hussites pre-date the Reformation, yet one can read a description of the Waldensians which says ". . . the Waldensian church is a Protestant community, Calvinistic in principle, before the Reformation."[1] The post-Reformation sectarians include the Anabaptists, Mennonites, Levellers, Diggers, and Millenarians. Troeltsch even discusses Methodists and Christian Socialists under this rubric.

Strictly speaking, the sect represents that kind of separatism which rejects both the world and the established church. Its members refuse to hold political office, take oaths, or participate in war. In an autobiography, James Luther Adams describes the religious orientation of his father, a Baptist country preacher of premillenarian persuasion. His father's attitude toward the world, in this case within the heritage of the Anabaptist tradition, illustrates the sectarian approach:

> My father was as otherworldly as the head of a family could possibly be. Very often he would tell us after family prayers before retiring at night that we might not see each other again on this earth. Christ might come before morning and we should all meet him in the air. He interpreted the World War as evidence of the approaching end of the present "dispensation." Later on, after he joined the Plymouth Brethren, he refused on religious principle to vote. He gave up his life insurance policy because he felt it betrayed a lack of faith in God. When he was employed by the American Railway Express Company he refused to join the union on the ground that it was a worldly organization with worldly aims. Indeed, he had taken up railway work because of his decision to follow St. Paul's example and refuse to accept wages for preaching the gospel.[2]

A sect has devotional, cultic, theological, and ethical characteristics. Its ethical concerns involve ways for setting ethical standards as well as strategies for implementing ethical decisions. Its reading of scripture as a moral law book usually belongs to the prescriptive motif. Moreover, the sect generally looks for the end of the age. Because it cherishes an eschatological view of history it does not feel as deeply concerned as does the church for the maintenance of justice and order. With the passing of the generations the eschatological expectations of the sect erode, and the sect experiences a lessening of its world rejection and becomes more and more like the church in its social outlook.

The sects are sometimes characterized as ascetic movements, a distinction being drawn between the intramundane asceticism of the sect and the extramundane asceticism of the monastic order. Troeltsch speaks of ascetic features of both movements, but very carefully distinguishes between them:

> The asceticism of the Church [i.e. of a monastic type] is a method of acquiring virtue, and a special high watermark of religious achievement, connected chiefly with the repression of the senses, or expressing itself in special achievements of a peculiar character; otherwise, however, it presupposes the life of the world as the general background, and the contrast of an average morality which is on relatively good terms with the world. . . .
>
> The asceticism of the sects on the other hand, is merely the simple principle of detachment from the world, and is expressed in the refusal to use the law, to swear in a court of justice, to own property, to exercise dominion over others, or to take part in war. The sects take the Sermon on the Mount as their ideal; they lay stress on the simple but radical opposition of the Kingdom of God to all secular interests and institutions. They practise renunciation only as a means of charity, as the basis of a thorough-going communism of love, and, since their rules are equally binding upon all, they do not encourage extravagant and heroic deeds, nor the vicarious heroism of some to make up for the worldliness and average morality of others. The ascetic ideal of the sects consists simply in opposition to the world and to its social institutions, but it is not opposition to the sense-life, nor to the average life of humanity.[3]

The distinctions drawn by Troeltsch between these two forms of asceticism work in the majority of cases and are helpful in distinguishing between the sect impulse and church-related monasticism. But American Christianity has produced several small movements in which the distinction between sect and monastic types of asceticism appears to break down. These groups include the several communities of Shakers and the celibate society founded by Conrad Beissel at Ephrata, Pennsylvania.

The Shaker communities played an unobtrusive but important role in American religious life, until they became extinct as communities in our century. The celibate life of the Shakers was governed by a series of Millennial Laws in which the community defined its sense of God's requirements for their corporate life. A number of these laws, which were generally given by verbal instruction and not printed nor published for wide circulation, pertained to the means by which men and women were to be kept separate from each other and all members of the sect were to be kept separate from the world.

Manual labor was central in the life lived by the Shakers, and the ingenious tools they created for use in an essentially agrarian economy attract more than a few visitors to the museums that have put them on display for the contemporary public. Work was done voluntarily as a symbol of consecration. Property within the settlements was held in common and a simple style of life prevailed. Shakers were known to be generous with outsiders, to have been fair and open in dealing with those making inquiries about possible membership in the group, and to care for one another with a concern which did much to ban anxiety from their minds. Their name reflects the fact that dance was used as a medium for worship.

Membership in the society was open to all comers, but under strict practical and religious conditions. A person seeking to join was required to settle all his debts, obtain the consent of any spouse involved, and provide for any children. Membership was open to families, in which case the children usually joined the community and grew up within its communal patterns, housed separately from the parents. During the period of trial, which lasted for at least a year, the decision to join the society required only that the available property of the new member be placed at the interim disposal of the society. When the decision to join was made, final title to property was given to the society on an irrevocable basis. Each person was expected to make a complete and unreserved confession and repentance of all past sins, a process which was believed to take great effort and much time. Anything deceitfully withheld was left to God to discover, though the actual confessions were given to elders of the person's own sex who were appointed for the purpose of aiding the new convert to make the necessary purge which opened "the door of hope." Shakers believed

> . . . the Pentecostal [i.e. early] Church was established on right principles; that the Christian churches rapidly and fatally fell away from it; and that the Shakers have returned to this original and perfect doctrine and practice. They say: "The five most prominent practical principles of the Pentecostal Church were, first, common property; second, a life of celibacy; third, nonresistance; fourth, a separate and distinct government; and, fifth, power over physical disease." To all these but the last they have attained; and the last they confidently look for, and even now urge that disease is an offense to God, and that it is in the power of men to be healthful, if they will.[4]

The Shakers admitted the legitimacy of marriage and property as belonging to a lower order of society but made no provision for the dual standard of the monastic tradition within their own group. Their life was marked by many virtues of potential use for all men: honesty, integrity, frugality without parsimony, temperance, kindness, diligence, freedom of debt, education for children, and care for the infirm and aged. Their communities were interracial, and members were drawn from among professionals as well as common people. The records show that joy and peace were frequently professed by the members, not always for merely ritual reasons. For a time the settlements flourished, spreading westward from the parent society at New Lebanon, New York. Today, the plain yet sturdy buildings of the communities have been put to varied uses as prep schools, museums, and work camps.

The Shakers were but one of many religious groups which lived according to ascetic standards. The community at Ephrata in Pennsylvania had a background in the Dunkard movement and an outgrowth in the Seventh Day Baptists. Its buildings are still standing and open to tourists. But Labadists, Rappites, the Society at Zoar, the Harmony Society, the Oneida Society, Amana, Aurora, Bethel, the Icarians, Bishop Hill, and Cedar Vale —all these and others which might be named—evidence the extensive influence of these movements in American religious history. To the extent that these movements practiced withdrawal from the world coupled to poverty, ascetic practices, and submission to group discipline, they show that the asceticism of the sects can be quite close to that of monastic orders even when the impulses and organizational ties of these two types of separatism are quite different.

In the sixteenth century, Jacob Huter, a Mennonite reformer, founded separate communities called the Bruderhof or Huterite communities. In addition to the pacifism and general withdrawal from worldly affairs practiced by all Mennonites, Huter required his followers to share their property in common, to refrain from economic attempts to obtain profit by any means, and to withdraw from all forms of political life. His followers settled in small groups and, seeking refuge from military service, moved from Germany to Russia, to South Dakota, and on to Canada.

In 1919 Eberhard Arnold, inspired by the practices and separatism of the Bruderhof, founded the Society of Brothers, colonies of which are found in several places in the United States today. Arnold took the idea of unity in love as his byword and refused to institutionalize the inner workings of these communities, yet he required adherence to a definite pattern of life based upon absolute love of God and of others—total surrender of the self. Property is held in common, all decisions are made by the canon of the unanimity, and families are brought up within a common pattern of shared responsibility.

The Society of Brothers regards its style of life as an alternative to the loveless, heartless realities of an entrepreneurial culture. The spirit of self-seeking, which is engendered by a system of private property and profit seeking, is considered to be at the root of all present problems, culminating in the ruthless regimentation of the totalitarian state. The Society of Brothers believes that the agrarian communal practices of their groups constitute an alternative to the service of mammon which is characteristic of our culture. When the self submits its will to that of the group, the possibility of true community is created. Work is done in common, goods are shared, decisions arrived at by the unanimous workings of the spirit, and an agrarian style of life followed as an example to the world. The communities support themselves by making wooden toys, which are believed to be as far removed as possible from potential use for military purposes. As a witness to God's uniting love the community considers itself to set forth in practice an alternative way to the self-seeking of the world. It also stays separate from the church and does not identify with cell-group movements or renewal patterns centered in the parish. The major difference between the Society of Brothers in this century and the Shakers in the last century lies in the rejection of sex by the latter. The Society of Brothers encourages its members to have children and to raise them in the communal patterns of the communities.[5]

We have examined enough material to see the degrees to which the sectarian impulse can go in practicing a rejection of the world. But we have only dealt with one segment of the sectarian phenomenon—with the type of sect which creates the very small intentional community and which sometimes rejects the practice of sex or the holding of private property. A bit closer to the normal patterns of the world are the Amish communities, which tend to be bigger, to allow the holding of private property (providing it is not used for ostentation), and which live in normal family units. There are many kinds of Amish, some who will not drive cars at all, others who will drive cars only if the bumpers have been painted black, others who make even greater concessions to the world. The Amish belong to the same Mennonite tradition in which the Huterites stand. One of their group calls itself the *Bruder Gemeinde*, or Brethren in Christ—a name which witnesses in a special way to the communal element which is so frequently central for intentional separatism.

Still closer to the world are those Mennonite traditions in which the traditional practices, like distinctive dress, adherence to a strict agrarian economy, and resistance to technological change, have undergone significant modifications. Nothing could be more misleading than to think of the Mennonites, even the stricter groups, as altogether cut-off from contemporary issues. Even the strict Old Order Mennonites have a college at Goshen, Indiana, and a publishing house at Scottdale, Pennsylvania. The more liberal General Conference Mennonites run Bethel College in Kansas and Bluffton College in Ohio.[6]

Central to the sect position is a belief in the importance of a distinctive Christian movement, the life of which is visibly different from that of the world. This theme is still reiterated by spokesmen for this heritage. In an address delivered to the Sixth Mennonite World Conference, Karlsruhe, Germany, in August 1957, the President of the Mennonite World Conference, Harold S. Bender of Goshen College Biblical Seminary, defended the historical position of the Mennonites. Bender explained how the early Anabaptists made their criticism of the classical Reformation because it accepted the realities of worldly culture even while professing to go back to apostolic Christianity. He flatly declared that the classical reformers, like Luther and Calvin, did not understand the Lordship of Christ, and said, "Christ had not been understood as Lord ever since the Constantinian synthesis of church and state (or church and society) in the fourth century was invented and put into practice."[7]

It would be grossly unfair to give the impression that the sectarian form of the separatist motif must consist of a nonreflective retreat from the world, quaint and dedicated, but hardly aware of what is going on in society. The Mennonite tradition is presently represented by a group of serious and well-informed scholars who are trying to restate the Mennonite approach to society in terms that are relevant to the issues of the contemporary scene. These scholars believe that the concept of the community brotherhood which pervades the Mennonite tradition is an important witness to a perennial and necessary element in the Christian tradition, and even in society at large.

Guy Franklin Hershberger, speaking of the duties of Mennonites in the face of the great economic and social changes which have taken place in the modern world, has this to say:

> These changes in industry, in agriculture, and in transportation have caused an increasing number of Mennonites to establish business and social connections outside the Mennonite community. This in turn has caused some of them to resort to commercial life insurance and similar non-Mennonite methods of aid and security. The security sought through these devices is legitimate enough; but the objection to them is that they are provided by companies organized on a commercial basis, having the profit motif uppermost, and employing methods out of harmony with the Christian way of "bearing one another's burdens." And while these agencies are offering their aid to Christian people, they also tend to break down the life of the brotherhood. The security sought is legitimate enough, but according to the New Testament way this security should be sought through the mutual helpfulness of the Christian brotherhood. It is essential, therefore, that every Mennonite community have an effective, working program of mutual aid, which does all, and more, than commercial life insurance and similar means of security do.[8]

The sect prompts withdrawal from the world of commercial self-seeking and coercion for the sake of fidelity to the Gospel. Many thinkers in the sect tradition, therefore, believe that they should urge other church groups to adopt the ethical standards of the Gospel, such as nonresistance and dependence upon the community. With increasing visibility, we find members of the Mennonite tradition seeking to influence society in regard to social issues. For example, in a pamphlet entitled *The Christian and Capital Punishment*[9] John Howard Yoder as a Mennonite theologian enters directly and forcefully into the discussion of capital punishment. He urges Christians of all persuasions to influence legislators to abolish capital punishment from the penal system. This is part of what he terms a "Christian witness to the state." Yoder suggests that the separatist is not called upon merely to lead a tranquil life within his own community, but to use his influence to prompt the state to keep violence at a minimum and to regard human life as inviolable.

Such efforts raise genuine difficulties for the Mennonite thinker. How, for instance, can he urge the state to adopt pacifist principles without changing his traditional formulation of pacifism in terms of withdrawal and nonresistance—adopting instead a pacifism of the operational type? How can he urge the world to follow standards which have characterized the sect when the very characteristics have been developed in terms of distinctive differences from the world? The sectarian theologian will answer that his primary judgments are derived from the Gospel ethic. If he can persuade the world to accept that ethic, the distinction between sect and world will vanish.

Paul Peachey has sought to work out a rationale for a social ministry by the Mennonites. His proposal deserves the most careful scrutiny because it, along with other works by Peachey, is a clue to a ferment at work in separatist intentionalism which is as important for updating and refurbishing this motif as the writings of more widely read theologians are for updating the institutional and operational motifs. Peachey is not alone in this effort. J. H. Oosterdaan and Frits Kuiper of Amsterdam, Holland, and H. W. Meihuizen of The Hague, along with John H. Yoder, Harold Bender, and J. B. Toews, are making suggestions along these same lines. They show us that the sect approach, even in a radical form, is not stagnant but living and seeking to be heard.

Peachey believes that living the Christian life should be an active service with social implications. While he admits that the personal relationship of each man to God is a central element in the religious life, he insists that

> . . . in this purely personal dimension the gospel is not exhausted; indeed it is not properly grasped at all. For in the gospel the emphasis on the individual is bound up inseparably with the accent on the neighbor. . . .
>
> In the present discussion we are asked to examine particularly the social dimension of our common Christian ministry. And so we ask: What does it mean to serve the gospel in relation to social needs and problems in our world? What does it mean for Christians to serve society?[10]

This last question is particularly significant from the lips of a Mennonite, for it may call forth interesting considerations of the contribution of religious separatism to the health of the social order.

Peachey discusses the role and function of the Christian community. He makes a very sharp distinction between the churches generally (as wedded to the culture) and the group which is loyal to the Gospel norm for the church. He asks the general question, "What is the social function of the church?," and finds three answers which apply to the traditional as well as the Gospel norm. First, the church should act as the conscience of society, because the word of God is preached within the church and here men become uniquely aware of his will for the world. "Thus the Church perpetually recalls the world from the errors of its social ways."[11] Secondly, the church is a component of society, sharing responsibilities for the making of social order. Thirdly, the church functions as a welfare agency. When these three functions of the church are pursued in what we might call the institutional motif, the church adjusts to the culture and subordinates its role to more inclusive efforts to achieve justice. Under such conditions the church comes to bless the collective ego instead of calling men to repentance. For this reason Peachey rejects the established or semi-established pattern of the church's relationship to the world. He declares,

> When we take up the gospel, however, we encounter a wholly other concept of the Church. To be sure, the Church is the "salt of the earth," the "conscience" of society. But this, and the other functions we here noted, is the outworking, in a sense the secondary result of what the Church *is*. That is, the *Church* is not an agency set up to serve the larger society in its own mundane ends. Much rather, the Church is the creation of a new society. Not a gradual amelioration of the old, but a reconstitution, a recreation, is the word of the gospel we heard at the beginning: "No man seweth a piece of new cloth on an old garment. . . ."[12]

Exploring the ways in which the same three functions of the church which prove inadequate when institutionalized can function creatively when recast in radical obedience to the Gospel, Peachey pleads for the church to be the conscience of the culture by calling it to a radical new alternative to the way of force presupposed in the threatened use of atomic weapons. He suggests that the church should actually become a structured interracial fellowship. Peachey feels that the Mennonite tradition needs reassertion as a challenge to the selfish claim of goods which infests modern life, especially in a capitalist economy. Noting expressions of renewal he feels to be necessary, Peachey observes:

> What is urgent throughout the world, however, is a renewal of the local congregation and recovery of its integrity; a recovery of a

whole life in which Christ lives and acts concretely. Church must once more become congregation (*Gemeinde*), in which every member comes to maturity in Christ, or to use a political term, achieves majority, not in the sense of casting a vote on the care of the church building, but in the continuous reshaping of the common life. We need congregations in which the members function responsibly to bind and to loose in Christ.[13]

This sounds remarkably similar to the calls for renewal which come from churchmen like Raines, but there is a difference. Peachey is calling for a more radical break with the culture, including the renunciation of military might and the profit system. Moreover, the community (*Gemeinde*) of which Peachey speaks is even more closely disciplined than cell groups usually are, for membership carries with it certain expectations that the Christian will radically re-assess his relationships to the world in light of his commitment to the Gospel. Most cell groups merely expect their members to bring Christian ideals to bear upon the situation in which they live, not to alter their situation or remove themselves from it. Peachey's work is significant, not only as a re-statement of his own tradition, but because of his efforts to set forth the challenges of that tradition to all Christians. Peachey obviously considers the sect-type of Christian social teaching to be the truest and most adequate expression of the Gospel ethic.

Peachey's thinking also differs from the thought of many institutionalists because he believes it very important for the church to live morally and to seek justice irrespective of how the culture lives. In an article on civil rights, written when the United States Congress was considering legislation to insure equitable treatment for all citizens in job opportunities, the use of public facilities, and voting rights, Peachey raised the question as to whether the churches were courting trouble by appealing for legislative means of securing racial justice when their own internal life was still far short of the ideals projected for the life of the community as a whole. Peachey obviously supported the aims of the civil rights legislation and did not urge its defeat or postponement, but he clearly declared that resort to legislation without inner moral renewal in the church's own congregational life was totally inadequate.

> Politically legislated desegregation is not of the gospel, however necessary it may be at this juncture. But if the churches, all the while failing to work out the disciplines of Christian obedience in the discourse of congregational life, mobilize their numbers to exert the direct political pressures which are the medium of public life, do they not offer stones for the bread the "racists" need? Will the assessments of the gospel be recognized as such when carried south behind the panoply of federal power?

Significantly, at this point the "institutional" and the "freedom" church are alike tempted. If only the saints could gain control of power from the state houses down! Ah, but they do control! The problem is rather that, as Dietrich Bonhoeffer once stated so pregnantly, "The claim of the congregation of the faithful to build the world with Christian principles ends with the total capitulation of the Church to the world." Accordingly, our real task is . . . to live obediently in a world we don't control. If this seems like a call for the church's "withdrawal," how does one properly characterize the performance of the churches during the century since emancipation?[14]

Peachey concedes the need to work for desegregation through legislative methods as a temporary necessity, but his heart is with the creation of a church in which the moral implications of the Gospel have been met. The church is the primary locus for the implementation of Christian norms; concern about the culture is derivative. A church thus defined belongs to the sect pattern, because priority is laid upon the moral attainments of the group's own members before attention is given to the creation of institutions or the use of power for the achievement of social justice.

The sect pattern is an important element in the Christian tradition and one not lightly to be dismissed because it is often retiring or removed from the main stream. The witness of the Quakers has been especially significant in American history for its insistence upon religious liberty and its opposition to slavery. The Quakers have consistently opposed the use of state power for coercing the conscience in religious matters, but they have also recognized the valid role of government in the maintenance of decent society. Robert Barclay summarized a Quaker attitude toward these matters in the fourteenth article of his *Apology for the True Christian Divinity*.

Since God hath assumed to himself the power and dominion of the conscience, who alone can rightly instruct and govern it; therefore it is not lawful for any whosoever, by virtue of any authority or principality they bear in the government of this world, to force the consciences of others; and therefore all killing, banishing, fining, imprisoning, and other such things, which are inflicted upon men, for the alone exercise of their conscience, or difference in worship or opinion, proceedeth from the spirit of Cain, the murderer, and is contrary to the truth: providing always, that no man, under the pretence of conscience, prejudice his neighbour in his life or estate; or do anything destructive to, or inconsistent with humane society; in which case the law is for the transgressor, and justice is to be administered upon all, without respect of persons.[15]

Quaker thinking illustrates the selective acceptance of the world. The Quakers reject war and coercion, but accept the role of government; they reject the institution of slavery but have generally accepted the capitalist economic system; they have rejected the hierarchical church and its sacraments, but accepted the meeting house and the leadership of its elders. This is not merely the consequence of the "sect cycle" at work in a tradition, though Quakers have been slowly affected by a process of assimilation into culture, but is the basic stance of an outlook which belongs to the right hand side of the sect spectrum. The American Friends Service Committee is a consistent expression of Quakerism, both in its works of healing, relief, and reconciliation and in its efforts to affect public policy on the legislative front.

One of the most eloquent expounders of Quaker doctrine, Gerrard Winstanley, was also a spokesman for the Diggers, another sect group which appeared in seventeenth-century Cromwellian England. The Diggers were strongly political in program, calling for a radical economic equality based upon a utopian communism which would redress the inequalities of the existing economic order. Winstanley had been reduced to poverty by a combination of cut-throat competition and absence from his trade to perform military service. Ending his life as a pauper, he came to realize the comfortless austerity of poverty at its worst. Thus, in the writings of Winstanley we find theological and political considerations closely related, with strictures delivered against both the established church and the established economic order of his day. He protested the Cromwellian commonwealth, in which there was a union of the church and the state, with the latter enforcing the desires of the former by the use of coercive power. But Winstanley believed there is a place for the office of magistrate in preserving public order, even though it has no right to enforce religious beliefs.

> O that our Magistrates would let Church-work alone to Christ, upon whose shoulders they shall find the government lies, and not upon theirs. And then, in the wisdom and strength of Christ they would govern Commonwealths in justice, love, and righteousness more peacefully.[16]

Winstanley's proposed commonwealth of justice, love, and righteousness is outlined in his pamphlet *The Law of Freedom*. This is a program of religiously inspired social reform, seeking to overcome the corruptions of kingly government by establishing a utopian rule inspired by the spirit of the Indwelling Christ. In the utopia all men will consent to membership in a free and equal brotherhood. Coercive law, hierarchical distinctions, and economic inequalities are to be overcome by the power of Christ as the Inner Light of the Reason.

Winstanley's hope for a new situation in which evil and injustice are overcome by the power of Christ looks forward to the same absence of coercion which George Herron believed to be possible within the perfect state. But Winstanley wrote as a sectarian; Herron, as an institutionalist. Hence, Winstanley thought of the perfect order as a creation of the Christian community apart from the world, whereas Herron thought of the perfect state as a creation of all men. Both expressions of utopianism are likely targets for the criticisms embodied in the operational motif, in which the exercise of power and influence is declared a necessary aspect of Christian social concern.

Intentional Groups with Special Emphases

Christians have sometimes gathered into groups around shared purposes or common interests. In the early medieval ages, for example, all those working on a particular kind of work bound together into guilds. These guilds served, not only to provide mutual aid and protection to the members, but to give religious meaning to their work. Guilds concerned themselves with the salvation of souls, the conduct of corporate worship, the giving of alms, and the performance of social services. They exercised discipline over their members, discipline considered to express a conscious Christian commitment. With the secularization of the culture, the consciously Christian and devotional aspect of the guilds gave way to the essentially protective stance of the present union or professional association, but in original form and conception the guild was a group that provided a community of discipline and renewal through which the Christian could implement his ethical decisions.

Unions, chambers of commerce, and professional organizations are now largely institutionalized. They discipline their members and even use power and influence in advancing their self-interests. Those Christians who think in intentional terms of renewal and dedication believe that such practices lack the distinctive elements which belong to Christian witness, and consequently have revived the guild concept. Some modern guild equivalents are distinguished by rigorous disciplines and social consciousness; others, merely by a general piety which believes spiritual renewal results in social betterment. Let us examine how the guild idea has reappeared in three vocational areas: education, the ministry, and business.

Shortly after the Second World War a group of interested teachers formed a fellowship of scholars from all the academic disciplines. They came together to explore the meaning of the Christian faith for the academic process, working in some ways as the faculty counterpart of the Student Christian Movement. There has been considerable discussion concerning the rationale of the Faculty Christian Fellowship which emerged as a formal movement from the impetus of this initial effort. Some have called for a rigorous covenant of discipline; others have been content to think of the fellowship as a professional guild linked only by common concerns about the relationship of Christian faith to the academic world. Werner A. Bohnstedt, speaking perhaps for a middle position, suggests that the name Faculty Christian Fellowship implies more than a professional organization, more than a collection of men engaged in the same job; indeed, a "fellowship where one member cares for the other and will stand by him in times of prosperity and in the days of trouble."[17]

In Bohnstedt's view the Faculty Christian Fellowship is a confessional group, bound together by a common loyalty to the Christian faith and dedicated to the exploration of its implications for the academic enterprise. It is also a group in which mutual aid and support of a personal sort take place. Speaking of his own experience, he writes

> We have truly become fellow-members, "members one of another" in our group and groups. Beyond the limits of academic specialty and ecclesiastic denomination, we are bound together by our common concern and our common searching for the clarification and solution of problems that confront us as Christian faculty people. The realization that we stand not alone, but have comrades in arms is perhaps the greatest reward that we can have in our groups. Here we find like-minded people, here common work can be done, and the *Ecclesia Militans* becomes a reality.[18]

The life of the group has not been developed along the lines of a closely knit intentional fellowship of the sort which Bohnstedt envisioned. But neither has the group become an action organization of a political sort—a Christian version of the American Association of University Professors. It has published a magazine in which issues related to theology and culture, theology and the academic enterprise, have been discussed with erudition. It has held national and regional conferences to explore these issues and renew friendships. But while it has not become a closely knit intentional guild in the pattern called for by some of its more enthusiastic sponsors, it has remained a confessional group with decidedly Christian aims and objectives, a confessional group which contains members with many persuasions and convictions about the interpretation of the Christian faith, but having a common mind to explore its meaning for the academic process.

In 1946 W. Jack Lewis became pastor of the Presbyterian Westminster Foundation at the University of Texas. He became convinced that the normal pattern of student religious activities hardly scratches the surface of Christian experience and action. In its place he developed a center for disciplined study and worship which trained a selected group of students in theology for Christian living. Study and community living were woven into a balanced pattern and the Christian student's duty to the university world was considered in the light of his developing awareness of the meaning of the Christian faith. Thus developed the Christian Faith and Life Community of Austin, Texas, a residential center for students taking courses at the University of Texas, who have agreed to study, worship, and live together under this covenant:

OUR CORPORATE STUDY

1. We covenant together to be present at the weekly lecture-discussions held each Monday evening from 9:30 through 10:45.
2. We covenant together to attend and participate in the hour and one-half Seminar per week as scheduled at the beginning of each term.
3. We covenant together to give a minimum of one hour of study each week to the assigned essays prior to the meeting of our seminars; to write a one page report on the one article so designated; and once each term to prepare and read a paper in our seminar as assigned by the instructor.

OUR CORPORATE LIFE

1. We covenant together to live self-consciously before the regulations of the University governing student housing and before the specific living arrangements of the men's and women's residence of the College House.
2. We covenant together to responsibly participate in the fifteen minute conversation periods regularly held at the close of the evening meal, Monday through Thursday.
3. We covenant together to be present at the special lectures and discusions held immediately after dinner on each Friday evening from 6:15-7:15.

OUR CORPORATE WORSHIP

We covenant together to attend the evening worship service of the College House, 5:15-5:40 p.m., Monday through Friday, either as a self-conscious participant or as an empathetic spectator. . . .

OUR CORPORATE MISSION

We covenant together openly and honestly to strive to discover anew and in depth what it means to be genuine free men in action— responsible, critically intelligent persons—in a university situation, in our family relationships, in our friendships, and in all the orders of social existence.[19]

The life of the community was used to develop an enriched and deepened experience of the vocation of each member as a student. In light of the theological insights learned in extra-curricular study the student came to see his whole educational experience in a new perspective. He did more than attend a conference once or twice a year. He lived and worked in a closely knit fellowship where the intellectual task of understanding Christian faith was taken seriously. As a pilot project which has been copied in a limited number of places, the Christian Faith and Life Community is a good example of the renewal group related to vocational concerns.

In the vocational area of the ministry the group approach that has been developed by the leaders of the East Harlem Protestant Parish deserves thoughtful inquiry. When Donald Benedict and George William Webber joined Archie Hargraves in a group resolved to minister to the slum areas of East Harlem, they early recognized that the demands and opportunities of the district could not be borne by three individuals working alone, or even as "friends." Something more sustaining was necessary, and so the Group Ministry of the East Harlem Protestant Parish was created. Each member of the Group Ministry bound himself to certain obligations of Bible study, financial frugality, and devotional life. Strength and reality were found in the meetings of the group, in the mutual support and encouragement of the ministers for each other, and in the direction which comes from deliberation over major problems. The group practiced the principle of the *Ordered* Day, which includes worship, periodic retreats for inspiration and planning, and the use of "Advisers" with whom confidences and failures are shared.[20]

The Group Ministry of the East Harlem Protestant Parish has been more than a staff which confers together about common problems; it has been a group which works in deeply felt personal commitments and shares specific spiritual disciplines and practices. Its life has not always been free of difficulty. In one crisis it was discovered that the professional staff was overly conscious of its group character and was cutting itself off from the lay membership of the parish. The death of one of its most cherished members in an auto accident forced the others to make a radical reappraisal of their own role and to find new meaning in the Bible study which they had previously found routine and wooden. The group has constantly reached out, but from a base provided by its own fellowship and disciplines. It has gotten into political action of various sorts, especially on issues where the demands of elementary justice in the local situation leave little room for a sense of ambiguity. It has not only sustained its own members, attracted new workers, and won the admiration of the parish and its friends, but it has provided leadership for similar experiments in other cities.

The Laymen's Movement for a Christian World, with headquarters at Wainwright House in Rye, New York, has sponsored a number of retreats for the discussion of business ethics. Devotional practices as well as ethical discussions are employed in these retreats, which place greatest emphasis upon the spiritual renewal of the individual so that he can return to the responsibilities of his job with renewed dedication and a high resolve to carry out his ethical ideals in daily decisions. Very little, if any, attention to the need for political and social renewal is evident in the program materials of the Laymen's Movement. Personal honesty, the cultivation of individual integrity, and the achievement of an idealistic concern about the impact of executive decisions are cultivated, but the radical challenge of existing society characteristic of the neo-Mennonite tradition or Iona would be quite uncongenial to the individuals who usually participate in its activities.

The Laymen's Movement for a Christian World is a spiritual kin to an older and a larger group inspired by the leadership of Frank Buchman. This movement has several names: Buchmanism, the name taken from its founder; the Oxford Group, a name identifying it with the place of founding; Moral Re-Armament, the title which best describes its program. While Moral Re-Armament has attracted men from several vocations and is not related simply to the circles of business executives, it has concentrated its work on the elite and placed its headquarters on Mackinac Island in Michigan—a place not frequented by the socially and economically disinherited segments of our society.

Frank N. D. Buchman emerged from a Lutheran pastorate in a small town of Pennsylvania concerned to renew the experience of heart-searching and commitment he felt to be missing in conventional religion. He found a reception for his ideas among intellectuals at Oxford University in England where Moral Re-Armament was launched as a movement in 1938, reviving an effort of some earlier years to excite the world about the need for changed lives and rededicated spirits. Like the Dominicans of an earlier century, Buchman gravitated toward men of privilege and eminence. He did so partly because of temperamental affinities for the upper classes, partly because he deemed it strategically helpful to have group members drawn from men of prominence, and partly because his ideas were congenial to men whose good fortunes were related to the *status quo*.

There is no doubt but what Buchman's emphasis was upon the individual. Buchman preached a message of individual renewal as the first step in social renewal. The individual is admonished to follow the four absolutes of perfect honesty, purity, unselfishness, and love. It is believed that men who abide by these norms can do much to overcome the divisions of the world. Strike deadlocks, report the spokesmen for the movement, have actually been broken when the four absolutes have been accepted by the antagonists.[21] One of Buchman's followers, Samuel M. Shoemaker, put the matter this way: ". . . give [men] new values which center in Christ, and you will soon get new relationships with one another and a new view of society."[22]

It is important to understand Buchman's outlook. It does not prompt negotiation as an end in itself. There is no counsel to compromise for the sake of agreement. The appeal to the four absolutes, addressed as it is to both sides, is believed to cut away the moral fog which breeds dispute and to allow truth to do its work. Industrial conflicts have been resolved "as management and labor began to think and act in terms of 'What is Right' instead of 'Who is Right.' "[23] When Moral Re-Armament issued a pamphlet in 1959 entitled *Ideology and Co-existence* the appeal was not for flexibility and willingness to negotiate issues of the cold war, but for moral resolve so firm and rigorous that the fiber of the Western world would outlast that of the Communist society. The individual who remains firm in his devotion to moral absolutes strikes a blow in defense of freedom.

The Oxford Group has been the object of much evaluation, most of which is either strongly critical or uncritically affirmative. The individualism of the movement, with its consequent tendencies to sanctify the *status quo* or to resolve issues on behalf of the established order has been the focus of some attacks. Other criticism has been concerned about the lack of a specifically Christian orientation in the movement, but Buchman himself cannot be fairly charged with this neglect. Propaganda of the movement has been accused of exaggerating claims. Finally, the movement itself has been peripheral to the life of the churches. While it has not declared its open hostility to the churches it has often worked without a specific tie to them and without relating its preachments about moral integrity to the ethic presented by the churches in the name of the Gospel. Moral Re-Armament makes much of the Sermon on the Mount, less of the *kerygma* through which the Gospel is proclaimed.

In an attempt to write a careful evaluation of the group and its accomplishments, Walter Houston Clark interviewed a number of individuals influenced by its work. He found some of these people strongly critical, others warmly enthusiastic, and still others neutral in their reflections upon the group. Clark is appreciative of the spiritual zeal accomplished by the movement through its efforts at renewal, which he finds to be in the same tradition with Spener and subsequent revivalist strands in English and American Protestantism. But Clark also has his doubts about the group's ability to keep itself from becoming a tool in the hands of men who may turn its approach to their own advantage by using spiritual renewal to engender conformity to the *status quo*. In summary Clark writes,

> We have nothing but admiration for the emotional drive and enthusiasm exhibited by the Group. The world needs more of such dynamism in the service of spiritual values, not less. But emotional drive unguided by the powers of the mind can become a danger, and even if some of that drive must be sacrificed, the critical faculty must not be put to sleep. The Group must be careful not to sell its soul to measures that, while they are means in its own estimation, may be ends for someone else. Specifically, what are meant are values such as social prestige, newsworthiness, riches, and political power.[24]

A member of Moral Re-Armament may not think of himself as separated from the world in the kind of ethic he follows, but he will probably think of himself as distinct from the world in the degree to which he adheres to his moral ideals. The traditional monk would hardly think of this moral rigor as an adequate separatism, yet the Buchmanite thinks of his witness and duty as implementing Christian goals through a special community of dedication, even as the monk does. Both feel that the world needs spiritual and moral refurbishing. The same impulse takes a radically different form in these contrasting expressions of the separatist motif, yet the belief that social health requires the inner renewal of the individual at the prompting of the special group is a common feature of both.

The separatist impulse has appeared with sufficient regularity in Christian history to engender the anticipation that it will continue to be a feature of the ethical outlook of at least some Christians. It seems to appear with renewed vigor when the distinction between Christian and non-Christian behavior tends to wash away. Whether it functions as antithesis or complement to other motifs may depend in large measure upon the way it is embraced and the way it is accepted by the majority of other Christians. Donald G. Bloesch, in his popular study of *Centers of Christian Renewal*, speaks of the renewal group as the lighthouse and observes that the pietist tradition always contains an impulse to separatism. Bloesch believes that the church has much to learn and to gain from groups of this sort, even those which break from its organization. He pleads with the special community to realize its vocation as a lighthouse by serving the church and hopes that it will not set itself up as a new movement. Then he declares,

> The church, on its side, must seek to relate itself to the religious community and to other para-parochial groups that seek to bring about church reform and renewal. The church must encourage the cultivation of special gifts and the growth of pioneering fellowships within its midst. Indeed, the church will retain its evangelistic concern and enthusiasm only if it makes a place for those adventurous souls who desire to abandon worldly cares and pursuits in order to be free for exclusive service to Christ and his kingdom.[25]

Whether a creative relationship between separatism and the larger religious community can be sustained depends not only upon the degree to which the renewal impulse is honored by others, but the extent to which it regards itself as a witness or corrective for existing practices rather than an alternative program which must be adopted by those who wish to be morally saved.

IV
Analysis and Evaluation

19

Polemical Exclusion in Christian Ethics

Each of the foregoing motifs has attracted its partisans and its critics. Each motif has drawbacks and each is open to abuse. The criticism of such abuse is a normal and legitimate aspect of Christian reflection, to be expected and respected. But there is another kind of criticism which stems from the impulse to defend a particular motif as normative for the Christian tradition, rejecting alternative motifs in order to defend its own. Indeed, some literature in contemporary Christian ethics consists more of arguments against rejected alternatives than of defense for what is advocated. Such arguments portray the motifs we have discussed as mutually exclusive rather than as complementary and create a mood of polemical exclusion in the discussion of Christian ethics.

Disagreements Concerning the Formulation of the Norm

Code morality is often ridiculous. In the attempt to deal prescriptively with every contingency which has or might arise, it endlessly elaborates rules and the interpretation of rules. These destroy freedom and even defy common sense. Cards get outlawed because they are connected with gambling, but the game of Old Maid brings forth no objections. Smoking of tobacco is considered sinful but corn silk is winked at. The Pharisee could drink the vinegar to cure his sore throat on the Sabbath but he could not gargle it. It takes very little sophistication to object to this kind of ethical myopia.

Codes may also be called into question when they lend themselves to a soteriology of works. Men who seek salvation through right actions must be certain which actions are right. The desire to know exactly the conditions which one must fulfill to be righteous is a major cause for the endless proliferation of petty requirements. John Calvin, who was not an outspoken critic of prescriptive ethics, put his finger upon a psychological truth about defined obligation when he noted the futility of defining re-

quirements with sufficient certainty to afford any man the comfort of
feeling his works guarantee salvation.

> If a man begins to doubt whether he may use linen for sheets, shirts,
> handkerchiefs, and napkins, he will afterwards be uncertain also about
> hemp; finally, doubt will even arise over tow. For he will turn over
> in his mind whether he can sup without napkins, or go without a
> handkerchief. If any man should consider daintier food unlawful, in
> the end he will not be at peace before God, when he eats either
> black bread or common victuals, while it occurs to him that he could
> sustain his body on even coarser foods. If he boggles at sweet wine,
> he will not with clear conscience drink even flat wine, and finally he
> will not dare touch water if sweeter and clearer than other water.
> To sum up, he will come to the point of considering it wrong to step
> upon a straw across his path, as the saying goes.[1]

When men rely upon codes and moral goodness to insure their salvation
or to prove their moral superiority to other men, codes become instruments of exclusion. Moral exclusiveness also arises from the desire to keep
conditions favorable for obedience to a code. The group which follows
the same rules both congratulates itself on its attainments and guards its
members from the temptations to misconduct which inhere in association
with those who ignore the code requirements. Such protective morality
becomes conservative, unbending, fearful of novelty, and afraid of interchange with other styles of life.

All these criticisms can be made without necessarily denying the valid
place for codes. They point out the misuse of prescriptive morality rather
than denying it a potential use. But there is another kind of criticism,
particularly widespread among contemporary Protestant theologians,
which looks at the foibles of code morality in order to deny prescriptive
morality any valid role in Christian ethics. Joseph Sittler declares that
any true understanding of the Christian ethic completely confounds both
a philosophical idea of natural law and the interpretation of the teachings
of Jesus as the "legislation of love."[2] Karl Barth elaborates three reasons
why there is decisive objection to even casuistical forms of prescription on
the part of Christian theology. In the first place, in casuistical ethics "the
moralist wishes to set himself on God's throne." The desire to know in
advance the entire scope and content of moral obligation seems to Barth
to create a substitute for the divine will—to place a fixed and unbending set
of prescriptions in place of the specific concrete command that comes
from God.

> [Casuistical ethics] is an undertaking in which man, even though he
> calls upon God's grace, would like to win clear of the occurrence,
> the freedom and the peril of this event, to reach dry land, as it were,

and to stand there like God, knowing good and evil. In it he thinks that he can be more than a mere recipient, beneficiary, or pure beginner. He feels and behaves—as though this were possible—like an ethical expert and a trustee.[3]

Barth also charges that any ethic which makes the command of God into a universal rule, or a "tissue of such rules," ceases to understand the living character of God. Generalized rules are foreign to the biblical ethic: "The commands of God in the Bible are not general moral doctrines and instructions but absolutely specific directions which concern each time the behaviour, deeds and omissions of one or more or many definite men in this historical context."[4] If any of the moral teachings of the Bible are divorced from this context, the whole nature of the biblical injunction is misunderstood. Finally, Barth charges that casuistical ethics interpose an alien and "other" reality between God and man. A man uses prescriptive laws to avoid the agonized decision-making which is imposed upon him in his freedom by God through His command. Action under God's immediate command, as contrasted with action in conformity to some defined obligation, demands that a man surrender himself utterly and completely to God. "Casuistry destroys the freedom of this obedience."[5]

In his criticism of moral theology Paul Lehmann examines the most flexible and sensitive kind of prescriptive ethic. Cognizant of all the richness of moral theology in the past and at the hands of its present advocates, Lehmann nevertheless concludes that moral theology is incompatible with a Christian approach to ethics because it leaves unchallenged the assumption that the ethical predicament can be solved by human powers, and like code morality, presupposes a solution to the problem of conduct apart from utter dependence upon God.[6] The import of Lehmann's argument leads to the same conclusion which flows from the arguments of Brunner, Barth, and Sittler: there is but one way of doing Christian ethics.

Many of these objections that apply to code morality can also be made of deliberative morality. Moreover, one kind of criticism raises issues about the adequacy of deliberative approaches with the intention to correct and supplement them. Another type seeks to discredit deliberative morality all together.

James Gustafson has raised the query: Do men really function deliberately when they arrive at ethical decisions? Looking at a specific problem, he observes,

> . . . in a labor dispute the opposing parties do not agree on a definition of justice, or the good society, and then deliberate about the economic consequences of such in the current dispute. If such an agreement were made, its ideological character (in the Marxist sense) would be

revealed quickly by the failure to agree on what justice or the good society mean in the particular context.[7]

Deliberations which search for ideals to be used in guiding social decisions are not so much objectionable as they are misguided. For example, both advocates and opponents of government health insurance can agree to the abstract ideal that all persons in serious need of medical attention should receive proper care, whether or not their personal finances permit them to pay for it. But while the two parties may agree about an abstract statement of the ideal, they disagree about the means for attaining it. Moreover, their disagreements reflect their own ideals and values as much or more than does their assent to the general principle. Those who support medical care through government programs speak of justice and democracy, care for the needy through regular systems of just procedure, etc. Those who oppose medical care through government programs speak of the dangers of regimentation, the problems of bureaucracy, and the importance of individual responsibility and initiative. Ideals tend to support and ennoble the positions in the controversy rather than to provide a common standard to which both sides can repair.

In the long introductory section to *The Divine Imperative* Emil Brunner contended that moral philosophy never comes to the consensus concerning the nature of the good which it takes to be basic to its very enterprise. A naturalistic type of philosophical ethic derives its theory of the good from the rules of experience, from the appreciation of what men find useful and pleasant. An idealistic approach, which stresses duty for duty's sake in response to the innate good, seeks an abstract and universally binding conception of the good. Not only do these two approaches disagree between themselves as to the nature of the rational good, even though both claim to be based upon reason, but they leave the tension between the external world of nature and the internal world of the self unresolved. "The philosophical ethic of reason," wrote Brunner, "which has arisen out of the need to give greater security to ethical thought than it possesses in its popular form, and to get rid of the contradictions which cling to it, is not only unable to do this since it has itself been split up into a number of systems based on reason, but the opposing views have now reached a state where it is impossible to reconcile them."[8]

Joseph Sittler feels that principles are often irrelevant to decisions. He illustrates his thesis with an incident from the novel *The Cruel Sea*. In the story, the captain of a destroyer must decide whether or not to drop a depth charge on an enemy submarine which he presumes to lurk under a place in the ocean where several hundred men who have abandoned a torpedoed ship are swimming in life jackets waiting to be rescued. The captain, feeling he must destroy the submarine even if it entails loss of life for the survivors of the abandoned vessel, says, "One must do what one must do—and say one's prayers." Sittler observes:

> . . . ethical decisions are never delivered from, and ethical achievements never add up to, a position elevated above faith's obedient placement within, and joyful acceptance of, man's creaturely situation. Just as no achievement can place a man beyond the daily need of God's judgment, grace, and forgiveness, so that no ethical decision is ever wholly true, just, or good—so, also, men's efforts will forever stand under both the thrust and the limitation of the same situation.[9]

The irrelevance of which Sittler is critical might be illustrated by imagining the ship's chaplain breaking into the command room of the destroyer and remarking that according to Adolph Harnack Jesus taught the infinite value of the human personality!

This illustration is, of course, drawn from a striking and unusual situation of crisis, in which an abnormally difficult and tortuous decision has to be made. In the book from which this illustration comes Sittler does more than indicate inadequacies in a deliberative approach to ethical norm-making. He attacks moral philosophy for stultifying the impulse of love by seeking the same detailed certainty that casuistry calls for. ". . . the desire to extrude principles from the Christ-life," he writes, "may be a form of man's hidden longing to cool into palpable ingots of duty the living stuff of love, and so dismiss . . . 'the Holy One with whom we have to do. . . .' "[10] Principles get in the way of service to the neighbor. Rather than providing a true alternative to the rigidities of code morality, deliberative ethics can become so concerned about rational principles as to be unable to do what is historically necessary in the crucial situation.

In addition to charging moral philosophy with irrelevancy and with getting between the self and service to the neighbor, Sittler also complains that it substitutes reliance upon principles for devotion to God. It is, therefore, idolatrous, and especially so when it claims autonomy for the reason. The very idea of a human reason that proposes to bring the revelation of God in Jesus Christ under a human test is a serious apostasy.

> There are evidences that our modern American enthusiasm for that aspect of Christian faith which is called *ethics* includes a covert form of idolatry—the more perilous because so disguised. There is a relation between the knowledge of God and the achievement and maintenance of human order; but God does not commonly make himself available to men who seek him primarily to achieve and maintain order. If God is sought in order to integrate the personality, the actual God is not God but the integrated personality. And when men are urged to renovate their religious values in order that the Republic may be more firmly glued together, this covert idolatry reaches a peculiarly pernicious and untruthful pitch.[11]

The foregoing has shown how certain relationalists exclude prescriptive and deliberative motifs. This kind of polemic is most obvious in contemporary literature, in which the relational case has been stated with considerable frequency. But relational ethics can claim no immunity from scrutiny and criticism, nor have they enjoyed any such immunity. In one kind of criticism of relational ethics difficulties and seeming inadequacies are examined without necessarily contending that the motif as such is wrong. Many theologians are worried because relational ethics do not seem to provide men with sufficient guidance. George Thomas puts the matter this way in criticizing *The Divine Imperative* of Emil Brunner:

> . . the crucial question that must be addressed to Brunner is, how can one determine one's *duty* without the help of principles? In the presence of conflicting claims from many different persons in a situation one cannot possibly meet all of them. It is not enough to say that one must open oneself to all of these claims and then listen for the command of God.[12]

John Bennett feels that relational ethics, particularly the situationalist versions, fail to provide the community with objectives and goals for which to strive. He feels that the principles set forth by the moral consensus of the Christian movement should provide a positive content to the analysis of any situation in which Christians must act. Bennett does not object to meeting the unique factors in each occasion, but he does not feel this requires the theoretical rejection of rules and principles. Instead, the Christian should bring something to the situation from the consensus and experience of the tradition. This may be formulated as principles or as some other kind of moral wisdom that seems helpful and authentic.[13] In Roman Catholic circles the criticism of situation ethics stems from a belief in objective norms. Karl Rahner, who is willing to consider the possibilities of incorporating some existential insights into a formal ethic, nevertheless denies that situations alone can determine the appropriateness of behavior. "This kind of situation ethics comes in the last analysis to the same thing as massive nominalism; it basically denies the possibility of any universal knowledge which has objective significance and truly applies to concrete reality."[14]

Meanwhile, in conservative Protestant circles, the objective character of ethical norms has been defended as part of a belief in objective revelation. This defense of objective norms comes closer to a polemic of exclusion than do the requests that relationalists consider factors they may have overlooked. Carl F. H. Henry has criticized the dialectical theology of Kierkegaard, Barth, and Brunner for abandoning the possibility of a rational knowledge of ethical standards, leaving modern man to flounder in a sea of relative judgments. Moral earnestness cannot long endure, he argues, on the basis of existential considerations alone, in a climate of deliberate anti-objectivism. While existentialism claims to impart freedom to deal with life in a new way, it surrenders its high status as a science of right and wrong. Existential ethics creates an artificial universe of moral relativism. Existence is made absurd, or "takes on" absurdity, by the very cultivation of this perspective. Its genuine rationality is deliberately obscured. This aids and abets the modern revolt against the moral.

> Say what one will about the passionate sobriety which Existentialism claims to impart to the moral life, there need be no doubt about the dispossessions it also requires. For existential ethics involves the loss of those cherished principles of action and sacred commandments which revealed religion has sanctioned; the loss of ethics as a science and the consequent surrender of behavior to rational inconsistency; the denial to Christianity of the right to vindicate the superiority of its ethical claim by exhibiting its coherent claim, in contrast with the logical inadequacies and incongruities of its competitive systems of morality; and the reduction of ethical earnestness to the subjective enthusiasm of theological Existentialism, which aims to inject hope into the world's moral despair but is precluded from giving a reason for that hope.[15]

This polemical exclusion of the relational motif is based upon an objective view of scriptural revelation. Conservative Roman Catholic theologians, who find objective standards based in the teaching authority of the church, engage in similar polemics against relational motifs. Unlike Rahner, who tries to correct existentialism when it goes too far, moralists like Ford and Kelley, who read the 1950 encyclical of Pope Pius XII, *Humani generis*, in a way that excludes all existentialist insights, side with conservative Protestants like Henry in insisting upon the objective character of the moral requirement.

Many critics of existentialist ethics write loosely and with unclear intent. Some writers, like Robert E. Fitch, come very close to a polemic of exclusion. Fitch feels that relational forms of contemporary Protestant ethics are contributing to the breakdown of standards, and protests:

> They all claim to be very much interested in conduct, but at precisely the point at which conduct threatens to take an unequivocal definition they draw back recalcitrant.
>
> The sacred self dispenses with principles as does the holy God. The Christian scholar and the Christian theologian want to get under them and behind them. The social philosophers want to internalize them and contextualize them. For none of these thinkers may the ethical reality be allowed, in Sittler's phrase, to "extrude" or to "dwindle" into particular counsels, precepts, duties. In brief, Christian ethics is a good thing until it becomes distinctively ethical.[16]

William A. Banner has argued that a valid sense of duty depends upon an objective ontological reality of the right and that relational ethics are fundamentally and dangerously wrong in ruling out the autonomy of moral judgments. They subordinate ethics into theodicy, into the situation in which God alone is taken as the source of moral vindication. Banner pleads for a new, or renewed, emphasis upon the objective nature of moral decision. Without human aspiration toward the moral good, ethics is impossible. Against the picture of the moral task presented by relational ethics, Banner declares:

> Love, justice, and mercy are the basic Christian moral ideas. These are to be understood in terms of modes of moral existence as virtues and modes of moral behavior as virtuous action. The goal of moral prescription is the highest life of man as certain states of character and certain patterns of conduct which sustain the highest life in one's own person and in one's neighbor. The moral life is a common life, with the basis for communication and community supplied through the recognition of an objective moral order which is independent of personal awareness of it. The Christian recognizes a moral order which is real even when it is not realized. In accordance with this order personal life is to be oriented and society is to be ordered and re-formed.[17]

Perhaps Banner needs to reflect upon the fact that a rational search for objective norms can also become a means of exclusion, particularly when it makes the principle of autonomy supreme. One form of ethical rationalism, Ethical Culture, may guard against this because of its willingness to tolerate such metaphysical "over-beliefs" as its members find personally meaningful. But does this really permit thoroughgoing relationalists to make common cause with its search for an autonomous ethic? Is the pluralism of Ethical Culture more pretended than real when its spokesman declares:

> . . . for Ethical Culture the attempt to lead an ethical life is not regarded as being contingent upon the acceptance or rejection of any one over-belief, no matter what the over-belief may be. Our common ground, our basis for coming together, is a commitment to the effort to live ever more ethically. In an infinite universe there is room for a great many differing over-beliefs. For Ethical Culture, the only ones to be rejected are those which dogmatically assert themselves to the necessary exclusion of any differing views.[18]

Lyman Bryson, speaking as the defender of a rational ethics, makes the tendency to exclusion even more clear as he notes that the rational method requires the rejection of traditional religious morality. Bryson draws a distinction between three types of "oughts": the religious ought, which is based upon supernatural sanctions; the moral ought, which is based upon tribal customs; and the ethical ought, which stands by itself on the grounds of reason. Religious oughts beg the question whether or not they can be considered universally valid, reflecting as they do mores that differ from culture to culture. Ethical oughts, clearly based upon reason, are best because they are autonomous. They have "strictly speaking, no sanction outside the self. A transgression will not be punished by an offended Deity, nor by an outraged tribe. The transgressor is more likely to be puzzled than shamed. And it is in this phase of judgment that reason is the only source of light or assistance."[19] This claim for the total adequacy of reason may display its own form of exclusiveness as much as does any theological motif that claims to hold the only clue to valid thinking about the ethical consequences of Christian faith.

Arguments Concerning the Implementation of Ethical Decisions

The institutional motif is probably the most traditional and widespread form of Christian social teaching. It often emphasizes the restrictive and negative functions of the state and thus breeds a social conservatism. Scholars have differed in their judgment concerning the degree to which this kind of thinking inevitably sanctifies the *status quo*. Troeltsch, for example, felt that Luther's influence was basically conservative, whereas Franz Lau, Rudolph Sohm, Hans Lilje, and Karl Holl tried to extricate Luther from responsibility for the use to which his teaching about the two realms was put by later followers. John C. Bennett credits Luther with some attempts to counteract the difficulties inherent in his views, yet declares, "Luther's emphasis upon order made him strangely indifferent to the problem of justice and the need of defense against the injustice of those who have political power."[20] Even where the theological tradition makes theoretical room for the overthrow of unjust rulers by the concerted action of the lesser magistrates, as in Calvin's teaching, the power of the magistrates is so honored and upheld as to create a basically restrictive situation. The teaching of obedience to civil authority appears with consistent regularity in the classical institutionalism of the Reformation heritage. Such teaching can lead to an acceptance of tyranny unless counterbalanced by positive emphasis upon the Christian duty to scrutinize and criticize the state whenever the authority which serves as a dike against sin threatens to become an instrument of oppression. But do not such conservative consequences flow most readily from taking the institutional motif to the exclusion of other patterns?

The Christian anarchist criticizes institutions in another way. Instead of warning against potential corruptions, he regards such institutions as basically demonic. Leo Tolstoy set forth such criticism in both his novels and his reflective writings. In *My Religion* he concluded that Jesus "absolutely denied the possibility of human justice."[21] The teachings of Jesus against exercising judgment over others rule out institutional actions of rulers as well as personal vindictiveness. "It is plain," he wrote, "that Jesus' words, *'Judge not, condemn not,'* were understood by his first disciples, as they ought to be understood now, in their direct and literal meaning: judge not in courts of justice, take no part in them."[22] Tolstoy believed that Christian thinkers since the days of the first disciples have failed to realize the direct import of Jesus' words in the way they were intended.

Likewise, Jesus' words "Resist not evil" make civil society impossible. Preferring the honest realism of the historical critics of Christianity to the compromise with statecraft made by most institutionalized Christianity, Tolstoy declared:

> The Christianity of our age and civilization approves of society as it now is, with its prison-cells, its factories, its houses of infamy, its parliaments; but as for the doctrine of Jesus, which is opposed to modern society, it is only empty words. The historical critics see this, and, unlike the so-called believers, having no motives for concealment, submit the doctrine to a careful analysis; they refute it systematically, and prove that Christianity is made up of nothing but chimerical ideas.[23]

Tolstoy considered the arguments by which Christians have justified civil structures, obedience to the state, and commerce in the economic order—and declared each argument faulty. Continued participation in these structures and activities is a subterfuge by which the real demand of the Gospel is avoided.

> The majority of civilized people have nothing to regulate life but faith in the police. This condition would be unbearable if it were universal. Fortunately there is a remnant, made up of the noblest minds of the age, who are not contented with this religion, but have an entirely different faith with regard to what the life of man ought to be. These men are looked upon as the most malevolent, the most dangerous, and generally as the most unbelieving of all human beings, and yet they are the only men of our time believing in the Gospel doctrine, if not as a whole, at least in part. . . . This remnant, in spite of calumny and persecution, are the only ones who do not tamely submit to the orders of the first comer. Consequently they are the only ones in these days who live a reasonable and not an animal life, the only ones who have faith.[24]

The chapter entitled "The Grand Inquisitor" in Fyodor Dostoevsky's novel *The Brothers Karamazov* inquires into the demonic temptation of the office, especially the office that is assumed in the name of spiritual responsibility for guarding the virtues of others. The spiritual enthusiasts of radical left-wing groups warned their followers to avoid the role of magistrate because it would cause them to lord it over their fellow men. They felt that the spirit should be free to express itself in the action of the dedicated individual without the restraints imposed by an office, the duties of citizenship, or even the rules of religious discipline. Mystical or spiritual religion is radically anti-institutional. "Its ideal is the untrammelled freedom of the spirit; not control, community discipline, and the strictness of the law of the Sermon on the Mount."[25]

In a contemporary attack upon the practice of capital punishment, Peter Berger has shown how the concept of an office can be used to justify actions which no man would make as an individual. Berger calls the justification for such actions "social alibis" and notes how frequently they condone the most demonic acts in the name of maintaining order. Noting that churchmen have often supported legalized capital punishment, he inquires,

> Leaving aside for the moment the difficulties which this traditional religious bloodthirstiness presents to adherents of a movement founded by an executed criminal, one may ask why this position exists and why it is so widespread among religious people. It is here that the relationship between religion and bad faith can be seen very sharply. We have discussed before how men put on magic cloaks for certain acts in society for which they claim moral immunity for their persons. But simple human conjury is not enough when it comes to some of the most terrifying acts. Now the alibi is not just that one does not do this personally but *qua* a particular kind of office-holder. Now the office itself must be transfigured by supernatural spookery. The act then takes on the quality of a divine intervention.
>
> It is in this fog of sanctified delusion that hangmen will shake the hand of their victim seconds before the execution, that priests will urge repentance on the victim to the last moment of the atrocity, that officials presiding over all this will afterward shake their heads and say, "I hated to do it!"—and that there will even be people who sympathize with them.[26]

Anarchists, like Tolstoy and Dostoevsky, are not any better pleased with the exercise of power and influence than with upholding structures of justice and order. The wrongs in one are compounded by the other. Indeed, since the exercise of coercion is the most demonic thing about an office, the exercise of coercion without the restraints and safeguards of the institution is even worse! The anarchist position is based upon a polemic of exclusion.

Except for those forms of the institutional motif that try to deny the necessity of power in the establishment and maintenance of institutions, the institutional and operational motif differ on the priority which they assign to the role of law and order in relation to power. This does not preclude arguments concerning which priority should be assigned, but it does largely mitigate polemics of exclusion. From time to time men have been prompted to underscore their understanding of the priority, as Jeremy Bentham did when he considered the responsibilities of a civil order for the fair and just treatment of prisoners:

> *Legality* (let it never be out of mind) is the object of inquiry here, not abstract *expediency*. So far as *security* and *economy* were concerned, legality and expediency seem to have been in a state of perpetual repugnance. *Legality* required that each man should be liberated from bondage the instant the time comprised in his sentence was at an end: *expediency* (had legality been out of the question) would perhaps have required that, in a society so constituted, he should never be discharged at any time.[27]

On occasion Paul Ramsey has felt it necessary to reiterate the importance of law in human affairs since some contemporary interpretations erode its centrality. His careful defense of the just war theory, refurbished for modern conditions, raises doubts about "realist" theories of international affairs which regard power as the ultimate sanction in the affairs of nations. His discussion of the sit-in insists that the exercise of power and influence must be willingly subject to law. While he finds a place for the sit-in as a means for creating the litigation by which the content of a law can be determined in the courts, he does not approve of a sit-in that claims exemption from the law by appeal to private conscience. Conscientious objectors—whether to participation in warfare or to ordinances which permit private proprietors to discriminate in choice of clients—must be prepared to accept the penalties for breaking the law. By a willingness to accept these penalties, such objectors uphold the sanctity of law even while protesting against particular requirements. On the other hand,

> It must be set down as a wholly unevangelical interpretation of man, of sin, and of the legitimate claims of social order by which anyone has come to believe that private individuals or factions or groups of individuals have a *right* to disobey human law by virtue of their appeal to a special knowledge of juster law that should, but does not obtain.[28]

Christian operationalists must be studied individually to determine whether they use correctional criticism or polemical exclusion. Some write about failure to use power in terms that are clearly polemical. Others simply urge their readers not to overlook the factors of power which are related even to institutional justice. Arguments of the latter type deserve to be taken more seriously than the former sort, for they warn against forgetting one polarity in a dialectic rather than presuming to set up a single understanding as adequate.

The correctional criticism of operationalism may include a theological questioning of its view of power. Nels Ferré has suggested that too much contemporary Christian thinking presupposes a naturalistic view of power.

> The distinctive dimension of the social action which can legitimately be named Christian is the activity of the Holy Spirit in relation to the Spirit of God. Too much of our thinking of late years along the lines of social action has been naturalistic. Somehow God has not been actually the prime mover, director and controller of human history as far as our practical considerations are concerned. We might have acknowledged this in theory, but even in this realm we have had a weak conception of the concrete and constant activity of God in history. God is great, beyond our every understanding, and His actual presence in history is its determining factor.[29]

James Luther Adams has drawn a distinction between power which is an expression of God's law and of God's love and power which is purely human manipulation. Adams accuses much social thought of ignoring the dimensions of God's law and love in the understanding of power. The result is a concept alien to religion, borrowed from the world of politics rather than understood with the insights of theology.

> When power is not considered in its proper theological character but only in its political, it becomes demonic or empty, separated from its end. Here power in the end achieves little but its own creation and destruction, and thus virtually denies itself as creative. In the human "order" this is what the Bible calls hardness of heart. The creative element of power is divine. The destructive element of power appears wherever power is divorced from an understanding of its source in the divine.[30]

Adams believes that many sociological definitions of power fail to see the dialectical dimensions of the sacred aspect. He is dissatisfied with Weber's definition of power as the "probability that one actor within a social relationship will be in a position to carry out his own will despite resistance. . . ."[31] Drawing upon illustrations of divine power from primitive religions and from prophetic belief in the power of God's historical actions, Adams develops a broader conception of power, a conception which includes the New Testament proclamation of God's dynamic work among men. He concludes, "Christian obedience looks toward the kind of social action and the kind of society that can provide the soil out of which the creative, judging, healing power of God may like a seed grow of itself."[32]

The polemics between institutionalists and operationalists, on the one hand, and the intentionalists, on the other, have often been sharpened by the emotion which is bound up in debates between pacifists and nonpacifists. To those who do not share its assumptions, the intentional motif with its impulse to separatism seems highly questionable because it abdicates responsibility in the world. From this perspective, the sectarian, the monk, and the separatist appear escapist, utopian, and unjustly perfectionistic. As Reinhold Niebuhr puts it, "The desire for perfection must . . . invariably express itself parasitically."[33]

But the separatist is not often an anarchist. While he hopes to remain aloof from the coercive measures which are used to support institutions, he is also very conscious of the values which inhere in structures of justice and order. He exercises strong discipline within his own religious community. He does not attack the place of the state in general though he may not participate in those functions of the state which stand at variance with the New Testament teaching about nonresistance. Writing as a Mennonite, Guy Hershberger summarized this position as follows: "Biblical nonresistance declines to participate in the coercive function of the state, but nevertheless regards coercion necessary for the maintenance of order in a sinful society, and is not anarchistic."[34]

Strangely enough, the most withdrawing intentionalism and the most realistic exponents of operations with power and influence are agreed in their diagnosis of the relationship of the Gospel ethic to the political affairs of the world. They both acknowledge that the Gospel ethic stands outside the possibility of direct translation into political strategy. But they make opposite responses to the same diagnosis. One withdraws from the political arena; the other modifies its understanding of Christian duty for the sake of achieving values that literal obedience to the love ethic of the Gospel cannot attain. Many of the most vigorous advocates of a realistic use of power respect the intentionalists who withdraw from the world for witness and dedication. The most formalized and hierarchical churches tolerate and encourage monasticism in their midst, defending and supporting it as a valid part of the whole.

Conservative institutionalism is likely to be especially hostile to all pacifism because it regards the refusal to use legalized force as a betrayal of the Christian's responsibility to the structures of justice in the world. But operationalism is apt to distinguish vocational pacifism, which it respects, from political pacifism, which it regards with critical suspicion. John C. Bennett, for example, takes political pacifists to task for advocating a kind of "unilateral disarmament which would increase the danger of aggression";[35] while of vocational pacifism he says, "as a matter of vocational concentration . . . it remains defensible."[36] The institutionalist regards the withdrawing sect as turning its back upon the very duties which are part of man's lot in the divine economy; the operational realist may, on the other hand, regard the sect as turning its back upon a sin-filled, yet necessary, process for maintaining tolerable harmonies amid conflicting vitalities. It is more difficult to be charitable with someone who is felt to be shirking duty than with someone who is deemed heroically loyal, even at the price of life itself, to an ethic of intentional purity.

High moral resolve gives birth to the intentional impulse. The problem faced by the group that would set itself apart from the world is maintaining its unique visibility. Troeltsch spoke of the "sect-cycle." The sect is born of the radical impulse, but eventually gets reabsorbed into the culture and tends to grow increasingly like the institutional church. Once in awhile, as in the Muenster rebellion, the sect adopts the operational pattern, but more often it moves toward institutionalization. As the sect becomes institutionalized, zeal wanes, moral rigor is compromised; the fathers make high resolves, the children find them hard to bear. The self-sustaining sect, without external authority to preserve internal integrity, tends to weaken with the passage of time.

Francis D. Hall has described this process as it works in the small intentional communities of recent popularity. Hall writes as a loyal participant in this form of Christian living. He outlines the values to be found in the intimate and dedicated group, but also notes its limitations. "If we think," he writes,

> of world society as a way of life that has found viability and some stability by building on the common decency of man and by counter-balancing rival, selfish claims through laws and courts of justice, we can think of intentional community as a pioneering attempt to find a new way of life built on love and self-giving. The whole history of intentional communities reveals, however, that the land on which they are built is prone to drougth, to earthquakes, and to volcanic explosions.[37]

Intentional community intensifies both the strength and the sinfulness of its human components. The intensification of the sinful factors creates unendurable pressures. The community usually dissolves through slow attrition and peaceful parting, and sometimes it blows apart with bitter recriminations. This consequence may be avoided if the community adopts countermeasures to curb the individualistic seeds of disruption. Such countermeasures are authoritarian in nature, as in monasticism. The abbot's rule is supreme, though hopefully not arbitrary. Groups without a central leader become preoccupied with the desire to make the community succeed, to ferret out all divisive elements in their lives. They end by sending away the nonconformists, by building a wall between themselves and the world. Like the monastic orders, the Shakers and Huterites were stable because they were authoritarian. They took into full covenant only those who survived a rigorous probationary period.

Those retreat and cell-group movements that suppose their disciplined style of living is a pilot achievement which should be universalized in the life of the church often overlook the fact that their very achievement is a function of exclusion. One cannot rely upon the right to exclude those who are unfitted or unwilling to accept special disciplines without presupposing the continued existence of an external world of the "less fit." Without such a world to absorb those who do not qualify for membership in the dedicated community, the dedicated community could not maintain the purity of its own life. The very logic of intentional dedication works at cross purposes with the hope of universalizing a given style of achievement. Such exclusion occurs less through verbal polemics than through community actions.

Moreover, to maintain a special group whose morals are self-consciously higher than those of the surrounding world is to heighten temptation to self-righteousness and self-centeredness. The intentional community easily comes to think of itself as something to be fostered and preserved for its own sake rather than for the service it renders to the whole community. Hall feels that this danger can be avoided if the intentional community is called to some service outside of its own purposes. "It is not to be wondered at that intentional community occupies only a footnote in world history, and that it has its greatest meaning when its corporate life is incidental to its work. When it seeks to be an end in itself the efforts prove too costly to justify, in terms of loss of valuable time, the energy and talents expended."[38] Does not this observation coincide with the observation that the search for adequacy in any single motif is abortive?

Perhaps all three traditional motifs for implementing Christian decisions assume that Christians have something which they are responsible for bringing to the world. There is another perspective, set forth in several ways, which seems to argue that the world has something to bring to Christians. Philippe Maury once declared, "Nothing human can be foreign to the Christian because in Jesus Christ the whole of mankind, with all its greatness and its weakness, is present."[39] Maury believes that men can come to know the Gospel as much through their experiences in the world as through the special quality of the church's inner life. Bonhoeffer emphasized much the same idea when he insisted that the church should lose its life—its institutional and ethical uniqueness—in its service to and through the world.

John A. T. Robinson makes the same plea in *Honest to God*. The church must strip down its religiosity, its piety, and its separatism in order to identify with the world. Ronald Gregor Smith has put the matter this way:

The real dialectic, as Bonhoeffer has sketched it, does not find God in the cult, taken by itself; nor in any form of pietism or socialism, which are just two forms of escape from one side or the other of the dialectic. But this dialectic of commitment to the world demands complete responsibility in and for the world, in all its interests and problems.[40]

In another place, speaking for himself, Smith notes that "We have been all too ready, especially since the great break through of the Renaissance, to fight a kind of battle against the world on behalf of God."[41]

The separatist fights a battle against the world for the sake of maintaining his own devotion to God at a special level of intensity. The institutionalist defends the outcome of battles that God has already won. The "realist" theologian who stresses the importance of exerting power and influence may fight battles as though God's work depends upon their outcome. The crucial issue in Christian thinking about these matters today may well lie in the question whether the battle stance that Smith rejects can be overcome by taking the traditional motifs tentatively, without claiming the validity of one to the exclusion of others, or whether we are called to an entirely new kind of thinking about the task of the Christian in the world.

20

A Prolegomena to Comprehensive Complementarity

The themes discussed in this survey are complex and varied, drawn from a long history and from a broad range of Christian experience. No attempt has been made to develop an interpretation of Christian ethics to set in contrast to the options presented. Should such an interpretation have been developed, if the motifs of this study have correctly identified the perennial possibilities, it would be similar to, or composed of portions from, the motifs which have been delineated.

We need not accept purity of method as the essential feature of a viable theological ethic. If theological thought remains dominated by the defense of particular motifs through appeals to revelation, reason, or tradition, it will be continually embroiled in scholastic battles over how ethical decisions ought to be made. Such debates, especially when they involve the pitfalls and abortive fruits of polemical exclusion, cannot contribute much to significant advance in Christian ethical understanding. Any single motif truncates Christian experience when it is taken as the sole way of approaching Christian ethics. Hence, deliberative ethics have the greatest difficulty maintaining a sense of religious meaning in actions which it judges entirely by canons of autonomous reason; prescriptive ethics are most subject to legalistic distortions when they seek to cover every contingent circumstance of life with an exact definition of the right; relational ethics are of the least guidance to men when they wear antinomianism on the cuff and are primarily, if not exclusively, concerned to reject the value of principles and codes in the making of ethical choices. Similarly, institutionalism embraced without correctives can result in oppressive conservatism; the operational motif can result in an overly power conscious, perhaps even cynical, judgment about the nature of political process; intentionalism can lead to moral narcissism or the abdication of social responsibility.

There are hopeful signs of a present discontent with the polemics of exclusion in Christian ethics. John A. T. Robinson thinks of the "new morality" as complementary rather than antithetical to the "old morality," and believes that they can come to similar truth from opposite directions.[1] James Gustafson has argued that the dichotomy between context and principles comes from a "misplaced debate," and has pleaded for a broader and more empirical way of identifying the different theological-ethical stances which can enter into various kinds of decisions.[2] Max Stackhouse has declared, speaking of the present social task of Christians, "A truly 'historical' theology of history for the new social gospel would not be caught designating one 'system,' or level of experience, as crucial and call that 'the essential one.' "[3]

There is another challenge to the dominant endeavors of contemporary Christian ethics—a challenge that is still more basic and fundamental. It declares all traditional approaches bankrupt and regards as futile any effort to decide which of them is singularly valid. John R. Fry has complained that theoretical discussions in Christian ethics ignore the every-day appetites and personal drives of individuals who respond to particular circumstances in terms of felt and unconscious needs. They deal with abstractions rather than looking at life and hence ignore "the immobilized, nameless, faceless, individual."[4] Kenneth W. Underwood, who has devoted much of his professional career to the study of the relationships between Christian faith and policy choices in contemporary society, puts it this way: ". . . we are in grave need of knowledge, not so much of how we think people in various positions of responsibility ought to act, and what they ought to bring to their actions in the way of religious principles, but of knowledge that tells us the actual basis or grounds of action of men in the major institutions and professions of the society."[5] Underwood is disturbed because theological ethics is seemingly oblivious to the knowledge about policy formation gained by the social sciences, whereas the social sciences, in turn, usually shy from value judgments which might be crucially helpful in policy decisions.

Perhaps a study mainly concerned to sketch the profiles of the past and present should hazard no observations about the prospects of the future. But it can express some predilections for what it would like to see happen and suggest the relevance of the past and present for the shape of the unfolding developments.

It is likely that increasing attention will be devoted to the psychological and sociological aspects of moral choice-making. This will call for much hard work—watching, listening to, and studying how men make decisions in reference to their faith commitments. Such understanding cannot come from the behavioral sciences alone, nor from the social sciences. It must include insights about the nature of religious concerns and the functional consequences of many ways of holding essentially sacred commitments. Merely external descriptions will not get at the root realities of religious

morality any better than "objective" types of anthropological and sociological studies of religion have themselves accounted adequately for the
dimensions of the holy. What is needed is a phenomenological understanding of moral decision-making as carried out in relation to Christian
commitment. Such an understanding could contribute to our awareness
of what Underwood calls "the actual basis of the grounds" of moral
actions.

Any accounts of the relationship of religious commitment to the
decision-making process, regardless of the extent to which they break
new ground in their descriptions of moral choice, will obviously be
dependent upon the historical and systematic categories which have seen
so much previous use in theological discourse. These categories must come
to be understood functionally as well as systematically, relating the ways
in which men employ their ultimate commitments in moral choices. Law
is a functional reality for the legalist; ideals are a functional reality for
deliberative thinkers; contexts and relationships are working realities for
still others. Similarly, there are men who are naturally inclined to respect
law and order; there are others who by temperament and/or training are
attracted to the exercise of power and influence; still others find the
impulse to withdraw into groups of renewal and dedication compelling.
Sometimes these factors work in concert, sometimes in tension with each
other. Often the behavior of men is less consistent than their theoretical
abstractions. It will be easier to acknowledge this fact about the motifs if
they are used functionally as descriptions of the way men arrive at
decisions than if they are used systematically as normative descriptions of
how men should make them.

Contextualism in our day is calling for a very valid emphasis upon the
actualities of circumstance. It is saying, among other things, that Christian
ethics is a community experience and should be functionally understood.
Does it not follow that we should study the kinds of processes with which
men actually work rather than argue for the abstract validity of one
particular way of explaining them? Contextualism is also saying that moral
decisions should be judged in terms of their maturity. Are we not thereby
obligated to understand the conditions which make for maturity and
health in the process of relating faith to ethics in any of the available
motifs rather than contending that such maturity is a function of one
particular motif?

Perhaps we should give increasing attention to the possibility that
different situations in life should be dealt with in terms of different kinds
of ethical response and not bind ourselves to any particular theory about
the one proper method. Are not certain matters most helpfully and simply
handled by laws; others, by principles; and still others, by the situational
approach? If so, then we should call for an even more contextual con-

textualism, one that refuses to be bound by the "in-principled rejection" of any particular way of formulating or applying Christian norms. Such a flexible, or nonideological, contextualism would not claim that it alone has the key to the application of love in relation to persons, but could embrace the valid contributions of any Christian ethic which bears fruit in neighbor love. If the fruit can be borne by a mature reliance upon rules, modified as necessary by casuistries, let it be respected. If the fruit comes from an idealistic or teleological ethic which handles these matters in terms of basic principles and their application, why cast it away? If the situation requires a contextual response to deal maturely with the contingent and unusual circumstances being encountered, let that be embraced in the freedom of the Gospel without requiring that the resultant way of dealing with the issue become paradigmatic for all Christian living!

The descriptive, pragmatic, empirical insights which we need will not themselves make ethics any easier. Nonideological ethics must not be offered as a scheme that removes the difficulties that other approaches have left unsolved. Tension and difficulty are inevitable aspects of the moral life—under any and all schemes. The hallmark of viable Christian norm-making should be a creative tension between a responsible sense of obligation to standards (however defined) and a creative freedom in circumstances. The law/grace and principle/situation dichotomies which have so often marked the discussion of the Christian life are witness to a perennial polarity in Christian experience. We cannot embrace obligatory standards in a way that destroys freedom of response; neither can we assert freedom in such a way as to take away the necessary guidance of obligation. The tension between obligation and freedom is always diffi-cult to maintain. When one aspect of the polarity is over-emphasized the other rises in reaction. Such a reaction may appear in more than one form. For example, appeal to principles against laws has often played the role on behalf of freedom which the appeal to the situation against principles plays in much writing in our day. Even prescriptive approaches have tried to correct their own rigidities through casuistries.

A mature Christian social strategy must take into account both the nature of the culture and the impulses of the Gospel. The purity/responsi-bility and world-affirming/world-rejecting dichotomies bear the same witness to a perennial polarity in respect to Christian strategy that the law/grace and principle/situation dichotomies bear in relation to Christian thinking about norms. We dare not adopt strategies which cut the tension between the Gospel and the world by permitting concern about either to remain unchastened. It may be necessary to acknowledge and nurture several responses at the same time, as Roman Catholicism has done with monasticism and mainline Protestantism has done more recently with its support of conscientious objectors to war.

The intentionalist is concerned (in a wide variety of ways) with the high moral achievements expected of the devoted disciple; his counterparts who think in institutional and operational terms are concerned about their responsibility in and through the world, even though they differ in their analysis of the means to be used for exercising that responsibility. The intentionalist can remind his fellow Christians of the dangers which inhere in the embrace of worldly instruments for the accomplishment of Christian goals while they in turn can remind the separatist that the price of purity may be too high in a world where significant values are served by compromise.

Perhaps the mutual self-correction between several motifs can be so embraced within the household of faith as to keep the polarities from excess most of the time. When the tension is forgotten, the main emphases swing from pole to pole, with attention placed first upon one facet of the truth and then upon another. The Christian movement may not consciously swing from one perspective to the other by premeditated design or a cyclical law of history. The polarity is too deep-seated to be regularized in such a fashion. Yet one emphasis may be closely followed by attention to the other in a continual vacillation of concern unless it is more wisely balanced by a dialectical understanding of the perennial values in each motif and the fruitfulness of mutual correction between them.

We need not fear nor be apologetic for relying upon complementarity, mutual correction, and even incommensurate theories for dealing with the relationship of faith to ethics. Other intellectual disciplines today rely upon the validity of complementarity. Moreover, in theology justification by faith may suspend the demand for final and absolute formulations. If in the realm of morals we "sin bravely," in the realm of understanding we can "know partially." Admitting the limitations in all our formulations we may search for more adequate understandings—acknowledging in their appropriate contexts the truth in a variety of efforts to set forth the relationship of Christian faith to the moral enterprise.

Notes

Note to Preface

1. Sidgwick, Henry, *The Methods of Ethics*. London: Macmillan, 1874, p. 10.

Notes to Chapter One

1. Titus, Harold H., *Ethics for Today*, 3rd ed. New York: American Book, 1957, p. 11. The fourth edition of this title, by Titus and Keeton, was published in 1966.
2. *Nicomachean Ethics*, Bk. I, Ch. 7, ll. 21-6.
3. Sidgwick, Henry, *The Methods of Ethics*. London: Macmillan, 1874.
4. Schuyler, Aaron, *Systems of Ethics*. Cincinnati: Jennings and Pye, 1902, p. 14.
5. Broad, C. D., *Five Types of Ethical Theory*. London: Routledge and Kegan Paul, 1930, p. 206f.
6. MacLagen, W. G., *The Theological Frontier of Ethics*. London: George Allen and Unwin; New York: Macmillan, 1961, p. 56. The reader must be aware that this use of the term "contextual" is altogether different from a use to be encountered later in connection with the relational motif.
7. Garvin, Lucius, *A Modern Introduction to Ethics*. Boston: Houghton Mifflin, 1935, p. 2. Italics in original.
8. Toulmin, Stephen, *An Examination of the Place of Reason in Ethics*. Cambridge: Cambridge University Press, 1950, p. 48.
9. Cambridge: Cambridge University Press.
10. Ross, Sir David, *The Right and the Good*. Oxford: At the Clarendon Press, 1930.
11. Prichard, H. A., "Does Moral Philosophy Rest on a Mistake?" in *Mind*, Vol. 21, Jan. 1912, pp. 21-37.
12. Ogden, C. K., and Richards, I. A., *The Meaning of Meaning*, 8th ed. New York: Harcourt Brace, 1956.
13. Ayer, A. J., *Language, Truth, and Logic*, 2nd ed. London: V. Gollancz, 1953.
14. Stevenson, Charles, *Ethics and Language*. New Haven: Yale University Press, 1944.
15. For surveys of the material briefly noted above, see: Binkley, Luther J., *Contemporary Ethical Theories*. New York: Philosophical Library, 1961; or Nowell-Smith, P. H., *Ethics*. Baltimore, Md.: Penquin Books, 1954.
16. Schlick, Moritz, *Problems of Ethics*, trans. by David Rynin. New York: Dover Publications, 1939, 1962, pp. 1f. Reprinted by permission of the publisher.
17. Hare, R. M., *The Language of Morals*. Oxford: At the Clarendon Press, 1952.
18. New York: Macmillan, 1950.
19. For an elaboration of this argument, see Holbrook, Clyde A., *Faith and Community*. New York: Harper, 1959, pp. 79-104.

315

20. Barrett, William, *Irrational Man: A Study in Existential Philosophy*. Garden City, N.Y.: Doubleday, 1958, p. 147. Copyright © 1958 by William Barrett. Reprinted by permission of Doubleday and Company and Heinemann Educational Books Ltd.
21. See Gustafson, James M., *Treasure in Earthen Vessels*. New York: Harper, 1961; and Winter, Gibson, "Theology and Social Science" in Jenkins, Daniel T., ed., *The Scope of Theology*. Cleveland: World, 1965, pp. 174-98.
22. Glencoe, Ill.: The Free Press, 1957.
23. A detailed examination of the writings of these men is beyond the scope of this work. Secondary exposition can be found in Loomis, Charles P., and Zona, K., *Modern Social Theories*. Princeton: D. Van Nostrand, 1961.
24. Cowling, Maurice, *The Nature and Limits of Political Science*. Cambridge: Cambridge University Press, 1963, p. 10.
25. Ibid., p. 171.
26. Berger, Peter, *The Precarious Vision: A Sociologist Looks at Social Fictions and Christian Faith*. Garden City, N.Y.: Doubleday, 1961, p. 64. Copyright © 1961 by Peter Berger. Reprinted by permission of Doubleday and Company, Inc.
27. Kolb, William E., "Value, Politics, and Images of Man in American Sociology," in *The Christian Scholar*, Vol. 44, No. 4, Winter 1961, p. 322f.
28. New York: Holt, 1929.
29. Lee, Robert, *The Social Sources of Church Unity*. New York: Abingdon, 1960.
30. Benedict, Ruth, *Patterns of Culture*. Boston: Houghton Mifflin, 1934, p. 1.
31. Ibid., p. 19.
32. Malinowski, Bronislav, *A Scientific Theory of Culture*. Chapel Hill: University of North Carolina Press, 1944, p. 3.
33. Ibid., p. 220.
34. New York: Holt, 1906.
35. Evanston, Ill.: Row, Peterson, 1963.
36. London, Macmillan, 1906-08.
37. Kluckhohn, Florence R., and Strodtbeck, Fred L., *Variations in Value Orientations*. Evanston, Ill.: Row, Peterson, 1963, pp. 1f.

Notes to Chapter Two

1. New York: Holt, 1935.
2. Otto, Rudolph, *The Idea of the Holy*, 2nd ed., trans. by John W. Harvey. London: Oxford University Press, 1950.
3. Calhoun, Robert L., "Moral Obligation and Religious Conviction," in *Confluence*, July 1955, pp. 174-93.
4. Toulmin, Stephen, *An Examination of the Place of Reason in Ethics*. Cambridge: Cambridge University Press, 1950, p. 219. For a discussion of the relationship between religion and morality in much the same vein, see Yinger, J. Milton, *Religion, Society and the Individual: An Introduction to the Sociology of Religion*. New York: Macmillan, 1957, pp. 24-8. Yinger's categories are conceived in much the same way as Toulmin's even though he attaches somewhat different meanings to them.
5. Eliade, Mircea, *Patterns in Comparative Religion*, trans. by Rosemary Sheed. New York: Sheed and Ward, 1958, p. xi.
6. Kristensen, W. Brede, *The Meaning of Religion*. The Hague: M. Nijhoff, 1960, p. 285.
7. In his book *Fear and Trembling* Søren Kierkegaard argued polemically that religion must be characterized by the priority of God's will over the ethical.

Kierkegaard's polemical contention should not be equated with Kristensen's descriptive assertion that religion always views things in this way.

8. Van der Leeuw, Geradus, *Religion in Essence and Manifestation*. London: George Allen and Unwin, 1938, p. 454.

9. Smart, Ninian, *Reasons and Faiths: An Investigation of Religious Discourse, Christian and Non-Christian*. London: Routledge and Kegan Paul, 1958, pp. 181f.

10. Tillich, Paul, *Morality and Beyond*. New York: Harper and Row, 1963, p. 15.

11. Ibid., p. 25.

12. Ibid., p. 24.

13. Tillich, Paul, *Systematic Theology*, Vol. I. Chicago: University of Chicago Press, 1951, p. 14.

14. Barth, Karl, *Church Dogmatics*, III/4. Edinburgh: T. and T. Clark, 1961, p. 3.

15. Barth, Karl, *Church Dogmatics*, II/2. Edinburgh: T. and T. Clark, 1957, p. 546.

16. *Church Dogmatics*, III/4, pp. 3f.

17. Knudson, A. C., *The Principles of Christian Ethics*. New York: Abingdon, 1943, p. 33.

18. Niebuhr, H. Richard, *The Meaning of Revelation*. New York: Macmillan, 1941, pp. 20f.

19. Ibid., p. 168.

20. Ibid., pp. 171f.

21. Beach, W., and Niebuhr, H. R., *Christian Ethics: Sources of the Living Tradition*. New York: Ronald Press, 1955, p. 4.

22. Ibid., p. 5.

23. New York and London: Harper, 1935.

24. Gardner, E. Clinton, *Biblical Faith and Social Ethics*. New York: Harper, 1960, p. 17.

25. Henry, Carl F. H., *Christian Personal Ethics*. Grand Rapids, Mich.: Wm. B. Eerdmans, 1957, p. 171.

26. Osborn, Andrew R., *Christian Ethics*. London: Oxford University Press, 1940, p. 9.

27. Ramsey, Paul, *Christian Ethics and the Sit-in*. New York: Association Press, 1961, p. xv.

28. Gustafson, James M., "Theology and Ethics," in Jenkins, Daniel T., ed., *The Scope of Theology*. Cleveland: World, 1965, p. 132.

Notes to Chapter Three

1. Aquinas, St. Thomas, *Summa Contra Gentiles*, Bk. III, Ch. 113. From Pegis, Anton C., ed., *Basic Writings of Saint Thomas Aquinas*, Vol. II. New York: Random House, 1945, pp. 223f.

2. Aquinas, St. Thomas, *Summa Theologiae* I-II, Question 20, Art. 1. Pegis, p. 351.

3. Ibid., Question 21, Art. 3. Pegis, p. 363.

4. Ibid., Question 58, Art. 5. Pegis, p. 447.

5. Bourke, Vernon J., *Ethics: A Textbook in Moral Philosophy*. New York: Macmillan, 1951, p. 238.

6. Aquinas, St. Thomas, *Summa Theologiae* I-II, Question 61, Art. 2. Pegis, p. 468.

7. Ibid., Question 62, Art. 3. Pegis, p. 478.

8. Ibid., Question 94, Art. 4. Pegis, pp. 777f.

9. Fitzpatrick, Joseph P., S.J., "Ethics of Roman Catholicism," in Johnson, F. Ernest, ed., *Patterns of Ethics in America Today*. New York: Institute for Religious and Social Studies, 1960 (distributed by Harper and Row), p. 32f.

10. Ibid., p. 39.

11. Bourke, V. J., see chart on p. 129.

12. "On the Function of the State in the Modern World" (*Summi Pontificatus*), October 20, 1939, from Freemantle, Anne, *The Papal Encyclicals in Their Historical Context.* New York: New American Library (Mentor), 1956, p. 264.

13. Haring, Bernard, *The Law of Christ,* Vol. I. Westminster, Md.: Newman; Cork, Ireland: Mercier, 1961, p. 294f.

14. Rahner, Karl, *Theological Investigations,* Vol. II. Baltimore: Helicon, 1963, pp. 227f.

15. Ford, John C., and Kelley, Gerald, *Contemporary Moral Theology:* Vol. I: *Questions in Fundamental Moral Theology.* Westminster, Md.: Newman; Cork, Ireland: Mercier, 1958.

16. See "Unchanging Ethics in a Changing World," in Maritain, Jacques, et al., *Religion and the Modern World.* Philadelphia; University of Pennsylvania Press, 1941.

17. Brightman, Edgar S., *Moral Laws.* New York: Abingdon, 1933, p. 265.

18. Rashdall, Hastings, *The Theory of Good and Evil: A Treatise on Moral Philosophy,* Vol. II. Oxford: At the Clarendon Press, 1907, p. 286.

19. Rashdall, Hastings, *Conscience and Christ.* New York: Scribner's, 1916, p. 10.

20. Smyth, Newman, *Christian Ethics.* New York: Scribner's, 1892, p. 3.

21. Ibid., p. 10.

22. Ibid., p. 11.

23. Ibid., p. 6.

24. Ibid., p. 7.

25. From an essay of R. W. Emerson, "Ethical Writers," in Whicher, Stephen E., and Spiller, Robert E., eds., *The Early Lectures of Ralph Waldo Emerson,* Vol. I, 1833-36. Cambridge: Harvard University Press, 1959, p. 370.

26. Emerson, Ralph Waldo, *The Conduct of Life.* Boston: Houghton, Mifflin, 1860, pp. 229f.

27. Tillich, Paul, *Love, Power, and Justice.* New York: Oxford University Press, 1954, p. 2.

28. Ibid., p. 11.

29. Ibid., p. 71.

Notes to Chapter Four

1. Harnack, Adolph, *What is Christianity?,* trans. by Thomas Bailey Saunders. New York: G. Putnam's Sons, 1901, p. 79.

2. Ibid., p. 73.

3. Ibid., p. 110.

4. Ibid., p. 78.

5. Ibid., p. 104.

6. For a brief discussion of Schleiermacher's attitudes toward moral philosophy, see Lehmann, Paul L., *Ethics in a Christian Context.* New York: Harper and Row, 1963, pp. 259-67.

7. *Christian Ethics.* New York: Abingdon, 1957.

8. *The Christian Way.* New York: Philosophical Library, 1949.

9. Knudson, A. C., *The Principles of Christian Ethics.* New York: Abingdon, 1943, p. 39.

10. Ibid., p. 154.

11. Thomas, George, *Christian Ethics and Moral Philosophy.* New York: Scribner's, 1955, p. 390.

12. Ibid., p. 420.
13. Garrod, H. W., *The Religion of All Good Men and Other Studies in Christian Ethics*. New York: McClure, Phillips, 1906, pp. 6f.
14. Liddell's translation: the sensible, practically wise, prudent man.
15. Garrod, H. W., *The Religion of All Good Men*, p. 15.
16. Osborn, Andrew R., *Christian Ethics*. London: Oxford University Press, 1940, p. 4.
17. Ibid., p. 11.
18. Ibid., p. v.
19. Ibid., p. 4.
20. See Ramsey, Paul, *Nine Modern Moralists*. Englewood Cliffs, N.J.: Prentice-Hall, 1962, Chs. 8 and 9.
21. Ramsey, Paul, *Basic Christian Ethics*. New York: Scribner's, 1950; London: S.C.M. Press, pp. 243f.
22. Ibid., pp. 112f.
23. Ibid., p. xiii.
24. Ibid., p. 344.
25. Ramsey, Paul, *War and the Christian Conscience: How Shall Modern War Be Conducted Justly?* Durham, N.C.: Duke University Press, 1961, p. 4.
26. Ramsey, Paul, *Deeds and Rules in Christian Ethics*, Scottish Journal of Theology Occasional Paper No. 11. Edinburgh: Oliver and Boyd, 1965, p. 12.
27. Ramsey, *Nine Modern Moralists*, p. 6.
28. See, for example, "The Sermon on the Mount," in Fosdick, Harry Emerson, *The Hope of the World: Sermons on Christianity Today*. New York: Harper, 1933, pp. 145-55.
29. See Kagawa, Toyohiko, *Love, the Law of Life*, trans. by J. Fullerton Gressitt. Philadelphia: Winston, 1929.
30. Niebuhr, Reinhold, *An Interpretation of Christian Ethics*. New York: Harper, 1935, pp. 8f.
31. Kegley, Charles W., and Bretall, Robert W., eds., *Reinhold Niebuhr: His Religious, Social, and Political Thought*. New York: Macmillan, 1950, pp. 434f.
32. Ibid., p. 442.
33. Niebuhr, *An Interpretation of Christian Ethics*, p. 37.
34. Niebuhr, Reinhold, *The Self and the Dramas of History*. New York: Scribner's; London: Faber and Faber, 1955, p. 232.
35. Harland, Gordon, *The Thought of Reinhold Niebuhr*. New York: Oxford University Press, 1960, pp. 19f.
36. Niebuhr, Reinhold, "Coherence, Incoherence, and the Christian Faith," *Journal of Religion*, July 1951, p. 162. Also found in *Union Seminary Quarterly Review*, January 1952, pp. 18ff.; and in *Christian Realism and Political Problems*. New York: Scribner's, 1953, pp. 191f.

Notes to Chapter Five

1. LeClercq, Jacques, *Christ and the Modern Conscience*. New York: Sheed and Ward, 1962, p. 68. Trans. copyright © 1962 by Geoffrey Chapman, Ltd.
2. Murray, John, *Principles of Conduct*. London: Tyndale, 1957, p. 24.
3. Ibid., p. 154.
4. Kirk, Kenneth E., *The Vision of God: The Christian Doctrine of the Summum Bonum*. London: Longman's Green, 1931.

5. Paulsen, Friedrich, *A System of Ethics,* trans. and ed. by Frank Thilley. New York: Scribner's, 1899, p. 222.

6. Niebuhr, H. Richard, *The Responsible Self.* New York: Harper and Row, 1963, p. 52.

7. Ibid., p. 54.

8. Philadelphia: H. Altemus, 1899.

9. Bosley, Harold, "The Christian Preacher and the Christian Ethic," in *Encounter,* Vol. 22, No. 2. Spring 1961, p. 123.

10. Dodd, C. H., *Gospel and Law: The Relation of Faith and Ethics in Early Christianity.* New York: Columbia University Press; Cambridge: Cambridge University Press, 1951, p. 14.

11. Ibid., p. 25.

12. Ibid., p. 72.

13. Ibid., p. 52.

14. Ibid., p. 72.

15. Ibid., p. 73.

16. Ibid., pp. 73f.

17. *The Ethics of Paul.* New York: Abingdon, 1957.

18. *The Meaning of the Sermon on the Mount.* Philadelphia: Westminster, 1941.

19. Schweitzer, Albert, *The Quest of the Historical Jesus.* London: A. and C. Black, 1910; and *The Mystery of the Kingdom of God: The Secret of Jesus' Messiahship and Passion.* New York: Macmillan, 1954.

20. Herrmann, Wilhelm, *Ethik.* Tübingen: J. C. B. Mohr, 1901.

21. *Law and Grace: Must a Christian Keep the Law of Moses?* London: S.C.M. Press; Philadelphia: Westminster, 1962, p. 117.

22. Wyclif, John, *On the Perfect Life,* in *The Trialogues* of Wyclif, ed. Robert Vaughan. *Tracts and Treatises of John de Wycliffe, D.D.* London: Blackburn and Pardon, 1845, p. 65.

23. Ibid., p. 179.

24. Calvin, John, *Institutes of the Christian Religion,* trans. by John Allen, Bk. II, Ch. vii, par. ii.

25. Ibid., II, vii, vii.

26. Ibid., II, vii, xii.

27. Reid, J.K.S., trans. and ed., *Calvin: Theological Treatises.* Philadelphia: Westminster; London: S.C.M. Press, 1954, p. 118.

28. Haroutunian, Joseph, and Smith, Louise Pettibone, eds., *Calvin: Commentaries.* Philadelphia: Westminster; London: S.C.M. Press, 1948, pp. 79f.

29. Calvin, John, *Institutes of the Christian Religion,* Bk. II, Ch. vii, par. xiii.

30. For a discussion of Luther's and Melanchthon's *Triplex Usus Legis,* see Ebeling, Gerhard, *Word and Faith.* London: S.C.M. Press, 1963, Ch. 2. Though the essay purports to deal with the Reformation, Calvin is not discussed!

31. Thomas, George, *Christian Ethics and Moral Philosophy.* New York: Scribner's, 1955, p. 123.

32. Henry, C. F. H., *Christian Personal Ethics.* Grand Rapids, Mich.: Wm. B. Eerdmans, 1957, p. 255. Used by permission.

33. Ibid., p. 303.

34. Ibid., p. 308.

35. Ibid., p. 334.

36. Ibid., p. 348.

37. *A Christian View of Men and Things.* Grand Rapids, Mich.: Wm. B. Eerdmans, 1952.

Notes to Chapter Six

1. Kirk, Kenneth E., *The Vision of God: The Christian Doctrine of the Summum Bonum*. London: Longman's Green, 1931, p. 111.
2. Goodspeed, Edgar J., *The Apostolic Fathers: An American Translation*. New York: Harper, 1930, pp. 33f.
3. Irenaeus, *Against the Heresies*, Bk. IV, Ch. 12, Section 3, in Roberts, Alexander, and Donaldson, James, eds., *The Ante-Nicene Fathers*, Vol. I. New York: Scribner's, 1899, p. 476.
4. McNeill, John T., and Gamer, Helena M., *Medieval Handbooks of Penance*. New York: Columbia University Press, 1938.
5. Ibid., p. 108.
6. Ibid., p. 158.
7. Davis, Henry, *Moral and Pastoral Theology*, Vol. III, 1st ed., 1935; 8th ed., 1959. London and New York: Sheed and Ward, p. 482.
8. Ibid., Vol. IV, p. 368.
9. Ford, John C., and Kelley, Gerald, *Contemporary Moral Theology*: Vol. I: *Questions in Fundamental Moral Theology*. Westminster, Md.: Newman; Cork, Ireland: Mercier, 1958, pp. 91f.
10. In *Select Practical Writings of Richard Baxter with a Life of the Author*, Bacon, Leonard, ed. New Haven: Durrie and Peck, 1835.
11. Part I, Ch. II, Direction XVII, in *The Practical Works of Richard Baxter*, Orme, William, ed. London: James Duncan, 1830, p. 153.
12. Ibid., p. 154.
13. *Select Practical Writings of Richard Baxter*, p. 458.
14. Ibid., p. 459.
15. Mather, Cotton, *Essays To Do Good*. New York: American Tract Society, n.d. pp. 18f.
16. Ibid., p. 19.
17. Mather, Increase, *An Arrow Against Profane and Promiscuous Dancing Drawn out of a Quiver of the Scriptures*, reprinted in Miller, Perry, and Johnson, Thomas H., eds., *The Puritans*. New York: American Book, 1938, pp. 411f. Reissued as *The Puritans: A Source Book of Their Writings*. New York: Harper and Row (Torchbook), 1963.
18. Willison, John. Albany: J. Boardman, G. J. Loomis, Printers.
19. Barclay, Robert, *Apology for the True Christian Divinity*. Philadelphia: Friends Book Store, 1848, p. 476.
20. The *Millennial Laws* can be found in Andrews, Edward Demig, *The People Called Shakers: A Search for the Perfect Society*. New York: Oxford University Press, 1953. The quotation is taken from the miscellaneous orders, pp. 278f.

Notes to Chapter Seven

1. Kirk, Kenneth E., *The Vision of God: The Christian Doctrine of the Summum Bonum*. London: Longman's Green, 1931, pp. 6f.
2. Ibid., p. 147.
3. Kirk, Kenneth E., *Conscience and Its Problems: An Introduction to Casuistry*. London: Longman's Green, 1927, pp. xvi and xvii.

4. Lehmann, Paul L., *Ethics in a Christian Context*. New York: Harper and Row, 1963, p. 295.

5. Bentham, Jeremy, *Works*, collected by John Bowring. Edinburgh: William Tait, 1838; reprinted 1962 by Russell and Russell, Vol. V., p. 224.

6. Ibid., Vol. III, pp. 1-29.

7. Pittenger, W. Norman, *The Historic Faith and a Changing World*. New York: Oxford, 1950, pp. 171f.

8. Long, Edward LeRoy, Jr., *Conscience and Compromise: An Approach to Protestant Casuistry*. Philadelphia: Westminster, 1954.

9. Fletcher, Joseph, "The New Look in Christian Ethics," in *Harvard Divinity School Bulletin*, Vol. 24, No. 1, October 1959, p. 17.

10. Ibid., p. 18.

11. Johnson, F. Ernest, ed., *Patterns of Ethics in America Today*. New York: Institute for Religious and Social Studies, 1960 (distributed by Harper), pp. 4f.

12. Ibid., p. 5.

13. Knox, John, *The Ethic of Jesus in the Teaching of the Church: Its Authority and Its Relevance*. New York: Abingdon, 1961, p. 65.

14. Visser t'Hooft, W. A., and Oldham, J. H., *The Church and Its Function in Society*. Chicago: Willett, Clark, 1937, pp. 193f.

15. Bennett, John C., *Christian Ethics and Social Policy*. New York: Scribner's, 1946, pp. 76f.

16. From Sanford, Elias B., *Origin and History of the Federal Council of Churches of Christ in America*. Hartford, Conn.: S. S. Scranton, 1916, pp. 497f.

17. Waetjen, Herman C., "Is the 'Imitation of Christ' Biblical?" in *Dialog*, Vol. 2, No. 2, Spring 1963, p. 125.

18. Ibid., p. 122.

19. Thomas à Kempis, *The Imitation of Christ*. Bk. IV, Ch. LVI, pars. 1b and 2, trans. by C. Bigg. London: Methuen, 1901, p. 284.

20. Beach, W., and Niebuhr, H. R., *Christian Ethics: Sources of the Living Tradition*. New York: Ronald Press, 1955, p. 357.

21. See Elert, Werner, *The Christian Ethos*. Philadelphia: Fortress, 1957, p. 253f.

22. See Henry, C. F. H., *Christian Personal Ethics*. Grand Rapids, Mich.: Wm. B. Eerdmans, 1957, pp. 132f.

23. Kierkegaard, Søren, *Works of Love*, trans. by Swenson, David F. and Lillian M. Princeton: Princeton University Press, 1946, p. 12.

24. Ibid., p. 87.

25. Thulstrup, Marie, "Kierkegaard's Dialectic of Imitation," in Johnson, Howard A., and Thulstrup, Niels, eds., *A Kierkegaard Critique*. New York: Harper, 1962, p. 277.

26. Ibid., p. 272.

Notes to Chapter Eight

1. Sittler, Joseph, *The Structure of Christian Ethics*. Baton Rouge: Louisiana State University Press, 1958, p. 25.

2. Muilenburg, James, *The Way of Israel: Biblical Faith and Ethics*. New York: Harper, 1961, p. 15.

3. Niebuhr, H. Richard, *The Responsible Self*. New York: Harper and Row, 1963, pp. 60f.

4. Ferré, Nels F. S., Lectures in *Minutes of the Thirty-Seventh Annual Meeting of*

the Presbyterian Educational Association of the South. Montreat, N.C., June 22-27, 1951, p. 48.

5. Lehmann, Paul L., *Ethics in a Christian Context.* New York: Harper and Row, 1963, p. 124.
6. Clark, Henry W., *The Christian Method of Ethics.* New York: Revell, 1908, p. 22.
7. Lowrie, Walter, "About Christian Ethics," in *Anglican Theological Review,* Vol. 31, No. 1, January 1949, especially pp. 4-5.
8. Bonhoeffer, Dietrich, *Ethics.* New York: Macmillan, 1955, pp. 8f.
9. *Filosofisk och kristen etik.* William A. Johnson has studied Nygren's thinking about such matters in a book entitled *On Religion: A Study of Theological Method in Schleiermacher and Nygren.* Leiden, Neth.: Brill, 1964.
10. Niebuhr, *The Responsible Self,* p. 57. Italics added.
11. Ibid., p. 87.
12. Lehmann, *Ethics in a Christian Context,* p. 144.
13. Bonhoeffer, *Ethics,* p. 245.
14. Niebuhr, *The Responsible Self,* p. 126.
15. Lehmann, *Ethics in a Christian Context,* p. 131.
16. Robinson, N. H. G., *Christ and Conscience.* London: Nisbet, 1956, p. 18.
17. Niebuhr, *The Responsible Self,* p. 45.
18. von Rad, Gerhard, *Old Testament Theology,* Vol. I. Edinburgh: Oliver and Boyd; New York: Harper and Row, 1962, p. 371.
19. Ibid., p. 371.
20. Ibid., p. 373.
21. Ibid., pp. 373f.
22. *An Outline of Old Testament Theology.* Oxford: Blackwell, 1958.
23. Eichrodt, Walther, *Theology of the Old Testament,* trans. by John Baker, Vol. I. London: S.C.M. Press; Philadelphia: Westminster, 1961, p. 374.
24. Manson, T. W., *Ethics and the Gospel.* London: S.C.M. Press; New York: Scribner's, 1960, p. 102.
25. Sittler, *The Structure of Christian Ethics,* p. 48.
26. Knox, John, *Chapters in a Life of Paul.* New York: Abingdon-Cokesbury, 1950, p. 154.
27. Knox, John, *The Ethic of Jesus in the Teaching of the Church: Its Authority and Its Relevance.* New York: Abingdon, 1961, p. 76.
28. Lehmann, *Ethics in a Christian Context,* p. 27.

Notes to Chapter Nine

1. Augustine, St., *On the Morals of the Catholic Church,* Ch. XI. From Oates, Whitney J., ed., *Basic Writings of Saint Augustine,* Vol. I. New York: Random House, 1948, p. 328.
2. Ibid., Ch. XII. Oates, p. 330.
3. Ibid., Ch. XV. Oates, pp. 331f.
4. Luther, Martin, "Treatise on Good Works," in *Works of Martin Luther,* Vol. I. Philadelphia: Holman, 1915, p. 191.
5. Luther, Martin, "Treatise on Christian Liberty," in *Works of Martin Luther,* Vol. II, p. 312.
6. Ibid., p. 328.
7. Ibid., pp. 331f.
8. Forell, George, *Faith Active in Love: An Investigation of the Principles Under-*

lying Luther's Social Ethics. Minneapolis, Minn.: Augsburg, 1954, p. 62. To substantiate his statement about Luther's judgment of the ethical standards of the pagan philosophers, Forell includes a reference to the *Weimarer Ausgabe*, 5, 137, which he translates as follows: "Hence it comes to pass that they most miserably crucify and murder the people by their lies and godless fables which they take from the morals of the philosophers, the laws of men, and their own precepts and traditions. . . ."

9. *Works of Martin Luther*, Vol. II, pp. 337f.
10. Edwards, Jonathan, *The Nature of True Virtue.* Ann Arbor: University of Michigan Press, 1960, p. 24.
11. Ibid., pp. 25f.
12. Ibid., p. 26.
13. Ibid., pp. 14f.
14. Edwards, Jonathan, *A Treatise Concerning Religious Affections*, ed. by Smith, John E. New Haven: Yale University Press, 1959, p. 347.
15. Ibid., p. 383.
16. Ibid., pp. 386f.
17. Edwards, *The Nature of True Virtue*, p. 18.
18. Watson, Philip S., in translator's preface to Nygren, Anders, *Agape and Eros*, rev. ed. London: S.P.C.K. House; Philadelphia: Westminster, 1953, p. viii. Used by permission of The Westminster Press and the Society for Promoting Christian Knowledge.
19. Nygren, *Agape and Eros*, p. 210.
20. Ibid., p. 218.
21. Ibid., pp. 733f.
22. D'Arcy, M. C., *The Mind and Heart of Love: Lion and Unicorn: A Study in Eros and Agape.* New York: Holt; London: Faber and Faber, 1947, p. 323.
23. London: Hodder and Stroughton, 1938.
24. New York: Oxford, 1954.
25. Ferré, Nels F. S., *Christianity and Society.* New York: Harper, 1950, p. 49.
26. Ibid., p. 58.
27. Ibid., p. 134.
28. Ferré, Nels F. S., "Theology and Ethics," Lectures in *Minutes of the Thirty-Seventh Annual Meeting of the Presbyterian Educational Association of the South.* Montreat, N.C., June 22-27, 1951, p. 48.
29. Sittler, Joseph, *The Structure of Christian Ethics.* Baton Rouge: Louisiana State University Press, 1958, pp. 56f.
30. Ibid., pp. 78f.
31. Ibid., p. 6.

Notes to Chapter Ten

1. Brunner, Emil, *The Divine Imperative: A Study in Christian Ethics.* Philadelphia: Westminster, 1947, p. 111. Copyright 1947 by W. L. Jenkins. Used by permission.
2. Ibid., pp. 117f.
3. Ibid., p. 118.
4. Ibid., p. 139.
5. Ibid., p. 134.
6. Ibid., p. 134.
7. Ibid., pp. 138f.

8. Ibid., p. 142.
9. Ibid., p. 150.
10. Ibid., pp. 150f.
11. Ibid., pp. 208f.
12. Pitcher, W. Alvin, *Theological Ethics in Paul Tillich and Emil Brunner: A Study of the Nature of Protestant Theological Ethics.* Microfilm dissertation, University of Chicago, 1955.
13. Philadelphia: Westminster, 1946.
14. Barth, Karl, *The Word of God and the Word of Man,* trans. by Douglas Horton. New York: Harper and Row (Torchbook), 1957, pp. 172f.
15. Ibid., pp. 169f.
16. Ibid., pp. 147f.
17. West, Charles C., *Communism and the Theologians: Study of an Encounter.* Philadelphia: Westminster; London: S.C.M. Press, 1958, p. 207. Used by permission.
18. Barth, Karl, *Church Dogmatics,* II/2. Edinburgh: T. and T. Clark, 1957, p. 587.
19. Bonhoeffer, Dietrich, *Ethics.* New York: Macmillan, 1955, p. 12.
20. Ibid., p. 18.
21. Ibid., p. 55.
22. Ibid., p. 142.
23. Ibid., pp. 244f.
24. Bultmann, Rudolph, *Jesus and the Word.* New York: Scribner's, 1934, p. 35.
25. Ibid., pp. 83f.
26. Quoted in Oden, Thomas C., *Radical Obedience: The Ethics of Rudolph Bultmann.* Philadelphia: Westminster, 1964, p. 145. Copyright © 1964 by W. L. Jenkins. Used by permission.
27. Lehmann, Paul L., "The Foundation and Pattern of Christian Behavior," in Hutchison, John A., ed., *Christian Faith and Social Action.* New York: Scribner's, 1953, pp. 93-116.
28. Ibid., p. 100.
29. Ibid., p. 102.
30. Lehmann, Paul L., *Ethics in a Christian Context.* New York: Harper and Row, 1963, p. 124.
31. Ibid., p. 131.
32. Fletcher, Joseph, "The New Look in Christian Ethics," in *Harvard Divinity School Bulletin,* Vol. 24, No. 1, October 1959, pp. 7-18; "Contemporary Conscience: A Christian Method," in *Kenyon Alumni Bulletin,* Vol. 21, No. 3, July-Sept. 1963, pp. 4-10; *Situation Ethics.* Philadelphia: Westminster, 1966.
33. Lehmann, Paul L., "The Foundation and Pattern of Christian Behavior," in Hutchison, p. 112.
34. Fletcher, Joseph, "Contemporary Conscience: A Christian Method," pp. 5f.
35. Kaufman, Gordon D., *The Context of Decision: A Theological Analysis.* New York: Abingdon, 1961, pp. 25f.
36. Rasmussen, Albert Terrill, *Christian Social Ethics: Exerting Christian Influence.* Englewood Cliffs, N.J.: Prentice-Hall, 1956, p. 166. Copyright © 1956 by Prentice-Hall, Inc.
37. Ibid., pp. 169f.
38. Miller, Alexander, *The Renewal of Man.* Garden City, N.Y.: Doubleday, 1955, p. 94. Copyright 1955 by Alexander Miller. Reprinted by permission of Doubleday and Company, Inc., and Victor Gollancz, Ltd.
39. Holbrook, Clyde A., *Faith and Community: A Christian Existential Approach.* New York: Harper, 1959, pp. 103f.

40. Gustafson, James, "Christian Ethics and Social Policy," in Ramsey, Paul, ed., *Faith and Ethics: The Theology of H. Richard Niebuhr*. New York: Harper, 1957, pp. 126f.

41. Lochman, Jan Milič, *Die Bedeutung geschichtlicher Ereignisse für ethische Entscheidungen*. Zurich: Evangelische Verlag, 1963.

Notes to Chapter Eleven

1. Troeltsch, Ernst, *The Social Teaching of the Christian Churches*. London: George Allen and Unwin, 1931, p. 461.

2. Ibid., p. 461.

3. Ibid., p. 743.

4. Ibid., p. 1008.

5. Ibid., pp. 331-43.

6. Brunner, Emil, *The Divine Imperative*. Philadelphia: Westminster, 1948, p. 291. Copyright 1947 by W. L. Jenkins. Used by permission.

7. Ibid., p. 291.

8. Cave, Sidney, *The Christian Way: A Study of New Testament Ethics in Relation to Present Problems*. New York: Philosophical Library, 1949, p. 171.

9. Elert, Werner, *The Christian Ethos*. Philadelphia: Fortress, 1957, pp. 79f.

10. *Society: A Textbook of Sociology*. New York: Farrar and Rinehart, 1937.

11. Brunner, *The Divine Imperative*, p. 224.

12. Ramsey, Paul, *Christian Ethics and the Sit-in*. New York: Association Press, 1961, p. 39.

13. Kenrick, Bruce, *Come Out the Wilderness: The Story of the East Harlem Protestant Parish*. New York: Harper and Row, 1962, p. 74.

14. Williams, Daniel D., "The Significance of St. Augustine Today," in Battenhouse, Roy W., ed., *A Companion to the Study of St. Augustine*. New York: Oxford, 1955, p. 4.

15. See Bk. XIV, Ch. 28.

16. Augustine, St., *The City of God*, Bk. XIX, Ch. 16. From Oates, Whitney J., ed., *Basic Writings of Saint Augustine*, Vol. II. New York: Random House, 1948, p. 493.

17. Ibid., Bk. XIX, Ch. 17. Oates, p. 493.

18. Augustine, St., "Letter to Marcellius," in Figgis, John Neville, *The Political Aspects of St. Augustine's City of God*. London: Longman's Green, 1921, pp. 57f.

19. Augustine, St., *The City of God*, Bk. XV, Ch. 4. Oates, pp. 278f.

20. Hardy, Edward R., Jr., "The City of God," in Battenhouse, pp. 279f.

21. Augustine, St., *The City of God*, Bk. XIX, Ch. 6. Oates, pp. 480f.

22. Aquinas, St. Thomas, *Summa Theologiae I-II*. Question 90, Art. 4. From Pegis, Anton C., ed., *Basic Writings of Saint Thomas Aquinas*, Vol. II. New York: Random House, 1945, p. 747.

23. Ibid., Question 92, Art. 1. Pegis, pp. 758f. Italics in the translation represent a quotation from Aristotle's *Politics*, I, 5.

24. Ibid., Question 95, Art. 3. Pegis, p. 786.

25. Ibid., Question 96, Art. 6. Pegis, p. 798.

26. Ibid., Question 97, Art. 2. Pegis, p. 802.

27. Ibid., Question 97, Art. 2. Pegis, p. 802.

28. Kelley, Alden D., *Christianity and Political Responsibility*. Philadelphia: Westminster, 1961, p. 78.

29. Excerpts from the encyclical from the Vatican Press Office translation circulated

by the NCWC News Service. Published in *The 1964 National Catholic Almanac,* Felician A. Foy, O.F.M., and St. Anthony's Guild, eds., Garden City, N.Y.: Doubleday. The selection from the introduction to the encyclical appears on p. 186 of *The Almanac.*

30. Ibid., p. 189.
31. Ibid., p. 191.
32. Ibid., p. 191.
33. Ibid., p. 194.
34. Ibid., p. 200.
35. Novak, Michael, "Break with the Past," in *Commonweal,* Vol. LXXVIII, No. 14, June 28, 1963, p. 375.
36. Schomer, Howard, "Toward Peace and Justice," in *The Christian Century,* Vol. LXXX, No. 22, May 29, 1963, pp. 703-6.
37. Herberg, Will, "The New Encyclical: A Question of Perspective," in *The National Review,* Vol. XIV, No. 18, May 7, 1963, pp. 364f.
38. Ramsey, Paul, "Pacem in Terris," in *Religion in Life,* Vol. XXXIII, No. 1, Winter 1963-64, pp. 116-35.

Notes to Chapter Twelve

1. Tawney, R. H., *Religion and the Rise of Capitalism.* New York: Harcourt Brace, 1926, p. 88.
2. Luther, Martin, "Lectures on Genesis, Chapters 15-20," from Pelikan, Jaraslov, ed., *Luther's Works,* Vol. III. St. Louis: Concordia Publishing House, 1961, p. 279.
3. Mueller, William A., *Church and State in Luther and Calvin: A Comparative Study.* Nashville: Broadman, 1954, p. 44.
4. Elert, Werner, *The Christian Ethos.* Philadelphia: Fortress, 1957, p. 412.
5. Luther, Martin, "Whether Soldiers, Too, Can Be Saved," in *Works of Martin Luther,* Vol. V. Philadelphia: Fortress Press, 1931, pp. 59f. Used by permission of the Fortress Press.
6. Forell, George, *Faith Active in Love: An Investigation of the Principles Underlying Luther's Social Ethics.* Minneapolis, Minn.: Augsburg, 1954, p. 135.
7. Brunner, Emil, *The Divine Imperative: A Study in Christian Ethics.* Philadelphia: Westminster, 1947, p. 291. Copyright 1947 by W. L. Jenkins. Used by permission.
8. Ibid., p. 335.
9. Ibid., p. 225.
10. Ibid., pp. 212f.
11. Ibid., p. 446.
12. Brunner, Emil, *Justice and the Social Order.* New York: Harper, 1945, p. 196.
13. Brunner, *The Divine Imperative,* p. 214. Italics in original.
14. Ibid., pp. 218f.
15. Ibid., p. 217.
16. Bonhoeffer, Dietrich, *Ethics.* New York: Macmillan, 1955, pp. 252f.
17. Ibid., p. 254.
18. Ibid., p. 199.
19. Ibid., pp. 256f.
20. Forell, George, "Realized Faith: The Ethics of Dietrich Bonhoeffer," in Marty, Martin E., ed., *The Place of Bonhoeffer: Problems and Possibilities in His Thought.* New York: Association Press, 1962, p. 218.
21. Bonhoeffer, *Ethics,* p. 299.
22. Ibid., p. 307.

23. Calvin, John, *Institutes of the Christian Religion*, Bk. IV, Ch. xx, par. xii. Library of Christian Classics Edition, McNeill, John T., ed., and Battles, Ford Lewis, trans. Philadelphia: Westminster, 1960. Copyright © 1960 by W. L. Jenkins. Used by permission.

24. Ibid., Bk. IV, Ch. xx, par. xxxi.

25. *The Modern Democratic State*. London: Oxford University Press, 1943.

26. *The History and Character of Calvinism*. New York: Oxford University Press, 1954.

27. *Democracy and the Churches*. Philadelphia: Westminster, 1951.

28. *Kircherecht*. Munich-Leipzig: Dunker-Humblot, 1923.

29. *Protestant Thought Before Kant*. New York: Scribner's, 1911.

30. Bennett, John C., *Christians and the State*. New York: Scribner's, 1958, pp. 40f.

31. Winthrop, John, "Speech to the General Court," July 3, 1645. Reprinted in Miller, Perry, and Johnson, Thomas H., eds., *The Puritans*. New York: American Book, 1938, pp. 206f. Reissued as *The Puritans: A Source Book of Their Writings*. New York: Harper and Row (Torchbook), 1963.

32. Miller and Johnson, p. 183.

33. Hooker, Richard, *The Laws of Ecclesiastical Polity*. The first four books of this work were published in 1594, the fifth book in 1597. The three remaining books were published eighteen years after his death from papers that Hooker left. In addition to the sections cited, pagination is given from an edition published in London by George Routledge and Sons, 1888. This quotation from Preface II, 1, p. 11.

34. Ibid., Preface, II, 4, p. 14.

35. Ibid., I, XVI, 1, p. 123.

36. Ibid., I, XVI, 8, p. 129.

37. Ibid., I, X, 9, p. 96.

38. Ibid., I, X, 13, pp. 101f.

39. Dooyeweerd, Herman, *A New Critique of Theoretical Thought*, trans. by Freeman, David H., and Young, William S. Philadelphia: Presbyterian and Reformed Publishing Co., 1953-57.

40. In Barth, Karl, *Community, State, and Church: Three Essays*, introduction by Will Herberg. Garden City: Doubleday, 1960, pp. 101-48.

41. Barth, Karl, "Christian Community and Civil Community," in ibid., p. 170. Copyright 1960 by National Student Christian Federation. Reprinted by permisson of National Student Christian Federation and Doubleday and Company.

42. Ibid., p. 168.

43. Ibid., p. 156.

44. Ibid., p. 151.

45. Ibid., p. 157.

46. Forell, "Realized Faith: The Ethics of Dietrich Bonhoeffer," p. 207.

47. Barth, "Christian Community and Civil Community," p. 177.

48. Barth, *Church Dogmatics*, III/4. Edinburgh: T. and T. Clark, 1961, p. 304.

49. Temple, William, *Church and Nation*. London: Macmillan, 1915, p. 67.

50. Temple, William, *Christianity and Social Order*. New York: Penquin Books, 1942, p. 42.

Notes to Chapter Thirteen

1. Troeltsch, Ernst, *The Social Teaching of the Christian Churches*. London: George Allen and Unwin, 1931, p. 991.

2. Smyth, Newman, *Christian Ethics*. New York: Scribner's, 1892, p. 144.
3. Ibid., p. 218.
4. Ibid., p. 245.
5. Ibid., p. 248.
6. Ibid., pp. 248f.
7. Ibid., pp. 254-92.
8. Ibid., p. 264.
9. Ibid., pp. 264f.
10. Ibid., p. 269.
11. Ibid., p. 273.
12. Herron, George D., *The Christian State: A Political Vision of Christ*. New York: Thomas Y. Crowell, 1895, pp. 47f.
13. Ibid., pp. 53f.
14. Ibid., p. 66.
15. Ibid., pp. 106f.
16. Ibid., p. 62.
17. Rauschenbusch, Walter, *Christianizing the Social Order*. New York: Macmillan, 1912, p. 125.
18. Ibid., p. 125.
19. Ibid., p. 126.
20. Ibid., p. 126.
21. Ibid., p. 127.
22. Ibid., p. 130.
23. Ibid., pp. 133f.
24. Ibid., p. 141.
25. Ibid., p. 148.
26. Ibid., p. 156.
27. Ibid., p. 408.
28. Muelder, Walter G., *Foundations of the Responsible Society*. New York: Abingdon, 1959, p. 78.
29. Ibid., p. 102.
30. Ibid., p 106.
31. Ibid., p. 108.
32. Ibid., p. 109.
33. Ibid., p. 116.
34. Ibid., p. 35.
35. Brookes, Edgar H., *Power, Law, Right, and Love: A Study in Political Values*. Durham, N.C.: Duke University Press, 1963, p. 27.

Notes to Chapter Fourteen

1. Miller, William L., *The Protestant and Politics*. Philadelphia: Westminster, 1958, p. 17.
2. Thompson, Kenneth W., "Prophets and Politics," in Cowan, Wayne H., ed., *What the Christian Hopes For in Society*. New York: Association Press, 1957, pp. 115f.
3. Muelder, Walter G., *Foundations of the Responsible Society*. New York: Abingdon, 1959, p. 62.
4. Niebuhr, Reinhold, *The Structure of Nations and Empires*. New York: Scribner's; London: Faber and Faber, 1959, p. 34.
5. Muelder, *Foundations of the Responsible Society*, p. 264.

6. Ibid., p. 265.
7. Niebuhr, *The Structure of Nations and Empires*, p. 262.
8. Muelder, *Foundations of the Responsible Society*, p. 268.
9. Niebuhr, *The Structure of Nations and Empires*, p. 293.
10. Muelder, *Foundations of the Responsible Society*, p. 60.
11. Niebuhr, *The Structure of Nations and Empires*, p. 33.
12. Kelley, Alden, *Christianity and Political Responsibility*. Philadelphia: Westminster, 1961, p. 87.
13. Shinn, Roger L., "Responses of Protestant Ethics to Political Challenges," in Lasswell, Harold D., and Cleveland, Harland, eds., *The Ethic of Power*. New York: Conference on Science, Philosophy, and Religion, 1962, p. 158.
14. Brunner, Emil, *The Divine Imperative: A Study in Christian Ethics*. Philadelphia: Westminster, 1947, p. 445. Copyright 1947 by W. L. Jenkins. Used by permission.
15. Sittler, Joseph, *The Structure of Christian Ethics*. Baton Rouge: Louisiana State University Press, 1958, p. 79.
16. Niebuhr, Reinhold, in Boulding, K. E., *The Organizational Revolution: A Study in the Ethics of Economic Organization*. New York: Harper, 1953, pp. 231f.
17. Ibid., p. 235.
18. Ibid., p. 238.
19. Niebuhr, Reinhold, "If America Is Drawn into War," *The Christian Century*, Vol. LVII, No. 51. Dec. 18, 1940, p. 1580. Copyright 1940 by the Christian Century Foundation. Reprinted by permission.
20. Niebuhr, Reinhold, *Moral Man and Immoral Society: A Study in Ethics and Politics*. New York: Scribner's; London: S.C.M. Press, 1932, p. 238.
21. Niebuhr, *The Structure of Nations and Empires*, p. 33.
22. Ibid., p. 61.
23. Ibid., p. 25.
24. Ibid., p. 105.
25. Niebuhr, Reinhold, *Christian Realism and Political Problems*. New York: Scribner's; London: Faber and Faber, 1953, pp. 120f.

Notes to Chapter Fifteen

1. Thompson, Kenneth W., "Prophets and Politics," in Cowan, Wayne H., ed., *What the Christian Hopes For in Society*. New York: Association Press, 1957, p. 113.
2. Ibid., pp. 112f.
3. Thompson, Kenneth W., *Christian Ethics and the Dilemmas of Foreign Policy*. Durham, N.C.: Duke University Press, 1959.
4. Lefever, Ernest W., "Politics—Who Gets What, When, and How," in Nelson, J. Robert, ed., *The Christian Student and the World Struggle*. New York: Association Press, 1952, p. 35.
5. Ibid., p. 38.
6. Ibid., p. 40.
7. Lefever, Ernest W., *Ethics and United States Foreign Policy*. New York: Meridian Books, 1957, p. 4. Used by permission of World Publishing Co.
8. Ibid., pp. 17f.
9. Muehl, William, *Politics for Christians*. New York: Association Press, 1956, p. 53.
10. Ibid., p. 56.
11. Ibid., p. 74.
12. Miller, William L., *The Protestant and Politics*. Philadelphia: Westminster, 1958, p. 90.

13. Miller, Francis Pickens, "Christian Ethics and Practical Politics," in Cowan, ed., *What the Christian Hopes For in Society*, pp. 44f.
14. Geyer, Alan, *Piety and Politics: American Protestantism in the World Arena*. Richmond, Va.: John Knox, 1963, p. 12.
15. Ibid., p. 23.
16. Rasmussen, Albert Terrill, *Christian Social Ethics: Exerting Christian Influence*. Englewood Cliffs, N.J.: Prentice-Hall, 1956, p. 119.
17. Muste, A. J., *Not by Might: Christianity: The Way to Human Decency*. New York: Harper, 1947, p. 74.
18. King, Martin Luther, *Stride Toward Freedom: The Montgomery Story*. New York: Harper, 1958, pp. 215f.
19. Ibid., p. 97.
20. Ibid., pp. 98f.
21. Philadelphia: Lippincott, 1934. The original edition carried a preface by Rufus Jones; a thoroughly revised edition, published in 1959 by Fellowship Publications, Nyack, N.Y., carries a preface by Martin Luther King.
22. Ibid., p. 125.
23. Ibid., p. 69.
24. Ibid., p. 52.
25. Shridharani, Krishnalal, *War Without Violence: A Study of Gandhi's Method and Its Accomplishments*. New York: Harcourt, Brace, 1939, p. 278.
26. Ibid., p. 293.
27. Muste, *Not by Might*. p. 80.
28. Ibid., p. 81.
29. Ricoeur, Paul, "The Historical Presence of Non-Violence," in *Crosscurrents*, Vol. XIV, No. 1, Winter 1964, p. 19.
30. Ibid., p. 22.
31. Ibid., p. 23.
32. Scottdale, Pa.: Herald Press, 1944.
33. Niebuhr, Reinhold, *Christianity and Power Politics*. New York: Scribner's, 1940, pp. 10f.

Notes to Chapter Sixteen

1. "Deposition of Henry IV by Gregory VII," February 1076, in Bettenson, Henry, ed., *Documents of the Christian Church*. London: Oxford University Press, 1943, p. 146.
2. "The Letter of Gregory VII to the Bishop of Metz," 1081, in ibid., p. 150.
3. Ibid., p. 151.
4. Ibid., p. 152.
5. "*Unam Sanctam*," ibid., p. 162.
6. Pope, Liston, *Millhands and Preachers*. New Haven: Yale University Press, 1942, p. 330.
7. Underwood, Kenneth W., *Protestant and Catholic: Religious and Social Interaction in an Industrial Community*. Boston: Beacon Press, 1957, p. 340. Copyright 1957 by Kenneth Wilson Underwood. Reprinted by permission of the Beacon Press.
8. Ibid., p. 345.
9. Ebersole, Luke Eugene, *Church Lobbying in the Nation's Capital*. New York: Macmillan, 1951, p. 177.
10. Harrison, Paul M., *Authority and Power in the Free Church Tradition*. Princeton: Princeton University Press, 1959, pp. vii-viii.

11. Ibid., p. 208.
12. Ibid., p. 216.
13. Ibid., p. 227

Notes to Chapter Seventeen

1. Troeltsch, Ernst, *The Social Teaching of the Christian Churches*. London: George Allen and Unwin, 1931, p. 331.
2. Hutchison, John A., *The Two Cities: A Study of God and Human Politics*. Garden City, N.Y.: Doubleday, 1957, p. 65. Copyright 1954 by John A. Hutchison. Reprinted by permission of Doubleday and Company, Inc.
3. Wyon, Olive, *Living Springs: New Religious Movements in Western Europe*. Philadelphia: Westminster, n.d., p. 31. Copyright by Olive Wyon. Used by permission.
4. Beach, W., and Niebuhr, H. R., *Christian Ethics: Sources of the Living Tradition*. New York: Ronald Press, 1955, p. 147.
5. Troeltsch, Ernst, *The Social Teaching of the Christian Churches*, p. 753.
6. Smith, Timothy L., *Revivalism and Social Reform in Mid-Nineteenth Century America*. New York: Abingdon, 1957.
7. Hoffer, Eric, *The True Believer: Thoughts on the Nature of Mass Movements*. New York: Harper, 1951, p. xii.
8. Ibid., p. xi.
9. *The Evolution of the Monastic Ideal*. London: Epworth, 1913.
10. Bouyer, Louis, *The Meaning of the Monastic Life*. London: Burns and Oates, 1955.
11. Kirk, Kenneth E., *The Vision of God: The Christian Doctrine of the Summum Bonum*. London: Longman's Green, 1931.
12. *The Call of the Cloister*. London: S.P.C.K., 1955.
13. Boyd, Malcolm, "The Taizé Community," in *Theology Today*, Vol. XV, No. 4, January 1959, p. 494.
14. Tertullian, *Prescription Against Heretics*, in Greenslade, S. L., trans. and ed., *Early Latin Theology*, p. 61. Philadelphia: Westminster; London: S.C.M. Press, 1956. Used by permission.
15. Law, William, *A Serious Call to a Devout and Holy Life*, Ch. 1, par. 7.
16. Ibid., Ch. 1, par. 8.
17. Bettenson, Henry, *Documents of the Christian Church*. London: Oxford University Press, 1943, pp. 359f.
18. MacLeod, George, *We Shall Rebuild: The Work of the Iona Community on Mainland and on Island*, rev. ed. Glasgow: Iona Community, 1962, p. 24. Used by permission of the Iona Community.
19. Morton, T. Ralph, *Community of Faith: The Changing Pattern of the Church's Life*. New York: Association Press, 1954, p. 92. The final chapter of this book, written by John Oliver Nelson, contains a brief survey of the intentional communities located in America.
20. MacLeod, *We Shall Rebuild*, p. 97.
21. Ibid., pp. 73f.
22. Emerick, Samuel, "The Role of a Church Renewal Center," in *Religion in Life*, Vol. XXXI, No. 1, Winter 1961-62, p. 29. Copyright © 1961 by Abingdon Press.
23. *The Kirkridge Style of Life*.
24. Raines, Robert A., *New Life in the Church*. New York: Harper, 1961.
25. Ibid., p. 78.
26. Ibid., pp. 81f.

27. Ibid., p. 82.

28. Spike, Robert W., *In But Not of the World: A Notebook of Theology and Practice in the Local Church.* New York: Association Press, 1957, p. 80.

29. Casteel, John L., "The Rise of Personal Groups," in *Spiritual Renewal Through Small Groups.* New York: Association Press, 1957, p. 24.

Notes to Chapter Eighteen

1. Ferm, Vergilius, ed., *An Encyclopedia of Religion.* New York: Philosophical Library, 1945, p. 817.

2. Adams, James Luther, *Taking Time Seriously.* Glencoe, Ill.: The Free Press, 1957, p. 11.

3. Troeltsch, Ernst, *The Social Teaching of the Christian Churches.* London: George Allen and Unwin, 1931, p. 332.

4. Nordhoof, Charles, *The Communistic Societies of the United States.* First published 1875. Reprinted by Hillary House Publishers, Ltd., New York, 1961, p. 133.

5. Further information about the Society of Brothers and the philosophy of the community may be had from the Plough Publishing House, Rifton, New York. The writings of Eberhard Arnold can also be purchased from this source, and are (significantly) hand set, hand printed, and hand bound. For a description of other communities in which the social and communal character of labor is upheld against what is deemed to be technological corruption, see Bishop, Claire Hutchet, *All Things Common.* New York: Harper, 1950.

6. For a scholarly study of the Old Order Amish, see Hostetler, John A., *Amish Society.* Baltimore: Johns Hopkins, 1963.

7. Bender, Harold S., "The Response of Our Anabaptist Fathers to the World's Challenge," in *Mennonite Quarterly Review,* Vol. XXXVI, No. 3, July 1962, p. 203.

8. Hershberger, Guy Franklin, *War, Peace, and Nonresistance.* Scottdale, Pa.: Herald, 1944, pp. 320f.

9. Newton, Kansas: Faith and Life Press, 1961 (Institute of Mennonite Studies Series, No. 1).

10. Peachey, Paul, "Our Social Ministry in the Gospel," in *Mennonite Quarterly Review,* Vol. XXXVI, No. 3, July 1962, p. 228.

11. Ibid., p. 229.

12. Ibid., p. 230.

13. Ibid., p. 235.

14. Peachey, Paul, "Christian Obedience in a World We Don't Control," in *The Christian Century,* Vol. LXXXI, No. 15, April 8, 1964, p. 460. Copyright © 1964 by the Christian Century Foundation. Reprinted by permission.

15. Barclay, Robert, *Apology for the True Christian Divinity,* Article 14.

16. Winstanley, Gerrard, quoted in Berens, Lewis H., *The Digger Movement in the Days of the Commonwealth.* London: Simpkins, Marshall, Hamilton, Kent, and Co., 1906. New edition: New York: Humanities Press, 1962, and London: Holland Press, Merlin Press, 1961, p. 55.

17. Bohnstedt, Werner A., "The Faculty Christian Fellowship: Its Meaning and Task," in *The Christian Scholar,* Vol. XXXVI, No. 2, June 1953, p. 150.

18. Ibid., p. 151.

19. The residential aspect of the student program is no longer operative. This covenant is taken from a "Letter to Laymen," *Journal of the Christian Faith and Life Community,* Vol. 6, No. 5, January 1960. For an evaluation of the curriculum and the theological perspective of the Faith and Life Community, see Rossman, Parker,

"The Austin Community: Challenge and Controversy," in *The Christian Scholar*, Vol. XLV, No. 1, Spring 1962, pp. 44-51.

20. For a discussion of the Group Ministry and its experiences, see Kenrick, Bruce, *Come Out the Wilderness: The Story of the East Harlem Protestant Parish*. New York: Harper and Row, 1962.

21. See Howard, Peter, *The World Rebuilt: The True Story of Frank Buchman and the Achievements of Moral Re-Armament*. New York: Duell, Sloan and Pearce, 1951, Ch. 1.

22. Shoemaker, Samuel M., "House Parties Across the Country," in *The Christian Century*, Vol. L, No. 34, August 23, 1933, p. 1058.

23. Howard, Peter, *The World Rebuilt*, p. 6.

24. Clark, Walter Houston, *The Oxford Group: Its History and Significance*. New York: Bookman Associates, 1951, p. 255.

25. Bloesch, Donald G., *Centers of Christian Renewal*. Philadelphia: United Church Press, 1964, p. 153.

Notes to Chapter Nineteen

1. Calvin, John, *Institutes of the Christian Religion*, Library of Christian Classics Edition, McNeill, John T., ed., and Battles, Ford Lewis, trans. Philadelphia: Westminster, 1960. Bk. III, Ch. xix, par. vii. Copyright © 1960 by W. L. Jenkins. Used by permission.

2. Sittler, Joseph, *The Structure of Christian Ethics*. Baton Rouge: Louisiana State University Press, 1958. See both pp. 70f. and p. 50.

3. Barth, Karl, *Church Dogmatics*, III/4. Edinburgh: T. and T. Clark, 1961, p. 11.

4. Ibid., p. 12.

5. Ibid., p. 13.

6. Lehmann, Paul L., *Ethics in a Christian Context*. New York: Harper and Row, 1963. See pp. 287-325.

7. Gustafson, James M., "Christian Ethics and Social Policy," in Ramsey, Paul, ed., *Faith and Ethics: The Theology of H. Richard Niebuhr*. New York: Harper, 1957, p. 128.

8. Brunner, Emil, *The Divine Imperative: A Study in Christian Ethics*. Philadelphia: Westminster, 1947, p. 44. Copyright 1947 by W. L. Jenkins. Used by permission.

9. Sittler, *The Structure of Christian Ethics*, p. 81.

10. Ibid., p. 49.

11. Ibid., pp. 12f.

12. Thomas, George F., *Christian Ethics and Moral Philosophy*. New York: Scribner's, 1955, p. 387.

13. From an address to the Society of Professors of Christian Ethics and Social Ethics, Philadelphia, January 1958.

14. Rahner, Karl, *Theological Investigations*, Vol. II: *Man in the Church*. Baltimore: Helicon, 1963, p. 219.

15. Henry, Carl F. H., *Christian Personal Ethics*. Grand Rapids, Mich.: Wm. B. Eerdmans, 1957, p. 140. Used by permission.

16. Fitch, Robert E., "The Obsolescence of Ethics," in *Christianity and Crisis*, Vol. XIX, No. 19, November 16, 1959, p. 165.

17. Banner, William A., "Christian Ethics and the Moral Life," in *The Journal of Religious Thought*, Vol. XIV, No. 1, Autumn-Winter 1956-57, pp. 14f.

18. Nathanson, Jerome, "The Ethical Culture Movement," in Johnson, F. Ernest, *Patterns of Ethics in America Today*. New York: Harper, 1960, p. 81.

19. Bryson, Lyman, "Rational Ethics," in Johnson, *Patterns of Ethics in America Today*, p. 111.
20. Bennett, John C., *Christians and the State*. New York: Scribner's, 1958, p. 39.
21. Tolstoy, Leo, *My Religion*, trans. by Huntington Smith. New York: Crowell, 1885, p. 26.
22. Ibid., p. 32.
23. Ibid., p. 42.
24. Ibid., pp. 234f.
25. Troeltsch, Ernst, *The Social Teaching of the Christian Churches*. London: George Allen and Unwin, 1931, p. 752.
26. Berger, Peter, *The Precarious Vision: A Sociologist Looks at Social Fictions and Christian Faith*. Garden City, N.Y.: Doubleday, 1961, p. 115. Copyright © 1961 by Peter Berger. Reprinted by permission of Doubleday and Company, Inc.
27. Bentham, Jeremy, *The Works of Jeremy Bentham*. Published under the Superintendence of His Executor, John Bowring (1838-1843). New York: Russell and Russell, 1962, Vol. IV, p. 275.
28. Ramsey, Paul, *Christian Ethics and the Sit-in*. New York: Association Press, 1961, p. 79.
29. Ferré, Nels F. S., *Christianity and Society*. New York: Harper, 1950, p. 152.
30. Adams, James Luther, "The Theological Basis of Social Action," in *Journal of Religious Thought*, Vol. 8, No. 1, Autumn-Winter 1950-51, p. 7.
31. Ibid., p. 9.
32. Ibid., p. 21.
33. Niebuhr, Reinhold, *Pious and Secular America*. New York: Scribner's, 1958, p. 115.
34. Hershberger, Guy Franklin, *War, Peace, and Nonresistance*. Scottdale, Pa.: Herald, 1954, p. 219.
35. Bennett, *Christians and the State*, p. 60.
36. Ibid., p. 168.
37. Hall, Francis D., "Pitfalls of Intentional Community," in *The Christian Century*, Vol. LXXX, No. 33, August 14, 1963, p. 1001. Copyright © 1963 by the Christian Century Foundation. Reprinted by permission.
38. Ibid., pp. 1001f.
39. Maury, Philippe, *Politics and Evangelism*. Garden City, N.Y.: Doubleday, 1959, p. 106.
40. Smith, Ronald Gregor, *The New Man: Christianity and Man's Coming of Age*. London: S.C.M. Press; New York: Harper, 1950, p. 106.
41. Ibid., pp. 98f.

Notes to Chapter Twenty

1. Robinson, John A. T., *Christian Morals Today*. Philadelphia: Westminster, 1964.
2. Gustafson, James M., "Context Versus Principles: A Misplaced Debate in Christian Ethics," *Harvard Theological Review*, Vol. 58, April 1965. Also available in Marty, Martin E., and Peerman, Dean G., eds., *The New Theology, No. 3*. London: Collier-Macmillan; New York: Macmillan, 1966.
3. Stackhouse, Max L., "Toward a Theology for the New Social Gospel," in *Andover Newton Quarterly*, Vol. 6, No. 4, March 1966, p. 16.
4. Fry, John R., *The Immobilized Christian: A Study of His Pre-Ethical Situation*. Philadelphia: Westminster, 1963.
5. Underwood, Kenneth W., "The Campus Ministries and the Ethical Questions of the University," an unpublished paper, p. 13.

Index